The Americanization of the Unconscious

THE Americanization OF THE Unconscious

John R. Seeley

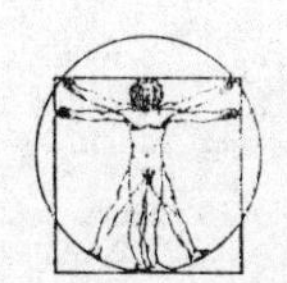

SCIENCE HOUSE, INC.
NEW YORK

To M.A.F., my father;
to G.B., my mother;
to M.M.S., my wife;
and for my children

Library of Congress Catalog Card No. 66-29488

Manufactured in the United States of America

Thanks are due to the publishers and organizations listed for permission to reprint the following:

"The Americanization of the Unconscious." From *Atlantic Monthly,* Vol. 208, No. 1, July 1961. Copyright © 1961, by the Atlantic Monthly Company, Boston, Mass. Reprinted with permission.

"The Psychiatrist as Reluctant Revolutionary." From *International Journal of Social Psychiatry,* 1965. Reprinted with permission.

"Social Values, The Mental Health Movement and Mental Health." From *Annals of the American Academy of Political and Social Science,* Vol. 286, March 1953. Reprinted with permission.

"The Future of Psychiatry." From *The University of Toronto Quarterly,* Vol. XXX, No. 3, April 1961, and *Psychoanalysis and Contemporary Culture,* edited by Hendrik M. Ruitenbeek, © 1964. Reprinted by permission of the University of Toronto Press, Toronto, Canada, and Dell Publishing Co., Inc., New York, N.Y.

"The Sociological Revolution." Unpublished paper presented at University of Florida, 1962, and in "Man in the Modern Age," Invitation Lecture Series, University College L. & A. Society, University of Toronto.

"Psychoanalysis: Model for Social Science." Reprinted from *Psychoanalysis and The Psychoanalytic Review,* Vol. 47, No. 4, Winter 1960–61, through the courtesy of the Editors of *The Psychoanalytic Review* and the publisher, National Psychological Association for Psychoanalysis, New York, N.Y.

"Social Psychology: Self and Society." From *Journal of Applied Behavioral Science,* Vol. I, No. 4, 1965, and *The Catalyst,* Summer 1966. Reprinted with permission.

"Personal Science." From *The Urban Condition: People and Policy in the Metropolis,* edited by Leonard J. Duhl, © 1963. Reprinted by permission of Basic Books, Inc., New York, N.Y.

"The Problem of Social Problems." From *Indian Sociological Bulletin,* Vol. II, No. III, April 1965. Reprinted with permission.

"Social Science: Some Probative Problems." From *Sociology on Trial,* edited by Maurice Stein and Arthur Vidich, © 1963. Reprinted by permission of Prentice-Hall, Inc., Englewood Cliffs, N.J.

"Applied Sociology as a Vocation." From *Reflections on Community Study,* edited by Arthur J. Vidich, Joseph Bensman, and Maurice R. Stein, © 1964. Reprinted by permission of John Wiley & Sons, Inc., New York, N.Y.

"Phylogeny and Ontogeny of Applied Sociology." Unpublished paper presented before Applied Sociology Seminar, Brandeis University, 1964.

"The Making and Taking of Problems." Accepted for publication in *Social Problems.*

"The Shaping of Human Nature." From *The Health Education Journal,* Vol. III, No. 1,

January 1950. Reprinted by permission of the Central Council for Health Education, London, England.
"Society, Social Pathology, and Mental Ills." Unpublished paper delivered as The McCuaig Lecture, Queens University, Kingston, Canada, 1962.
"Hostility in Modern Society." From *The Health Education Journal,* Vol. III, No. 2, April 1950. Reprinted by permission of the Central Council for Health Education, London, England.
"Progress from Poverty." From *Liberation,* Vol. 11, No. 5, August 1966. Reprinted by permission of *Liberation,* New York, N.Y.
"Crestwood Heights: A Transaction." From *Reflections on Community Study,* edited by Arthur J. Vidich, Joseph Bensman, and Maurice R. Stein, © 1964 (as "Intellectual and Libidinal Dimensions of Research"). Reprinted by permission of John Wiley & Sons, Inc., New York, N.Y.
"Mental Health and the Law: *Lex Salutis.*" From *University of Toronto Law Journal,* Vol. XV, No. 2, 1964. Reprinted by permission of the University of Toronto Press, Toronto, Canada.
"The Law of the Retardate." From *Mental Retardation,* Vol. 14, No. 2, 1964. Reprinted by permission of the Canadian Association for Retarded Children, Toronto, Canada.
"Parents: The Last Proletariat?" From *Food for Thought,* Vol. 18, No. 7, 1959. Reprinted by permission of the Canadian Association for Adult Education, Toronto, Canada.
"Education: What For?" From *The School Review,* Winter 1958. Reprinted by permission of The University of Chicago Press, Chicago, Ill.
"The Facts of Life." From *Toronto Educational Quarterly,* Vol. 2, No. 1, Autumn 1962, and *The Education Digest,* Vol. XXVIII, No. 6, February 1963. Reprinted with permission.
"Mental Health and the Secondary School." From *The Teachers College Journal,* Vol. XXXV, No. 3, December 1963. Reprinted by permission.
"Education for Mental Health: An Experiment." From *Canadian Education,* Vol. 7, No. 3, 1952. Reprinted by permission of the Canadian Mental Health Association.
"The Forest Hill Village Human Relations Classes." From *Understanding the Child,* Vol. 23, No. 4, October 1954. Reprinted by permission of The National Association for Mental Health, New York, N.Y.
"A Controlled Experiment." Paper, co-authored with Dr. Thomas J. Mallinson, delivered before American Psychiatric Association, Atlantic City, N.J., 1951.
"Guidance: A Plea for Abandonment," and "Guidance and the Youth Culture." From *Personnel and Guidance Journal,* May 1956 and December 1962. Reprinted by permission of the American Personnel and Guidance Association, Washington, D.C.
"Planning for Mental Health." From *Planning 1964.* Reprinted by permission of the American Society of Planning Officials, Chicago, Ill.
"Adolescence: The Management of Emancipation in History and Life History." Paper prepared for plenary session of International Congress for Child Psychiatry, Edinburgh, Scotland, 1966.

Contents

I : The Revolutions: Psychiatric and Sociological

1. The Americanization of the Unconscious 3
2. The Psychiatrist as Reluctant Revolutionary 18
3. Psychiatry: Revolution, Reform, and "Reaction" 36
4. Social Values, the Mental Health Movement, and Mental Health 48
5. The Future of Psychiatry 64
6. The Sociological Revolution 79

II : The Psychoanalytic Stance of Social Science

7. Psychoanalysis: Model for Social Science 99
8. Social Psychology, Self, and Society 108
9. Personal Science 131
10. The Problem of Social Problems 142
11. Social Science: Some Probative Problems 149
12. Applied Sociology as a Vocation 166
13. Phylogeny and Ontogeny of Applied Sociology 211
14. The Making and Taking of Problems 224

III : Society in Psychodynamic Perspective

15. The Shaping of Human Nature 239
16. Society, Social Pathology, and Mental Ills 246
17. Hostility in Modern Society 267
18. Progress from Poverty 280
19. Crestwood Heights: A Transaction 296
20. "Lex Salutis, Salus Legis . . ." 314

21. The Law of the Retardate and the Retardation of the Law 317
22. Parents—the Last Proletariat? 322
23. Education: What For? 331
24. The Facts of Life 338
25. Mental Health and the Secondary School 348
26. Education for Mental Health: An Experiment 353
27. The Forest Hill Village "Human Relations Classes" 366
28. A Controlled Experiment 378
29. Guidance and the Youth Culture 386
30. Guidance: A Plea for Abandonment 402
31. "Planning for Mental Health"—Paradise Stormed 418
32. Adolescence: The Management of Emancipation in History and Life History 436

IV : Epilogue

33. The Beneficial Encounter 449

I

The Revolutions: Psychiatric and Sociological

1

The Americanization of the Unconscious

America is the world's Wonderland. In all the shadings and nuances of the word, she is before all others the world's producer of wonders, and a matter herself of wonder to the alien, and, a fortiori, to herself. Amazed and amazing, bewildering and bewildered, fascinating and utterly fascinated as she sees herself, either directly or reflected in the eyes of others, inexhaustible in her variation, beyond plumbing in her subtlety, inscrutable, unfathomable. . . . Words fail, but interest never flags. Of only one thing can we be sure: that the face she presents to the world—the simple, plain-spoken, direct, homely, straightforward, practical face—is the least of her aspects and serves chiefly to conceal the complexity within complexity that is characteristically hers, and beside which China seems patent and India obvious. The myth of simplicity which she has woven about herself and persuaded others to weave about her serves as a penetrable mantle that calls attention most to what it is ostensibly designed to conceal.

Anyone who attempts to describe America therefore runs the risk of revealing himself simple-minded, of being taken in by appearances, of taking a part for the whole, of taking a fleeting mood, moment, or flicker for the enduring set, process, and stance. Despite the risks, the chance must be taken—and this is one of the ploys of the game that delights Americans—if anything at all is to be said of the modern world over which in one sense, she hovers, and which, in another sense, she infuses and transforms.

The very title of this chapter points to something distinctly, if not exclusively, American: the intellectual centralization of self-analysis as a collective and personal preoccupation, the pouring into it of vast libidinal investment and the receipt in return of endless emotional gratification. The love affair between America and its image is unlike any under the moon or sun. Every other nation holds before itself for relatively lengthy periods a rather steady image of its collective personality, clear-eyed or distorted. Some move from phases of self-glorification to phases of self-denigration: from Rudyard Kipling, say, to the Angry Young Men. Some brood endlessly on the mystery of their being, but always sinking deeper into a mystery that is always the same. Some romanticize, or, as in Canada, pursue frantically a national identity which eludes perception because it is pursued. But only in America does one turn and turn the corporate image before all the available transforming mirrors of this frame of reference and that. Other peoples glory also in their singularity, but since the singularity of America is its variation, how could America fail to glory precisely in that?

Such desperate overcomplication in the object doubles for the would-be analyst the temptation to oversimplify. One is tempted to "account for" America, and thus to kill the very idea of it, by reducing description to a small set of worn-out, and even originally misleading, terms. Every characterization becomes thus a caricature, and while Americans are sometimes taken in, so that they begin to act as they were said to be, more often they smile indulgently and turn their interest to the next "reflection." There are, however, a few things that might be said about America that would at least be free of the limits of such common clichés as "pragmatic," or "practical."

It might be said that Americans who take no one seriously —almost never a European, and rarely one of their own—are hero-makers and hero-worshippers. The statement understates the case. An air of Messianic expectation pervades the culture—as one would expect in a society where the conventional belief is in fundamental equality. The secular version is the much-worn log cabin to White House, but this masks rather than reveals the much deeper conviction that some much more general and profounder savior from something more pervasive than the moment's political problems will any moment appear and be recognized. The excessive and unadmitted expectation accounts in part for the typically rapid rise and fall of the hero: over-rapid rise, because the expectation creates the necessity to project onto the candidate the preshaped halo; over-rapid fall, because such distortion of reality cannot long be maintained. (I know the habit is to account for such phenomena in terms of the highly developed communications media, the maneuvers of publicity, the harsh glare of the resultant spotlight. But the media are means, not purposes. One does not develop a far-flung net of detection to observe what is not of paramount interest.)

It might also be said that Americans who believe in "the pursuit of happiness" (life and liberty appearing merely as necessary conditions therefor) far from behaving hedonically, flee happiness (both pleasure and joy) and seek unremittingly for "illumination." Work and study—things that may not be spoken about seriously because they are serious—represent the Royal Way. The amount of popular and semipopular literature read annually that is in essence philosophic or that looks to the provision of high general answers to profound life problems, would, if it were published as "religious publication," as it properly should be, outweigh the publication of any other kind of literature here and now, and the publication of any similar literature in any country at any time in history.

Indeed, Americans, who have disestablished religion, tend in a profound sense to make a religion of everything. It is true, no doubt, that to a very large extent they have made what they call "religion" shallow, but if this is not precisely because they have made other matters, which other nations treat lightly, most profound, at least the two tendencies reinforce each other. It would be but a slight exaggeration to say that Americans are the most unsecular people on earth. If devotion to an Idea, if ardor in its affectionate development, if the rendering of the idea immanent in the body of thought of the time, and if the pervasive embodiment of the idea in behavior, are, as I believe, the hallmarks of a "religious" attitude toward it, then ideas are religiously treated in America. It is true that one religion readily succeeds another, but this is rather from the devotion to the general religious quest than from disloyalty to the particular religion abandoned. "God by God goes out, discrown'd and disannointed, But the soul stands fast that gave them shape and speech."

Lastly, contradictory but coexistent, just as everyone who is anyone becomes a hero, so everything that is anything tends to become an industry. By an industry I mean nothing more than some enormous organization (as in any modern nation it must needs be) in which some input is put in, brought under a process characterized by a maximum of "rationality" (minute subdivision of labor, immense organization, and exact adaptation of calculated means to ends), and thereby some output put out. Whether the matter is child-raising or "higher education" or "entertainment" or the production of a new generation of non-Momistic mothers—or even religion in the narrower sense—almost inevitably it is so organized and so put into "production."

Into a culture thus constituted in its general workings was implanted about 1909 a cultural seedling, the thought and technique of Sigmund Freud. In almost any soil the seedling was bound to become a mustard tree, with room for all manner of fowl to lodge in its branches. In America—the analogy begins to fail—it was to transform and be transformed by the society.

The *practice* of psychoanalysis underwent almost no change in the transplantation, except that for reasons that have more to do with politics than culture, it fell almost exculsively into the hands of doctors. (It should be remembered that Freud to his life's end tried to live down his definition and attitude as a physician in favor of a redefinition as a psychologist-philosopher of theory and unquestionably a prophet-priest of practice.)

It was the theory—by far the more important part—that was to be modified and made over, and to modify and make over men, theories, and institutions.

Freud's doctrines as they reached these shores were, by implication, stern if not gloomy. Since his own writings fill a good-sized shelf, and professional commentary upon them a good-sized library, it would seem idle to attempt to reduce them to a paragraph here. The leading ideas that are of interest here concern the instinct theory, the "institutions of the mind," and the nature of man and society.

Man, as Freud portrayed him, comes to the world with a full accoutrement of instinctual drives. Pleasure (or happiness) lies in the satisfaction and gratification of these instinctual demands which are in principle insatiable: more particularly the pandemic demands are for outlets for sexuality and aggression. It is in the very nature of man, in Freud's view, that he cannot live outside society, while at the same time it is in the very nature of society to require renunciation of instinctual gratification, the only source of happiness. (Even if man were able to live "outside of" society, Freud leaves us cold comfort: it is also in the very nature of pleasure itself to require mounting tension as a prelude to relief, so that the desired and the undesired are even "in raw nature" inextricably intertwined.) In any case, since society cannot survive without taming the instinctual demands, and indeed subverting them to its uses, it achieves its ends, at the expense of individual happiness, by routinely, radically, and inevitably dividing the psyche against itself. This double assault upon the possibility of any sensible degree of happiness—the truncating of the individual's opportunities for gratification, together with the internalization of the conflict that "really" lies between him and his fellows—is carried out and completed upon the helpless infant by the unwitting adults.

The first figure in the drama of the child's ontogeny is the "id," an institution of the psyche, largely unconscious, representing in principle unlimited demand for the gratification of sexual and aggressive instincts. The nature of the environment requires from the child sufficient appreciation of that which is independent of his wishes so that he does not totally stultify his own search for gratification by the use of inappropriate means. A second institution, custodian of "the reality principle," is thus differentiated in the "ego." But dominant in the child's significant environment are those who can and do most obviously give and withhold gratification, mete out reward and punishment, the custodians of the culture, the surrogates for the society's interests: the parents or their deputies. In the course of time, the watching, warding, judging, criticizing, ruling, governing behavior of these virtual jail-keepers of the instincts are "internalized" in yet a third institution, differentiated out of and set over against the ego—the "superego," again mostly unconscious, but not the less censorious, vigilant, and punitive for that. The ego now has an additional reality to deal with: the conflict between the excessive demands of the id for gratification and of the superego for the limiting or extinction of these demands. A great deal of the limited energy available to the ego is thus consumed in ceaseless adjudication between one party that would empty life of pleasure and the other that would rob it of safety. The child is finally his own prisoner, jailer, and the mediator between the two. By a final and exquisitely ironic twist, the very aggression that is thus cut off from its gratification becomes the very source of the energy of the superego, so that the psyche is indeed "the plough-cloven clod, and the plowshare drawn thorough. . . ." What is to be inferred with regard to man and society, Freud says in one of the starkest of his works, *Civilization and Its Discontents*. The burden of the volume is that as man seeks to defend himself against disaster-bearing nature and against the disease- and death-bearing body, the very necessities of the defense organization (society and culture) require the attenuation of sources of satisfaction to such a degree that the life thus secured is mostly precarious, and, even when stable, scarcely to be endured. He leaves both the survival of civilization and the capacity of men to survive under it as open questions.

The popular myth is that these gloomy doctrines running into the irrepressible optimism and meliorism of the American people underwent characteristically American reversals and came out transformed, pupa into butterfly, in the much more palatable dogmas of what were politely called "The Revisionists": Horney, Fromm, Sullivan, and others. It is true that a "Revision" occurred: a revision perhaps as radical as the one that produced Marxian materialism out of Hegelian idealism, but what made the "Revision" possible and necessary had little to do with American optimism directly. In any case, as will later appear, what is most interesting and most "American" is not the revision as such, but the subsequent "psychoanalyzation"—horrible coinage, but what word will serve?—of American thought, institutions, and life.

In the first place, the words were hardly cool on Freud's lips, the ink hardly dry on his pen, before "revisionism"—or, as he looked upon it, apostasy—set in, even in Europe. Unlike Christ, eleven-twelfths of whose disciples remained formally firm in the faith, Freud lived to see proportions almost reversed: Jung, Adler, Ferenczi, Reich, Reik, Rank, and Stekel, to mention only the most eminent. In a sense though, tragically, he did not "see" it so—revision was a movement that the Master himself set off both by his method and by the power of his example, and he had as much chance of stopping it (short of force) as Luther had of limiting Protestantism to his own first great Protest. So the fact of revision is not purely American.

Nor is the direction taken by revision so easily to be explained. It would be impossible to do justice to the theories of any one of Horney, Sullivan, or Fromm in a short chapter, let alone to all of them. Each developed a connected viewpoint either implicit or explicit, and, in the case of Sullivan—the least known of the three—something that approached a new systematics. More of Freud survives in all three than any one of them is ready to admit—so much, indeed, that one can see a distant ecumenical reunion in the far offing, perhaps a century off. What binds the major Revisionist schools together, in the same kind of radical-variation-within-basic-similarity as binds American Protestantism, is a sizable shift from a biological determinism to or toward a cultural and social determinism, together with (necessarily, I think) a preoccupation with "the self" as the unit of concern and investigation, the central element in theory, in contradistinction to the preoccupation with the fate of instincts and the squabbles of the psychic Trinity. This is not to say, of course, that any one of the Revisionists "denies" instincts, though all reduce the role played by infantile sexuality and aggression. It hardly goes too far to say that what was peripheral in Freud's developed work—ego-function, the role of ego-ideals, etc.—becomes central for the three, and what was central for Freud becomes peripheral.

Since society and social relations—"interpersonal relations" as Sullivan significantly calls them—are thought to be more readily amenable to rational improvement than biologically "given" instincts, there is unquestionably a greater air of optimism in what the Revisionists say, and an unmistakable foundation for meliorism for those so inclined. Indeed, in Erich Fromm, the message moves very nearly from historical analysis (in *Escape from Freedom*) to a combination of character typology, philosophy, and institutional analysis (in *Man for Himself*) to a virtual trumpet call to (a quite particular) social reform as the means to psychological health (in *The Sane Society*).

What made this particular line of "Revision" necessary and

possible was the prior existence in America (and nowhere else) of a fairly well-developed body of fact and theory in the social sciences generally, more particularly in sociology, anthropology, and "social psychology." It was the collision with this rival episcopate, already considerably entrenched in American affections, already turning its microscope on American life, and already holding out the promise of offering America more images of more of its illimitable aspects, that gave the Revisionists the impulse, the possibility, and the model for their subsequent development. The existence of this body of specialists, their particular orientations, and the actual and potential public interest in them are, of course, consequences of American affluence, the necessities of self-understanding posed by the melting-pot, by rapid social mobility, and by all the characteristics of American culture pointed to at the beginning of this chapter. But it was the collision of European psychoanalytic theory and "case material" with American social and social-psychological theory that gave the revision its form and preoccupation and part of its content. Indeed, from the time of the collision, neither was ever again quite the same thing. Much social science (part of it properly and part of it improperly) continued with studied inattention to psychoanalytic theory; some psychoanalytic theory continued in studied disregard of social science; but a great deal of each now took a new turn, fertilized by the other; and out of the fertilization grew a new child that might, almost indifferently, be labeled social-psychoanalytic theory or psychoanalytic-social theory.

It is hard to see how, in a social-scientific community sensitized by the work of a long line of social psychologists reaching from Baldwin to George Herbert Mead, the central problem of the organization of the self stated in terms of role-taking and role-generalization could be long evaded by any group claiming to understand the genesis of personality. The interest of Charles Horton Cooley in "the primary group" and its relation to "the social self" was contributory to the focus on "interpersonal relations" which Sullivan was so expertly to fill out. The hard-won anthropological and sociological materials were ready to cross-question any general theory of human nature or human development that was too narrowly based on a single society, a single class, or an otherwise "biased sample." The parents needed each what the other had: adequate case materials, particularly of sufficient depth and intimacy, were lacking to give body to the rather lofty generalizations of social psychology; adequate formalization of the relation between social process and psychological process had been lacking in most psychoanalytic thought.

The interplay between social science and psychoanalytic theory becomes too complex at this point to follow much farther. It issues at one point in the anthropologically informed psychological theories of social character of an Abraham Kardiner; the psychoanalytically sensitized anthropology of a Margaret Mead; the Revisionist-sensitized social character typology of a David Riesman; the exquisitely sensitive playing back and forth between person and society, concrete and particularized rather than abstract and general, of an Erik Erikson.

. . .

In a fashion somehow also typically American, orthodox Freudianism—*echt Freud*—survives and develops. There is inter-sect antipathy, but characteristically no Wars of Religion. Indeed, the True Church not only survives and develops, it flourishes and is favored by the hard-core social scientists over the offerings of the Revisionists, who are rejected partly on intellectual grounds and partly on the emotional ground that they make things—including especially the life of the social scientist—too easy. Nobly, quixotically, or masochistically—view it how you will, and it has touches of all three—the biologically trained psychoanalysts struggle with culturism and sociologism while the sociologically trained social psychologists struggle with biologism. The psychonalysts come to terms with what David Riesman has called the "dirty secrets" of sociology: social class, ethnicity, and the like; the sociologists come to terms with the corresponding dirty secrets of the analysts: sex and aggression. The preoccupation of each with the supposed preoccupation of the other can be "explained" sociologically or psychoanalytically, and appears equally interesting either way, but this is not the place to explain it.

Much more dramatic than any of this analysis of Analysis and its fate among the professionals is the story of its destiny and development into something immanent in American life, interfused with all thought and activity, making over the society in as radical (and as shallow) a way as had earlier the official religions: Christianity and (nice contradiction!) liberal, capitalist democracy.

Perhaps this is the point at which to set up some contrasts. How far in Europe have the views and preoccupation, of "mental health" spread, ramified, infused the views of ends or means of educators, city planners, makers of social policy generally, parents, writers, politicians, administrators, executives, and so on—in short, nonpsychiatrists?

I do not wish to caricature, but cannot avoid doing so in a sketch. A summer's extensive and intensive survey trip revealed that Europeans had access to, had read, and were highly "interested in" our social science and psychoanalytic literature, American and—what there is of it—Canadian. They regarded it predominantly in a "detached" way: an interesting expression, symbolically, of America, and no doubt, a good enough account of American life. But they saw it neither as directly applicable to them nor as providing a model of sorts which they might apply to their own self-study. (Actually, excellent similar studies had been made of European life by Europeans, but they were less widely known or appreciated.)

They have excellent "mental health" enterprises—indeed some so excellent that the best here suffers, I think, by comparison—but little or no tendency to "generalize" either by reproducing copies of the dramatically successful enterprises, or by "drawing out their principles" and seeking to apply them over a wide range of life, let alone to re-examine general social objectives in the light of them. There is remarkably good research; but the people who knew or cared about it were largely the professionals, and then either (as in England) in a task-oriented sense or (as in Germany) in a dominantly philosophical one. It is as though the movements of thought which in America (in *these* matters) are almost instantaneously communicated to every cell of the body (a sort of intellectual-emotional metastasis) were there contained, dammed off, localized, and allowed to exert a general influence only gradually, if at all. The remark of a very literate, sophisticated, old school teacher may be allowed to stand as typical: yes, she knew a good deal about Freud; no, it had little to do with "*Erziehung*," the bringing up of children. (We found the same sharp split in France between problems of "therapy" and problems of "development.") Our teacher and her contemporaries had even once taken a course on the *Geisteskrankheiten*, but she spoke of it with the same reminiscent delight and the same air of separation from the everyday concerns of life as if she had been speaking of a course in Egyptian hieroglyphics. In fact, it had for her something of just that travelogue quality: interesting, quaint, but happily remote and someone else's worry.

More typical of America—and only faintly exaggerated in the one direction as the previous anecdote is in the other—would be, to take one institution, the school faintly adumbrated in my book *Crestwood Heights*, but to be found in purer form in numberless suburbs in the United States.

In the "pure form," not only means and methods but goals and criteria of performance have been made over in terms of available psychoanalytic understandings. Just as religion has become a way to Peace of Mind—thereby emptying it of specifically religious content—so education has become the way to strength of soul, to "positive mental health," to "maturity." It is not that teachers are preoccupied by pathology; they are too healthy for that, though their rather general viewing of children as "problems" (paralleled by parent perceptions in the same terms) begins to border on that danger. It is rather that everything is seen, "understood," and acted upon (as far as reality permits) in terms of the depth drama actually or possibly underlying any act. Little behavior is taken at face value; almost without consciousness of alternative possibilities of perception, everything very nearly is "interpreted." The role of the teacher as a "parent-surrogate" is understood and accepted. It is expected that "hostility" will be "displaced" upon her, that drawings, essays, polite exchanges have "covert" meanings much different from their "overt" content—and much more real and much more interesting. The "libidinal" give and take that accompanies all communication (or motivates it?) is noted, albeit less easily accepted. If Johnny throws a spit-ball at Mary, nothing so ordinary as "mischief" is afoot. The possibilities have to be (are joyously) entertained that Johnny is "working off aggression," compensating for deeply felt "inferiority," asserting his "masculinity" in ways "appropriate to his developmental stage," "testing for limits," or, in characteristic upside down way (and perhaps most likely), saying to Mary in a circuitous and hence safe way, "I love you." And so not only for students, but for the interrelations of staff, and of all to "authority." The "mental health" of the staff as a prerequisite for the mental health of the pupils is a matter of focal concern —not, of course, in the bare sense that teachers should not be mentally sick, but that they also should be positively well, continuously "growing," always "developing" and "maturing"—and manifestly happy, continuously emotionally rewarded, in so doing. I will not go on. The rest spells itself out. Except perhaps that I should note again what I have noted elsewhere: that in such schools the parents (or at least the mothers) must be continuously caught up in the enterprise to a point of unexampled intimacy, and in a role partly of lay assistants in the child's upbringing and partly of apprentices or pupils.

What is true for the school is true for the church, for industry (on the white-collar side, at least), for the family, and even to a sensible degree for the "peer-group" institutions among the youngsters themselves. The explicit awareness of high school kids—and those in the elementary school, down to kindergarten—of the depth-psychological world they now inhabit, is exquisite, and many of them know their gamesmanship better than the adults.

This development in America—and it has still to run the major part of its course—makes for a change in the very nature of the society, comparable in the magnitude of its effects with the original American Revolution only as the strong and streaming sun with the pale and puny moon. That was a revolution of mere *externa;* this of *interna, ultima, privatissima.* We are confronted by the possibility— perhaps now the inescapable necessity—of a highly self-conscious society of highly self-conscious individuals, a society that must sustain, cope with, or use all the new possibilities of "vertical" complexity in addition to the pre-existing ones of "horizontal" complexity. We have added a dimension; and there is no more radical act. We are in the process of producing, if we have not already produced, a distinctively American Unconscious.

Such a society has the possibility of approximating a "therapeutic community"—or, rather, a community favorable to the emergence of a humanity more humane than any we have ever known. It has also the possibility of becoming a "manipulative society" in which the minor clumsy attempts depicted by Vance Packard in *The Hidden Persuaders* are perfected to the point where resistance is virtually meaningless; a society in which, moreover, the threats of manipulation from without are countered but fatally compounded by self-manipulation, which is also full in the current American stream. The dice are heavily loaded in favor of the latter risk, the risk of catastrophe, by the American devotion to mastery as the *Deus deorum.* Only if we can bring out of the consulting room into the society (as well as the *ideas* we have already brought out) the intelligent affection that contains and domesticates the otherwise threatening possibilities of insight, only if we can institutionalize these in public life (revolutionizing other institutions in the process if necessary), can we hope that we have called out the forces of life rather than tapped upon the door of death's angel. Insight is mere technique: Eros and Thanatos still dispute whose, and their representatives in us will determine.

2

The Psychiatrist as Reluctant Revolutionary

I hear psychiatry is having troubles. Not technical troubles: what to take from or give to whom to make whom feel better in what ways. Nor the troubles of weakness: how to get together what resources in what concentrations, where, in order to defend against what dangers, real or imagined, in what order, in what strengths, on what fronts, when. But the troubles of strength: the troubles that accrue with and derive from being a force in the world—or a threat of force.

I hear, first, that psychiatrists are being noticed, which is in itself a danger signal, next most monitory only to being taken note of, and then served notice upon. No longer just nuts or nut-doctors whose activities can be indulgently smiled upon as analogical to those of the more harmless of their patients, but people whose activities, on the contrary, threaten the society in precisely the same way but on a deeper level and greater scale than the less mild, less lovable, less easily contained and warded off of those whom they treat or segregate or both.

I hear next that men call psychiatrists—or some of them—demagogues. A demagogue commits the very crime for which Jesus was executed: "He stirreth up the people." He is a false leader; false not only because he does not derive his just powers from the consent of the governors, but false because he speaks in a new vocabulary, on the basis of a claimed new authority, fanning the fire of old resentments into the light of new hopes. It is thus not only—and not so much—the content of the new message, whatever it is, but the appeal to a different authority, that is the essence of the charge. For an appeal to a new principle is in principle itself the overthrow of an existent order. It is indeed a treason—to something.

I hear they say worse. I hear they say psychiatrists are subversive. Not subversive only in some vague and general sense—say, the sense in which poets and painters are, as they always are, subversive—but subversive in the quite specific way that they sharpen the edge of discontent, honing it upon the edge of the possible and pointing it upon its causes. More especially, they say, by their very interest in discomfort, more particularly evitable or reducible discomfort, psychiatrists threaten to make the latent manifest—and the diffuse focused. Such opening and organizing of perspective—even if one does no more—is as much a prelude to action as a hammer tap is to clonus. The minimum, not fully formed, action to be feared is the expression of restiveness, the milling that precedes all radical reorganization, the milling that not only leads to "noncooperation" but is itself the first stage of it. The latent—perhaps not clear and present, but visible and imminent—danger is that men so moved may be less than enthusiastic collaborators in the designs that their present and traditional masters have upon them—always, of course, for their own good. They may thus, because of psychiatry, inadvertently strike from generous hands the proffered cup of their own salvation, which is what the Southern Negro seems to be doing at the present moment, partly as a consequence of the Supreme Court decision, which itself is unobscurely related to doctrines as to the nature of man stemming unambiguously from the direction provided by psychiatrists. It is a very serious situation.

Lastly, I hear that they say—though I suppose these are footnotes or supererogatory charges—that psychiatrists are presumptuous to meddle in such matters as they meddle in, that they covertly represent special interests, and that they serve, in the present, functions much like those served by the Communist Party in the past, and the "communist conspiracy" even now: the very shape, shade, epitome, and spearhead of everything that is wrong, dangerous, ill-conceived, ill-intended, ill-executed, and pregnant with unnamed and indefinable catastrophe!

How have psychiatrists come to this pass? Who has brought them to it? What may they do? And how shall they extricate themselves?

I gather that psychiatrists are not undivided in the enthusiasm with which they welcome this revolutionary role or the ascription or imputation of it to them. I gather that some, at least, all of the time, and all, at most, some of the time, had rather see themselves simply and singly as healers of the sick and curators where they cannot be curers. I understand that many have not wished to seize greatness, either for good or for ill, and still less to have greatness for either thrust upon them. There might even exist desire among those who wish to define their whole function as the cure, care, and keeping of this patient and that one—to divide and cut themselves off from those who think otherwise, lest there arise not only guilt by association but harm by association—which so easily flows out of it. There are those, I am told, who wish to cut deep in the definition of their function, and those who do not want to cut deep, doubting the profit, wisdom, or possibility of so doing. There are those, similarly, who wish to sweep wide, and those for whom the mandate for each to sweep only before his own doorsill is already too extended an injunction.

It is easy to sympathize where one cannot solve. What must be the state of a profession, and what the agonies, internal and external, of its practitioners, when some, seemingly, would content themselves with a little supportive "psychotherapy" here and there, now and then, or perhaps a little pharmacoassistance discreetly administered, while others dream and hope—and, worse, talk—of replanning the world, not merely in its full global extent at the surface, but also and simultaneously (and thereby) at its inmost reaches and deepest depths. I sense that there is something short of utter unity between the starry-eyed and the dusty-handed; and that, as always in such conjectures (reversing Macaulay), those in front cry "Forward" while those behind cry "Back!" Indeed it is possible that the van and the rear each feel that the other has compromised the army and put the war itself in jeopardy—more particularly so since the line of march or defense or attack is not agreed upon, and hence no agreement is possible as to which is rear and which van, which forward line and which base. An army so situated is not merely encompassed, but in danger of rout. It must at the very least determine—discover or rediscover—its direction before it can organize its defense and then its line of movement.

What the direction must be—it is trite, perhaps, to say it—is an element in the set of what is possible. If the set contains only one element, then, of course, the decision is already made once the set is defined. If it contains even a limited number of elements, then the decision is facilitated by restricting attention to what is worth considering. Perhaps we can, by surveying what *can* be, assist in the choice of what is to be. At least, for the reluctant and eager, the pacemakers and pacebrakers, alike, we ought to determine in what sense psychiatry is or is not of its nature and essence revolutionary.

It is sometimes—indeed very often—helpful to be clear about terms, at least key terms. What is a revolution? What is a revolutionary? A revolution is a radical change in the social order, commonly sudden of seeming onset and sometimes fulminating, at least in its early course. By a radical change is meant a change that reaches wide and deep: wide, so that many are affected; deep, so that something more than what men consider trivia and details are altered and overset. By the social order (in which are included the associated abstractions called the economic and political orders) is meant an insitituted, going, and expected arrangement for the differential distribution between aggregates of men (thereby defined as "classes") of whatever there is to get. Whatever there is to get is what men value. What men will value is partly a function of their natural nature—as air while they live, and life itself under most circumstances—and partly a result of what they have been taught to desire or made (by their early formation) to "need."

Harold Lasswell, in an excellent introduction to politics, tells us that politics is the art of getting the most of what there is to get, and that what there is to get is income, deference, and safety. For his purposes at the time these definitions were good and sufficient. But for our more general purposes they will not do. For what "income" is is not self-evident: as we know from anthropology, it may be the right to give away more than others; for a masochist it may be humiliation and pain; and for a mother the child's taking suck (his income, incidentally, and hers simultaneously). Nor are "deference" and "safety" self-evidently self-defining. What deference is depends upon a prior libidinal distribution that is in turn related to the earliest libidinal investments, failing which no "source" can be sufficiently endowed with value or meaning to make an appropriate gesture that could carry the gratificatory quality of "deference." And "safety," is notoriously dependent for its definition on the meaning and significance given to its cognate term (in a ground-figure relation) "danger"—which is itself socio-psycho-biologically defined, except at the margin, by the whole early ontogeny. At best, then, these words figure as containers of variable content—content so variable that what is contained may in one case be the opposite of what is contained in the other. Can we find less variable definitions of "what there is to get"?

I think we may do so—though it may seem strange doctrine—by being plainly and radically subjective. By subjective I mean only that we choose terms that plainly imply that they are oriented from the viewpoint of the actor, unlike, say, "income," which appears to be gauged from the observer's point of view. (This is only to say what is, I think, obvious: that social affairs are only or ultimately to be understood phenomenologically.)

Suppose we take it that the things that there are to get are such things as "love," "security," "self-love," and "self-respect," "legitimacy" or sense of right-being and right-doing and right-having—or some such list. Clearly, these are at least defined from the viewpoint of the actor—though this is not to say, of course, that every actor invents his own criteria or levels of satisfaction, at least not altogether. There may even be universal and unalterable elements in the definitions, such that, for instance, adequate expressions of love cannot be separated from adequate dermal contact; but the important thing is the element of variability that leaves considerable room for definition and redefinition, personal and social, private and shared, of what it is that is the sign and signal, the substance and reality of each. For so it is. What is income is, again, a matter of what is defined to be income: at the right moment, in the right place, for the right person, the right to go to one's "premature" death as a Kamikaze pilot, borne upon, and bearing with one, the eternal afflatus, the divine wind. And so for all such terms. It is not even evidently necessary—as long as the other "beliefs" are consistent—that the terms refer to a known and evidently existent world: "safety" lies in "salvation" in a world not seen of eye or sensed of touch, "beyond" and "above" this one, and at the risk of every earthly possession, the "soul" only excepted and the body less than nothing—for those who believe so, collectively or idiosyncratically.

If all or any of these things is substantially true, then it must be obvious that there are at least two ways to make a revolution in the sense that I have defined. One would consist in leaving the going order of goods—the "valuation scheme"—essentially intact, while rotating the prerevolutionary elite out of their preferential positions and rotating a new elite into their preferred places. (By an elite I do not mean to make a value judgment here, but only to define the relative monopolists of valued life-chances in any order.) This is the "classic" model, I suppose. But the alternative form is equally clear, and perhaps at this point in our history much more cogent. In the alternative form, by a transformation of valuation—no matter how accomplished—we leave the *ci-devant* elite sitting precisely where they were, while revaluing goods so that theirs are generally downgraded in value while those of others are heightened. No one, for instance, needs to take away titles of nobility from their legitimate possessors in order to effect a revolution of sorts, once the general value put upon such titles has been changed from positive to negative. No one needs to alter anyone's ancestry, and still a revolution has been effected, once it has become disvalued (by fiat) to be the child of bourgeois or kulak, and valued to claim proletarian or peasant origin. The "first shall be last, and the last shall be first" effect has been had in the instant and by virtue of the fact of transvaluation. We even saw it happen with money—itself, in our society, the supposed measure of value—in the German inflation: the possessors of stocks, money, bonds, found themselves poor, naked, and despised as well as despoiled beside the meanest owner of the merest spot of land, the shabbiest cloak, the driest crust of bread. The redefinition of values, in a crisis of circular failure of faith, entirely overset, virtually reversed, the elite-mass, exploiter-exploited, relationships. If the illustration seems remote or far-fetched, remember we have been watching a less dramatic but nevertheless consequential similar transformation and reorganization as city-periphery has come to be preferred over city-center as a place of residence. We do not have to water the desert to make it blossom like the rose; we merely have to shift our preferences, alter our valuations, to bring the wild wasteland to the height of value and endow its possessor with the bounty of unearned income and windfall capital gain.

But what is so obvious even of hard and economic goods

like land is a fortiori and more dramatically true of socially defined goods like ancestry, accent, place of origin, skin color, manner of making a living, type of service rendered in return, output and input in general. In less than a generation, a change in the climate or scheme of valuation can make it a matter of shame instead of pride that one's sole output is one's decorative gracefulness and one's corresponding input a carefully selected, tasteful sufficiency of the best there is to get—from caviar, to esthetic and educational "experiences," to rest in the best cemetery. Indeed, even more rapidly, what is seen and said to be tasteful and graceful may so come under review and revision that the former virtuosi of the corresponding arts are rendered rapidly not so much obsolete as counter-exemplars, illustrations for the instruction of others in what not to do and be, social dinosaurs by pure redefinition.

In the power to revalue lies, therefore, along at least one axis, the power to revolutionize. Shifts in legitimation *are* shifts in value. And legitimation is a function of definition and redefinition—definition of what things *are*, in themselves and in relation to each other, and hence and independently, of what they are worth. A little different light on the same activity makes today's good mothering tomorrow's "momism"—and it is already something different and worth something different in the moment, the very instant, of redefinition. The very identification of an unknown or undeclared relation is in and of itself a revolutionary alteration of the related identities, once revealed and made known; thus what it is to be a son or a daughter, a father or a mother is something quite other after Freud, and more so after his followers-after. Definitions distribute goods, and redefiners alter distributions.

A revolution is thus essentially achieved when a new viewpoint—or perhaps I should say, worthpoint—succeeds an old one in a society, just as a recovery is actually achieved when the corresponding events occur in the patient. All else is consolidation or effloration, though it is not to be discounted because it merely follows. But the revolution may be said to have occurred already when ideal succeeds ideal, or idol replaces idol. Actualization is a matter of time and circumstance, and while not trivial, is essentially incidental.

The ideals that are open to change are in number virtually infinite, but only a few are consequential because they carry the others, by logical implication or practical necessity, with them. The central, prepotent or paramount or master ideals are those respecting the ideal man, the ideal society, the ideal or ideals of interpersonal process, and, perhaps most basic, the ideal outlook or perspective. The first three are intimately interconnected; and all three rest in a sense upon the fourth.

Changes in such central ideals may come about by the explosive eruption of new revelation of an essentially religious or poetic nature, or by the slower and more erosive action of philosophy, amateur or professional. But increasingly, since the seventeenth century at least, in the West anyway, the principal agent of transformation has been that loose aggregate of nevertheless distinct activities we call "science." Indeed, the institution of science as the preferred or ultimate or bedrock ideal perspective or outlook is the first great revolution of our era; and the extension of some or all of the scientific outlook, with or without modification, to the affairs of men, is the second and more far-reaching transformation. More patently, of course, does it carry with it the risk or certainty that in the new perspective the ideas and ideals of man, society, and interpersonal process may themselves be transformed, so that the whole core value-system is under total and simultaneous reconstitution. The third revolution may be said to occur when the powers and potencies of this new outlook are brought into conjunction with the notions of care and the Hippocratic tradition: a powerful conjunction or confluence of two old and well established traditions with a new one.

In the confluence or collision, both the nature of knowledge and the criteria of care are themselves somewhat transformed. The scientific outlook is in some peculiar sense truth-bound rather than truth-limited. This in itself is a dangerous social doctrine, and when we come upon it, it is already no longer merely a doctrine but an embodiment in an ideology, a set of practices, roles, persons, and institutions. The notion that it is better to know than not know, without restriction or taboo, is so new an idea in the world that no society in history has substantially instituted it, and none, of course, does unreservedly yet.

Nearly related, but not quite the same thing, is a strand in the scientific outlook that seems intrinsic to it, that for want of a better name may be called holism. The understanding of any part of anything even partially seems to require the understanding of any relevant whole of which it can be seen to be a significant part, and that whole in turn comes to be seen as a part of some still conceptually larger whole. Thus historic interests cannot be restricted to the biased history of our nation, and sociology cannot get along without comparative material from other times and places, and psychology cannot be understood outside social contexts, which cannot themselves be appreciated outside *their* contexts—and so on. One may for practical reasons momentarily narrow one's gaze, but one lives and breathes forever in the shadow of the all-else, and one knows that what one sees in constricted perspective must in the next moment be re-placed somehow in that seamless everything in which it inherently belongs.

The foregoing fact—and the peculiar nature of the "generalized other" to whom he is responsive—makes it particularly difficult for the scientist to be partial (in either sense) or partisan in his interests or evaluations: not that he is not, but that these partialities suffer relatively rapid attrition. This too makes him as it were a resident of a foreign country, for it is the normal accompaniment of any other "social status" to have and require a peculiar and more parochial ideology and outlook, and to look rather to the continuous building up of the same than to its reduction or confounding in an outlook more general.

Last, though it may be no more than the sum of the above, there is some unfortunate tendency in the scientist, I believe, to a kind of urbaneness or civilizedness, that tends to make him in every locality in some sort a stranger, and in every era born somehow out of due season.

What characterizes the outlook spills over, where there is any close conjoining of the two elements, into the canons of care. Every right-thinking man in the street knows that some are more deserving of care—or, at least, deserving of more care—than others. (Such an inclination would seem to be a datum of siblingship in the Western type of family, if it has no other roots.) Moreover, the man in the street has a pretty good idea, a strong suspicion at least, as to who it is that deserves more care, or better. But, with rare exceptions at the very margin (as when a choice may have to be made between mother and child), medicine knows no such necessities, or proposes to act as if in a different and otherwise governed realm of freedom. It is hence a perennial difficulty to restrain attention to a particular patient, a particular class of patients, patients from a particular region, or patients in any particular situation. Indeed, it goes somewhat against the grain to define the term "patient" too narrowly so as to exclude the unwilling (as in vaccination in some cases) or the not-yet or not-at-all sick, as in preventive programs like sanitation—physical, or if we know enough, psychological.

The "caring" activity and orientation, in turn, tend to make over the scientific activity, obviously in the direction and content of its interest, but also, I think, to some degree in its style and tone so as to render it a somewhat more apt instrument for the investigation or study of human as against nonhuman behavior.

So we have a new outlook. And, for better or worse—and some evidently think worse—it diffuses. Human scientists, especially of the caring variety—or those who mix both roles

—come willy-nilly to be examples, good or bad, which some emulate in attitude or practice or doctrine, as they understand them and as best they can. It is a serious problem. But it does not stop there. The trouble is not only with the air of inquiry, nor even its association with a caring activity and orientation.

The trouble is deeper. The very nature of the inquiry, for some of the reasons previously sketched, begins to make over the ideals tenable for man, for society, for interpersonal process, for much else.

In the first instance, in the first shock of encounter, the ideals that men may (and, finally, can) hold are altered by double redefinitions of the possible: double, in that they both limit and expand possibility. By the mere tracing of intrinsic consequences it becomes speedily evident that there are constraints, hitherto unsuspected, on possibility: perhaps it becomes evident that you cannot have a given this in association with a given that, say, harsh, early and "effective" toilet-training together with genuine generosity or the feeling of authenticity in such giving as there is. It may also become evident that dispositions toward the body are incapable of divorce from dispositions toward all else, so that certain possibilities are ruled out as viable schemes. Similarly, new possibilities may be opened up to exploitation because they are recognized in the course of systematic inquiry. Thus, for example, the possibilities of satisfying fatherhood may be expanded by the recognition that it is not necessary that all the present roles be bound up in one bundle, and that indeed in some societies, quite viably, the disciplinary function for instance can be separated and discharged by the child's mother's brother (or child's mother's sister's husband even!).

So tenable ideals are altered by redefined possibilities. But there is more than this. As inquiry establishes new links between any two or more events or conditions, one of which may be thought causal to or inseparable from the other, the values of each or all are made over. Thus punishment as an aid to "discipline"—or even as a preferable elicitor of desired behavior—may be revalued when its connection with other events and dispositions or states that we also care about has been established, and some of these connections may be quite surprising, new, and unexpected. Any preferred practice may thus be dethroned, rather suddenly sometimes, because it has been shown that the king's prosperity depends on the poverty of his subjects.

Now it would be bad enough if these painful and revolution-causing changes in perspective and perception occurred essentially at random, so that one never knew from what direction the next impact might come, but so that in some sense they might be thought to balance or cancel each other. But, in general, they do not. There is a direction in what is discovered. The direction is toward the necessary inclusion in any conclusion that makes sense of more and more. The stone that the builders rejected is not by any means to be rejected without consequence, and consequence consequential and undesired. More and more of what Riesman calls "underprivileged orders of data" must be rehabilitated, legitimated, and taken into account. It is not possible to despise the senses and still have every choice practically free in the realm of thought and feeling; not every attitude to the body, or even every conception of it, is to be reconciled with every attitude to what is held to be nonbodily. It is not possible to retain the oppressed in oppression—personally or socially—without grave and inevitable consequences for the oppressor. It is not possible to have prisons without imprisoning the jailers. It is not possible to be sadistic without being masochistic also. It is not possible to deny without simultaneously also asserting—at least anything that matters and that is true in whole or in part.

Need I go on? The establishment of interdependencies makes it ever more difficult to treat, and treat of, "others" as external and irrelevant to one's self and one's concerns. Humanity tends toward emergence as a brotherhood less because it is so recommended and ever more because as we knit up the remote consequences of proximate acts we see that we *are* so interrelated, whether or not we like it. Thus virtue becomes prudential (but leaves further room, I hope, for further virtue). Sympathy enlarges partly under necessity, but also fed by desire.

I must turn aside for a moment because, though I indicated the gap, revolutions for their full run and consolidation require more than changes in viewpoint.

A full-scale revolution, from its inception to the full extent of its run, requires ideologists, agitators, organizers, and charismatic leaders, as well as followers, footnoters, and countless others.

The *ideologists* are required to systematize and give force to, to organize, fill out, and particularize, intellectually—and also to integrate emotionally, "passionize" and impassion—the meaning of the message as it is received in general. They must supply, and furnish defense for, the creed in detail, and the rhetoric that in its pity and passion communicates and fires it: what, in another vocabulary, makes it relevant to and fit for action.

The *agitators* are required to institute the condition of "education" and freeing from previous definitions, investments, and bondages, that make possible the institution of new loyalties, and corresponding directed activities. It is they who mobilize, within and between persons, the resentments and hopes, the visions of heavens and horrors, the expanded affiliative and reduced disjunctive dispositions, the thanatic and libidinal possibilities, on which personal and social and political reorganization depend. It is they who call out and echo the wave of the future, if such it be.

The *organizers* are necessary to form in minute particularity the formless. It is they—compromising the pure doctrine with "the world," it is true—who make the transition from a moving idea to an idea in movement, and then to a movement embodying an idea. They sacrifice immaculacy for the sake of effect, but since both are desired they are brokers between them. They are the indispensable unlovely unloved without whom nothing can be brought to birth and with whom nothing can be uncontaminated. They are the men of the world who have contact with what is not of that world, and they benefit and damage both, but they cannot be done without.

Finally, *charismatic leaders* are required—for reasons so psychoanalytically obvious that it would be supererogatory to state them—to catch up, act out, exemplify, symbolize and embody in their persons, and to sanctify, en-magic, im-poetize in their acts, the inner meaning and outer scope of the movement in all its aspects. Personalization is of the essence; and, given the charismatic aura, virtues and vices alike (so only they are colorful and personal and not fundamentally incompatible with the direction or drive of the movement) are indifferently serviceable for anchoring-points, identifications, and reassurances. Remember Martin Luther whose fits served him probably at least as well as his physics!

Against this cast of necessary revolutionary agents we ought to cast the variety of psychiatric practitioners in order to see how badly—if that is the way one views it—they are already or inevitably entangled in revolution, or, *per contra*, how and in what way they may extricate themselves, and save the good name of psychiatry for other (perhaps undefined) purposes.

So far as I understand the profession, psychiatrists are all variously or in various combinations therapists, would-be preventors, educators, consultants, researchers and story-tellers. By "story-tellers" I am, of course, implying no mendacity, but rather that in speech and print they give severally accounts, to which others may have access, as to what they have been about and perhaps what they are intending. (Their patients are, of course, also supplementary story-tellers in the same sense, either informally in face-to-face gossip, or more formally as in, say, *The Fifty Minute Hour*, or, earlier, *A Mind That Found Itself*). Not in any of his roles is the psychiatrist entirely free of potential revolution-tending danger, but it is out of the ineluctable necessity of publication that he becomes a member of an exoteric instead of an esoteric revolutionary sect.

I think I know and understand the unease many psychiatrists feel as they move across the continuum (if it is, in fact, that) from containment, through mitigation, improvement, or cure, to "secondary" or "primary prevention" to "positive mental health." I know the parallel unease that accompanies the transition from a limited relation to one patient, to such "units" as families, communities, institutions, work-places, industries, Peace Corps, foreign or domestic, "international arenas" to "worlds," sane or insane. Nearly everyone must feel that the *internal* risks (internal to the profession, and to each of their consciences severally) which attend extension along both of these continua have to be added to the *external* risks of attack (just, they may feel) as they move in the same direction. Even a statement along the conservative lines of "What Psychiatry Can and Cannot Do" may seem of little help—or less than none. The very locus of that statement—in *Harper's Magazine*—serves as much to indicate what psychiatry is actually doing (whether it "can" or not) as it does to mark some desire for retrenchment.

I think the beginning of wisdom—as also of some partial moral relief—lies in the recognition that psychiatrists are *not* entirely free, severally or collectively, to define their own roles. They may, of course, *say* what they are in any way, limited or extended, that they please and that they can severally conclude or collectively agree upon. But what they are is not in any necessary relation to what they say they are. What they are is, in part, a function of what they actually do, as I have already indicated, and partly a function of what others say they do and believe they do. What they are is socially defined, and in that social definition theirs is only one voice.

less powerful partly because less united and less powerful (because the needs of others are here more powerfully at play), than would be the case in reference, say, to surgery or, perhaps, internal medicine. (Pediatrics shares, in this respect, some of their situation, and is widely practiced *in extenso* through the medium of Pocket Books.)

It may seem "presumptuous" that *as psychiatrists* they or some of them should think they have anything (or, at least, much) to say about "poverty" at a time like this when the word is emerging as a banner for all sorts and conditions of men to operate upon society in all sorts of ways under all sorts of programs. But how can they responsibly still their voices? Who is to represent what they know of biological or psychological or social poverty? Who is to say, what is obvious, that we are not really so much interested in the reduction of poverty as such, but—insofar as this is not just another political gimmick—in the reduction of human misery and the increase of human satisfaction, only related in a loose way to poverty? Who is to speak with expertness as to how human misery is represented in the inmost and most real reaches and depths of the personal life? This is not to say that they have the last word. (Even if poverty did not, as it does to a degree, make the poor miserable and the miserable poor, we would have a right and a duty to eradicate it because it makes the nonpoor miserable—or should.) But they have a word. And who, if not they, is to speak it?

It must seem clear enough that I do not think they can altogether escape their revolutionary effect, although they may have some choices as to revolutionary roles, and a little control over pace and substrategy.

Part of the problem may be seen, insofar as it is open to rational decision and control at all, as a problem in the division of labor. They are not alone professionally. Applied sociologists and applied anthropologists share with them, as perhaps do others, the conjuncture of the "scientific attitude" trained upon the affairs of men, with the fatal caring disposition. And beyond the professions themselves there is potentially a structured body of laymen, spokesmen and intermediaries.

But here they encounter, I believe, as do we all, a very real dilemma. They may not wish to play the roles of any or all of the revolutionary functionaries: ideologists, agitators, organizers, suppliers of charisma. Nevertheless the roles will be played out, and the question then becomes one of who is to fill them. Broad choices exist between relative withdrawal from this socially secondary process and relative immersion so that they attempt to fill the roles themselves. In the center might be a policy wherein most of the roles were filled not by psychiatrists, but by persons largely of their choosing and legitimation. In the first case, withdrawal, psychiatry will have no control and no "responsibility"; in the second, playing the roles themselves, psychiatrists will have considerable control and virtually sole responsibility; in the last case, little control and much responsibility.

But perhaps "control" and "responsibility" are relatively empty words in this connection. No one is going to have much of the first, or ever does in any rapidly moving revolutionary situation. And responsibility will in such situations be attributed and exacted for in a way that has no really rational relation to reality.

This is not the happiest situation for the kind of decision that, trained as we have been, we like to make and have others see us making. But I fear that is the situation that we are in. It will probably call not so much upon the analytic skills that have been our professional point of pride as upon practical arts in which we are not much practiced, since they are primarily the political arts. Perhaps, at least, psychiatrist and sociologist can help each other. And perhaps we can work out new relations to the whole society that will serve to put both theoretic and practical problems in a different perspective. I believe the problem to be urgent in my own field, sociology, and it seems, only more evidently, urgent in psychiatry.

3

Psychiatry: Revolution, Reform, and "Reaction"

Just as in the "natural" course of events every person knows least about himself, his "real nature," his effect on others, his "function" in the world in which he lives (indeed, what world it is that he lives in), so too, and for analogous reasons, for all social groups, and not least for professions. The view a profession has of itself—or, to be more exact, the shared views the professionals hold, in virtue of which they recognize each other as colleagues—has the same relation to reality, and a similar set of functions, as has a person's unreconstructed self-image. It is to function as a guide to salability, or at least negotiability, internal and external, which is to say primarily that it is to be a polite, politic, and political version of and front for the underlying realities. It is a presentation—a guise in which—a disguise for—what is to be presented, partly by selection out of what is present, partly out of what can be made to appear so.

There is the same problem for the profession as for the person of being, in a dual sense, hoist by one's own petard. First, in both cases the representation taken (for mixed motives) at its face value by others comes to function as a radically coercive set of expectations, so that what it is to be a doctor, a teacher, a John Smith is no longer largely a matter of choice for the doctor, the teacher, or John Smith respectively. Second, in both cases the representations "take in" (though they do not include) the representers, so that they come to mistake their masks for their persons. Bankers may really come to believe that bankers are acquisitive, while the most cursory survey may indicate that after a lifetime of dealing in debits and credits (referring even then to very abstract titles) they have acquired little (besides ulcers) and have been able to accept, and thus genuinely acquire, less than an "exploited" blue-collar worker.

The pains and gains of probing any further are also, in the case of person and profession, somewhat alike. There can hardly be a question that in most cases most of the time the going pretenses allow the person, social group, or profession to "function well enough." To function well enough means essentially that day-by-day routines can be carried out, some considerable smoothness, coordination, and articulation can be preserved, costs can be overlooked, neglected and forgone possibilities kept at least invivid, and the whole chain of tragedy, destruction, other-crippling, and self-truncation that is the attendant upshot, ascribed and written off to such "other causes" as fate, miscalculation, or the malign propensities of alien or enemy others. But it is in most cases most of the time "a stable system" of a sort, and we do have sufficient reason to value stability that we ought not lightly to disrupt it unless we can show credible cause. Unless things are going very badly—as in psychosis, or family disintegration, or a powerful attack on the medical profession—it is difficult to show such credible cause. We are left with mere faith—which is necessary, but, like love, "not enough"—that things would be plausibly better under or after examination, peculiarly and painfully self-examination. I believe, however, that things *are* going sufficiently badly—as attested by wars, pervasive fears, chronic and acute, clamorous competing claims by all parties and professions to have a line, if not the line, to salvation, and the like—to justify some self-examination on the first count alone.

Not that we should take it that under social examination,

any more than psychological, what is to be discovered need be (except in a very special sense) self-damaging. Just as patients may conceal their tenderness as well as their aggressiveness, and turn out to be both better than they feared and worse than they believed, so may professions turn out to serve purposes or perform functions both more and less worthy or needed or self-pleasing than they supposed.

I take it that what is true for other professions, including my own, is true also for psychiatry. And I take it that, even where psychiatric sensitivity is so exquisite that virtually nothing significant in the doctor-patient relation escapes the doctor—I take it, even then, that it does not follow that the relation of the profession to society is necessarily at all clear. It is on this supposition that I make bold, as a would-be friend to and student of both society and the psychiatric profession, to speculate about the two and their relations in the following way.

Note at the outset the magnitude, rate of growth, pervasiveness, reach, and novelty of psychiatry, whether viewed as profession, doctrine, or practice.

I know that, as far as size is concerned, psychiatrists are sometimes seized with visions in which it becomes clear that even to do the most narrowly defined of their jobs—to care, say, for the frankly mentally ill—they would have to double, treble, or n-tuple the present size of the certified profession; visions in which they sometimes see themselves as a beleaguered little sect, lost till recently in general medicine, itself lost in a barbarian, pagan, and superstitious world. They are quite right in these visions. It is so. There are not enough good men to go around. And there never will be, because there never can be, because in this way of figuring as soon as we came close we would redefine what it means to be a good man.

But what a peculiar way to count—unless they intend it as a professional strategy, like self-deprecation in a patient who knows no other way to ask for praise. It is as though the

Church at the height of its power had counted over its saints, seen their insufficiency to the needs of the day for sanctification, and concluded to its own weakness or the world's irredeemability. The saints are not the Church, by definition, and neither are the certified psychiatrists psychiatry. The Church is not even properly bounded by its membership, for that requires commonly a formal act of adherence, and informal acts are functionally no less efficacious. The boundary of the Church is where its sway of influence runs out, where conduct, including belief and the mordant pangs of conscience, is no longer substantially ordered by and conformed to what it stands for and believes in. (It may even be, thus, that in evil times the true church is altogether or substantially outside the Church, and for all I know it may be so even now.)

And this has little to do with whom psychiatrists will recognize or admit to colleagueship or license to practice. Those are their prerogatives, and the degree of finickyness that is appropriate to a given profession at a given moment is a matter of strategy that I do not wish to enter upon here. Psychiatry may bound its formal or nominal membership as it will, but it cannot easily limit the number of those who judge their attitudes by psychiatry's, who seek to pose in its posture, who adhere to and base their conduct upon what they take to be its (most recent) doctrine, let alone the growing number of those who do so without self-conscious awareness of the source of their modeling or the capital or vatican of their "profession." The profession, thus properly numbered by the number of those who profess its professions, perhaps not in all pristine purity, runs into millions, or more likely, hundreds of millions.

Note that this is not an idle distinction, something true for every profession. Mathematics, despite the spread of much low arithmetic and poor algebra, is not followed and attended by a mass following of more or less mathematically thinking and mathematically self-guiding people. Hardly anyone has a clue to what the mathematical orientation is, or what it can do, or what it is for, or the beauty and delight of it. Nor is everyone in some notable degree a classic historian, a cytologist, or an expert in Sanskrit. Even a learned psychiatrist might know next to nothing of Sanskrit and be little affected by what little he knew; but our Sanskritologist would have to be confined in his ivory tower to the point of illiteracy to know but little of psychiatry, and be uncomprehending to the point of idiocy to be little affected by whatever he did know.

So psychiatry is a peculiar profession which has a cloud of witnesses quite uncommon, and a numberless host of co-believers, sharers in the mystery, and, licensed or not, copractitioners. The ultimate test—that some vast majority of those who oppose psychiatry orient themselves not so much on a competitive doctrine but on their opposition to it ("Down with Mental Health!")—indicates the particular place of prominence that, sought or unsought, is psychiatry's.

Nor is this a matter of mere externalities—like the Church's adopting the habits and manners of the Roman rulers to whose powers it succeeded—though it is that also. These outward signals are indeed signs of inward and invisible graces, even if not as inward or as graceful as we might wish. People widely do, now almost by first nature, regard themselves, conceive themselves on the lines of a "psycho-dynamical psychology" directed in a "therapeutic" direction and taking for granted as presupposition what is in psychiatric theory given as conclusion. And as toward themselves, so in some degree toward each other. And not necessarily from above down only, but also and frequently from below up. So that one may observe adolescent children, for instance, not only making valid and insightful diagnoses—if I may use the term—of their parents' condition, and their own, and the interplay, but additionally taking serious and sometimes weighty therapeutic responsibility and acting thereupon with quite consummate skill. Or so I judge.

So psychiatry is a profession of magnitude and pervasion. As for novelty, I perhaps do not need to press the point. But as someone recently pointed out in reference to King Henry VIII who left a trail of blood, misery, disease, and schism and a divided nation behind him, the very question of what was wrong with him in the modern, post-psychiatric sense could simply not have occurred to anyone—because the world to which it refers, while it existed, existed in everybody but existed *for* no one. And that is less than fifteen generations back. Grandeur can now in principle be distinguished from grandiosity, and while men do not yet govern themselves accordingly, now that they know that answers are available they will not long content themselves with mere questions.

I have only made these general points in case one is generally insufficiently impressed with the size, reach, depth, and first-order consequence of psychiatry as a movement in the world. Moreover, I wanted these generals as background to and foreplay for some particulars. The particulars have to do with the social consequences, intended or unintended, of psychiatry's practices.

At this point, I fear, I have to distinguish among its practices—the things psychiatrists do, in a variety of combinations and mixes. Among them I find prominent the following. Some refine and elaborate or extend theory, either directly or as incident to other activities. Some illustrate and enrich theory by the provision of ever fresh or ever more dramatically detailed, and hence in one sense more comprehensible, case material. Some educate in these or other ways, by writing or speaking—or example, even—either in pair-relationships, or in larger groups or aggregations or publics. Some practice psychotherapy which, in many cases, is a microscopic—but all the more important, for that—mix of all these things. Some draw the seeming implications as they appear for public policy of what they observe in their consulting rooms and in the republic—what Scott Buchanan calls "the public thing." Some go beyond drawing implications and publishing them, to other and closer arts of suasion, a more direct intervention in the shared life of institutions. Others become administrators. Still others become sorters of men, or assistants or accomplices in their sorting. And some, I am sad to say, become keepers of men in the same sense as zoo-keepers are keepers of animals, and jailers and wardens are of boys and girls, men and women.

I am sure I have slighted some practitioners by the omission of vital functions, but, even so, I am forced by the needs of brevity to do further violence by lumping all this vast variety of different activity into three gross categories: their function as theorists and case-reporters; their function as policy-makers and policy-changers; their function as sorters and jailers.

Broadly speaking, let me say that in these three roles respectively psychiatrists appear vis-à-vis the world as revolutionaries, reformers, and reactionaries. By a revolutionary I mean someone who oversets the fundamental criteria by which men habitually govern themselves. By a reformer I mean someone who makes or procures changes in the operation of important institutions in important ways without, however, directly challenging the going order at its base. By a reactionary I mean someone who comes along to restore *a tergo* what a society has actually or latently already progressed beyond, someone who not merely stops up the womb of human and humane development but attempts to cram back into it the already delivered fruit thereof.

Let me deal with the last first since—quite evidently—I like it least. And briefly.

The presenting problem is the following. In a given society those who have the power to do so exact from those who have not the power to refuse a patterning of conduct (sometimes extending even to speech and the showing of feeling) which bars some lines of behavior and requires others. Some yield to the exaction and some do not. In a sufficiently advanced stage of civilization an attempt is made to distinguish those who cannot yield from those who will not. The distinction is pragmatic: those who *can* not yield are those who do not do so after every sanction the society is willing to use has been applied—plus those who are somehow judged to be like them. Those who *will* not yield are the residue. In general: those who will not yield, so distinguished, are the criminal and delinquent; those who *can* not are the ill and defective. (The difference between the last two is also pragmatic: a defect is a disability—a state of *can* not—that there are no means available and allowable to change.)

Both ways, men are classified and restricted. Both of these are police operations. Police operations, etymologically and otherwise, mean policy operations, politic operations, operations of power, operations directed to discipline, order, and control *for* some community, operations, then, in behalf of some men on and against one man. There are, of course, important differences. But the identities are even more significant. The psychiatrist becomes gentle jailer, polite policeman. His patient is no longer, except marginally, his client. He serves the public order—with such kindness, at best, as that constraint permits. He is open to the corruptions of power, peculiarly so, more so than the more worldly warden. For his ward is—by definition—weaker, and, to escape, must yield not only outerly but innerly. The wildest tyrants in their wildest fantasies have not required more. Indeed, their fantasy is for the first time somewhat filled out: conduct that might be sufficiently convincing of the inner conformity required to pass muster for a Grand Vizier may well not get by the oblique eye of a Rorschach. In preserving and promoting such an institution in the world, in serving or assisting it or what is like it, the role of the psychiatrist is, in the deepest sense, in the service of reaction.

And by "what is like it" I mean all those organizations that "employ"—that is, use—men, conceiving of them as "employees" (useds) or "potential employees" (usables) or "personnel" (man-matériel). Try to hear it, what is being said, with an unspoiled ear: Men have uses! (How would you respond if someone asked: How can I use this baby? or this little girl? or boy? Why do you respond if the object is "these men," "these women"?) All the various assistances psychiatry gives to the sorting, selecting, transfer, and other associated categorizing and locating processes are in principle no different from the labeling and relocation by ward (as reward or penalty) that is provided as a pattern in the mental hospital.

Let me turn with relief from these enterprises to those that constitute the psychiatrist's principal effect, what I have spoken of as willingly or unwillingly "revolutionary": his direct effect in psychotherapy (when properly practiced); his indirect effects as he publishes in whatever degree the general results or dramatic details that flow therefrom.

The most far-reaching effect is, of course, the redefinition of what man is. To be a man, following the vision from Vienna, is to be something else again from what it was before, incredibly more credible, released by several degrees of magnitude from the principal imprisoning pretenses of the past. And, moreover, furnished forever in principle with a key to that prison, though by no means have all doors yet been opened, or even noted. I will not belabor the point, for a great deal has been said and written about the Freudian revolution, though, even so, not enough. For in a very real sense not one stone is left upon another in the ancient walls, temples, and such as remain are destined, one may see, for a different use. Let me turn to less obvious but perhaps nearly equipotent effects.

For men do not live by the bread of abstraction alone but by every word that cometh out of the mouth of the concrete actors who constitute history as they speak and act the vast drama of their little lives. So that what it is to be man is defined and enriched no less by those truer autobiographies that come out of the consulting room as case material, than by what is inferential in or explanatory of what occurs there, by way of heuristic concepts or metapsychological entities. Not just the theory of "the vicissitudes of the instincts," not merely the fascinating forms of the compromises and "resolutions" and their consequent structurings of lives and life chances *in abstracto*, but all the complex, concrete, unique outworkings as dramatically presented in the ongoing drama—these restructure and reform and redefine our life and our lives. Not the theology only, but the rich and encrusted hagiography of everyman, is and enters into the reconstitution and illumination of the life, lone and shared, of every person-participant.

But beyond—or below—theory and concrete embodiment lies the propaganda of the act, the force of psychiatry's example. The existence in the world—the same world where men have uses!—of the therapeutic alliance serves to raise an uncomfortable question about every alternative relation. For the core of it is an interpenetration and interplay between the actual best in one person and the latent best in another, with no other aim in view but the release in the one who—momentarily—has the less to give of that latent best crying for its own liberation into reality. And that operation underwritten not by a judgment of relative worth but by a presumption of absolute value. And the reward not in money (which merely makes it possible), nor affection which sometimes hampers it, nor honor which is at best a by-product, but in pure joy in pure liberation: For the patient:—"And my growth have no guerdon but only to grow. . . ." For the true psycho-curator: "And the lives of my children made perfect with freedom of soul were my fruits."

I say that that relation, established and re-established, enacted and re-enacted every day, challenges and calls into question every other relation and joint enterprise. For, first, it is infinitely generalizable and extensible wherever, as is always the case, there is a difference in degree and kind of needs between persons from moment to moment. And second, it becomes increasingly clear that most of the things we say we value can be had under the sign of that relation and no other, so that we are driven either to abandon age-old hypocrisies or to run the risks of authentic, unarmed, and beneficent encounters in the authentic. And as we do the latter, the domain of the genuine is extended, and the realm of the false and the tawdry manipulative is shown in sharper shadow for what it is. So that the very underpinnings of what most men do most that is most harmful simultaneously to themselves and to others are undercut, and the structures erected on them rendered untenable and untenantable. And as the country of the soul is mapped, the country for the soul, the meaning of the long-sought civilization, comes into sight and may be occupied.

Last, from this peculiar and most unlikely perspective, the couch actual and virtual, comes, curiously enough, the crucial information as to how things are going in the ordinary affairs of men. For institutions and customs and social practices are not, or not only, what they patently (and, particularly, rationally) seem to be. A family is not (or is not simply or only) a social "arrangement" for getting sex regulated, children bred, born, and raised, companionship established and cared for, love in its multiple meanings deepened and channeled—or any such list of "functions." For the family—and any other institution—is in one sense consumed by each of its members, and in another sense the stage for and context of them, and in yet another an interpenetration with as well as a mode of expression of their lives. And the meaning—in each of these meanings—of what it is, is neither what appears at the face, nor what is to be "more carefully observed," nor even what can with skill be introspected—but more than these and less, and certainly quite other. The family is most crucially—but so is the state, the school, the colleagueship, the group of friends—a conversation unconscious to unconscious, direct and indirect, a provision for heredity (continuity and variation) at an ulterior and quite decisive level. And knowledge of what that conversation is—and hence of what the institution *is*—can come or does come to us only by the processes by which we explore the unconscious or its manifestations, prototypically the psychoanalytic methods. And the relation between what men say there—and, indeed, in both senses of the word dis-cover—and what they say in everyday and ostensible conversation is so oblique and multiplex, that we can hardly even regard the two as complementary revelations, and can hardly help but regard the first as giving the "true" or "real"—or certainly, crucial—meaning of the second. However that may be, let us say conservatively that the ostensible meanings, serving motives, functions, and effects of institutions from war to monogamy, from courtship to combat—are so little and misleadingly given, both in general and in particular, by their evident and everyday appearance, that social policy founded on such shallowness and distortion is quite inevitably disaster-bound failing the corrective—let us call it that—that comes to us from that other world.

And that other world is the domain of the psychiatrist as such (and not, let us say, of the psychologist, no matter how skilled and "psychodynamic") because knowledge of it is to be had when and only when life is faced as a problem and not as a question.[1] And where there is a problem—or most specially, *the* problem, who am I? What must I do?—there is an agony. And where there is an agonist, there is a problem of soul-healing in the problem's resolution—a psychiatric contest and opportunity in the widest sense of those words.

So I see psychiatry, I am sure, through my own distorting lenses. There must be in my picture omissions and misbalances. But, in its large lines, I think, after long and tender study of the object, the picture I present is valid—at least in the sense that a vision of the flower's possibilities is possible on the basis of what is only promise in the bud.

[1] A beautiful elaboration of the distinction occurs in Abraham J. Heschel, *Who Is Man?*

4

Social Values, the Mental Health Movement, and Mental Health

Any attempt to describe the relations between social values and mental health must take account of the social movement that marches under the banner of "mental health" or "mental hygiene." That movement is itself an expression of, and a result of, a revolution in social values; it also affects social values, and, presumably, mental health. I should like, therefore, first to state briefly how the sociologist looks at the relation between social values and personality, and what he knows about it; second, to turn attention to the origin and growth of the mental health movement in relation to general changes in the values in our culture; and, last, to raise some questions about the effects of the movement both on values and on mental health.

I have written from two points of view. *As a sociologist*, I have attempted to view the matter as dispassionately, not to say coldly, as possible—in effect, to view the movement as if I were a detached outsider. *As a citizen*, and moreover as a person in intimate touch with and sometimes involved in the movement, I have written also from the perspective of the "insider." I feel confident that the reader will easily disentangle what is said from one viewpoint from what is said from the other, and be able to make due allowance for the bias inseparable from each view.

HUMAN NATURE IS SOCIAL NATURE

It is the general viewpoint of the social scientist, his proper professional bias, that man is human in virtue of his *social* nature: "human nature is social nature." Unless the meaning of this statement is clearly understood, it may seem to claim either too much or too little: it may seem presumptuous and imperialistic, or trivial and tautological.

As to the first, the social scientist does not deny or ignore the fact that man exists as a physical object, that he can be dropped and smashed like a crystal goblet. Man does exist as a physical object, and if a physical force is sufficient, as the flight surgeons can tell us, his physical and human nature will be radically and sometimes irreversibly altered. Similarly, the social scientist does not deny or minimize the importance of the fact that man exists also as a biological object. The extraction of a few cubic centimeters of fluid or tissue will change the wonder of a biological going concern, an organism, into a mere aggregate of unstable chemicals; and, with that transformation, human nature will disappear.

What the social scientist is contending is that no matter what light may be shed on man's nature by *any* analysis (not merely present analyses) that is couched in the terms of physics or biology, these sciences furnish explanations only of *necessary* conditions for the behavior of human beings as human beings, and not explanations of *sufficient* conditions. There are physical, chemical, physiological, and anatomical conditions without which a man cannot exist or continue as a man; but no compilation of such statements of conditions will account for that in him which is distinctively human. We may account in physical-chemical-physiological terms for the fact that men grow periodically hungry, but this they share with the animals. But to account for the fact that they—or some of them—will go into a restaurant, read a menu, smile seductively at the waitress, have a moment of guilt or elation about that, and then proceed to order lobster Newburg because it is a prestige-laden food (as against, say, shepherd's pie), we have to turn to an order of explanation that is not physical-chemical-physiological, for these are distinctively human acts.

To the charge of triviality (that the social scientist is saying what everybody already knows, namely that social behavior is a "part" or aspect of human behavior) the answer is that this is not what the social scientist means, either. He means that (given the necessary physical and biological conditions) *all* that is distinctively human about man must be wholly and solely accounted for in terms of his social nature. He means that man is made human by humans, and in society. He means that it is in social life, and only in social life, that the welter of mere potentialities with which man is born is organized and given form and operability and access, via communication, to a share in the common human life and, via that, to a human life of his own.

This general view is buttressed by large-scale observations of the process in differing societies and by a limited amount of evidence as to what seems to happen to people who by some freak of fortune have become isolated from the humanizing (or socializing) process at some critical juncture. On the basis of this view, the social scientist is faced with the task of describing in some more useful detail just how the process proceeds—what are the relations between "culture" and personality, "social character" and social organization, personality organization and disorganization and their social correlates, if indeed they are correlated, as the general outlook would lead one to suppose.

WHAT WE DO NOT KNOW

We are here at a very unhappy stage in the development of our sciences—unhappy, that is, for those who feel, properly I think, that the questions are of overwhelming import and their answering of considerable urgency. I can hardly doubt that such feelings are justified at a time when attempts to rationalize social life founder on the intractabilities of personality organization and when attempts to improve the quality of personality organization come to grief on the brute rock of social organization.

It would be going much too far to say that we know very much about the relation of social values to personality organization and disorganization. We do *not* know what kinds of "cultural discontinuities" or "contradictions" are "dysfunctional" from either a social or a personality viewpoint. We *do* know that the distress of many who select themselves as patients is focused around such contradictions, but we can hardly say that the one is the cause of the other, or what contributory elements there must be in the situation before such social factors can appear as personality stresses.

We have much reason to think that personality breakdowns are relatively infrequent in groups whose morale is high; that "morale" is a name for the powerful feeling released in the individual who feels himself a member of a strong and important group; and that such unity is frequently a product of (as well as a cause of) the sharing of social values felt to be important. (The stress, it should be noted, is on what is *felt* to be so, rather than on what a detached observer might regard as the facts.)

We are somewhat chastened by the knowledge that the group in question may be, to the outsider, imaginary (for example, a man and his guardian angel, his totem, his idol, or his deity), or that it may be a group immediately present but of no discernible enduring or explicit purpose.

WHITHER GOES THE PROCESS?

Thus far, we cannot even clearly distinguish between those forms of disorganization (personal or social) which are necessary phases of reorganization, improvement, and "growth" (and therefore "benign") and those phases which are the beginnings of continuing disorganization, disimprovement, and, finally, the disruption of the person or society.

It is easy, of course, to be wise after the event, but it is not then that knowledge is needed. Is Billy's stuttering at this stage a sign of coming reorganization of speech habits with markedly increased ease and fluency, or is it the beginning of a process that will hardly permit him to speak at all? Is the crime or delinquency of a Chicago slum in the 1920's to be viewed as a *necessary* part of a process in which slums will finally be torn down because they are socially too costly, and replaced by places humanly habitable? If so, it is about as "pathological" as the baby's cry that tells us he is hungry and needs to be fed. Or is the delinquency a sign, on the contrary, that life in large cities is inimical to personality organization and social organization alike, and therefore either itself pathology or the evidence of it?

Both views are tenable, and are held; and which of the two is chosen depends in large part on the time span that is taken into account, as well as on the author's spoken or unspoken guess as to where the whole process is taking us (or being taken by us). If we view the phenomena as part of a process of "revolution" with a probably improved state at the end, it is difficult to view them much differently from the process of formation of antibodies in the face of mild infection—"good" coming necessarily out of "evil." If, on the other hand, we view the phenomena as part of a process of "the breakup of the Western world," they may well appear either as parts of or signs of the general lethal disease.

None of us, I think, knows the answer. The important point is that, except after the event, it is difficult to distinguish disorganization from reorganization. Even where the distincton can be made, it is often easy to distinguish in a particular case (for instance, this patient) but not in general; or in general but not in any particular case.

SOCIAL VALUES AND THE MENTAL HEALTH MOVEMENT

Despite this mountainous lack of knowledge, there has grown up in the Western world an increasingly powerful movement concerned with problems of "mental health." The growth of that movement is of extraordinary interest to the social scientist whether or not he is directly interested in mental health, and since it affects the layman deeply and is likely to affect him more, it should also be of extraordinary concern to him. Let us therefore examine the origin, the nature, and the effects of this movement.

When the going and settled order of the Middle Ages was disturbed and broken up, perhaps chiefly through the introduction of money, there was radical change in an old social structure, the feudal order, inevitably involving changes in the economics, the politics, the ethics, and the theologics of all the Western world. Unavoidably, man's relation to things, man's relation to man, and man's relation to what he projected as the ideal had to alter.

How men did things to and with things altered; these alterations constituted the "revolutions in technology." *What* men knew about things altered, enlarged, and expanded, giving birth to natural science viewed as a body of knowledge. And *how* men knew about things changed; natural science as a method came to dominate over revelation and tradition, and the testimony of scientists came to have greater weight than the opinion of priests or ancestors.

In the relation of man to man, somewhat the same sequence followed. Men, related to one another primarily by force, authority, tradition, and love, were reorganized in relations that depended more nearly on force, advantage, calculation, cupidity, interest, distrust, and fear. The market became the dominant institution, virtually replacing all such mystical bodies as family, church, and, later, guild. Similarly, what men knew about themselves and one another changed, giving birth to the social sciences viewed as a body of knowledge. And the ground upon which they accepted or rejected knowledge about themselves or one another changed to some degree also as the social sciences provided new methods of securing reliable knowledge about man. This revolution is by no means complete, and the traditional sources of knowledge still compete openly and forcefully in both popular and scholarly literature for the right to have their testimony accepted and its source accredited.

In the realm of value, or the ideal, the revolution is hardly well begun. Save for the obvious passing of the dominance of the one institution, the church, which formerly exerted almost undisputed sway in defining both what is and what ought to be the order of goods, nothing is clear. That no church any longer organizes the lives of men in so many respects or at so deep a level as the church once did, it would be difficult to doubt. But what has passed clearly—and, the author believes, finally—from the church has devolved exclusively upon no other body, nor has it even become dominantly concentrated in any. Who today has the right—for whom—to an authoritative pronouncement of what is the good life, of what is the order of the virtues, of whether there is a supernatural order, and if so, what it is and whether it matters? Has scientist, priest, artist, philosopher, psychiatrist, or Man of Distinction this right?

Into this power vacuum the mental health movement has been drawn—together with a variety of competitors from neo-orthodoxies to new inventions, such as the omnicompetent State. With one foot in humanism and the other in science, it seeks to perform, and to a degree does perform, many if not most of the functions of the relinquishing institution—plus, perhaps, some others. A revolution in social values is what gives birth to the movement, and it is a revolutionary doctrine that the movement is moved by and expresses.

The power vacuum created by the bankruptcy of other institutions, however, furnished only the condition in which a new institution could "move in," and does not fully explain it. There are three other roots of the mental health movement in the "great revolution."

First, such a time of radical and widespread change is likely to be (or to be *felt* as) a time of acute stress and deep distress.

It will in and of itself (and it has done so) cause people to turn sustained attention and effort not only to the life without, but also to the nature and vicissitudes of the life within. And the latter is precisely the area of specialization and concern of the mental health movement.

Second, such a time will tend to call out (and it has) a spate of new social inventions—ways of dealing with human problems; and these, if they appear at a sufficiently rapid rate, will in turn call out mediators of the new ideas. And this is precisely where the mental health movement operates—between the scientific pen and the lay eye.

Third, whether or not there has been a net increase in misery of a psychological nature, the existence of a movement directed to its remedy or alleviation will tend to focus concern upon the problem; that is, in effect, to expand the market which it is equipped to supply.

This will tend to be more readily possible in a situation in which there is a diminution of suffering from natural disaster, famine, or the want of material objects. Lightning rods, ever-normal granaries, and the mass production of goods *permit* us to pay some increased attention to the inner life. The mental health movement *encourages* us to do so; the nature of present-day life virtually *forces* it upon us; and the disappearance of the formerly accepted and accredited ways of so doing inclines us to the trial and adoption of new methods. So we move from the "cure of souls" in either of its senses to "psychotherapy" and "mental hygiene"; from preoccupation with salvation to preoccupation with adjustment or peace of mind; from the attack upon evil to the war against anxiety; and from obedience in a service which was perfect freedom to a search for autonomy in a freedom without which no service can have dignity.

That the situation described presents some remarkable parallels with the situation confronting the early Christian Church should occasion no surprise. That the general shape and form of the resultant movement should in many vital particulars resemble those of any other church ought also to occasion no great astonishment.

Like the early church, the mental health movement unites and addresses itself to "all sorts and conditions of men," so only they be "for" mental health as they were formerly for virtue and (more mildly) against sin. Like the church, it consists of a body of laymen and specialists, with the latter having as their special charge the psychological welfare of the former, to be worked out, however, by both together. Like the church, there is a "fellowship of all believers" that transcends great variety of belief, but differentiates from the unbelievers—those who are against "all that" or simply not for it.

As in the church, a vast variety of activities are carried on whose principal unifying element is that they are all thought to lead in some degree to the furthering of the common end, though they are not all of equal importance; the monastic work of research, somewhat abstracted from the trials, tribulations, and rewards of this life, is frequently thought more important than the life of teaching and rescuing "in the world" with double risk of reward and seduction.

But much more important than these incidental analogies is the fact that the movement occupies or seeks to occupy the heartland of the old territory. The protagonists and practitioners of mental health are increasingly called upon to pronounce on what used to be called moral questions, in the small and in the large, in general and in particular.

The pronouncements cover matters of both substance and method. Breast feeding of infants, for instance, is currently "good," not under divine dispensation or because it is "natural," but because the mental hygienists say—probably quite rightly—it will help to produce a "good" child from the viewpoint of mental hygiene. The production of "good" children in another sense—what used to be called well-behaved children—by bad means such as fear or conditioning or seduction is held to be bad because it militates against integration, which is close to the mental hygienist's *summum bonum.*

Divorce is good or bad, not in and of itself, but insofar as it increases or decreases the mental health of the parties thereto; or, in a rare, wider view, all the parties concerned, including nonparticipants.

To say these things is by no means to attack or make fun of the mental health movement—quite the contrary. What is being said, in effect, is that of necessity it has the form and flavor of a church: organization, a message or mission, a set of central values, committed servants—lay and professional—activities, orthodoxies and heresies, celebrations and observances, excommunications at need, and the felt power in moral matters to bind and loose.

This is also not to say that there are no distinctions to be drawn between this movement and the movements it wholly or partly replaces. There are profound and important differences. How else and why else should it be on the wax as they wane?

First, the values embodied in the movement are this-worldly and secular, as opposed to other-worldly and supernatural. Second, it is man-centered—sometimes perhaps too narrowly (taking account only of this patient, and taking the social context for granted), but often with a wide view and a full sweep. Third, it is to an unusual degree nondogmatic (unless the dictum that there is to be no dogma is itself held to be a dogma) despite what has been said above about orthodoxies and heresies. In close touch with the changing deliverances of science, it has itself to partake to a large degree of the tentative attitude, and in this respect it resembles more the mystic wing of the churches which for analogical reasons had to keep themselves largely unfettered and open to "the free sweep of the spirit." Fourth, its role is to facilitate an ongoing process, to remove obstacles to action and enjoyment, to free and liberate rather than enmesh and enchain.

The mental health movement has thus arisen out of a collapse of ancient social values, it has caught up, shaped, and embodied new ones, and has made of "mental health," however vaguely apprehended or defined, an important if not dominant social value, and seen to its incorporation to a degree in the beliefs and practices of other institutions.

THE MENTAL HEALTH MOVEMENT AND SOCIAL VALUES

In the process of its own growth, the movement has, as already intimated, had reciprocal effects on the general social value scheme. To a very large degree, as the mediator of the inquiring spirit of the social sciences, it has acted with the other "acids of modernity" as a solvent of hitherto stable beliefs. Where are yesteryear's open champions of obedience, of the innate superiority of men over women, of the quiet, well-mannered child (at any price), of belief in "original sin" or the fundamental baseness of man (or virtue, for that matter), in the unitary character of intelligence, in corporal punishment, in proprietary rights in children and women? They are still with us, as the wheelbarrow is compresent with the airplane; but in much the same places.

The mental health movement has not unaided made these beliefs and a thousand others unfashionable, not to say disreputable, but it has helped. But it has done far more than render discreditable beliefs discredited. It has created or helped create something that is new in history, or as new in history as anything ever is. It has focused attention on the inner life—or perhaps more exactly, the inner life in relation to the outer. And while every church has sought to do that, the difference is that this movement is in somewhat more intimate contact with scientific methods of discovering what the inner life is.

This is a difference indeed—a difference that makes a difference. For good or ill, the movement is a mediator or interpreter of the scientific message, rather than an opponent of it, giving ground gracelessly and step by step.

The movement has not only focused attention on the inner life and its quality, but it bids fair to make that the touchstone of all other goods. This also is not new. But again, what is new is the gradual development of methods of increased sureness and reliability for the discovery of what that inner life is really like. "Know thyself," said the Greeks; but they hardly suspected the structure, not to say the content, of that which man least knows and most needs to know—his "unconscious."

This concentration upon, and heightened consciousness of, the nature of mental life is now so widespread as to ensure an appreciative audience for "New Yorker" cartoons about psychiatrists, Hollywood films about alcoholism or amnesia, mothers'-aid books about the emergent little superegos and their resurgent little ids.

On the whole, the mental health movement has been content with its role of facilitation of ongoing process, and has had very little to say about final ends, or ultimate values. There are, of course, striking exceptions, as when a leader in the field says that Santa Claus (and his equivalents) must go, and as a consequence finds leagued against him a powerful combination of the sophisticated who have much to lose and the unsophisticated who have nothing to lose but their strains. But the two persistent positions taken by the majority in the field have interesting consequences.

The first of the two positions states or takes for granted that mental hygienists are not concerned with ultimate values as such: they function at the *means* level, and their aid should be equally welcome under almost any scheme of ultimate values. The church, industry, the Nazi party, the socialist society, all have mental health problems, and the mental hygienist can help all equally. Some have reservations, but the position is essentially that within a wide range of moral schemes, or in all of them, mental hygienists can aid and operate.

This is not quite moral indifference, though to many it will seem so. It is the precise analog of the position of at least one church: that it is above and beyond politics, and that—provided certain of its criteria are met—it can live in any form of polity and reach a concordat with any bargain-keeping government.

The alternate position consists largely in the attitude that ultimate values are matters for continuing discovery, and that therefore the business of the mental hygienist is to facilitate and further the endless common search. In this view, no values are ultimate; all are tentative and temporary, *except the values implicit in and necessary to the method of discovery itself*. This view puts a high premium on curiosity, honesty, intelligence, care, and boldness; and also, by implication, on due humility and proper responsibility in the human enterprise.

It may be felt that there is a great and unbridgeable gulf between these views; I feel that there is; and that this represents the latent first great schism within the movement. But in at least one important respect, the effect of each view upon social values has been, unwittingly, much the same.

That joint effect has been to shake confidence in any existent scheme of ultimate values, to lead people quite generally to conclude that such questions are unanswerable and that the answers are matters of indifference. No mental hygienist known to me actually holds such views; many people known to me draw such inferences from what mental hygienists say.

Selection between the two positions is as difficult as it is important, for the second is quite capable of making the search for ultimate values central to the human enterprise, which is where, in my judgment, it properly belongs. But the first position has behind it the authoritative weight of the medical and priestly tradition that the profession is there to serve all comers, regardless of the use to which they intend to put regained health or grace. The alternative is very uncomfortable ethically and politically. Ethically it raises the problem of forgiveness: to whom, under what circumstances, may the means of health or grace be refused? Politically it means the return of the power to bind or loose to a body of professionals, with all the risks of corruption of one side and spoliation of the other that such power situations always have implied.

No matter which course is chosen, the effects on social values are already profound, and are likely to be increasingly so as money and power and prestige accrue to the movement, as they may well do at steadily increasing rates.

THE MENTAL HEALTH MOVEMENT AND MENTAL HEALTH

It remains to say a word, stemming largely out of what has been said, about the effects of the movement on that which it intended most to affect, namely, mental health. In the case of particular patient and particular therapist, it is difficult to doubt the high frequency of efficacious work. But it is rather with the general effect of the movement that we must be concerned.

Here, as elsewhere, we are largely in the dark; and yet a more important field for research could hardly be marked out. It is nearly always the unintended consequences of social policy, rather than the intended ones, that raise profound and harassing practical problems, and it would be strange if this were not so in the case of the mental health movement.

In areas where its effects have been concentrated, such as one of the communities once intensively studied by my colleagues and myself, these effects are very striking. They are so striking, indeed, that some of us had the feeling of being confronted with a social invention whose disturbing size and power may well be at least equal to those of the industrial revolution itself.

What seems to be emerging is a situation in which laymen —ordinary men and women—in their everyday activities are coming into possession of and using a new body of knowledge and techniques of analysis with reference to themselves and to one another. The importance of this may not be immediately evident, but the effect is almost as though another dimension (and another complication) had been added to life.

Self-consciousness in the ordinary sense, when it emerged

in the process of evolution, meant inescapably the loss of that pristine innocence and naïveté which is the exclusive prerogative of non-self-conscious animals—an innocence and naïveté to which we all occasionally have deep-seated and understandable yearnings to return. It is very largely the burdens and pains of that loss that it is the business of mental hygiene to deal with. Self-consciousness, man's distinguishing gift, is also his primal wound. Undue self-consciousness is fatal to spontaneity, and heightened self-consciousness is a burden not lightly to be borne.

But as mental hygienists, we have now added to ordinary self-consciousness a self-consciousness of a different kind: different in its accuracy; different in its penetration and depth; different in that it continuously tears away the veil of privacy from what was hitherto private; different in that we are ourselves self-consciously engaged in building it up; and different in that we know that our immediate associates and friends are so doing, and that they know we know. This is, in some important sense, a radically new way of life.

What this does to the mental health of people going through the process is difficult to assess. That they are obviously relieved of some tensions and difficulties seems clear; that they are new-burdened with others seems evident also. That this is an additional stress for the neurotic and the near-neurotic seems likely. That it furnishes a new channel for old anxieties, and perhaps a particularly difficult and dangerous one, is hard to doubt.

But none of these would recommend against the process, even if the worst were assumed in each case. We cannot at all clearly distinguish between the pains of transition and the pains inherent in the new state of affairs itself. Much of what we see, we can be sure, is ascribable to the fact of change and not to the new state that may follow. We would be as wise to condemn the surgical knife because it hurts as to concentrate exclusively on the pains of change. The key question for policy is whether or not the new state is better (from a mental health viewpoint) than the old; and to that question we have no answer better than faith or guess.

But it is no longer even a question for policy. No known man or body of men now has the power to arrest the flow or alter the general direction of events, even if, on mental health grounds, that should be indicated. If we, the mental hygienists, should amputate our writing arms and seal our reluctant lips, the field would fall to the quack and the charlatan, and the principal difference would be that the self-consciousness would be worse-founded and more misleading. There is no choice open in that direction for us, any more than there is a way of abdication for the physicists in the face of the atomic bomb and its more violent variants.

What is really needed is that we should lay upon ourselves the same self-consciousness (and the responsibility that it carries with it) that we have laid upon others. We can no longer afford to shoot psychological arrows in the air and be satisfied that they "fell to earth I know not where." We need close and continuing research contact with the proximate and remote consequences of what we have said, so that, while we cannot control the wide sweep of events, we may make adaptations in particulars and cause the effects to be no more painful than they must be. To act otherwise is to act irresponsibly and to invite, if not to guarantee, disaster. The disaster would be that the very means of man's liberation, self-knowledge, would have become the instrument of his enslavement and the procurer of his impotence. This is not what we set out to do.

5

The Future of Psychiatry

I come among psychiatrists as a "friendly stranger"—which is also, I take it, the position from which they speak to their patients. The role of the stranger, as Georg Simmel has so well described it, is that of the person who is simultaneously near and far, who accordingly sees some things and misses some, and sees yet others in a perspective different from our own. I need hardly press my claim to the title: I am no biologist, no physician, and my concerns are chiefly with society and social theory rather than with men in their severalty, and practice with its problems. Nor must I press my claim too far: not to the point of utter strangeness. I have lived among psychiatrists for twenty years now, either as a guest in their scientific house or as host to them in mine.

I have qualified the word "stranger" by the word "friendly" for good reason. By the use of that word I imply the existence between us of a disinterested love—a congeniality, tempered and enlivened, fed and restrained, by what I believe to be our dedication to a common obligation. If I urge anything upon you, it is only in virtue, as Polanyi would say, of a commitment to ends that are sufficiently universal to command and unite us both. Is this not also the relation within which, and the ethic under which, your practice is conducted? Is it not true, as I heard someone say recently, that we have the right to seek to change only what we love? Is it not also true that

* A lecture given on the twenty-fifth anniversary of the Psychiatry Service at Massachusetts General Hospital.

we may say we love only what we are willing to take responsibility for changing?

Last, let me warn in preface, that what is in form a prediction is in fact a plea. In stating a belief about the future of psychiatry, I am in fact seeking to give effect to a hope. I am making an assertion that tends to tip the balance of action in favor of its own confirmation. A psychiatrist who tells his patient, explicitly or implicitly, that he expects him to recover, is counting upon what appears as a statement of fact to have a consequence in what it purports to predict. So am I. We hold up mirrors, but the reflections from them inescapably and sometimes profoundly alter the objects reflected. Therapy counts upon the fact, and social science must come to terms with it.

The practice of psychiatry is, I am sure, full of satisfaction —win, lose, or draw with the patient. There is joy in success; heightened interest and determination in the face of failure. It is only when we try to make what we do intelligible that the difficulties multiply and, for good reason, the anxiety mounts. This difficulty is common to all professions. All have secrets: some to be concealed from the public, some from colleagues, some even from oneself, the *ultra-privatissima*. But psychiatrists who believe in uncovering when covering hampers performance may be under special mandate to steel themselves to its pains. In any case, since I also believe that the future of psychiatry is bound up so much more with clarification of theory than with inventions of practice, I shall assume that the pressures of necessity are added to the fortitude and patience for which I ask.

Foremost among the insufficiently aired or examined questions in psychiatry is the one concerning its relation to other medical specialties. It has fought so long and hard for a place in the medical sun, for recognition as a respectable specialty, that it has emphasized its similarities almost to the point of denying difference. Yet it differs from the others more deeply than they differ from each other, and that distinction is of the essence, not the accidents, of psychiatry. Other specialties differ from each other by distinctions in space—the human geography seized upon: GU, GI, ENT, and so on—or distinctions in time such as pediatrics or gerontology. What psychiatry deals with essentially has no locus in space and no focus in time. It differs in the most radical of all possible ways, since it treats of and with man as human, a being in a moral order, as against the natural order, biological or physical.

Psychiatrists in their role as general physicians may *in that role* deal with their patients as machines or organisms, that is, as objects. But to the degree that they do so they are either merely (as general physicians) creating suitable conditions for their true work as psychiatrists, or using mechanical or biological means to communicate a human message. Such a conjuncture of roles or mixture of means may be practically inescapable, but practical convenience should not be allowed to obscure theoretical clarity. That which is essentially psychiatric in the compound act is that in which a person is dealt with as a person by a person, that which lies wholly in the dimension of the distinctively human, that which is altogether in the order of choice and value.

For this reason, because of the order of reality addressed, psychiatrists are inevitably allied with and fraternal to all others who deal with man as man: priest, king, philosopher, teacher, preacher, pundit, and propagandist. The psychiatrist alone, in this sense, represents humanity in the court of medicine; and only in the sense in which medicine, in general and regardless of means, is itself an organization of tender loving care, does he represent medicine in the court of humanity. The psychiatrist is thus cast in the role of ambassador in two countries of a third country yet to be defined. He may expect the privileges of embassy—some diplomatic immunity, a chance to be heard on occasion—but he must not be surprised to be regarded as "strange," to be only partly understood, to have such views as are understood taken account of rather than adopted. Even these privileges may only accrue when the identification is clear; an undeclared ambassador may seem something less to others as well as to himself.

Once the distinction is clear, the chances of peace, order, and good government in medicine are vastly increased. We might, moreover, have a less divided performance, a more vivid self-image for ourselves, psychiatrists and social scientists alike. There might even ensue a cessation of attempts to state perfectly valid human insights in pseudo-physical, pseudo-biological terms—a procedure that robs them of their immediate power of conviction without establishing them securely in the forum of science.

It follows, I think, that theory *in* psychiatry is social theory, and theory *about* psychiatry is philosophy. Physics and biology bear on another and circumambient realm. The practice of psychiatry is hence social practice, and physical and biological practice come in as mere *mise-en-scène*, mere condition-creation for psychiatry itself.

It is difficult to overstress the point. Might I be permitted an analogy from education, which also has the perennial difficulty of disentangling from the myriad things that educators do those acts or aspects of acts that can rightly be called "education." One condition for effective teaching usually is that the child can see a classroom's length to the blackboard. If he is unable to see so that the teacher can teach, the eye problem may be mechanical and amenable to surgery or correction by spectacles; or it may be physiological and tractable by vitamins or other ingesta. But surgery-doing and pill-giving are not education, even if (which God forbid) the teacher does them; they merely establish conditions favorable to the pursuit of it. Even should the teacher argue (as all might and some do) that first aid given by him shows love and hence establishes a relation inside which education can proceed better or deeper, surely this does not mean that the administration of first aid *is* education. It means, at most, that a teacher should or must sometimes perform *other* roles for the sake of his distinctive and unique one. Whether he separates or mixes roles in practice is a matter of practical convenience and must be judged by practical tests; whether he distinguishes his roles theoretically is a matter of vital moment. If he is not clear, at least in his thinking, he confuses himself and others. And confusion is precisely that which an educator—like a psychiatrist—is mandated to dispel.

You may wish to maintain that physical, biological, and social interventions are so closely linked in the equivalence of their effects that I have overdrawn a distinction to make a point. A little improvement in surgery or pharmacology might soon make it possible, by a surgical nick here or there, a tablet or capsule now and then, to banish anxiety, allay the consciousness of guilt, evoke euphoria, release energy, engineer mood, and so on. (I am told that a little alcohol will, even now, do these things for some.) What then becomes of a distinct moral order? Is psychology not reducible to physics and chemistry?

I think not. I agree that we could remove from the universe all generically psychiatric problems. One way would be to exterminate all people. If that seems a trifle radical, a competent corps of anesthesiologists together with a team of specialists in intravenous feeding could, no doubt, remove from the world all psychiatric problems—except their own. But, obviously, such interventions remove psychiatric problems in precise proportion as they destroy human nature. Less radical interventions simply alter the base from which psychiatry has to operate. Like other forms of increase in affluence, or available possibilities, such means augment rather than diminish the problems with which psychiatry has to deal. As long as humanity remains, irreducibly psychiatric problems remain: they have to do with what man can do with himself as a human being, not as a machine or an animal. The better he is cared for as machine and animal, the more open his human potentialities, the greater his psychological vulnerability, probably the more numerous and the greater his psychiatric problems.

So much for the relation to medicine.

The distinction drawn does something more, however, than redefine the relation of psychiatry to medicine. The fact that psychiatry deals with men as members of a moral order alters every important perspective we have upon it. It raises new epistemological problems: problems of the kind of knowledge we can have of such a being in that capacity. It raises new conceptual problems: questions about the meanings to be attributed to key terms such as "health" and "disease." It raises ethical questions, having to do with the criteria for success, the warrant for interventions of various extents, and so on. It raises linguistic questions: what is a vocabulary appropriate to catch what we want to talk about?

Let me begin with some assertions in a philosophy of knowledge—not, be it noted, a psychology of knowledge. There is a difference between the consequences of a mistaken conception of its "object" in physics and a mistaken conception in psychology or social science. A mistaken idea in physics leads to inconvenience for the scientist, but does not affect the behavior of physical objects. A mistaken idea in psychology, in contrast, is not only inconvenient to the knower; it limits or traumatizes both the knower and the known, and is thus not only scientifically but morally a wrong. In "taking a view" of man, and of the relation of human science to man, we have to confront simultaneously scientific and moral criteria of rightness: a right view is a good view, and a wrong view is not simply erroneous but bad.

I shall maintain that the right view—the view justified by the facts—and the good view as to the object of a science of man are one and the same. I shall also maintain that the sciences of man share one object or purpose, equally centrally, with the practice of psychiatry. The object is nothing more nor less than to liberate or free man, to increase the range, significance, and importance of his choice.

How is such a view to be reconciled with the prevailing view that the object of any science is the discovery of determinate connections? Obviously, if this definition of science is insisted upon, it would be better to renounce the use of the word "science" than to twist our perception of what is the meaning of "human" and "social." The difference may cut deep enough to call for another term, and some of the reasons are obvious.

In physics, the statement of law that relates volume, temperature, and pressure neither frees nor binds the action of molecules. But, of course, the molecules do not hear us, and we, the speakers, are not molecules. When we state "a law of human nature," even if correctly, human beings do hear us, and we are human beings. The very statement of the law alters the nature of what we are speaking about, and virtually invites, or sometimes directly effects, an escape from the determinacy that it is supposed to establish or describe. Let me illustrate. A really naïve and tradition-bound culture has as its culture-bearers persons whose lives are indeed to a sensible degree "determined by their culture." If prediction is the aim of science, we can probably very well predict about them. If determinacy is the test, we have determinacy. But along comes an anthropologist and states as a law that human beings are tradition- and culture-bound. Eventually his "subjects" hear him or read him. Knowledge of what he has said is now "in the culture" so that if his people are "culture-bound," they are now bound by a radically different culture. Moreover, they, having this knowledge, are by that much radically different. So that what is bound as well as what binds is changed. Once a "tradition-bound" culture has, as an element in it, the knowledge that it is tradition-bound, the society concerned is well on the way to the probability or necessity of self-regulation by some other mechanism. Tradition, in virtue of knowlege as to its effective control, is in movement toward the loss of effective control.

The social scientist has thus a most peculiar role. When he speaks, as a human or social scientist, he is standing in one sense outside and above the system he is talking about. But if he credits his own performance, he must, as Polanyi also maintains, credit the capacity of others to do the same. We must therefore accredit also the capacity of others to alter or negate the very regularity that we reported upon. What we do then, in making our assertions about human behavior, is to shape steps upon which men may eternally climb out of the very pits in which we observe them.

I am thus asserting what I believe to be a fundamental metaphysical statement: that when we talk of man or men we are speaking of utterly indeterminate, absolutely infinite systems —at least as far as the long-run future is concerned. When we talk of atoms, we may with reasonable confidence hold that the laws of gravitation will be the same in a million years as now. When we talk of man, we cannot even predict to 1984; or, if we do, we may ensure by so doing either that it turns out as Orwell sketched it, or that precisely that fate is avoided.

A human system is thus one in which any statement about the system is vitally *in* the system, immediately or in the next virtual instant. Such a system has indeed a history, but cannot have scientific laws analogical to those of chemistry and physics. It is not merely that the system is open or has feedback. The very statement of a determinacy or determinate relation feeds back not into a mechanical and deterministic process, but into a creative, building-up act, the living of a life, which the asserted determinacy really must deny as its premise. You cannot say to a child something as simple even as "If you hit your little brother you'll feel ashamed" without *in the statement* altering him, you, and the probability of the stated association of events.

This view implies another (a statement about human nature thus implying another about the nature of human knowledge of matters human). Clearly, the human knower stands outside the human known, whether the known is another or himself. Even if, in the same instant or the next, he takes cognizance of himself as knower and himself as known, it is now a new knower, now outside the first knower and the first known. And so infinitely. Human knowledge thus appears as a flickering snapshot of a movement that in the next instant falsifies its own picture. Knowledge of things human is thus journalistic, that is, more or less true but only for its instant, rather than timeless, as in physics or chemistry. These observations are not merely about matters of fact in metaphysics and epistemology. Do they not point also to the very views that you would wish the patient to have of himself? Would you not regard the seizing of them in their full implication as among the criteria of practical success in therapy? Surely it is an aim of therapy to reduce the role of determinacy, to open and free the patient for choice. And a necessary condition, if not a sufficient one, for such reduction is that the patient should come to some such belief, or faith rather, in himself. Is this not part of what you wish, yourselves, to communicate?

There is another curious aspect about the facts in which we deal. It was implicit in my remark on the place of faith in therapy. Patently, facts emerge from the infinite flux of reality *as facts*, only in virtue of our interests. What may have been true with reference to falling apples from before time was becomes a "fact" only when someone implicated directly or vicariously in a line of action needs to establish what the facts are to permit the activity to go on or build up.

The most important human facts, as Polanyi says, only appear in passionate conviction and commitment, which, of course, lie beyond mere interest. Much more: the facts are *constituted* by the passionate commitment. This is not quite Berkeley's problem of the tree in the quad, but very near to it and much more credible. A love-object does not exist except in virtue of our love toward it. As a hunk of matter or an animal or even a person it may exist independently, but as a love-object it is whole and entire the creature of our passion. Similarly, justice exists and is real so far and only so far as men are devoted and dedicated to it. It, too, is literally the creature of their passion, as, I suggest, is everything we care for or ought to care for. As we give our passion rein, we people a universe that is otherwise empty of objects worthy of our interest.

Inquiry into human affairs, or reporting about them, cannot therefore be "objective" or "detached" or unimpassioned if it is not to miss the very things we set forth to seek. Inquiry can be "disinterested," but that is very different. May I claim again that these views, if true, are not merely philosophical assertions, but crucial and decisive communicanda in therapy. Faith is neither mere knowledge nor belief, but belief wedded to passion: belief of a kind capable of self-confirmation, wedded to passion sufficient to tip the balance toward confirmation. And faith is surely the tendril on which life winds to light; failing faith, life fails of its vitality.

This brings me to another connected point, central to psychiatric practice, and distinguishing psychiatry again from all other medical specialties. Psychiatry is the only specialty in medicine in which the theory of the subject is itself the remedy or a substantial part of the remedy. It is as though the surgeon were to cut open the patient with his theories and suture him with his hypotheses. The surgeon does not; psychiatrists do. Inescapably, the psychiatric patient gets better or worse, by coping with the psychiatrist's view of himself, of man, of society, of reality, of what is "appropriate" and "inappropriate." His psychiatrist's theories and commitments, taken as a unity, are the cast and splints within which and upon which, if at all, psychic limbs are sufficiently straightened to permit natural or better-than-natural growth to be resumed. Indeed, transcending the analogy, the cast may become bone of the patient's bone. So the therapist's theory about man and the psychiatrist's moral position are not just "basic" to psychiatry; they are "in" and "are" psychiatry. This truth also is, I trust, a communicandum of therapy.

I cannot continue without touching upon the matter of health and disease, since it is concern with these that distinguishes the psychiatrist among the other "caretakers," as Erich Lindemann has happily called them. Even in the biological order, the terms are hard enough to define. In the moral order the difficulty is even greater. In biology we usually have readily available well-founded criteria of normative performance for the biological class of which our specimen is a sample. By a disease we mean any long-standing process that grossly militates against such performance—if the process is economically remediable. (If it is not economically remediable, we call it a defect.) Veterinarians are thus able to act with relative certainty and uncomplicatedness. Even a pediatrician dealing, *qua* biologist, with an age-sex-height-weight problem in a child has relatively little difficulty. When we as men seek to deal with men as men a host of problems arise. Every previous criterion loses its simplicity.

In reference to the moral order we can define a normative process, but we cannot see its end because nothing is visible except as we are in it, and the end retires and enlarges like an expanding horizon as we advance. The normative process is one of socialization, followed or accompanied by trans-socialization. The presocialized, potential person, brought into a set of relationships with actual living, loving persons, is caught up in a meaningful role in an ongoing complex of social acts, and is introduced to and made at home in a culture. This is stage one. Some never get so far. Some do in a fashion, but fall back or fall out. Some go farther, and this is stage two. This is the stage or process in which one's relations to particular and living persons are transcended: not thus devalued but given increased value and meaning. This is the stage in which the role assigned is transformed and transfigured by reference to a view of the universe, and hence not simply accepted as assigned by "society." Neither Riesman's gyroscope of superego nor radar of peer-group reference largely guides action. The culture is transcended, ceases to be the placenta of psychological life, and becomes a domain for esthetic or ethical or other value-giving operation. The result is not merely transcendence of, but change and enrichment of, the culture without limit. This view at least leads away from the moral dilemmas and ambiguities of operation of an adjustment psychiatry—a fit servant only of a totalitarian state.

But if this is the normative process (the process of being caught up into an actual and also an ideal society), surely not everything that falls short of it is to be labeled disease or defect, at least in the sense that it falls into the psychiatrist's particular sphere of concern or area of operation. How we are to draw a working definition of "disease" from such a statement of the ideal requires that we turn for a moment to consider the relation of ideals to action.

A number of obvious things may be said at once. The want of a clear ideal is one way to self-destruction. The wrong relation to or conception of the role of the ideal is another. Unguided action is self-defeating. Action directed merely to momentary melioration is unsatisfying. What an ideal should do is to define a structure and establish an order with reference to what exists and what does not yet exist. Action directed toward achievement of an ideal all at once—or indeed toward everything it implies, indifferently and in any order —implies at worst paralysis and at best diminution of attainable goods. Hence counsels of perfection are counsels of despair.

We must therefore unquestionably do first things first. We must seek to remove present, blatant, manifest, remediable evils before we seek to bring into being remoter potential goods. We may *say* with W.H.O. that we are dedicated to health as a positive, ideal state rather than a mere nonnegative condition. We may cherish and be cherished by such a vision. But it is to be noted that under that mandate they have gone off to deal first and energetically with yaws, TB, malaria, and malnutrition.

One additional reason for orderly advance in the field of mental health is the very dynamic character of the norm, already alluded to. It seems obvious, but it needs saying, that every gain in "mental health" opens to greater clarity the psychic eye that may see and define what ideal "mental health" is. The norm thus moves, enlarges, and in a sense becomes more distant as we move toward it. This view both implies and assumes what I mean to imply and assume: an infinite moral space which is man's natural and inescapable home. The problem is how to live in it, duly awed but not so overawed as to lose the capacity for present expansion into it. A clear image of what is involved is not so much (or not only) a matter of progress in thinking about it as of progress in the achievement of it.

What are the most blatant remediable evils I must leave to the psychiatrists to determine. (It is not obvious that mental illness, so-called, is the number one enemy in their field.) But that they must order their enemies, and adjust their strategy and logistics to that order I do not doubt. I am only made uneasy by statements that indicate it is time to shift our attention from disease cure, palliation, mitigation, or prevention to the realm of "positive mental health." Only a part of my concern stems from the lack of clarity attaching to the notion.

There is a deeper difficulty lurking in such ideas, one pointed to in the realm of politics long ago by Karl Popper in *The Open Society and Its Enemies*. He makes out, I believe, an altogether convincing case. He maintains that when the State seeks to go beyond the task of removing or preventing present blatant evils on to the establishment of the good life for its citizenry, their freedom and the openness of the society fall first victims to the attempt. Since this freedom and openness is to me a more general good than any good the State might seek, the State's claims to eminent domain everywhere, even if beneficent, cannot be countenanced. What is true for the superparental figure, the State, is, I think, true in the everyday life of everyday parents, and for those of us who operate in between. We are gardeners not sculptors, in the figure of Homer Lane, an illustrious predecessor of all the wise caretakers. We uproot weeds, we loosen soil, we remove obstacles to growth; we do not push and pull the living substance into neater shapes.

I believe, then, that while the psychiatrist is obligated to remember, to be guided by, to be passionately committed to maximum, open, wholly ideal norms of health—and to make that passionate dedication visible—he is warranted in interference, especially autogenous or unsolicited interference, only to remedy or avert or mitigate gross and obvious evil. This remark may not be nearly as trivial as it sounds. I have heard at least one planner in recent months lay claim to the role of trustee for a new and not very clear utopia. I have heard more than one psychiatrist assert the same. I have heard at least one proposal for merging the two roles. And I am not unfrightened as I hear echoes in these dreams of the moral foundations that every would-be autocrat is forced to lay down for his legitimation.

This brings me to an attempt to restate the criterion for psychiatric success. I once asked one of the greatest men in the field how he knew when he had succeeded with a boy. In a language typical for him, he answered cryptically and profoundly, "Vulnerability, I suppose." What he meant became clear as the conversation proceeded. A boy who was "better" was a more voluntarily "open" boy, a boy not frozen or carapaced in rigid defenses, a boy who could and would be willing to be wounded again for the sake, presumably, of a good greater than mere security. I am drawn to that view.

But what *is* that greater good for which we have a right to ask that a man should be willing to be wounded? Perhaps it is the same good that, in another sense, is said to render him invulnerable. It must be not only a reward-in-prospect sufficient to make vulnerability tolerable, but a reward-in-retrospect that makes any and every further advance in this direction possible. What is that good? It has many names, but an anthropologist's term will serve. We may call it "kinship." The opposite of kinship is "alienation," and when psychiatrists were called "alienists" (even if for another reason) the core of their mission might have been more clearly implicit in their title. Truly, nowadays, psychiatrists are first (and often, sole) kin to the most alien; they are also the means whereby these are transformed with diminishing alienation into a kinship, greater without limit.

The notion of kinship excludes the necessity or transcends the limits of adjustment and "fitting in." Kinship not only permits and tolerates otherwise intolerable differences, it values them because it refers all differences not just to the two-point "interpersonal relation" involved, but to a third point, the family, which orders the other two in the realm of value. The appropriate third point of reference for patient and psychiatrist is never necessarily or ever exclusively the existent family, society, or social order. Indeed, these function, in the realm of value, as instances and embodiments merely of that moral order and that wider fellowship to which they point—the dead, the living, those who may yet live, and those who can only be imagined in the quickened heart. It is alienation from *that* fellowship and order that is, I hazard, not merely the cause, but the criterion, of the sickness psychiatrists seek to combat. And the criterion for their success is not that where id reigns ego shall be, but that where alienation ruled kinship shall triumph.

It will be obvious to many that no man can effectively recall another into such kinship in virtue of mere knowledge about it. We cannot call others into a kinship not our own. I said earlier that right knowledge is in psychiatry the essential tool. I am now saying that what the psychiatrist *is* is equally essential. This is so not only because what he is is a measure of his capacity to use what he knows. It is true because in matters human what we know and what we are are not separable and different. The illusion that they can be is one master-illusion with which psychiatry deals. The future of psychiatry is thus inseparable from the one process by which psychiatrists and those they affect grow without limit into knowledge quickened by passion, and passion given form by knowledge.

6

The Sociological Revolution

Just as in the latter half of the nineteenth century a Darwinian tidal wave passed across the world, upheaving the depths of thought and feeling, and even religion, just so a psychoanalytic massive movement of the waters marked our entry upon this, our century. And, hardly less noticeable, so a sociological disturbance of seismic proportions marked the middle of the century we are now in.

We are wont to complain at, but actually we are very nearly accustomed to, the changes wrought by technology, changes that make over the face of the nation, like that of a wealthy dowager, every few years. Yesterday—the figure is by now almost hackneyed—a man exploded a little volatile fluid in a cylinder capped by a piston linked to an axle bearing a wheel. Today, as a consequence, our nation is netted—like that same dowager's varicose-veined leg—with a complex of roads that laid end to end would reach from here to the moon and back a number of times; the roads are be-blobbed with huge urban aggregates, cities so-called, places rendered unfit first for animal and vegetable and then for human habitation, choking in the traffic that brought them into being like a man suffocating in his own bloodstream; and the highways rimmed with billboards bearing untrue, meaningless, and unwanted messages in every blaring tone of vulgarity and ugliness, matching the gas stations, motels, and bric-a-brac, debris, and garbage required to sustain and nourish that intermittently nomadic way of life that—nostalgically now—we were wont to call the motor age.

Or, again, yesterday a current alternated briefly in a vacuum tube or caused a notable effect in a little crystal sandwich, and today as a consequence the age of automation is upon us, no minor revolution now to render surplus the labor of slaves and horses (as did to a great degree the industrial revolution) but a major turn in the history of men that may not merely render the greater part of them surplus, but render them surplus to a large degree in terms of their only specific contribution to the evolutionary sequence, their point of pride, their power to think, that which made them credibly able—for a little while—to assert themselves only a little lower than the angels. Right now giant computers—over their domain of competence surely better machines than we are men—are charting the courses of international strategy, planning for a future at least ten years ahead, as well as predicting the proximate outcome of the present states of the nation's economic affairs. Indeed, in principle, there is now no obstacle to the eugenic breeding of computers: the programming of one computer to build an improved computer, programmed to build a still better computer. No computer has yet had a mystical experience or reported a feeling of union with the fount of all Being, but perhaps the day is not far off: the computer is in the infancy of its evolution. Reversing Oliver Wendell Holmes: three generations of idiots may be enough, but three generations of mechanical superbrains is but the barest of beginnings.

Yes, technology has had some not inconsiderable impact. But it was and is my argument that besides these obvious and far-reaching transformations, less obvious but much more far-reaching are the transformations of ideas that I alluded to at the opening of this chapter: the evolutionary revolution, the psychodynamic revolution, the sociodynamic revolution. For the technological volcano can at best spout things and ideas about things, modifying the environment, it is true, and radically so, but relatively safely, for it is a modification proceeding inward only from the outermost shell. We should not underestimate its effects, for just as the automobile that only aimed to reduce time-distance finally made over sex behavior, the family, and the city, so the computer that was initially only a more rapid adding machine cannot fail finally to alter self-images, dwarfing all our capacities for the ordinary tasks of reasoning and affecting profoundly our picture of our neededness and utility.

But powerful as such an attack is, it is at most remote from an attack at the core—man's conception of what he is and ought to be—and, in a sense, oblique to any line through the core. The other transformations I have spoken of—one of which I propose to touch upon, and one to treat at some length—are cardial rather than epidermal, very much at the heart of the matter.

The three revolutions have one thing in common—the treating of man *as a natural object:* Darwin, with regard to man as a species (and an organism), an operable biological mechanism; Freud, with regard to man as a psyche, an operable psychodynamic mechanism; the sociologists—properly enough taken as a group, since no comparable great name emerges—with regard to man as a member of society. In one sense the Darwinian revolution underlies and provides a model for the other two; in another sense they differ sharply from it as well as from each other. The communality lies in the mode and form of "explanation," the difference, in what it is that is explained.

Before we turn to an examination of the "new order" of thought perhaps we had best allow ourselves a backward glance at the old, that which was overthrown by the scientific soviets of soldiers and laborers. The old order of thought consisted not of an explanation—at least not in the modern sense of that term—but of *an account*, in dramatistic terms, of "the world and all that therein is." Life, history, cosmology were cast in the form of a drama, intelligible only in terms of *motives* and not to be reduced to terms of mere motions, a terminology in which the notion of an *act* (in its several senses) is central, and a movement apart from an act is an accident in or aberration from the dramatically unified action. The proper question of moment with reference to an act is "why?" The only answer that can be returned with reference to a movement is "how?" In the first account the "how" appears as a matter of quite minor interest: *how* the point of Macbeth's dagger pierces Duncan's epidermis, steel being harder than skin, hardly catches the playgoer's attention, let alone occupies the focus of his concern. The piercing is made intelligible not in terms of the physical properties of steel and skin, nor of the mechanical capacity and advantage of the wedge, the dagger, as a splitting mechanism, but in terms of the ongoing drama—the act, agent, or actor, purpose, scene, and agency, in their active unity, and in that order of emphasis.

For my purpose here it does not matter in what terms the drama is cast, if only the dramatic explanation itself is retained. The terms may be those of the medieval Western synthesis in which all things work together for good, and the dramatis personae are men under God, in their hierarchy headed by His vicars, lay and ecclesiastic, with the remainder of the Creation as scene and agent (or, perhaps, audience and witness). Or the terms may be the Manichaean ones of a principle of good in eternal lock with a principle of evil, man's choice being to assist the principle of his choosing and thus to enlist in the battle and affect its outcome. Or the terms may be nonsupernaturalistic—which is not to say naturalistic—in which man is the measure of all things ("Beside or above me naught is there to go"), and his task, not given but adopted, is that of the playwright-actor, to act out in terms of the lines he has himself written the very play in which he is playing for the sake not of something beyond it, but of the play itself. It does not even matter if the principal protagonists are abstractions such as "the nation"— personified, of course, and calling men into "their" service, perhaps even monopolizing the sense of vocation as well as the legitimate employment of violence—provided still that the form is dramatic and leaves to act, actor, and purpose the unconstricted scope they respectively require.

What is important here is not the differences between these "plays"—important as those differences may be for other purposes—but the difference between them as a logical class and their rival lines of explanation, also taken as a logical class. For the dramatistic accounts invite *involvement*, while the naturalistic ones, if appreciated, presuppose *alienation.* It is not proper, and it is barely possible, to be even a spectator at (let alone an actor in) a drama without that participation therein which is, I think, our distinctively human capacity; but it is barely possible, and certainly not proper, to share even vicariously in the accidental occurrence of mutations together with the elimination of the more unsuitable of them.

It had never been argued, I think, in any dramatistic account—and it was never implicit in any actual drama—that scene and agency were irrelevant to agent or purpose or act. The very care exercised in "stage-setting" in actual dramatic presentation suggests that due weight had always been allowed to the implicit if not explicit assertion of the interdependency. It is in the expansion of the scope of action of scene (or agency) from relevance to the determinative role that the dramatistic account ceases to be dramatistic and becomes, in the terminology I have been using, *naturalistic*. It is one thing to say of an actual play that the size and form of the stage facilitate or limit the action, that the hangings help achieve (and declare) the mood, that the actors cannot walk through the table but must take account of its properties by going around it, that they are constrained by the range and power of their own voices or the lever-properties of their own limbs. These facts must be—always have been—not only "recognized," but rendered contributory to the action itself.

It is quite another thing to say that the play can be, should be, must be explained in these terms, i.e., that what "appears to be" meaningful communication, purposeful action is "really" not a playing at all, but a playing out of the properties of this (accidental–there is no other term!) conjuncture of scene and agency. Indeed, on this view, there is now no play, no theater, and the very terms "scene" and "agency," which presuppose a play, are inappropriate. The force of a science of psychology or a science of sociology is precisely in this direction, and it is hard to see how, once the view has been adopted as presuppositon, limits to its operation can be set.

The prototype of a scientific psychology may be seen to be implicit in Pavlov's experiments with his demonstrative dogs. You remember the experiment. It is a "natural property" of dogs to salivate, when hungry, at the sight of meat. By presenting another "stimulus," the sound of a bell, in a proper time-relation to the original stimulus, the meat, the dogs can shortly be brought to salivate at the sound of a bell without sight of the meat. (They cannot live off the bell tones, but that is another matter.) We now have a new dog with new properties, a so-called conditioned reflex, over which (it being a reflex) he has no control, and into which (it being conditioned) no element of dog-purpose enters. It is obvious that such stimuli can be linked into chains so that, by proper presentation, the changing of a light could come to function as a substitute stimulus for the ringing of the bell, which had been itself a substitute stimulus for the smell of meat. And it is not difficult to offer this scheme as a paradigm of learning, animal and human.

We are going, if we are thorough, to have one difficulty with this as a general scheme, but perhaps the difficulty can be brushed aside (as it must be, of course, if the scheme is to survive). What are we to substitute in the general scheme for the purposing experimenter in the original, particular, and Pavlovian scheme? The answer is that the "purposing experimenter" is an illusion, or what amounts to the same thing, unnecessary for the explanation in the new vocabulary. For it must be obvious that what he is doing is no different in kind from, though it may well exceed in complexity, what his dogs are doing. His "response"—the experiment on the dogs—lies at the end of a much longer chain of successively conditioned stimuli than theirs, but in principle and practice, in substance and significance it is a process of the same kind. And, to be consistent, what lies at the source of the process by which he became conditioned? Not, in any intelligible sense, a purposing parent-educator who, by choice, conditioned his child that way, but another set of conditioned stimuli—response chains, necessarily responding (out of their previous conditioning) to him as a stimulus and thereby conditioning his responses—with the effects observed. What we mistook for an ongoing drama with live actors, purposes, a play, is then nothing more than an endless (and beginningless) interaction of stimuli and responses for which people, if they are required as terms at all, are the stage (the scene of the events) or the agency (the means of the events). Anyone with a sense for the dramatic might in passing note the irony: in his attempt (as an explainer) to come to terms with life (as an actor), man has not only explained himself but explained himself away. And this "explaining away"—to the explanation of which we shall later have to return—is the hallmark of science as applied to man. It is all—or at least it is the essence—of what science has to offer.

When I referred to the second revolution as the Freudian one—rather than the Pavlovian—I allowed myself some literary license; and I also took the historian's liberty of attending to a widespread and more familiar and—outside the U.S.S.R.—evidently more appealing school of thought. It is not quite as convenient, however, for the analysis I want to make.

For the Freudian theories which have, in my opinion, well nigh overturned the world, represent a strange mixed bag of dramatistic and naturalistic representations. It is the dramatistic element that procures the saving "well nigh," and the naturalistic element that provides the overturn.

The Freudian literature (indeed Freud's writing alone) is

so rich that one hardly knows where to begin, where to point, saying "Lo, here the seeds of our revolution." One might note to start with that the total effect of his work is to convince us that little of what we believe to be true of ourselves—and still less of what we would *like* to believe—is true.

The prized "innocence" of the very young reveals itself on even cursory inspection to be a jungle of erotic and aggresive impulses and activities, only thinly disguised and barely if at all inhibited. The real baby—unlike the baby growing out of our need to see what we want to see—arrives, not trailing clouds of glory as he comes, but equipped for, and from the first moment embarked on (if he is a male) an aggressive design upon his father in furtherance of his erotic designs upon his mother.

The relative, even if admittedly tarnished, innocence of the no—longer—very young turns out to be not even that—much less indeed than that. The "explanations" we give ourselves for our conduct turn out to be "rationalizations" by which we merely seek to make reasonable what is essentially not reasonable, and right what is neither wrong nor right but just there. For our true "motives," those things that really move us, are (for the most, and therefore the vital and significant, part) "unconscious," and we are so provided with means to prevent their becoming conscious that only rarely and by the greatest misfortune are we forced to confront the inner reality which our self-deceits normally effectively and mercifully hide. Our "highest" productions are also not as they seem: our religion is itself an illusion, a shared illusion, an outgrowth of our neurosis; and our poetry is in essence a perfumed set of veiled illusions, veiled because we cannot bear to see naked, and allusory because we are not permitted to speak directly of, that to which the veiled allusion alludes.

The greater part of behavior turns out to be not what it seems to actor or beholder, but an integration into a system—a rather precarious system at that—of "defense mechanisms," designed to protect us against the collapse consequent upon too illuminating a beam of truth falling upon the structure of self- and other-deceit.

Our wit is in reality a compromise between inadmissible aggression—inadmissible, that is, even to consciousness, not just restrained from behavioral expression—and necessary social self-protection. Our dreams speak of the unspeakable, literally, and would have no need to exist but for that necessity. Our most prized virtues are commonly mere "reaction-formations" to opposite impulses in us so powerful that their containment has called out—unconsciously, of course—these elaborated counterrevolutionary forces and precautions. What we take for adult love is, as often as not, narcissism masquerading; we look into the eyes of the "love-object" and behold either ourselves, or the selves we fool ourselves into thinking we are.

Even that on which we most pride ourselves *internally*, our conscience or "superego," is nothing more than the voices of the elders, again mostly unconscious, instilled in us by a confidence trick, speaking to us spuriously in a voice we take to be our own, and designed to stand between us and our health, between us and our pleasure. That on which we pride ourselves most *externally*, our civilization, is the source of our sicknesses and our discontents, the very organization that we designed to protect us being, in fact, the very instrument of our undoing.

For two quite different reasons these adversions have never been allowed to exert their full force. The basic reason is that somehow Freud—happily for humanity, unhappily for logic and consistency—never quite brought himself to close all loopholes or drive his arguments to their logical conclusions. The second reason, closely related to the first, is that the whole theory has been closely related to an art—"psychotherapy," "psychoanalysis"—that must deny as its premise what the theory appears to assert as its conclusion: that, in the service of blind instincts, behavior is determined unconsciously in one generation. Freud was too faithful a physician, too good a doctor, to let his doctrine carry him so far. At every point where a more thoroughgoing naturalist might have found himself driven into the naturalistic Pavlovian box, some reservation, some qualification, leaves a role, albeit diminished, to the human actor as dramatistically conceived. Nothing is to be withdrawn as to the life and death forces, Eros and Thanatos, contending with each other within man as the theater or stage for their struggle; the instincts urge ever blindly to their satisfaction and are themselves not to be domesticated, and only riskily (and precariously) penned. For the unanalyzed, the way to understanding is forever and formidably barred, and only the few for one reason or another are capable of analysis; hence far the greater part of human conduct is to be viewed necessarily as the jerkings of puppets on strings they know nothing of, and held not by a purposing actor but by "life forces" that, like the ebb and flow of cosmic tides, are "just there." It would probably be fair to say that the Freudian doctrine does not quite eliminate the three first terms of our pentad (act, actor, purpose) nor, therefore, quite extend into totality the scope of operation of the remaining two terms (scene and agency); but the scope of the first is radically restricted, and the range of the second enormously enlarged.

Even so—even with this vital exit meticulously held open—the View from Vienna has altered, virtually revolutionized, our views on practically everything of moment. It is difficult, psychoanalyzed or not psychoanalyzed, not to see onself (and be seen) in psychoanalytic perspective. One may be as opaque to oneself (and others may be as opaque to one) after Freud as before him; but it is impossible *after* him to be unaware of the opacity. If dreams have become reality and reality largely dream, we may still have no way of getting from one to the other at will, but we cannot escape the knowledge that we are dealing mostly in counterfeit coinage in transactions that, whatever else they may be, are but rarely what they seem. The everyday world if not radically "debunked" has become thoroughly disenchanted.

I will not press the point in connection with everyday

matters, though the importance of the transformation can hardly be overstressed. The man who wrote *The Psychopathology of Everyday Life* prepared the way for the perception of everyday psychopathology of life. We no longer need to "detect," we cannot close our ears to latent meanings behind manifest declarations or to the deeper symbolism of the simplest acts. All poetry, all painting, all sculpture, all playwriting, all criticism of all art almost, moves, no matter what words it chooses, in a vocabulary that is essentially Freudian, telling of a dialectic that elaborates the descriptions he developed.

Nowhere is the consequence of this transformation more evident, and of greater practical consequence, than in the expanded meaning of the term "disease" (or disorder, or some other ethically neutral equivalent) to cover more and more of human behavior formerly judged to be morally evil. The beginning lies in the legitimation (as a disease) by Charcot, Freud's tutor, of hysteria, thitherto clearly enough *not* a disease since no medical probe then (or since) has uncovered any physical substrate for the behavior in question: the very criterion until then of what was meant by a disease. What might otherwise be regarded as willful or weak behavior—the neuroses, the psychopathies, narcotic addiction, alcoholism, delinquency, criminality, fanaticism, authoritarianism, almost all persistent forms of "failure" (in the older vocabulary)—became rather rapidly redefined as diseases, in whole or in part. The scope of the concept of culpability, in law and ethics, was sharply constrained and is on the way to still sharper curtailment. It is difficult to see how, in principle, along lines already conceded, we can avoid defining as disease any line of behavior that persists in the face of mild and humane sanctions to secure its change. Even the simulation of mental disease is, as Szasz points out, held by many psychiatrists to be a sufficient sign to infer insanity in the simulator: for who is so crazy as to want to seem crazy unless he is crazy?

I am not inviting you here to bemoan or bewail this *boule-*

versement, this oversetting of pre-Freudian norms. If we have not eliminated cruelty to others, we have eliminated all shade or shadow, ethical or "practical," of justification for it. If we have not yet become able, each of us, to "accept" and be kind to himself—as Erich Fromm puts it, to be *for* himself—we have no warrant in any reasonable construction of how we came to be what we are, to be other than accepting and affirming, and no reason to hope for any good practical result by being otherwise.

But this is a two-edged sword. We have been robbed of our justification of our prized injustices, but—on the strength of the theory itself—we are not much affected by such intellectual insights, and can hardly avoid them, recognizing that our brutality is for its own sake (not, as we should like to think, in the service of some higher cause). Hence our guilt can hardly fail to increase, and it is out of increased guilt that increased brutality grows. . . . And, in another sense, the sword of our liberation is sharp at two edges: for we can hardly hope to minimize culpability without simultaneously diminishing competence: what says "you are not guilty" says also "you cannot help yourself." If we increase the range of operation of scene at the expense of actor and purpose—indeed, if we largely explain and explain away actor and purpose in terms of scene—it would, indeed be a subtle casuistry that would apply the argument in mercy as man moves toward the dark, and refrain its application, for edification, as he moves toward the light!

The blow struck at the going line of explanations and expectations by psychology was rendered puny in scale, I think, by the blow from sociology that was to follow. For sociology was to claim for its explanatory domain not only the behavior of men in all its distinctively human aspects, but finally the very explanation systems themselves. Since for sociology the society is the scene (*and* the actors, purposes, agencies, and acts), it would seem that little or nothing is left that is in need of being explained away.

The domain of sociology is marked out by a claim innocent enough in appearance: it seeks to be (it "is") the science that explains the behavior of men insofar as such behavior is affected by their membership in groups. Alas for modesty, it turns out in the sequel that this means all human behavior, except for that realm, relatively trivial in interest, that might be marked out by reflex at its pinnacle and mere chemistry (or electronics) at its base. The whole realm of "the meaningful" is in; only the inframeaningful is out.

I shall sketch only briefly here the domain of sociology. Let us begin at the beginning—with society.

The fundamental notion of sociology is "the society," viewed as an organization of interdependent roles. It is the roles and their organization that persist through time, that shape the behavior of the actors (and, as we shall later see, the actors themselves), and that account alike for the significant variation between societies and between persons in any one society. If you look at a "primitive" society you can see more or less clearly how the defined roles, for instance, of Chief and Medicine Man not only structure and give form to behavior, perception, and expectation at a given moment, but operate through time in such fashion that one Chief is more like another ten generations back than he is like his contemporary Medicine Man or Warrior. When men act, we should have to say, they act in roles; the roles that they are to act in are provided for them by the society; the roles are so intermeshed that any alteration in one necessitates alteration in all; and acting out of role is, when the society is effective, punished or attended by social death proportional to the degree of deviation, so that the role-system may endure. Where a "deviation" is widespread and cannot readily be dealt with as a rare aberrancy (as, for example, homosexuality in some societies), it is itself institutionalized, that is, made into a role, and hence reintegrated with and made contributory to the role-system. The interdependency of roles, the consequent effective division of labor, ensures the interdependency of persons, making conformity to expectation both "natural" and "rewarded" and departure therefrom unnatural and hence properly to be punished. (Indeed, the punishment seems "natural" as much as being burned is a natural consequence of putting hands in fires.) But more than external conformity to other people's expectations is required for (and found in) a properly operating society: the social character that makes the "required" behavior at least acceptable, and at best the highest delight, the natural source of satisfaction, must be instituted in the members of the society by the natural operation of the society. So the society, viewed as a system, institutes in persons (who are the mere means to its persistence) those qualities that require the role-system and its permanence as the context that makes life viable, in either the practical or the ethical sense.

As pervasive and general, as all-explanatory as the term "society," is the necessary accompanying term "culture." Indeed, the terms are coextensive, and the realities to which they refer are coconstitutive. "The culture" is, in brief, the society's patterned way of doing things, including more particularly "communicating" things, in the wider sense of that term. What is done, said, thought, felt, insofar as it is at all intelligible, is patterned, and insofar as it is patterned, *is* the culture. The culture is that which is "shared"; the members of a society are those who "share" in its culture; the sharing is what the society, dynamically viewed, *is*. (Do not think, please, that *over against* this realm of the shared and cultural and social there is to be set a realm of the private. What we think of as "private" is still in a most thoroughgoing sense social: a mother holding a child does so in a patterned way; a holy man having a mystical vision "sees" what his culture has taught him to see, even when it seems to him astonishing and unexpected. Even inventions and discoveries, innovations, occur simultaneously to many people because at a given moment they are what the *system* requires.)

The culture is not merely a set and patterned way of doing

things, but it always includes a set of explanations of *how* things are done as a set of justifications of *why* they are done as they are done—including finally justification of its own justifications by a religious system. The force of this observation may be noted by juxtaposing two dicta springing from crosscultural comparison: (1) there is no mode of behavior approved in one culture that is not disapproved in some other; (2) there is no culture that lacks a convincing argument as to why its practices and beliefs are the supremely (or only) right ways of doing and believing. Even hypersophisticated societies like our own, which can afford themselves social critics, do not escape the charmed circle of culturalism. For the canons of criticism, the criteria of evaluation are themselves in (and fundamental to) the culture, so that all the critic is doing is accelerating a process that takes place anyway based on what William Graham Sumner used to call "the strain to consistency in the mores." (The mores are those shared views about the good, or right or seemly which, in every society, are "beyond discussion.") And in just the same way that we cannot touch the role-system without altering all roles, so also we cannot disturb a culture element without repercussions upon all others and a threat to the viability of the system. And it is precisely to preserve their culture that men are most willing to die and be killed, for life (or such life as men think worth living) depends on the integrity of the culture.

Nor is the relation, the fittedness, between the needs of the social system and the "needs" of its members as perceived by them in large outline at all any mystery. For the "nature" that persons have, their "human nature" itself, is precisely what they get by participation in, by being caught up into, the social process whose continued operation *is* the society extending through time. Apart from those blind urges that depend on the mere biology of the organism, everything that belongs to the person, everything that makes him a *human* being, is an outcome of his socialization, that is, of his being lived and loved into humanity by those whose nature and behavior he assimilates precisely as he is assimilated. There is a detailed and dramatic social psychology of such role-taking for which the name of George Herbert Mead will be forever famous, but the place for such detail is not here. It is a psychology both necessary and sufficient, I think, to account for the differences between human nature and brute nature by tracing the coemergence of mind, self, and society in the process of role-taking by a form that can learn to take a role, take the role of another, and finally behave toward itself as another form. In that process is instituted the most distinctively human characteristic, the articulation point between "I" and "we" (as well as the "ground" for both), the calling out by a social process of a self that can be a self to itself!

The logic and the mode of analysis that had proved so helpful—and in many ways so comforting—in application to alien and so-called "primitive" societies could not, in the nature of things, be withheld from application to our own. Indeed a diversified society like ours, while it no doubt has its (hard to discover) unities, may on another view be seen to be but a loose congeries of subsocieties, largely alien to each other—"alien" meaning, as it always does, not just strange but inimical.

And the moment this view is taken it is impossible not to explain and explain away their modes of behavior, and more particularly the manner in which they explain and justify their conduct. The general view may be stated as "what you think depends on where you are," which comes close to saying, "it is not you that thinks your society, but your society that thinks you."

The arch-polemicists of this view were perhaps Marx and Engels. Noting how class views always, at all times and places, served class purposes (which is to say always exploitative interests), they reduced all ideas (except their own) to mere "ideology." "Ideology," it might be said, is an organized (and closed) explanation system that serves a society or a subsociety (a "class") and cloaks an interest. It is to be dealt with, not by discussion of its validity, but by "unmasking" the peculiar function it has in securing for someone differential material (and nonmaterial) advantage. The view feeds anger because what you say is generally only an oblique way of seeking your own advantage; but it also feeds pity because you can no more help thinking so than you can having been born to whomever you were born to.

It could not be, of course, that so potent a political argument could be left to the Marxists, though they long monopolized it. If aristocratic and bourgeois views can be shown to be mere ideology, how can proletarian views be seen as different except by a special argument that is itself part of the proletarian ideology, and that has the same formal character as the special arguments by which each of the other two "proved" their exclusive justification?

Indeed how can any argument escape the "ideological" imputation, and hence reduction from the realm of argument as ordinarily conceived, altogether. Note that we are not saying merely that there is an element of limitation, of parochialism, in all contentions, and that this is to be progressively escaped. We are saying that the very criteria of validity, the categories of analysis, are primarily (if not exclusively) *strategic*, hence political, hence to be judged pragmatically—and clearly pragmatic judgment turns on who you are and where you stand with all the illimitable limitations implied by both.

It is time to abandon for now our little revolutions. Society—blessedly perhaps—has a way of coping with new ideas, particularly ones that might subvert it altogether, by selective inattention or by managing to maintain at once two or more incompatible perspectives. Sometimes this playing for time pays: the Micawbers are not always wrong, and "something may turn up." But most often such ideas unattended too long prepare the way for real and bloody revolutions, battles of bullets—not ballots—conflicts which under modern conditions we can less and less afford.

Such ideas, as we have discussed, bear upon the roles, and deeply affect the enterprises and self-conceptions of all of us. We are constrained, I think, to contribute our mite to Sumner's "strain to consistency in the mores." A first step might be to examine what we now believe, and how those beliefs, if altered, affect our vocations and professions, both as to what we do and as to what we may legitimately profess.

II

The Psychoanalytic Stance of Social Science

7

Psychoanalysis: Model for Social Science

Relativity is more than a theory in Physics. It is a quite general position to which one feels constrained to adhere. In just the same way that a statement about the velocity of a physical body is meaningless without reference to the relative position and velocity of the observer, so also any general proposition (and perhaps also any particular one) about human affairs is meaningless, rather than true or false, without reference to the philosophical position from which the statement comes.

Human knowledge—and perhaps the external reality to which it is supposed in some sort to correspond—has often been thought to be hierarchichal in its "natural," or most convenient, organization. On one, most common, variant of this view, Philosophy is the "Queen of the Sciences," mandated to examine for validity the assumptions upon which the other sciences rest. Indeed, there is a tendency—I think Bertrand Russell represents it rather well—to define Philosophy as being distinguished by its capacity or duty to discharge this obligation.

It is a strange hierarchy, however, in which with no difficulty whatever, we can see any one of the general sciences as being superordinate to all the rest. From the viewpoint of sociology, to take an example, the behavior of philosophers, including most particularly their products, the contending philosophies, are social data to be explained in sociological terms. Karl Mannheim epitomizes this point of view, though he neither originated it nor was able to accept or extricate himself from the position into which it placed him. The conclusion he should have drawn, as a sociologist, was and is that a philosophy is a social product, a function of a given society in a given time and place, an ideology whose warrantability or unwarrantability rests upon its relation to the society to which it appeals. Indeed, he went so far (but only in premature alarm) to try to save himself from the "relativism" to which he saw himself thus condemned.

It is quite possible to turn the tables and to examine philosophically the warrantability of Mannheim's whole argument in philosophic terms, and many philosophers have not unnaturally concluded that it cannot be maintained. But this counterattack can again be examined in terms of sociology of knowledge, and "accounted for." And so on. The whole philosophic enterprise may be entirely included in the study of sociology, and the whole sociological enterprise is a matter of philosophic enquiry. We have the logical paradox that two "sets" are wholly included within the same set, and yet each is distinct—something that the merest tyro in the mathematical theory of sets will tell us at once is impossible. But so it is. And also for each of the corresponding metasciences: the sociology of sociology, and the philosophy of philosophy.

What has been said for sociology is, even more familiarly, true for psychology. It would be a very modest psychologist who would not see in any philosophy a vast, individual or collective, projective system: a tale told in reference to the nearly blank "TAT card" that the universe represents, a tale whose telling yields a rich story about the teller and very little about the card. It would be a not very immodest one either, who would assert that *in principle* and forever this is bound to be the case. Given the very nature of "the card," it is not now and cannot ever be more than an ostensible stimulus to people to report obliquely upon their need and preoccupation systems under the illusion they are asserting something about the card. An equally modest philosopher would wish to bring under analytic scrutiny the notion of "projection." He might even demonstrate that the use of the construct tells us more about the needs of the user than about his object matter, and hence that if the concept is valid at all it is invalid altogether, since it undercuts its own roots like the statement, "Everything I say is always untrue."

It is in the midst of unresolved—and, I believe, unresolvable—difficulties of this kind that we are required to examine such a question as "what is the scientific status of psychoanalysis?" For to ask the question so is to tip some sort of precarious balance. At least to ask the question, outside the context of its companion question, "What is the psychoanalytic status of science?" is to define beforehand and inequitably who is to be plaintiff and who defendant, and, more important, who is to combine the role of judge with the role of making out his own case.

It ought hardly be necessary for me to urge, in a psychoanalytically oriented group, that science (as a body of knowledge or an activity) is itself a matter of psychoanalytic investigation and attention—just like eating, or toileting—rather than (or as well as) the touchstone against which psychoanalytic theory may assess its merit. And yet it is necessary, because quite obviously the periodic, strenuous, and sometimes strident efforts of psychoanalysis to have itself defined as scientific indicate a situation which, if it occurred in a patient, we should regard as meriting our close attention, to say the least. What would we not all suspect? Passivity? Idealization of the nonego, accompanied by underlying hostility? Lack of a solid identity, based upon some failure to work through the premature and cloudy introjections of infancy? Reluctance or inability to recognize one's own potency or strength except insofar as it can be redefined in terms of resemblance to or dependence upon "the parent?"

Most obviously, science is, to begin with, an extreme and elaborated manifestation of the secondary process. It deals with its materials, as it becomes more and more scientific, by a process of severing successive roots in or connections with the primary process, or indeed with reality in any degree of fullness. For very remote, perhaps dubious, and certainly manipulative or instrumental ends, it moves by a succession of abstractions into a realm of equations, relation to which, let alone cathexis upon which, is impossible. It is not difficult for me as a person to relate as a whole person to this table as immediately apprehended by any of us here. The set of equations that expresses the dance of the atoms that is this table from the viewpoint of physics can only appeal to one very limited side of me. It is hardly an exaggeration to say that as man probes into reality through science he is alienated from reality in a most radical and, I would add, very probably dangerous, sense. It is not, as has been so often stated, simply that his familiar world becomes, under the moving illuminations of science, an unfamiliar one; it is, more radically, that the very basis of the scientific outlook requires an increasing distance of the observer from the observed, which it becomes progressively impossible to bridge as the science advances, so that man's relation to his universe becomes ever more secondary, remote, cold, tenuous, unsatisfactory, and, perhaps, impossible. He cannot be "at home" in a universe that he must leave in order to describe. Whether he finally returns home or not, he subsequently maintains (in it or out of it) the view that he got by looking upon it as an outsider.

What is said so far is certainly true for the physical sciences (including the biological ones in the ordinary sense of that word) and when we attempt to cope with corresponding problems in the social (or human or behavioral) ones, the difficulties multiply even faster.

It is not at all clear that a science of man, in the sense in which we have been using the term "science," is at all possible —or, if possible, possible without destroying the object of the investigation, in this case the investigator and his species, which of course, also then implies impossibility. I am not thinking here of such relatively trivial objections as the complexity of the subject matter; all subject matters are as complex as we please to make them! Nor am I thinking of such momentary and historical objections as the present weakness or crudeness of our tools of observation. The difficulties are problems in principle.

The first point—which has an analog in biology, but not in physics—is that man is at all times and places an actor in the only and once-and-for-all drama that we call history. With reference to practically everything we are interested in here, this is a germane, if not pressing, consideration. There is a locality, a temporalness in most of our propositions about man that is the exact antithesis of the generalizations in physical science, which correctly assume for their (practical) purposes repeatability of experiments and (practical) identity between units. In the human world, in contrast, not only is each actor caught up in this general drama, but—as I need hardly emphasize here—he is caught up in his family's history, and, most dramatically, in his own, so that today's "objectively identical," "stimulus," or "response" cannot be effectively identical with yesterday's, if only because it has followed it in the experience, the historic experience, of a history-sensitive organism.

The second difficulty, which has no analogue in biology or in physics—despite the Heisenberg indeterminacy principle—is of the very essence in determining the status of a putative "human science": it lies in the fact that almost any "fact" stated about human beings is almost certain to be "heard" by them, to alter them in the hearing, and so to falsify, in the long run or the short, the statement made. Post-Freudian man is different from pre-Freudian man, at least by access, direct or indirect, to the Freudian word; and to that degree, the Freudian picture is either no longer true, or simply incomplete. (Some of my psychoanalytic friends say they encounter new difficulties in practice in the interweaving of defenses with psychoanalytic sophistication that Freud's patients could never have had. The tablets cannot be brought down by the same or another Moses from the same Sinai twice.) This is a characteristic of news—and of the statements from the head of the couch—but not of the propositions of a general nomothetic science.

A third difficulty, closely connected with the second, lies in the peculiar problem posed by adopting for human behavior the terminology of determinism, even a "probabilistic" determinism (whatever that may be), in reference to beings whose most immediate intuition of themselves, in their most important matters, is the overwhelming intuition of choice. Indeed, failing full faith in such an intuition, our discussion here is empty of exactly the meaning we apprehend it to have—a weighing procedure capable of affecting what we shall shortly think and proximately practice. Such is, over a wide range of behavior, the nature of human nature, that if we here determine (by choice) to think of our behavior as, in general, determined, then will it indeed be so determined as a consequence of our choice. We can indeed, by sufficient intellectual faith in our impotence, effectively ensure it by our self-castration. Whether men would long listen to such an apostolate of apostasy from the immediate promptings of their own potency is another question, but certainly in all other respects it is a tenable position. Indeed it is the only position that a generalizing, nomethetic science of man can hold, and it is this, perhaps more than anything else, that casts doubt upon its possibility.

If one is ready, on the strength of these contentions or others, to doubt whether a science of man cast in the form of the sciences of things is either profitable or possible, it may yet be expedient to ask what sort of a "science," using the word now in a more equivocal or ambiguous sense, of or for man might be possible.

I think we have a great deal to learn both from the physical sciences and the emerging, but seriously disoriented social ones, that is of utility in human affairs. I should be the last person, either in theory or practice, to undervalue exactitude of conceptualization as far as it can be pushed, meticulousness of reasoning, and the ultimate submission of the results of the process to some relatively public test of reality—experimental, or as close thereto as the nature of the subject will allow us to get. Half the nonsense written and spoken in the social sciences today is there for the want of decent attention to the simplest such canons of orderly procedure and thought.

I should not expect too much, however, from such a procedure.

Given the necessarily time-limited and place-limited character of its conclusions, I should expect that every "finding" would be but a momentarily valid picture (like a snapshot of a growing child) of a state passing from an evanescent present into the memory of the past and the material for the future. I should think that, with rare exceptions, even what is momentarily true would emerge out of an endless, continuing conversation between society and its scientists (or would-be analysts) in which conversation the scientist is as much reforming as informing the society (or helping it to inform and thus reform itself). I should expect that that part of social "science" which was operational, in the sense that it is at all in the mainstream of the culture, would be that part of the body of knowledge immediately relevant to critical and crucial personal or social problems, already manifest or latent. I think we should re-encounter in such a science such familiar phenomena as overdetermination, i.e., multiple lines of explanation each of great convincingness and with power of illumination but not, in the ordinary sense, capability of proof or even decisive test of preferability as between them. We already have established the phenomena of self-confirming predictions (or even postdictions) and problems in the ethics of research and publication analogical to those of the psychotherapist with his patient.

I have gone too far now to refuse to pose openly two clearly related questions:

(1) Is psychoanalysis not, perhaps, pursuing strange and futile gods in its constant attempts to make itself

scientifically respectable on the model of the nonhuman science?

(2) Would it not be well for the social sciences to ask themselves whether or not they have in psychoanalysis a more apt model for getting what they want than they have in the dominantly dilute physical science models they now so largely ape?

I shall not seek to answer either question fully here. Should I attempt it, I would have to deal first with the interfusion of each into the other that already exists: the pseudoscientism that Freud (and his followers) never entirely escaped, and the "analytic" orientation that pervades some social science without explicit acknowledgment of its parentage or identity.

If time permitted the pursuit of the second question much further, I should be inclined to start with some "psychoanalytic" questions or ones analogical to them. Is not much of the product of present social science suggestive of that detailed knowledge of the trivial or esoteric, together with a curious blindness to vital fact, obvious and near at hand, which must be neglected because fixity of method will allow no account to be taken of what most needs to be taken account of? Is there not at the core of the social science we know, the analogue of the patient's treating himself as mere object, and the analogue of the illusory hope of his coming into such power over himself that he becomes, in some indefinable (because impossible) sense, the servant to his own ambitions? Is there not, in effect, at the heart of the model, both alienation and hope of omnipotence, the second on the ground of the first—and destined to defeat because of it?

I cannot help feeling that my questions are well on the way to answering themselves. At least, many social scientists, among them the best and wisest, have been the ones most engaged with life, most likely to speak of it in the terms of reportage "from within" (as well as with a dash of detachment "from without"), least scientific, least oriented toward such engineering terms as "control," most oriented toward more biological or aesthetic modes of thinking. The names of Charles Horton Cooley, Park, Redfield, Fromm, Erikson, Riesman, Margaret Mead, Malinowski, Herbert Blumer—in unordered series—come to mind. Their methods could, I think, find point-for-point matches over the wide range within the psychoanalytic movement—but not within neurology or biochemistry. Perhaps what is wanting is the open recognition of an identity or affinity that, like so many recognitions, has its difficulty precisely proportioned to its importance.

8

Social Psychology, Self, and Society

Social psychologists find it hard enough to talk to each other. The languages they use range from something that looks and sounds like the writing and talk around the launching of the Venus-bound spacecraft to something that looks and sounds like what must have been the spectator talk after the first presentation of a play by Sophocles or Shakespeare. I do not even faintly exaggerate. On one wing we would find a discussion that requires, for its understanding, a comprehension of modern mathematics, one that is couched and written in almost pure mathematical terms. On the other wing we would find material that taxes not mathematico-logical competence, but human range, empathy, and dramatic insight: capacity for appreciation, if you will. In the middle we would be subject, in the attempt to understand what was being said, to minor strains comparable only to those called for in mastering Newtonian physics, elementary chemistry, or any other semi-strange way of talking about semifamiliar material.

If these strains attend communication *within* the profession, what must be the strains of attempting to communicate with an audience outside the (divided) "mystery?" The question is not only *how* should one tell, but *what* should one tell?

Perhaps the easiest thing would be to follow the pleasure principle, to tell the audience what it would like to hear so that it might be gratified and, being gratified, might applaud, thus making everybody happy all around. This course is very tempting, particularly since experience teaches that what audiences in general like to hear is something that assures them that something useful (to them) is being produced and that there is some assurance that the supply of such products is likely to become more plentiful and less costly. By "something useful," they usually mean, in reference to the social sciences, something that will alleviate their miseries, particular or general, or increase their psychic or material incomes.

I think I *could* (in a technical sense) follow this course. It *would* be possible to point to the multiplication and proliferation of social psychologists, social psychological books, journals, articles, or associations, a proliferation that follows rather exactly the rate at which fruit flies multiply in a bottle. In technical jargon, this looks at first like an exponential curve, becoming rapidly visible as a logistic one. If this multiplication did not, by itself, reassure you, I think I could point to the educative effect of all this by demonstrating (by word count or "content analysis") the growing use in novels, in talk about practical affairs such as education or race relations, of social psychological terms or views. So, *if* being used is a sufficient criterion for usefulness, I think I could convince you that social psychology is finding increasing use, and should hence be regarded as increasingly useful. If you are too sophisticated for that, I do not doubt that I could introduce you to some nonundesirable uses of the stuff: I guess prisons are less patently brutal in some places, mental hospitals less obviously inhuman, schools less directly child-destroying, family life less pervasively or nakedly mutually exploitative, and so on. Whether or not social psychology is the cause of these things, it does figure largely in their explanation and justification, and hence enters into their support in a way that is not to be discounted altogether. (Affluence and safety can also be great engenderers of debrutalization, perhaps not by themselves, but obliquely in terms of the other things they permit.)

I should be happy to do all this, except that if I allow the argument one way, I have to allow it the other: the very things of which we are wont to complain most in American society find, no more and no less, their justification—if not their cause—in social psychology. Any Madison Avenue conference —the ultimate aim of which is to part you from your money by making you feel that X's soap or Y's automobile is indispensable to your femininity or masculinity (respectively, I hope)—is founded in thoroughgoing fashion in the self-same social psychology. The procedure of the advertising or the public relations strategy, or of the conference itself—as well as its aim—is so affected. The aim is still primarily piratical, but out of Freud via Dale Carnegie: Freud, in the insight into the sexualization and libidinization of all things; Carnegie, in the smooth uses of such insights for such high ends as the general good (of the pirates concerned, of course). The *method* is out of Freud (on group psychology) and Cooley (primary or face-to-face groups) via Lippit and Lewin and the Group Dynamics Laboratory of Bethel, Maine, via the theorists about "leadership" and "small groups," the students of "group process," "consensus," and the "engineering of consent."

It may appear to you that I have, so far, said only that although social psychology shows great growth and grasp, it is, like any other science, "ethically neutral," and has hence been productive so far of great good as well as high harm. It would usually be added that what men do with a science, say chemistry—whether, for instance they make cheap, sure, abundant equivalents for mothers' milk, or whether they devise "nerve gas" or "truth serum"—is something that it does not fall within the province of that science to explain (let alone affect or control). This habitual stand is relevant for chemistry, but is commonly uncritically carried over to social psychology. Surely it will not hold. If men put the first deliverance of social psychology to use to destroy (or support) each other, then surely this too is social behavior, and surely it is thus within the realm of social psychology. It is hence incumbent upon social psychology at least to *explain* this use in its second deliverance. Failure to take this view is itself a curious piece of social behavior, and must itself come in for a social psychological explanation. And what if, further, the very nature of the first deliverance should turn out to affect the probability that men would find fine, as against fatal, uses for it? Does this leave us with a science of human behavior, insofar as it is socially affected, that is in any important way comparable to any of the sciences we are accustomed to consider? I think not.

But I see I have already begun to do what I simply intended to warn you I was going to do: to exhibit, as far as I can, some of the difficulties and distresses within the house of social science, rather than to demonstrate the achievements already achieved and the promises (prematurely, I think) held out. I choose this course—I prefer to pursue this thornier path—not simply because I believe that a public is entitled to a proper reply to a well-posed question, but also because I think the only sure defense against the public danger posed by a *pseudo science* of human affairs is a superior understanding on the part of the public of what is at issue.

I am thus driven to write of remote and abstract and, perhaps, difficult matters instead of near and concrete and easy things, pleasant to hear and reassuring to remember. I am driven to write, at least briefly, of the philosophy, politics, psychology, and sociology of social psychology, all of which sounds (and is) formidable. I can touch only briefly on each problem, but enough to assure you, perhaps, that not everything is so safe and settled in the social psychological house as to require your uncritical subservience on the ground that the experts are united and must know what they are doing. As a matter of fact, I think the opposite holds: roughly, where they are united, they do not know what they are doing, and where they know what they are doing, they are not united.

The first problem is doubtless to agree on what social psychology is. In the *Handbook of Social Psychology*, Professor Allport of Harvard, who is about as wise a man in these matters as anyone, takes about seven hundred fifty words to tell us he has not a clue. First he says it has no sharp boundaries; then, that in many respects it is indistinguishable from general psychology; then he speaks of its "apparent lack of autonomy," finally giving it a "focus of interest" in "the social nature of the individual person." He then makes a bolder stab by saying that most social psychologists regard their discipline as "an attempt to understand and explain how the thought, feeling, and behavior of individuals are influenced by the actual, imagined or implied presence of other human beings."

I do not know how most social psychologists view their craft, but there are some very tender, crucially tender points, sore points, in the Allport definition. The first thing to notice is that even before we begin we are committed, on this view, to *assuming* an "individual human being" in the actual or virtual presence of other "individual human beings," and we are simply asked to explain the influence of this presence on the thought, feeling, and behavior of one of them. But what influences the one is not the *presence* of the others; it is *their* thought, feeling, and behavior—which is the very thing to be explained. Moreover, *their* thought, feeling, and behavior are influenced by *his*, so that they are not data, not independent variables, not things that can be used *either* to understand or to explain. Somehow, we are all tangled up and had better make a fresh start.

Let us say that a social psychology is an attempt to account for behavior insofar as it is shared (which is what makes it social) in terms of meanings (which is what makes it psychological). What is excluded is only a very narrow range of happenings: if a stone "accidentally" (that is, in a meaningless way) falls upon my kneecap and produces a reflex jerk directed toward no one, we are outside the realm of social psychology. When the same effect is produced by a doctor to whom I am a patient, part of the behavior (the naked reflex jerk) is outside, but a much greater part of the behavior (my unspoken comments, how I represent my feelings to self or others, indeed what I apprehend to have happened) is social psychological matter.

But the very words qualifying the behavior at interest—"insofar as it is social"—are a far cry from Mr. Allport's relation of the individual to other actual, imagined, or impliedly present individuals. It seems so close to common sense to postulate such individuals that it is very hard to shake the sense of it from scientific discourse, let alone from everyday account, but shake it I must. The individual he speaks of is not only social in his origin—so that we would have to inquire into his origin before we so blithely take him as a datum—but he is social in his immediately present nature. By "social in his present nature" I mean two quite different things, both of which leave little of Mr. Allport's individual as a datum. I mean first that psychologically he lives in a society, just as organically he may be said to live in action. His relation to society is not to be viewed as similar to that of an island in a sea, or to an island in an archipelago. I mean "in" in the same sense as Jesus' observation of God: "I am in the Father, and the Father in me." If we say analogically (with Dewey) that community exists in communication, we do not mean that the two can be abstracted from and viewed as mutually influencing each other, but that they are one and the same thing in different manifestations. Indeed, they *constitute* each other, without separability or residue. Thus, when we say men live in society, that *is* what we must mean. The wave is not to be *related to* a perturbation in the medium; it is not only a perturbation of the medium, it *is* the medium perturbed.

The second sense in which man is social is not only in relation to that "them" in whom (psychologically) he lives and moves and has his being, but also in relation to that which he sets naïvely *over against* them: whatever he refers to as "I."

For to this object, if such it be, he also sustains a social relationship. He talks to himself. He also feels about and responds to himself, and he may have feelings about his feelings. But a system that works like that is what we *mean,* when we are at all clear, by a "society." Hence, the self not only lives in a society of others but *is* itself a society of selves. Moreover, what he will regard as, think of, feel as, *or* behave toward as *self*, and what he will regard as *other*, will fluctuate from stage to stage of "his" development, and from moment to moment at any stage. The "genuine voice of self" at this instant was once taken for the alien voice of other, and may yet later be felt to be ego-alien (even though coming from within); and, per contra, the voices the others use may speak in the very tones of self at an earlier day. The self that approves and rejects the innumerable other selves of the selfsame self is but one self in the company of selves, giving and withholding friendship and recognition, just as, on Mr. Allport's model, the "individuals" are figured as doing between them—except that, unlike him, we recognize that they do not exist apart from the company they keep.

Something in Western thoughtways makes this line of thought extremely difficult, and it may be that the very sickness of Western society (exaggerated pride and shame, self-esteem and guilt, ulcer-pregnant sense of responsibility) stems from it. Somehow, in Western thought, as in that of a small child, society is set outside and over against the self, with some ridiculous and indefensible boundary drawn at the anatomical (and hence irrelevant) skin. It is intolerable that science should reinforce such views. Anyone who has lost a loved one—a supposed other—should know better.

It is not merely, as Donne has it, that "no man is an Island entire of itself." The very way of thought, and with it what makes Donne's reminder necessary, is a first-order misconception that permits little thereafter to be rightly conceived. Does anyone doubt that at this moment he is in life and life is in him; that he is simply not intelligibly he apart from life; that the terms cannot be counterposed or used to explain each other; that life does not exist apart from him and his like? Self and society are similar terms. I am in the society that is in me, as I am, and can only be, in that grace (small though it be) that is in me. The very conception of a counterposition of the two shows so poor a socialization as to make its proponent a good spokesman neither for himself nor for his society. The magnitude of the self, if one can speak of such things, is measured by the society it incorporates. The magnitude of the society, if one can speak of such things, is measured by the selves that it unites. "The society" is the name for the "unity," but "the selves" are that in which the unity is seen as multiple. There are as many societies as there are selves, and as many selves as there are societies. It is as idle to ask which is prior or preponderant, or which influences the other and how, as it is to ask the same questions of the life and the living, the breathing and the breath.

It may seem that—right or wrong—I am making too much of a single point. After all, it may be said, what we do in such cases is to take the rival conceptual schemes—say, wave theory and particle theory in all-but-recent physics—draw deductions from them, test the deductions, and qualify the one and disqualify the other. I am sorry to say that I fear that in most cases, or in most cases that matter, we cannot test theories about human beings in this way. (Such a view of the relation of theory to actuality in reference to human beings does not test but begs any question as to the soundness of the views I have just set forth.)

If we exist in each other, as I suppose, then it cannot be other than that we are affected in what we are by what others think of us, by their hypotheses or theories regarding us, so that the hypothesis to be tested affects the data that are to make the test. We are not, in my vocabulary, merely "affected" or "influenced," we are *altered* as a region in a field of forces is altered by a change in a line of force passing through it. It is not, again, that one *causes* the change in the other, but that the single event may be referred, indifferently, to the line or to the region.

Again, on this view, a theory about human beings, if widely held, tends to bring about its own confirmation (or, sometimes, disconfirmation). (This follows from the hypothesis, but we are all familiar with instances. The only value that money has, for instance, lies in our belief that others believe it to be valuable. It functions as, and can function only on, faith; the faith alone gives it its functional value. Without that, it is mere burning paper, and poor at that.) So a theory that picks up from the widespread Western intellectual belief in a postulated (and thereby instituted) individual-as-over-against-society, is not testable against a contrary theory. If a theory starts out from a naïve preconception in physics, the data repudiate the theory if the theory is wrong. If a theory starts out from a naïve preconception in social psychology, not only do the initial data tend to confirm it (since men are largely what they think themselves to be) but the preliminary confirmation, once published, tends to reinforce the inadequate self-conception and society-conception, and hence, on subsequent tests, tends to lend ever greater plausibility to error.

One might ask how I can maintain at one and the same time that men *are* largely (or, worse, wholly) what they think themselves to be, and that they are, nevertheless, in error in thinking what they now think and are "really" something quite other. The difficulty sounds more formidable than it is. Imagine yourself coaching a child to pitch a baseball. He makes several wild throws, is discouraged, and says *in virtue of his discouragement*, "I can't pitch!" A true report of the state of affairs. One coach may say (on hypothesis): "No, you can't," and, depending on his relation to the child, may make him angry enough so that all of a sudden he can, or discouraged enough so he "really" cannot. Another may say (on hypothesis): "Sure you can, Jimmy," and in a sudden access of strength as the counterpart of faith, Jimmy may really be able to. So the hypothesis constitutes the new fact (not merely "causes" it), and it *is* simultaneously true that (a) Jimmy cannot really pitch, except (b) on the hypothesis that he can.

Now I agree that not just anything the coach said, no matter how close his relation to the boy, would be subsequently (let alone immediately) realized. What he can assert not only must be within the realm of the possible, but also must reflect accurately *and* call out, a latent fact about the boy, a fact that only requires accreditation to make it manifest and supervenient. The company of the coach, insofar as the boy lives in it, effects a reorganization in (more strictly reconstitutes) the company of selves in the boy, shifting executive possibility from one to another.

The central fact that emerges out of this is that the test of fit of a hypothesis from among a very large variety of hypotheses is, in social psychology, not so much the selection of a scientific guide to study as it is actual embarkation on a program of action. It is not, as in physics, so much a question of hard data to which the hypothesis conforms ill or well according to well-known intellectual tests. For such problems, we have standard tests of "goodness of fit." In social psychology, the data (people, society) fit themselves, ill or well, to the hypothesis, and the tests of "goodness of fit" are not merely (or only trivially) scientific, but ethical and aesthetic as well. It is not only—not even primarily—how closely do hypothesis and data conform to each other, for in time no doubt they may conform quite well to each other. (Parents who believe ill enough of their children long enough may finally come to have children it were well to think ill of.) The question of overwhelming force is whether the data are *constrained* on the hypothesis: and this judgment requires canons of goodness and beauty that are not to be derived from what is manifest in man, since, *ex hypothesi* it deals with what is latent, what the hypothesis may call into actualization.

On this view, a social psychological theory—or, more especially, a set of premises underlying a theory—is in appearance an opinion on the facts, but in reality a fiat, good or bad, effective or ineffective. No less than a statement of the rights of man, it is a proclamation: an attempt to institute what ought to be in the form of a statement about what is. If on either ground (moral appeal or assumed factuality) it is taken to be acceptable, what it "says" comes to be true by the data's conforming themselves to what was hypothesized about them.

I will not go on, for it is clear enough without filling out detail that the social psychology that hoped to bring good into the world by first divorcing itself from ethics and becoming "scientific" merely succeeds in being ethically blind, that is, it has effects for good and evil at random—and mostly for evil, since good, like aesthetic pattern, rarely comes out of a random process. That it paints for us pictures of the world—all, I think, equally credible or incredible, all equally supported or unsupported—and that these pictures negate and deny each other, is not to be wondered at. Shall we live, subjectively, in the world of radical pessimism of Sigmund Freud, as in *Civilization and Its Discontents*, where the sacrifice of pleasure which is all that we *can* value is the price to be paid for civilization and culture and all that we *should* value? Shall we live in the halfway house of Anna Freud, the revisionists, the new ego psychologists, where a sort of precarious light of human hope filters onto and throws into bolder relief such ego functions as we would like to identify with? May we inhabit with impunity the nearly light-filled house of a Maslow or the house of a Fromm, overlit with resolute optimism? As the record shows, what we dwell *on* we shall dwell *in*. Where should we like to dwell?

Or do we have a choice? If a social psychology is a science that deals exhaustively with the cause-and-effect relations in the "mental" or meaningful life of persons, seen now severally and now as a system, then surely it must account, in cause-and-effect terms, for beliefs. And the beliefs to be accounted for are not just political or religious or magical beliefs, nor are they the beliefs of distant and alien others in far times and distant places. The beliefs to be accounted for include our social psychological beliefs!

So the social psychology must surely account for itself and explain its own deliverances in much the same terms that it explains its first-order subject matter. For whatever the social psychologist says or does (not only "as a human being" but in his "specialized role") is also a product of a society, a social system, a role playing, an attempt to maintain or alter specific personal and social balances or patterns. The ground upon which the social psychologist is to stand—presumably uninfluenced or little influenced by the actual, imagined, or implied presence of other human beings, while he explains how all this works—has never been defined! I venture to suggest that, on his own hypothesis, it cannot be defined.

If it were otherwise, I am not sure that, given the social scientist's heaven, we should want to enter in. (Of course, our wants might well be irrelevant.) If the result were one kind of science, like astronomy, I suppose we should merely be enabled to stand by, watching with awe or horror, while those stellar bodies, ourselves, rushed toward spectacular cataclysm (if that is in the cards), or brilliant boreal display (if that is the way the cosmic social psychological ball must bounce). If the result were the other kind of science, like chemistry, where control of the conceptual scheme leads to mastery of the material, the consequences would seem to be even more catastrophic. For if the knowledge leads to genuine control of the process, the question of who is to have this knowledge and be capable of this control becomes crucial. If it is to be some select social group, then some problems of enslavement for the others arise—even if the knowledge is used for their good (if that term still has an intelligible meaning). On the other hand, if the knowledge is everyman's possession so that he has mastery or control over himself, are the consequences much less disastrous? For what is this within you that is to have the mastery over that that? Are master-and-slave relations in the psyche or among the selves any better than in the external world? Is it not rather that we are driven to protest and resist the imposition of such order between us precisely because it would have, as an equally intolerable consequence, a parallel order within us. (Incidentally, I believe that when we do welcome the one it is also because we would welcome the other.)

There is a still more curious consequence to be anticipated, I think, before we start to dream social psychological dreams of self-mastery. What is mastered is generally doubly dead. Insofar as it is mastered it is dead to itself, for by life we *mean* what is unmastered, what has a life of its own. But also, insofar as it is mastered, it is dead (lifeless) to its master. It is without interest. The mastered *is* the lifeless. Even a slave, a prisoner, a victim, a dog, is of interest only insofar as it is not mastered, insofar as whatever is mastered opens up new possibilities in the unmastered.

So the counterpoint to mastery is apathy in master and mastered. On the astronomical model for social psychology we *might* retain a spark of lively interest as we observed ourselves bombinating through historic space. On the model of chemistry, we should, I presume, have much to care for and nothing to care about. Which is perilously close to where we are. No, I think, it will not do—it will not do at all.

Let me start again.

When, as social psychologists, we come upon men as a subject of interest in a formal and ordered way, we are already men ourselves. They and we are members of groups; neither we nor they have ever encountered an individual. We and they are in the life that is going on, the common life, the society, and it is in them and us, and we are in one another. The life is ongoing, bearing us with it, as it is itself also nothing but the movement in us, abstracted in another way. *In medias res*, in the middle of the battle, someone bethinks himself (or is bethought) a little. What he thinks is given by the turmoil, and is a part of the turmoil, as the bubble is in the river and part of the river. It is, as it were, an eddy, damping out the effect of a motion here, contributing to another there. One of these eddies is social psychology.

Let me return now to more prosaic language, the figure having presumably served its purpose. If I have firmly located social psychology in the social process itself—*in* history, *in* the culture, *in* the politics—it remains to say what differentiates it from the undifferentiated social swirl.

What differentiates it as a special sort of social activity is the company, the society in which it occurs. It—or rather the social psychologist whose activity it is—is deeply implicated as already indicated in the society of his day. But he is also intimately implicated with other social psychologists. And, beyond this, he is implicated, in a sense I shall presently indicate, with an unseen company. An analogy with the religious person comes readily enough to mind: he too participates in the world, in the militant and present church, and in the church triumphant, that anticipated but effectively present future that assumes the full flowering of what is now but seed and soil.

The difference between the social psychologist and the religious person is that the former looks forward, if he is sane, to no day of judgment, no apocalyptic transformation of the states of affairs and the rules of the game, an eternity in which there is no church triumphant, but the sole triumph is the maintenance of its militance. He looks not to solutions, let alone total solutions, but to resolutions, *ad hoc*, and for now. His problems are not analogical to the discovery of how to split atoms, but to the discovery of how to further justice. Concretely, justice is furthered *in a given case*. The problem arises afresh with full and equal acuteness in the next and in every new case. Methods may carry over from case to case, but even this cannot be counted upon. The doing of justice alters the capacity to do justice, the ability to perceive more clearly what is there and not there (the real and ideal, the actual and potential) and therewith even the method. Nothing endures but the battle and the quest.

It is in such an enterprise—and, moreover, such an ideal enterprise—that the social psychologist is located. Even when he does not teach, even when he thinks himself most a scientist, he is first, last, and all the time an educator, a person whose profession and pride is the enlargement of other persons—and therewith himself—in a quite particular way. The means of enlargement are quite literally those of revelation. Revelation and *exposé* are not synonyms but polar opposites. Revelation occurs in a relationship and has a matter or subject. The relationship is necessarily social, but more than that, it is ideally social, that is, loving or caring. The subject, as far as social psychology is concerned, is just such relations, in general and in particular—the variety of them, the conditions of them, the obstacles and aids to their furtherance. On this view, the social psychologist, when and if he is an expert about society in psychological perspective, is a society maker: he brings into being—"the community exists in the communication"—a society more dedicated to seeing itself now detachedly (for the sake of its commitment), now committedly (for the sake of its detachment). This is a peculiar society: the social psychological society, the society that cares enough for what it is committed to, to bring its commitment and its service in that commitment into review as detached as is at the time possible. To put it another way, the task—and in any case the effect—of the social psychologist is not to bring into being a body of knowledge that stands over against and describes the society in some static fashion. On the contrary, in history and for history he enters into history for the sake of making it. He does not just social psychologize. He social psychologizes *something:* the society. For better or for worse he inevitably renders it other. If he thinks himself not so involved, the result of his effort will be nugatory or noxious; it will come to nothing or worse. As he engages thus with the society out of which he has (momentarily and in part) differentiated himself, he is altered and made over, as they are, by the consequences of his own acts. This in turn means a new social psychologist facing a new society and a new social psychology, and so on indefinitely, if neither brings the other to catastrophe.

The same dangers and imminences of catastrophe, as well as the same potentialities and probabilities of benefit, attend social psychologizing as attend the private psychologizing we call psychotherapy. The analogies are nearly exact. (The major disanalogy is that the social psychologist can rarely observe and almost never so quickly correct for the effect he has on his "patient.") Otherwise, point for point, social psychologists and psychotherapists may not aimlessly heighten awareness. Each must select what is cogent from among a potential infinity of "true" statements respecting the "patient" or subject, and must place these in a selection from among another infinity of contexts, or under one of an indefinitely large number of constructions. What is cogent is given not only by the state to be described, but by the general character of the state it is desired to bring into being. The context in which material is to be seen and the construction that is to be put upon it are governed likewise by these aims. But the aims are not given in any specificity or fullness or detail beforehand. They emerge with clarity only at each reconstructive step, and then only for the next step or those most proximate to it. Thus, what is relevant, as well as what is tolerable—at least nondisruptive—emerges as specific directive only in its own historic moment.

This is not, say in the one case, any more than in the other, that what is to be done is *determined* by the situation: such a criterion would once again make a machine of the actual society. Certainly what is to be done is rooted in and conditioned by the presenting problems, the surrounding circumstances. Nevertheless, it is surely obvious that the psychotherapist appeals from what is patent in his patient to what is latent; he interferes, he intervenes, and his intervention involves discrimination. (There is nothing virtuous or desirable in something merely because it is latent.) From among latent potentialities, he *selects;* and he selects in terms of an implicit agreement that he and the patient share, an agreement that is the unspoken social contract that combines the two into a society in some full sense. What he develops in the patient, when he is successful, is an added ability to complete some commitment to which both are committed. The completion of the two-man commitment is the full development of the two-man society. Initially, the physician sees so much more clearly than his patient what is at stake, what is at issue, what is the confusion of commitment with countercommitment, that in a sense he leads and seems almost to control the process. Gradually his power and potency in this respect come into the possession of the patient, so that the processes he cherished and fathered can go on in the patient in his virtual presence and no longer need its actuality. They two are an enduring society—like the Christian forever in the company of the saints. Psychotherapy is at an end.

For all points save this last, the relation of social psychologist to society is an analogue (without the overtones of imputed sickness here of Larry Frank's "Society as the Patient"). In the interaction between social psychologist and society psychologized, there is a constant, heightening interchange without necessary terminus or canonical end. What is to come out of the interchange is the development of the society in a quite particular sense. The quite particular sense is in the direction of its immanent but latent best. (Mere development of the society as a criterion would have led the social psychologist of that day to further Nazism, had he lived in Germany, and would have led us to sanction his actions whether we lived there or not.) The invocation of a notion of the best as central implies that in some nonarbitrary, not wholly culture-bound fashion we know either what is best, or both what is better *and* that successive moves toward the better do cumulate in a movement toward the best. The first is, I think, improbable. I do not know whether the second is true or not, but I believe so, and I believe the belief has the quality of many such beliefs: a tendency to bring its warrantability into being as a consequence of belief itself.

The position is full of risk. Even taking it for granted that the social psychologist has steeped himself in his culture without losing himself in it, that it is a culture that does not of its very nature blind him to its own potentialities or blunt his creativity or intuition—even assuming all these things, the margin for error is immense, but the alternatives are worse. The alternatives are (a) no social psychology, which is not now possible, or (b) a random process that merely heightens oscillation to the point of upset, or (c) a social psychology of built-in bias that develops the existent society to its logical conclusion, which is to say its ossification, devitalization, and death.

I think we have thus no choice but to go forward in fearful boldness. Even without such a vision, even blinded and bedeviled by imagining itself as "science," social psychology (by smuggling in the implications of the position I have sketched while denying it as a premise) has made progress, has mapped and marked out little islands of probably true and perhaps nondamaging knowledge. But without sound foundations it cannot, I think, proceed far, or insofar as it can, the farther it goes the unsafer it becomes—and renders the society.

What is the bearing of all this on "present-day barriers and tensions between groups"? This is a fair question, and I must attempt an answer no matter how inadequate: inadequate, partly because I do not know, partly because another chapter at least would be required for even a sketchy reply.

The first difficulty I have with such problems—as with the alleged problems of delinquency or alcoholism or inadequate family life—is in getting from the problem-bearer a reasonably clear statement of what the problem *is*. I mean this not unkindly: we exhibit, all of us, the same kind of confusion in our own personal lives, even in something so relatively simple as our hopes and fears for our children—let alone in world affairs or intergroup relations. When we examine such "aims" we often find, I think, that they are too vague to guide conduct, or that they are specific but self-contradictory, or in conflict with other aims equally prized, or good enough and clear enough but not really ours.

Now, as to "intergroup tensions and barriers," let me state what I think the problem *is not*—or, at least, ought not to be. The problem is not (or ought not to be) to institute world-wide (or society-wide) homogeneity, not even with regard to very important matters: matters as important as the proper cooking of food, the proper care for children, or the right view of Mr. Kennedy (or perhaps I should say the Messrs. Kennedy). Indeed, the view that this *is* the problem—the non-coexistence theorem—is of itself probably the greatest single contributor to the really dangerous elements in the situation.

But if important differences are not to be eliminated—if they are to be first tolerated and later treasured—there must be, by practical as well as logical implication, "groups" to sustain and nourish such differences, indeed rather to increase than to diminish them. And a group logically and practically implies a "barrier," just as a family implies a barrier. ("Barrier" is only a name for a boundary that, at the moment of speaking, we dislike.) And barriers imply tensions, indeed are properly *defined* (whether in physics, psychology, or sociology) in terms of tensions. (Tensions are names for momentarily disapproved forces. Boundaries are lines or zones in a field of such forces.) Nor is it possible, I think, to eliminate hostility or its being brought to bear where it is naturally brought to bear, at just such boundaries—where, if only because of ineradicable ambivalence, what is seen at one moment as the rose hedge that defines, borders, and protects my garden is at the next moment seen as the thorn wall that keeps me from expanding as I should wish into my neighbor's yard.

I do not think then that we ought to wish—and I do not think that except in moments of confusion, weariness, or despair we do wish—to eliminate differences, groups that embody difference, borders, or barriers that are the conditions for group existence, tensions that define the boundaries, and even hostilities that attend the tensions. All talk directed to these ends I regard as folly or, in rare cases, villainy. By attaching hearts to what we cannot have—and what would ill serve us if we could—they at least confuse counsel, and at worst bring on the ultimate despair out of which regress rather than progress springs.

This view moves me to restate the problem in a fashion that can at least, I believe, yield some warranted hope and some guidelines for concrete acts.

The ultimate aim must be redefined as a state of affairs in which, under a set of clearly transcendent or supervenient values, differences, no matter how important otherwise (as both valued and disvalued), are held, *really* held, to be of minor import in the context of the larger commitment. A thousand everyday instances abound: a teammate of Jackie Robinson's, no matter what his views on color or race relations, can hardly help wishing him success when he is at bat, and the supervenient interest in winning the series turns upon his next movements. What is needed is the generalization of that situation, preferably *above* the level of the common enemy or common danger formula: "There are no race relations under bombing attacks." The generalization has the force, if not the form, of a universal religion, a passionately held view around which behavior and personality are organized, a view that, in terms of timeless and spaceless, transcendent loyalties, is able to afford, indeed even warmly welcome, differences simply because they are not, cannot be, of a kind that threatens the higher (or deeper) unity. If this sounds abstract, difficult, or farfetched, ask yourself if the principle is not the very one upon which you operate in your family when you are operating as you would wish. The very difference of the beloved is—most of the time—the ground for the love; the love is the ground for the boldness to be different wherever, as nearly always, difference demands courage for its sustenance.

Now it is one thing to define a desired end state, no matter how ill or well, and quite another to define how we might move toward it. The end state is far off: what we need now are guarantees for the process by which it might be gradually approached. Two quite different—sometimes fatally incompatible—elements are required in conjunction to guarantee the process. The elements are in strict analogy with the corresponding process in international relations. There must be force—influence, persuasion, of course, but ultimately force—to prevent a forcible solution in its own favor by any party. We cannot as yet, unfortunately, have a parliament without a sergeant-at-arms. The force should be sufficient to make recourse to force or fraud practically unthinkable. The problem is not even properly presented for solution as long as a nonpeaceful process is a thinkable solution.

On the other hand, within the arena for nonforcible solution, created and held by force, a process diametrically opposite, in essence an ecumenical process, must be fostered and served. An ecumenical process is not a process to confound differences but to find supervenient, far supervenient, identities. I do not know much about how it is done, but it is not done in disloyalty to love or truth or faith, even though loyalty to each does invite or seem to invite disloyalty to the other two. Conferences that blur differences, or by the use of ambiguous terms turn them into pseudoidentities; meetings that invite one, under the impulse of momentary good fellowship, to mistake passing goodwill for permanent love—all these are useless, and worse. The search is for understanding. The understanding cannot be subserved by pretense or tactical maneuvering for short-range comforts. The love that the understanding requires cannot be had before the understanding, but the understanding cannot be had without some preexistent love or the intimation of it. The faith is not justified without the confirming understanding, but the understanding cannot be begun without a burning faith in its possibility. It must thus be a process in which step serves step, each making the next possible. It is a creative act whose precise end, as against its general character, cannot and ought not to be foreseen.

It can be furthered and assisted, I think, by a social psychology of the kind I have defined, where the social psychologist involved is clearly *in* the act, committed with his brothers, and finding with them what it is that his commitment has committed him to as he goes along. Such a posture removes us, I believe, from the all-too-present temptation so to act that we are merely teaching groups how to conduct their external relations to their own best advantage, or to contain or manipulate each other, or to pay spurious tributes to brotherhoods they are not able to bring into being because they have not been brought out of a brotherlike process. Perhaps only a handful can be found to engage in so totally taxing an activity. Perhaps a handful would suffice.

My general position is really very simple and, I think, it is the direct implication of the central message of the great names in social psychology. From W. I. Thomas' recognition of the centrality in social action of "the definition of the situation," I derive my view of the social psychologist, the redefiner par excellence, as social actor, indeed superactor. From George Herbert Mead's insistence on Mind, Self, and Society as coemergents, I derive my view that the social psychology—what is in the social psychologist's mind and the mind of his readers, eventually the society—is and can be only a coemergent with a new personal and social self, that is, with the remaking or continuous making over of self and society. From Freud, the *magister magistrorum*—the man who most clearly, in "thinking" about men, made himself (and them) over—I derive my view of the unity, the mutual and reciprocal coconstitution, of personal and social psychology: not two subjects but one, like the same geometry reversing the places of theorems and postulates. (If I am in error, do not blame them; what I say I "derive" I might just as well have said I imposed as construction, but then, as I have been saying, it is just that kind of act that social psychologizing is.)

A social psychology so seen and thus founded has not even been well begun. The view, if accepted, like the mystical experience, makes all things new. It brings the social psychologist and the social psychology within society. It does *not* make value a scientific problem, but makes social science a value problem. It makes teaching preaching of a quite peculiar kind. It entails the taking of a value position, not merely in embracing the calling (the universal of dedication to truth or science or whatnot), but in each particular scientific act (a thoroughgoing political position). It implies more of the stance of the warrior and less of the attitude of the entomologist than we care to think or wish to admit. It recommits us to the battle from which, in the belief of many, science was to provide the escape. It returns us to the ambiguities and agonies of life. It robs us of a precious—because psychopathic—defense. It makes us men among men and not demigods above them. It returns us to humility. It restores mutuality: social psychologist and social psychologized dwell in each other and have no existence *as such*, apart from their so doing.

I think such views are implicit in the warmest, gentlest, clearest of them all, Charles Horton Cooley. We have a long way to go back, I think, before we can again move forward. To that retreat, for the sake of such sound advance as is possible, I invite alike my colleagues and theirs—the society of which they would like merely to speak, but *must* choose whether to hinder or help. The nirvana, the neutral ground, does not exist. Once more, what is brought from the heights is not peace but a sword. Once more we hear ". . . he that is not with us is against us, and he that gathereth not with us, scattereth abroad."

9

Personal Science

Two varieties of "rational intervenors" lie at the ends, so it seems, of the spectrum of rational intervention: on one side personal psychiatrists; on the other, city or system planners.

As a first approximation, let us examine psychiatrists—not as persons, but as role players in a division of labor—as occupying a curious, anomalous, interesting, and effective position: a strategic stand.

Looking backward, they represent the virtual impotence of the psyche; looking forward, its virtual omnipotence. In the early stages of therapy, the psychotherapist as virtual attorney for the prisoner, his patient, brings to the patient a vivid realization of his own inevitability as product of a conjuncture of forces he had no power sensibly to affect. The relief from (irrational) guilt, the capacity to perceive the self as it is (or at least in some reasonable relation to reality) depends upon a lively perception of self as product, a substantive shifting of blame onto, at every point, "the environment," as over against the ego. The culmination of this procedure would be attested by the return of a soul-deep "yes" to the question, "Canst thou say in thine heart thou has seen with thine eyes, with what manner of art, thou wast shaped in what wise. . . ?"

In a second stage of therapy—now with society rather than the patient as the client for whom he is attorney—the "participation" of the patient in the process that is simultaneously his achievement and his fate is brought into focus. That psyche which was, most emphatically, product is now seen partly as producer, calling out (in virtue of what it had been made to be, but nonetheless therefore was) the shaping responses that would further make it what it would be. The psyche is no longer seen altogether passively as ". . . fashioned in love on my bosom and shown on my breast to the skies," but author and authored, maker and made—"I, the plough and the furrow, the plough-cloven clod and the plough-share drawn thorough; the germ and the sod. . . ."

Near the end of therapy, no matter what may be *said*, the virtual omnipotence of the psyche is asserted. One is where one is, one does what one does, one's experience is such as it is because most generally this is what one wants. Not that the therapist denies "reality" or permits his patient to do so, but that he now represents a special aspect of reality, its virtually infinite capacity for transformation in experience as a function of the manner of its apprehension. It is not precisely a directive to count "the world"—the world as the unregenerate see it—well lost for the sake of that inner world that is the ultimate only home, but it is a clear enough directive to remold the world in perception as an indispensable prelude to doing anything worth doing about it. The attitude is a secular analogue of "Seek ye first the Kingdom of God and His righteousness and all these things shall be added unto you." It *is* an enjoinder to seek an inner order as a precondition for effect upon the world, or, even failing that, for riches that the world can neither give nor withhold. At the very least, there is a selective focus upon the fact—the fact *constituted* by faith in it—of agency, upon those aspects of experience that are brought into being, that are given their existence by human endowment.

The test of the success of such a procedure is the relative diminution in importance of what might be called the brute world *as such*. When a friend of mine contended that his test for therapeutic success was increased vulnerability in his patients, he meant that he counted upon an increased *willingness* to be wounded (for the sake of other goods), which is only another name for increased invulnerability, in the sense of relative indifference to, and diminished importance of, pain.

The generalized upshot of the whole procedure is a double reduction in the significance of the external world: its importance is reduced in that the agent's paramount role in defining and regulating its impact is given due place, and its significance is reduced in that the caring eye is focused (not altogether, but primarily) on the inner experience which is a transmutation rather than a reflection of the outer.

Paradoxically, it is thus (and perhaps only thus)—in this or some closely analogical way—that the world, the world that matters, can be made over, reconstituted, transformed, and re-formed. It is first diminished, abandoned, left, until—following a transformation that is in but not of that world—it can be returned to, reengaged, re-wed, and finally transfigured.

Social planners begin at a different point, move by a different procedure, and come by a different conclusion. If the psychiatrist's first object of attention is the incredible internal chaos created in the individual psyche by the efforts of the well-intentioned people who have deliberately directed their attention upon it, the planner's first arresting object is the equally incredible external chaos men create for each other in the pursuit of lives and careers that may well make sense for each of them severally. It is this luxuriating foliage of success and achievement, the other-choking consequences of individual potency and production, the jungle of embodied goods and assets that confronts him at the outset.

In a sense, then, he comes first upon man the producer, rather than man the produced, but man as the producer of the ills from which he suffers: the congestion, the disorder, the all-pervading nexus of unintended and unwanted consequence, and hence ultimately the victim, the helpless and hapless product of his own production. The problems that arise for him are primarily problems of public acts rather than private feelings, problems that *do* have their roots in the world of brute fact, and their solution, if any, there also. The planner comes thus in the second instance to the position that the psychotherapist came to in the first: to man as the captive of, the product of, forces or situations that not only transcend but, in their immensity, dwarf the resistive resources of the individual. Indeed, it is, on this view, "the environment" that endows man with its characteristics and, for any individual, in effect brings him into being, maintains, and alters him. If anything is to be better for anyone in any large sense, the improvement must proceed from (and ultimately be reflected in) the reorganization of that external environment in ways that will conduce to, if not directly cause, the internal satisfactions that it is idle or self-defeating to seek directly. Not only is no large-scale individual regeneration necessary as a prelude, but it is, *ex hypothesi*, impossible. Such personal regeneration as is necessary will flow from the rearrangement of objective circumstances, and that rearrangement does not necessitate any radical increase in individual rationality. What it does require is a social division of labor in which the burden of ratonality is—in a rational recognition of one's own permanent irrationality—externalized, thrust upon a body of professionals, and hence set beyond one's own capacity to mismanage. In effect, one is to become rational, not by some internal and personal struggle, but by setting in motion a public process that, once started, one cannot arrest—a process in which one selects an elite to procure for oneself and others that environment that is most conducive to rational behavior and to other major satisfactions.

Whether or not it is thought that I have exaggerated, it is impossible not to distinguish two dominant themes—two themes that have played in and out in the lives of all of us, like a bad (or, at least, not-so-good) bigamous marriage (or, perhaps more to the point, like a prolonged oedipal struggle). One theme virtually asserts that "if each before his own door sweeps, the village will be clean"; the other, that if the village institutes a proper sanitation service, each one will be clean—at least as far as his dooryard, and probably beyond. In dogmatic form these views are asserted not simply in terms of "if," but in terms of "if and only if"—that is, a way becomes The Way. One formula runs roughly: good persons (or "mature" or "productive" or whatever new word for "good" you want) make a good society, which inevitably makes a good physical ordering—or, if not, it does not matter since virtue is its own sufficient reward. The other, obviously: a good physical order leads toward a good society, which produces (or educes) good persons—or, if not, it does not matter since a good external order is a—perhaps sufficient—good in itself.

By and large, we dignify theories of the first kind, if they are well developed, by calling them religions; and we denigrate theories of the second sort by calling them ideologies. We are, of course, in origin and dominant outlook (or certainly for polemical purposes), a religious society. An ideological society (for example, the Soviet Union) would view the matter otherwise—again for polemical purposes. I have to enter the stricture because closer examination reveals what may be called a countertheme to each: in the West, where people are supposed to account for circumstances, a great deal of weight is allowed in the adjudication of guilt or innocence to the theorem that circumstances account for people; in Soviet (and Chinese) trials, per contra, where circumstances are held to account for people, problems of personal guilt seem to be of focal if not exclusive interest.

In any case, we find ourselves in some uneasy relation to the two types of theory or clusters of theories, and to the practices based upon them. One manifestation of the unrest is the phenomenon just pointed to: the holding to one theory while behaving in terms of the unacknowledged other. Another is a sort of migration or wandering back and forth between the two in the lives of persons, and in the history of society.

The equal emphasis on movement *back* and *forth* is not quite right. The two-way wandering occurs, but there is, or seems to be, a net migration toward the planner-ideological end of the spectrum and away from the psychologist-religious end. There seems to be a greater appeal for those at or near the religiopsychological pole in the goings on near the other pole. Indeed, there is some reason to think that this is the direction in which entropy lies, although it is always possible to interpret the data otherwise. One might view (Western) history as a succession of runnings down toward the external-naturalistic ideology, interspersed with a series of windings up by great religions or secular-religious figures (I would count Freud and his immediate, though not postmediate, followers among them) returning the society to a more charged, a less natural, a more improbable state or position.

If this is true in whole or large part, it would be interesting to speculate about the reasons for the greater attraction in one direction. The fact of the attraction may be taken, of course, as a prima facie warrant of desirability—or, as on the face of it, a ground for caution, if not suspicion. Examination of the nature of the attraction may illuminate even when it cannot settle the issue.

It is not too difficult to begin a listing of the evident virtues of the institutional position. The immediate relief from a burden of guilt and responsibility is very like that of the first stage of psychotherapy, but enduring or permanent. It *is* so much easier to institute and institutionalize outside controls than inside ones, that once the idea has occurred to one, one is left wondering at one's prior folly. It *is* so much easier to love men in general and at a distance than to love anyone in particular and near at hand that if both are equally effective it is the better part of the most elementary wisdom to choose the former.

There is, of course, not only psychological but material

economy: it is in every sense cheaper to institute a process for the millions than to make a similar number of parallel individual efforts. That is, perhaps, one reason why Americans who say they believe in education turn out upon examination to believe only in schooling, which is sometimes a mere condition and more often a sure preventive of it.

These virtues are, however, but pale gleams beside the central shining star of attraction, the *virtu virtutis*, that, like another brighter pole star, sheds its light directly over only one pole. Perhaps it is a cluster of virtues—perhaps I should have chosen Ursa Major rather than Polaris for my figure. The cluster had best be labelled "scientific," with all that the term popularly connotes.

The scientific virtues are not only incomparable but perhaps innumerable; the song of their praises should be a never-ending lay. There is a sense, a proper sense, I think, in which one may say that the matters of scientific discourse—indeed the scientific discourse itself—are out in the plain light of day instead of somewhere in the stilled gloom of the nonscientific crypt. The references are to things seen rather than shades—or shadows of shades—sensed. The world is the world of common consent (even if common sense must, by training, be rarefied to ensure it), and the reassurance in it is a communal reassurance which is harder to doubt—or is it?—than a self-reassurance. It is a world of reliabilities. Indeed the test of survival within it is precisely that. It is a bounded world—free to widen or contract its boundaries, but clearly bounded. It is a world of certainty, even when the certain is extended only over a probability table—or a set of probabilities of probabilities. It is essentially a democratic, nonelitist world, where the passport of average intelligence renders every man approximately equal in his potentiality of compassing what is known. It is a world in which steady pedestrian work assures almost anyone a reasonable return in terms of a visible pile of amassed factual crumbs. It is a world where very ordinary virtues pay, higher virtues are hardly required, and ordinary vices are hardily insured against by being robbed of their normal payoffs. It is a world where the views reached seem—in some extraordinary or transordinary sense—independent of the self, hence not the responsibility of the self, hence not to be held at personal peril. It is—largely—a certified world.

I do not deny that such a world exists—in reference to physics. I do not deny that insofar as it exists we should be drawn to it. However, in reference to the affairs of men, with regard to the social sciences, and such planning and managing procedures as are founded on them, the picture is far different: the phenomenal world is a phenakistical one.

Not in any important point of comparison is there any resemblance between the natural and the social sciences. As crucial a formulation as any in the social sciences is W. I. Thomas' recognition that social action depends on what he calls "the definition of the situation." If I extend my hand toward you and you define such a movement as the beginning of a friendly approach, the probability of one chain of actions over another is quite different from what it would be if the extended hand is held to prefigure—and *therefore* likely does prefigure—an attack. Nothing objectively in the situation affects the outcome. If I hug a teenager it may be most proper if I am defined as her father, but so improper as to lead toward jail if I am defined otherwise, and the difference is held to be critical. Such definitions are, of course, social definitions rather than idiosyncratic ones, definitions held in consensus.

It would be entirely wrong to think of a society as an aggregate of persons, though I know such a view is common. The society *is*—it extends as far as, it lives and moves and has its being in—the shared definitions of situations. At the center of that network is—as for the person—its self-definition. Now whatever else the social scientist does, he *redefines* and thereby, and insofar, alters the society. Indeed, insofar as he *does* function as a social scientist, he does nothing else: even when he seems to function otherwise, when he "merely" records the going definitions of his society, he has altered the general level of self-consciousness in reference to the definition, he has brought it into or to the threshold of critical awareness, and thereby altered it functionally about as radically as it can be altered. So the social scientist is, in the very performance of his scientific role, a social actor, a crucial actor, a mover and shaker, parallel in function to any formally designated politician, and probably eventually more powerful. Who was it said, "Let me write the songs of a nation. . . ?" In our day, he should have said, "Let me write its definitions . . ." for the right to define is the right to make and unmake, create or destroy.

Even when this inescapable entanglement in action is recognized, a second effort is made to save some special, extraordinary, and in some sense superior status or standpoint for the social scientist. It is held, briefly, that he is under the discipline of his data (and his method) and that these drive him to a position very little dependent on his personal predilections and preferences. It is usually allowed that "interest" may well direct inquiry up to the point where an object of attention is selected, but that beyond that point the scientific process somehow takes over and controls outcome.

Even if the claim were conceded, it would be almost infinitely damaging to the asserted role of the social scientist, for the right to attend to this and not that *is* the right to direct attention hither and not thither (that is, to adjudicate on the basis of personal sensibilities and preferences). Suppose a judge declared a free power to direct attention upon whatever in the evidence interested him; it is a near equivalent to a proclamation that he will decide the outcome in terms of his private program.

But the claim cannot be allowed. The scientific process does *not* somehow take over once the object is focused under the eyepiece. For there is still the selection of the light in which the object is to be viewed, the context in which it is to be seen (actually *put*) and the setting of canons for discrimination between true and false, or more and less plausible propositions.

It is not that "reality" constrains the social scientist in no way at all but that the constraint is not much (if at all) tighter than the corresponding reality laid upon the artist, say a portraitist or painter. There is in each case a literal infinity of nonfalse representations that can be made. *Which* will be made in actuality is as poetic in motive and as political in effect as any other essentially expressive action. For that is what it is: a ritualized acting out of an internal choice or necessity, in which the ritual in some sense orders and hence renders comprehensible, while in another sense it frees and hence allows the largest latitude for the personal. (I shall not document these statements here, but it should be obvious that one may, for instance, "account for" delinquency, say, in countless ways: as an expression of the delinquent's wish, character, or need; as a consequence of his parents' acts or unconscious motivations, or those of their parents; as a result of differential association or communication; as a function of the slum, or the economic system, or advertising, or the police system, or the rating and dating scheme; as a result of want of care on the part of folks stolen from or beaten up—the victim makes the crime!—or the presence of alleys or want of light at the site; as an artifact of unreasonable laws . . . and so, literally, ad infinitum. The putting of all these true propositions together in one book—as in most texts on the subject—does not alter the status of the whole over that of the parts, for the ratio of one to infinity is the same as the ratio of ten to infinity. It should be obvious too that what is selected for exposition out of this interminable tangle is free neither of personal motive nor of political consequence: indeed, it arises almost altogether out of the first and eventuates almost altogether in the second. (The word "almost" is meant to cover the barring of patently false propositions, which is indeed one of the virtues of social science over less scrupulous propaganda.)

I have not presumed explicitly to adjudicate between two competing emphases in the generalized melioristic enterprise that we all share. We are all, I am sure, would-be orthogenists—most so, those who would deny it. The poles represent selective concentration upon the system of the person as the unit and an *art* of improvement upon it at one end, and selective concentration upon a transpersonal system—the social, political, economic, cultural order—and a *science* about, and an engineering of, it at the other. I have not adjudicated, but clearly I have tried to affect an outcome, for all the usual reasons—personal, political, and, ultimately, poetic. I have tried to ensure that, as far as my words have weight, none should too readily transfer residence from one pole to the other on the intimations of some chamber-of-comerce-like folder that hints that things are far different and far better at the place one is not at. It is not so. All the agonies that attend any art anywhere, all the necessities and all the constraints that what one is lays upon what one does, all the dubieties of what one senses over the certainties of what one sees, all the hazards of commitment and the helplessness of fate, all these and more attend no less those who would deal by reason with the many at one time than those who would deal by intuition with the ones at many times. However, if we propose to enhance goods or mitigate ills, let us at least not continue in the illusion that there is some position from which, some method whereby, or some system wherein the costs upon us personally may be reduced and some cut-rate victory be won. That it might be so is an enduring hope, but since nothing in history or prospect warrants it, perhaps it is merely a will-o'-the-wisp that it were better to chase no further.

10

The Problem of Social Problems

I could perhaps be forgiven for using—as an occasion to say something I wanted to say anyway—a pregnant editorial statement[1] over the signatures of Drs. Roucek and Mohan: "[If] . . . sociology is to be a science and if it could help society, it must stop worrying about the *nature* of social problems and should start solving them."

The statement comes at the end of a masterly brief review of the roots, origins, and history of sociology, and is meant to mark a turn in that history, the contemporary or modern mood.[2] My first response is like Ruskin's alleged reply to Tennyson as they sat down to chess, and Tennyson said "May the best man win!" Said Ruskin, winningly: "Oh I hope not."

For if this is the contemporary or coming view I think we are begun on one more byway, embarked again on a false track when the road lies otherwise reasonably plain before us. Perhaps I can clarify what I believe to be at issue by examining simply some of the terms of discourse, and stating how, I believe, the realities to which they refer are related to each other. Although the editorial is written by sociologists for sociologists, and therefore the meaning and implication of terms ought to be self-evident or conventionally agreed, I am not sure that this is always the case. Before we rashly conclude

[1] Joseph S. Roucek, Raj Pal Mohan, Editorial, "From Ideal to Real," *Indian Sociological Bulletin*, Volume One, Number Two, Jan. 1964, p. 4.

[2] In contrast to "The armchair speculations of their academic fathers." *Ibid.*

that the problem is to solve problems rather than ponder their nature, perhaps we ought to answer in some way the following questions: What is a "social problem"? What is sociology? What is the relation of sociology to society—and to a "social problem"? What is a "solution"? How independent are the problem-solving and nature-determining processes, the second of which is, on the editorial argument, to be given up in order to advance the first? These questions, too difficult to receive adequate treatment short of a book, deserve at least brief answers here.

First, what *is* sociology? Sociology is a name for the produce and process of sociologizing. Sociologizing is what men do when they give themselves and each other a would-be general and orderly account of their relationships. The product is a lore. Like any other lore, it is an element of, and within, the culture. Unlike any other lore, it is the lore about the culture itself. The process is a social action, its most striking and evident aspect taking the form of a conversation between those more or less specialized to this task ("sociologists," whether formally so designated or not) and those less so specialized. But the conversation is, be it emphasized, only the apparent, manifest element in a social action that has all the characteristics of any other social action.[3] Sociologizing becomes "scientific" when it is carried on under, or continuously corrected by, canons that more or less resemble some of the procedures of "science."

Now a society is a body of men fashioned (in their social nature) in a given fashion and related to each other in a given way—the fashioning and the relations being coemergents or, better, coconstitutents.[4] The relations exist in the consciousness of the relations, just as, to quote Dewey, community exists in communication. To put it another way, the relations that

[3] See, e.g., Talcott Parsons and Edward A. Shils (Eds.), *Toward a General Theory of Action* (Cambridge: Harvard University Press, 1952), especially pp. 53–109.

[4] Prima facie, the relations of which an object is capable turn on the nature of the objects to be related. But, more profoundly, in man the social nature is the history of the social relations had and being had.

constitute the society are the relations as they are represented chiefly in consciousness—or at least in conversation, in its broad meaning. But the representation of these relations in conversation (intrapersonal or interpersonal) is, in ground and emergence, the sociology as lore, and it is also the sociologizing as process—according as we mean by "representation" the process or the product of representing.[5]

Thus the sociology is the society (or that which renders the aggregate a society), and men are members of a common society by virtue of their possession of, and proceeding upon, a common sociology.[6] The distinction between the thing represented (society) and that which represents it (sociology) attenuates or disappears where the reality is largely or wholly constituted by its definition, as, for example, with a friendship or any other concrete "social relation."

Were we momentarily to restrict the term sociology to mean the more *formal* and specialized part of the conversation in society having society for its subject, we should have to say that today's sociology is (or legislates, or brings into being, or is the ground of) tomorrow's society. The specialization and formalization of such a sociology heightens the tempo in which the society builds itself up into a society and increases the complexity of what it means to be a society of that kind.[7]

[5] The dual meaning of "representing" should be noted: presenting *again* and presenting *anew*. Thus we recognize the mimetic and poetic, imitative but reconstitutive aspects, that are both invariably, knowingly or unknowingly, present in all presentation. Whatever we aim to mimic we succeed only in making over.

[6] It will be said that they have much else in common of course. But that "much else" either flows into or flows out of the common sociology. Their common interests may be said, for example, to bind them together, but obviously the common interests are almost wholly matters of social definition, and where they are not, they set limits to possible sociologies.

[7] The metasociologist who—as here—reports upon, theorizes about, or comments on this state of affairs, further furthers both tendencies—in a sense brings into being a metasociety. The society that has a professional sociologist reporting to it is significantly a new kind of society. The society that has someone observing and reporting upon *that* process is a society of another level of complexity. And so, indefinitely.

Now, what is a social problem? Social problem is a term in the sociological conversation that defines some aspect of life as being suited to a certain kind of treatment, handling, or response. To term something a social problem is (successfully or unsuccessfully), by abstracting and naming, to *enact* a reclassification of some part or aspect of the common life in order to alter the response it will receive, or the relation in which it will stand to other parts of the common life. To call something (e.g., unemployment, population movement) a social problem is thus already, to that extent, to reconstitute the society by redefining the activity.[8] Sociologists are not thus "confronted by pressing social problems" [9]—except insofar as they "confront" the work of other sociologists. Otherwise, they *create* the social problem out of some aspect of the social life, i.e., they give it form as such, which is all that makes it a social problem.

Unfortunately, confusion is worse confounded because sociologizers appear to mean at least four different things by their legislative acts: that a problem is a problem from, in, of, or for the society. For example, if it were to be said of neurosis (as it is said of alcoholism) that "neurosis is a social problem" we might mean (any or all) that: (a) the genesis of the problem is social, (b) the consequences are social, (c) the remedy is of a kind that only "society" can give effect to, (d) the problem is nothing but (or is "fundamentally") a relational malfunction, i.e., a social perturbation.

The presence of a legislative element in all four cases should be almost equally plain since all distinctively human problems are social in their genesis, consequence, and medium of action, and the question of a "remedy" (which is bound up with questions of cost, and cost for whom) is the most patently judgmental of all. If they are all social problems in one of these four senses, then to designate any specific problem as

[8] A current case in point may be noted in the new and fashionable "problem of leisure."

[9] Roucek and Mohan, *op. cit.*

such is, by fiat, to give it a special status by election from among its rejected fellows. Thus crime is a social problem while university administration is not.

How legislative and consequential such definitions may and must be is illustrated by the alternatives, as, for example, in defining delinquency (as against, say, parental neglect or poverty) to be "a social problem," or unemployment (as against, say, idleness or vagabondage or vagrancy). Even before study, reporting, or recommendation of a "solution," the very cutting *out* of the problem in conversation is, insofar as it reaches (i.e., insofar as it becomes an operative element in sociologizing) a cut *in* and reorganization *of* the society.[10]

Now as to what is a "solution," it must be almost trivially evident that the answer is dependent in the first instance on what the problem is initially stated to be. It is in this sense that the solution, or, at widest, the solution set within which the solution is to lie, is contained or implicit in the "definition of the problem." And it is for this reason—*naming* it as a problem, after naming it as a *problem*—that we have a second act of legislation in the specification of what the problem *is*, after having specified that it is a problem.

More carefully considered, the word "solution" is as misleading in reference to social affairs as was the word "problem" (which can hardly help but carry with it its mathematical connotations) to begin with.[11] What *is* possible is not a solution but a *resolution*—more in the sense of a triangle of

[10] I happen to think that delinquency is a very bad thing to abstract and define as a social problem, but to say so is to define my own politics and to indicate what I want solved (changed) instead. If I say, in the accepted (and misleading) vocabulary, "Not delinquency, but X is the problem," it should be evident that I am not speaking descriptively but legislatively or hortatively. No less if I accept the going definition. It might be thought that we should address ourselves to more fundamental (or radical) problems, but that too is a special political view.

[11] Perhaps we should have repudiated earlier the usage by which a social problem is thus misnamed, but one must begin somewhere. It is not properly a problem but an issue—which is what is at issue here. And the power to state what the issue is—to define issues—is a supreme political power. In many cases, such power is decisive for the outcome.

forces, or, better as the new outcome in a conflict or adversary process. Indeed, specifying the criteria for a solution merely continues the legislative process that begins with defining something as a problem and then saying what the problem, more specifically, "is." We have strikingly before us, now, all these processes, with reference to Negro-white relations in America, and Hitler recently gave us a sufficiently graphic demonstration of the political motive and effect of his freedom to name, define, and specify the solution of what he named "the Jewish problem." [12]

The common test of a solution is that it "works," i.e., that it fits the object in hand. This is the test of "objectivity." We test our solution against an object, i.e., against that which *objects* to a false or ill-fit solution. But where the object is man—the problem of a social problem—it is man that objects; and such objection, because we are socially involved also, we call "opposition" or, if we are tricky, "resistance." So the test of a solution (or resolution) is a power test, i.e., a test of the relative capacity to make effective objection. A resolution is, thus, that redistribution of effects (seen as returns and costs) that will lead those who have access to the (audible) defining process to cease defining the new distribution as a problem. A solution to a social problem is thus a partial and temporary settlement. Like any other settlement, it remains such as long as the parties to it (or such parties as choose to make themselves party) remain settled.

The relation of sociology to a social problem may now be succinctly stated: sociology defines a state of affairs as a social problem (vests it with the title in virtue of which, like the President, it is what it is). Sociology then specifies what the

[12] Hitler rose to power as his own sociologist, his political power and his power to give new sociological forms to (German) society and to give the society new social form proceeding *pari passu*. *Mein Kampf* is, *inter alia*, a sociological treatise. We deem it bad partly because of its politics, which are not ours, partly because it does not meet the canons of civilized discourse. The most monitory fact, however, is that men on a grand scale came to be what Hitler said they were before the event, i.e., the degree to which his "bad" sociology came to be social fact.

problem "is"; and, within this now limited leeway, it specifies, at best, the resolution set.[13] The resolution set depends on the previous sociologizing, operative as the value-and-belief system of the society or that part of it that is party to the problem. Whether or not a given redistribution falls within the resolution set is, again, not merely a matter of the interests at issue as naïvely given, but is a matter also of articulation by the sociologist. "Articulation" means here both "expression" in suitable and persuasive form and, thereby, appropriate linking with the social process out of which it arises and into which it must reenter. Indeed, in a sense, the resolution of a social problem is such a rearticulation.

The beginning—and hence also the end—of any solution of any social problem is thus an appropriate definition of its general and particular nature. The dual test of appropriateness is conformity to a desired political outcome within the realm of political possibility. Political possibility is structured by the pre-existent sociologizing which it is the aim of the present sociologizing to alter. The alteration desired is to unfix the ascription of "problematic" from this state of affairs (and to attach it to that) by altering the state of affairs in virtue of altered definitions and their "consequences" in action and its further reflection.[14]

[13] Generally, because of ignorance, want of imagination, etc., the resolution set may be falsely or, more commonly, only partly, identified.

[14] I should like to acknowledge the assistance of Dr. Fred I. Greenstein in clarifying my expression of view, though, of course, I must remain responsible for remaining confusions and opacities.

11

Social Science: Some Probative Problems

I want to raise, rather than settle, some difficulties that have, for me, been hardy perennials in my own attempt to see myself as a social scientist; to locate myself in social, moral, scientific, or epistemological space. At most, I hope, in Mr. Oppenheimer's words, "to begin a conversation among us."

In presenting these problems I may well be showing considerable bias. There may well be, within the social scientific enterprise as a whole, subenterprises to which my perplexities have no relevance. If so, I should be grateful for clarification of what these subenterprises are, what constitutes the *principle* on which one set (to which my perplexities *are* relevant) can be separated from the other, and how the conjuncture of the two sets in an enterprise that receives *one* single social definition affects the whole and the parts. I shall not attend, at first at least, to that part of social science, if any, to which my critique is irrelevant, but for brevity and simplicity's sake, I shall talk of "social science" when I mean that part of it to which the critique *is* germane—leaving due qualification for the discussion later.

In what follows, I am simply going to assume that the social scientist I am talking about talks, tells, or publishes (that is, he does not keep all his observations, reflections, and findings to himself). I am also going to assume a literate society that reads or listens, and hence *eventually* knows what he said. I am, however, going to treat the problem of time as not of great importance, so that initially at least, I shall regard as "virtual instantaneity" the period from observation to writing to publication to restatement in, say, *Life*, to republication in the *Reader's Digest*, to summary in the editorial page or advice to the lovelorn column in the community throwaway newspaper. Indeed, at first, borrowing from physics the right to postulate a perfect friction-free machine, I ought perhaps to postulate a sizable cadre of social scientists who tell all and who are heard telling all instantaneously by all. Some of my problems fit that model; some have to do with departures from it.

Let me start with what might be called the *uniqueness theorem*. All institutions, except perhaps conceptually the church, have in effect a mandate to serve the society by discharging their part-functions *within* the widest agreed social definitions. The church furnishes a nice ambiguous case: in its heyday, before social science, it did, in form and fact, appeal to an order held to lie beyond (above) society, or indeed humanity, in terms of which it could and did criticize society—no holds barred, no values excepted—and even depose princes and unmake kings. By self-definition, widely conceded socially, it lay (as it saw itself and was seen) outside the mere society of men, even outside of humankind. Today—insofar as, by the action of social scientists, the church is seen and sees itself as (merely) a social institution— it does not differ *in this respect* from other social institutions such as the school or the underworld. Artists similarly lay claim to some transsocietal *Standpunkt*, but their claim is barely audible and hardly allowed. The social scientist on the contrary must—*conceptually* must—be conceded the right or given the duty to bring the whole society under review (from some standpoint yet to be defined). The notion of being a social scientist, a scientist of society, cannot be divorced from the notion of the right and duty to study the whole society (all society, all societies) if only because a mandate to study a part might very well be nugatory except in the light of knowledge regarding the whole. So the social scientist *uniquely* has as his mandate the study of the society that gave him his mandate (as well as other societies). This raises, I think, some peculiar problems so far barely touched. Given a supernatural order and a process of revelation taking place in essentially a different medium (the spiritual) it is conceptually easy to study and bring under criticism or judgment the society of men as a human (mere human) society. But what is the analogical ground on which the social scientist is to stand—something transsocial—while he performs his function? Science itself is surely not sufficiently transsocial, as any student of the psychology or sociology of science (let alone the politics or sociology of sociology) will tell you.

Among the possible attempts to avoid this perhaps insuperable difficulty, probably as famous a solution as any is that embodied and self-consciously discussed in Gunnar Myrdal's *An American Dilemma.* The argument is probably familiar to you but let me summarize it briefly: the standpoint from which the analysis of the Negro-white problem is conducted is the identification in American life, but particularly as it bears on the problem, of at least two mutually incompatible value commitments, such that further action to serve the one implicitly disserves the other. This seems very good. (It is, incidentally, part of the strategy we use with counsellees, patients, ourselves, and friends.) But note how little it really solves the problem I have posed. What the author does is to take a peculiar pose or posture: he *pretends* to take at face value what (some) Americans *say* in their perhaps better moments—"the American dream"—and then confronts them with what they say and do in their worst. This is nothing short of psychological warfare on Americans—cruel and unusual punishment: cruel because so subtle and difficult to resist and helpful-seeming; unusual because there are few capable of forcing so devastating a self-realization on so many. How does the social scientist console himself in this situation where it should be clear at least that he is taking for granted a value for consistency of behavior that few people would really hold and a disvalue on ignorance that most people, if they understood themselves at all well, would put great stock in? He consoles himself—he must do so—either by recognizing his frank partisanship with the underdog (at present, generally, the Negro) or by appealing, from the general social investment in inconsistency and ignorance (both of which allow the pleasures of impulsive behavior), to something he believes to be intrinsically better or higher. But that "better" or "higher" is either the personal or professional commitment of the social scientist *as over against* the society (or all but some subsegment of it). For if it were the commitment of the society generally there would be no need for *him* to appeal to it: it would be operative. And if not—if, like the American dream itself, it is either a commitment for all men only some of the time, or for some men all the time—then he is again intervening in its behalf in the name of something still higher (in his view)—for example, that a society "ought to" pay more attention to its highest values. I think that on any construction, Mr. Myrdal appears as a preacher or parent or therapist (a subtype of both), and his excellent sociological study, nevertheless, as a tract.

Most other attempts to find a foundation fail in the same way, I believe, if we are not willing to concede that the social scientist must find for his mandated role either (a) a "transsocial" position, yet undefined, or (b) merely his own personal position (which necessitates redefining his function). The commonest attempts smuggle in pretenses that men do generally desire to be consistent, rational, good, mature, scholarly, philosophical, which patently they do not, or else the occasion for the exercise would seem to be wanting. Let me leave it at this: the social scientist does and must criticize the society from a viewpoint that he cannot justify by an appeal to the society as it is—apart from his *mandate* which *he* defines as he goes.

Let me turn now to a difficulty closely connected with the foregoing. Certainly in some, probably in most, very likely in all of his activities *as a social scientist*, the social scientist, by what he does, inevitably intervenes in, interferes with, meddles in, the social process.

One of the points I tried to make on an earlier occasion bears repetition here. What people do with their new potencies of atomic fission is not, whatever else it is, a problem in atomic physics. But what they do with Mr. Warner's reports of class in America *is* a sociological problem (in part, even, a further problem in "class in America"); and what they do, each of them, with Mr. Freud's allegations regarding psychopathology in everyday life is a psychological problem (and, indeed, a further problem in the psychopathology of everyday life). It is certainly a further problem for the science in terms of accounting for the behavior. I think it is a problem also for the planning or social engineering or political action—which is usually thought to be separable from the scientific problem itself, though I cannot help seeing the distinction as obscure, if not untenable. At the very least, the view taken leads me toward an *inexhaustibility theorem:* the subject matter of something cannot be exhausted if the first description both alters and, in any case, increases the subject matter to be described. (One version of the inexhaustibility theorem would go, "You cannot describe a culture when every description is by definition in the culture as soon as it is made.")

The inexhaustibility theorem appears to me to open toward a *freedom theorem*—an antidote to radical determinism—on the only intelligible basis I have been able to give it. If every theory (or most, or some theories) regarding human behavior, enters into human behavior as a "new factor" then there is no sense in which the behavior can be said to be determined in any definite (finite) sense. Empirically, it seems to me that an assertion, even if initially fully justified by inference from all previous cases, such as that boys feel unlimited rivalry with their fathers in reference to their mothers, may and frequently does enter into the behavior of any of the three parties in a very short interval in such a way as to make necessary its own qualification. It may, for instance, so affect pride, anger, felt potency, or anything else as to change *in and of itself* the *cetera paribus* on which it originally depended. It is a little like telling a student, "You are a failure." God knows—or at least, I don't—what the consequences for his success-failure outcome may be. This is less Merton's theory of the self-confirming prophecy than a generalized theory of *inevitable intervention.*

Let me develop this theorem just a little further. It seems to me that sociologists—and psychologists and other social scientists analogically—broadly do three things. They state (or *define* or recognize) *problems.* They write what I shall call, analogically with elementary geography, *sociography.* They do *sociology.* By "sociography" I mean an enterprise of description—perhaps an idiographic enterprise; by sociology I mean an attempt at a causal analysis, a nomothetic enterprise. In all three cases, they make, to my mind, a decisive intervention, one attended by very difficult intellectual problems of self-location, and ethical problems of warrantability.

I shall deal lightly with the first case, though it is no light matter. The very recognition of something as a scientific instead of some other kind of problem marks a shift, an implicit act of legislation so profound as to deserve the title revolutionary. Nothing, I should think, except the commonness in our day of these acts of scientific territory seizing, could obscure the radical change involved, a change that by itself threatens to shake the foundations of the present society and to erect a new one of unforeseeable characteristics—perhaps an iatrocratic one—in its place.

Numerous illustrations will occur to us all. A recent one is alcoholism: the minute alcoholism is *defined* as a problem for science—even before any causal connections are established, let alone controls or remedies found—*in virtue of the definition* of what alcoholism is held to be, and therewith attitudes to, practices upon, and even custody of, care of, and responsibility for the alcoholic are immediately implicitly, and later explicitly altered. *The social relation is altered by the definition per se;* society is reconstituted out of the simple fiat (if effective) that alcoholism is a problem for science. With "mental disease" and "neurosis" as forerunners, with "sexual deviation" trembling on the border of redefinition, with delinquency half in, half out, but coming in, with no bar in principle to the admission under the rubric of any desired or undesired condition—"authoritarianism," for instance—is it not visible, almost patent, that more and more is being defined out of the old and nonscientific society and into the new one taking gigantic shape in its womb? I see no bars in principle. If the causes of authoritarianism can be scientifically determined, why cannot the causes of democratism; and why cannot the one be countered while the other is nurtured—except, of course, that an induced or caused democratism is not what we really wanted to begin with. (We may have to return to this point—the point of what someone recently called the "morality pill.") All I want to establish for now is the *science-as-legislation theorem:* that "recognition" of a problem as scientific at all legislates a revolutionary difference into human affairs as clearly as any nineteenth-century Act of Annexation did in affairs political.

I now want to deal with what looks like the most innocent, most innocuous, or least interventive aspect of our trade: mere sociography or psychography: description of what is, map making, if you will, or data assembling and ordering.

The description of a vital human activity, in and of and by itself, constitutes, in my opinion, an attack upon that activity, both from the viewpoint of the participants and from the viewpoint of the disinterested (neither participant, nor social scientist) observer. To the degree that it is a successful description, ethically neutral, deadpan, it tears apart for the participants the veil of unreality that is the foundation of the activity. A scientific description of our behavior in this room might well yield us something, even something of considerable worth, but could not leave something that was also valuable here unaffected for the worse. Everyone purports to value light, but too much light is pitiless glare, and what goes on during and after the glare cannot be what went on in the welcome and familiar twilight. How could a love relationship survive, for instance, an extended equitable enumeration of the characteristics of the beloved? How does other-directed behavior survive its categorization (stigmatization) as such? What becomes of the organization man once he is identified by self and others as such? I am almost tempted to analogize: the light of social science is ultraviolet; the bacteria cannot survive the light; life cannot live without bacteria; social science sterilizes; the sterility kills.

We have long confronted this problem as the problem of "unmasking." I think nearly every description, again in and of itself, of any vital social or psychological matter involves or risks such unmasking. In both sciences we have comforted ourselves (I think, falsely) by protecting the identity of the unit we are describing (the patient, person, community, or factory). I suggest it is a false comfort, only because it is insufficient: it avoids the inequity of fining a particular speeding motorist, as it were, by fining them as a group. Whether, finally, our initial operation results in a new (descriptive) image of parents, doctors, academics, teachers, professional men generally, business men, executives, unwed mothers, suburbs, churches, parishes, community chests, neurotics, alcoholics, pedophiles, hoboes, slums, gold coasts, Americans, Japanese, Indians, Protestants, Catholics, Jews, fundamentalists, or mystics, the living conditions for definable classes of people are altered, generally, I should think, in the direction of a more complex, strenuous set of demands accompanied by a diminished armamentarium of available defenses.

It may or may not be significant that a long-standing point of friction between Americans and Russians in Geneva has been the issue of *inspection.* As Kenneth Boulding has repeatedly pointed out, we have little or nothing of a sociology or psychology of inspection. Social and psychological descriptions are not merely inspection but *reported inspection.* It is not even clear which way, ethically and psychologically, the categorical, nonpersonal form of the reporting works. For the true professional, perhaps a description (a potential exposure) of the enterprise—the Church, the teaching profession, his type of community—with which he is associated is infinitely worse than an exposure of himself as a mere actual repository of an ideal embodied in the naïve social definition.

Again, we cannot, I think, console ourselves in any easy way. We cannot, as indicated above, get off the hook by shifting focus from individuals to groups or categories. Nor, which may be less obvious, by shifting from persons or institutions to types of behavior—say, antagonistic cooperation, or sibling rivalry, or gamesmanship—without again encountering the probability that we merely make life harder for everyone, or, more commonly, for some who share preferentially in the behavior in favor of those who do not. Nor may we comfort ourselves, I think, by believing that in time we will get around to everyone in all respects, so that at least we will hold the balance of disadvantage even. There is an infinity of possible categorizations to be viewed in an infinity of possible perspectives, and there will not be an infinity of infinities of monographs written or read. Thus we exert a judicial function in deciding what to describe. Description is like taxation; the right to describe absolutely is the right to destroy absolutely.

What we do, in practice, is, I think, to intervene (by description) against some bad guys in favor of some good guys—but by unacknowledged canons and on no ordered, let alone explicit and shared, principle.

If sociography and psychography are implicit interventions, what is to be said of the bulk of psychology and sociology, if by these we mean the sciences that trace supposed cause and effect relations in their fields?

A fortiori, these represent not mere findings, but findings *for* and *against*, judgments as well as verdicts, and, in their redefinitional effects, acts of legislation as well.

Let me assert first that there is a fatal peculiarity about the normal notion of cause when an attempt is made to apply it in the social sciences. I take it for granted that in society as in nature everything is related to everything else and hence in some ultimate, metaphysical sense everything is the cause of any one thing. By "*the* cause" or "a cause" we mean in science, however, as in practical everyday life, that particular thing which it would be most convenient, economical, or efficient to change in order to secure a desired change in what we are pleased to call an effect. Thus mosquitoes, if we do not mind exterminating them, are "the cause" of malaria in men; though apart from this canon of convenience we might equally have said that blood or man was the cause of malaria.

The differences on this score between the natural and social sciences is that, in the former but not in the latter, there exist two plain, open, and public canons of causal selection: there is, first, a basic judgment for man *against* the rest of the animate, and, a fortiori, the inanimate universe; and the second is that, in general, there is an economics mediated by a single fungible medium (price in money) that permits, or appears to permit, comparative measures of convenience and inconvenience in terms of relative costs. (A whole set of social conventions underlies this procedure, but the natural scientist is not bound to examine these.)

However, the minute we try to apply this mode of reasoning in the social sciences we are faced with two problems: one perhaps only technically difficult (interconvertability of costs or disutilities), and the other, I think, insuperable. For when we say "convenient" in the social sciences, we must further ask, "*convenient to whom?*" And unless we can either identify a general interest—which we have so far failed to do—or a supervenient criterion (such as pleasingness to God) we cannot fail, in effect, in attributing causality, to award costs to *X* out of the social, psychological, or material pocket of *Y*. For by the very act of picking out of the infinity of actual causal connections some one or ones as designated and hence recognized causes, we are altering definitions, redistributing tasks and responsibilities, increasing and decreasing prestige or repute, changing balances of psychic and social incomes, assets, and liabilities.

Take the problem of accounting for delinquency, as an instance. Admittedly, this is selected from the field of social problems, where the procedure is most evident, but an attempt to account for apathy or anxiety, or administration or bureaucracy would serve nearly as well. As I have said elsewhere, the cause of delinquency, other things being equal, is any one of the following: poor street lighting, alleys, immigration, paternal infidelity, differential association, neurotic acting out, broken homes, the American income distribution, lack of alternative meaningful activities, advertising and display, failure to nail down prized objects, the slum, the ecological organization of the American city, materialism, its opposite, preoccupation with one's worth as a person, the law itself, the absurdity of society or the human condition, the want of religion, the nuclear family, the political system which needs crime which needs a training ground, prisons and reformatories, schools that engage few or no loyalties, the perversity of the individual delinquent, or his parents, or theirs, psychological ignorance, the unconscious wishes of those who deplore the activity or condemn the actors. "Choose your pick," as they say. There can hardly be a question that all are involved, and an infinity—literally—of other candidates for causal ascription besides. And each of these causal factors is also connected, for the purposes of science, with an infinity of other causes. The selection for reporting, and hence attention, of any one cause—say the ghettoization of Negroes in the Black Belt, leading to rent extortion, leading to overcrowding, leading to heightened necessities for certain types of experiences and escapes—is as clear an act of judgment (in the legal sense) as if when a bridge collapsed a judge were to select a particular passenger over it as the cause of its downfall from the combined excessive weight of all of them.

The selection of any one of these for study is a political act, an expression of a political position—a power-redistributing value function that the social scientist knowingly or unknowingly holds. Let me leave this here for now as the *cause-tax or etiology-fine theorem.*

Another problem is the *ceteris paribus,* or context-taken-for-granted problem. Let me suppose a sociologist or psychologist interested in the rehabilitation of the imprisoned delinquent. He might be asked, and he might assent, to study any of the following roughly ordered problems: How, after we have thoroughly strapped a defiant child, can we mitigate his feelings so that he is not led by them into the vicious cycle of further defiance and increased punishment (surely a humane desire, within its context)? Or, how can we find a substitute punishment for strapping that would have the same effect—the breaking of resistance—without the too-patent sadomasochistic risks (surely also humane enough in its context)? Or, how can administration be smooth and overwhelming without resort to patent punishment, defined as such? (I think this is the commonest type of problem our clients bring us.) Or, given morally meaningless confinement, how can we minimize coercion? Or, given the need for order and the absurd rules of the society, what alternatives can we find for confinement (e.g., free marijuana)? Or, what alternatives are there to the absurd rules, given the present sociopolitical structure, or, what alternatives are there to that structure, given the need for national stability in the face of the cold war? Or, what alternatives are there to cold war, given no radical reconstruction in the minds and hearts of men?

With every shift in context, it is obvious that the whole scientific problem shifts. With every success at an early level in the list, the likelihood that a subsequent item might be successfully examined is reduced. If a really successful outcome for strapping could be assured with the aid of science (as perhaps it could) the view that we might need to reexamine larger problems would be most unlikely to find research funds or listeners. So the problem of where to cut into a social problem, what other things to take as being equal, is in effect an act of intervention tending to ensure that they remain not only equal but unchanged. One way to reduce theft from department stores, for instance, would be to institute a pay-what-you-like system (including no payment) with losses turned into profits by tax-subsidies. Why not? But the problem is not usually posed so. Which means that the problem as set is within a complex net of assumptions and goals, the *ceteris paribus*, that in effect constitutes an invitation to join the conservative party. So the way to deal with alcoholism is likelier to be found by science to be the setting up of more clinics where the socially hurt can be reconciled to their fate and persuaded to find substitute comforts, than it is to be the elimination of the sources of anxiety, aggression, self-denial, and self-castration that appear (to me) to underlie all or most self-defeating self-indulgence. Even when we shift away from the study of *problems*, defined as such, the study of persons, or small groups—again, all other things being equal is the very precondition for the study—we flee, I believe, in motive, as well as in effect, from the larger questions, just as we divert resources, and, worse, attention from these much more far-reaching matters. American sociology and psychology go that way, I believe, not on the mere ground of scientific safety or ease of management of the problem, but from covert alliances with the going order, in its major aspects, already in the heart of the scientist.

It does not need emphasis that just as the best is sometimes the enemy of the better, so most often the better is the enemy of the best. A sure-fire psychotherapy might well put off for three thousand years any attempt to cope with the institutional ways that ensure the breakdowns that the therapy deals with. I will leave this as the *accepted-context-equals-alliance theorem*. Communists used to use the phrase "blunting the edge of revolution" for the effect of minor (or perhaps particularly major) reforms, and while we may not wish to espouse the politics, the perplexity remains whether we are electing to deal with a narrow-context social problem or a sociological problem. One is more likely to stand in the way of more radical action, the other in the way of more significant knowledge.

Let me drive home the point of the context once more, but in a different way. A social scientist studying, say, the psychology of resignation in the context of Belsen is doing something far different from someone studying the same problem in the context of midtown Manhattan, or for that matter, Lhasa, Tibet. No less with the development of learning theories that explore the analogies of human learning with the behavior of machines, pigeons, or students of Zen.

Nor can we comfort ourselves with the consolation that we all act freely on manifold interests and that these individual impulses can be ordered by the market, intellectual or commercial. Our interests are themselves potential matters of scientific investigation and would turn out to be closely connected with a personal politics that gains no advantage from being inexplicit, if not denied. The actual and practical upshot seems to me even short of Louis Wirth's attribution to the whole of the term "an omnium gatherum"; it fails the completeness of the first term and the orderliness of the second. Indeed, its first-order social consequence—and it may not be unintended, it may be the very condition under which we are socially allowed to practice—looks very like the scattering and frittering away of most of the best minds of any given generation over the whole field of the variously trivial. Perhaps not; perhaps there is more order or sense than I see; but my first impression is that the result would well justify the opening stanzas of Ginsburg's *Howl.*

Another set of problems flows out of the interpenetrations of knowledge and commitment. In general knowledge flows only out of commitments (or implies them) whether one is more or less witting as to the nature of, or basis for, the commitments in question. It goes without saying that the commitment is or may well be made over in the light of the knowledge gained on the basis of it.

I want to drive the point home somewhat further by beginning with the problem of psychoanalysis—of any school, as far as I know—and raising the question of what kind of social knowledge is not analogical *in the process necessary* to reach it. I do not wish to enter here into any discussion of any particular psychoanalytic tenet. But the formal status of the knowledge is *ex hypothesi* that it cannot be embraced (or tested) until certain kinds of experiences have been had that alter (probably irrevocably) the intelligence that proposes to assess them. It is open to those who have not made the commitment nor had the experience to say either that the deliverances are false or not demonstrable. But this will no more—and properly so—shake the devotees, than the like arguments against the existence of God shake the religious. Indeed the arguments are formally similar in that a first act of faith brings into vision (what appears to the participant as at least as uncontestable as everyday or scientific vision) an object or class of objects, that justifies a further venture of faith, that brings into sight more objects or more of the same object . . . and so on, indefinitely.

This form of discovery—if you are willing to admit the word—is not limited to psychoanalysis. Nothing short of a mature mind is capable of defining (or even recognizing more than perfunctorily) what a mature mind might be. But such a definition in effect moves ahead of, rather than behind, the maturing mind. The insight contributes to the maturity and thereby brings new visions and the necessity of redefinition into sight.

We commonly attempt in sociology at least to pay tribute to something of what is involved by speaking of the process of "participant observation." Sometimes we speak as though we could occupy a position anywhere on a scale from total observation without participation to total participation without observation, and for limited purposes this may serve us well enough. But it seems to me there is a class of matters in which nothing but total, unreserved participation will bring the object to be observed into sight in anything except a fatally distorting light. The model might be the mystical experience. I doubt that it can be had on the basis of a trial or limited or divided commitment; neither perhaps can a love experience, although obviously celibate sociologists could write some things learnedly about love and marriage. But the central social facts—love, hate, friendship, enmity—are constituted by faith, and entered upon, for any purpose except most trivial comprehension, in ways that set up the process of building knowledge on faith and faith on knowledge in a succession of steps that simultaneously opens one to some observations while blinding one to others. The most obvious statement might be that we can understand nothing until our modes of perception have been ineradicably set in many ways by some culture; but once this process is well begun, we can understand some things and not others. The knowledge has thus, essentially, in its very structure, the nature of a historic or ontological process, in which successive steps in the activity produce irreversible changes in the actor, so that the convention that approximates reality in the natural sciences—the contrary of Heraclitus' assertion that you cannot step into the same river twice—has no counterpart in the social sciences, or finds only a minor echo there. Insofar as this view is adopted in any large part, I should think it ought to give a quite different perspective upon a career in social science and the training appropriate for it, and upon the meaning of contrasting deliverances by different social scientists. (Commonly, these are viewed as erroneous judgments on one part by the other, or are explained away in terms of a sociology of knowledge. But the possibility that they may be equivalid as consequences of different commitment-knowledge sequences, while invoked as a criticism in terms of ideology, is rarely allowed as legitimate and desirable as well as, perhaps, unavoidable.)

There are a number of other problems about which I have sometimes puzzled, but which I can only allude to here.

There is the problem of publication and, insofar as knowledge is useful or even comforting, the problem of redistributing power (or gratification) in certainly unplanned and perhaps undesired ways. (The laissez-faire effect is to secure and maintain a Pareto curve for the distribution of vital knowledge of self and others.)

There is a problem connected with the activity itself in its bearing on social stability: social change is already quite directly tied to the technology change, in turn directly tied to quasiautonomous natural science research. We are just entering the period in which the society will be ever more rapidly changed (and shaken) by the much more far-reaching products of social scientific research. But again, this problem is not the natural scientists' concern as such, whereas it is ours *as such*. In Lenin's words, "What is to be done?"

There is the problem connected with the ambiguities of the notion of mastery in relation to social affairs. With the aid of social science, what is to be mastered by whom and with what conceivable results?

There is the opposite problem, the impotency-perception problem, as thinking in terms of causes and effects—the essential vocabulary of science—gradually replaces thinking in terms of agency, the essential vocabulary of action and drama.

There are some interesting problems about mutual inclusions and imperialisms, as when philosophers bring sociological or psychological reasoning under their scrutiny, while simultaneously their behavior in so doing is grist for the sociological or psychological explanatory mill.

One could go on indefinitely, and any stopping-point is arbitrary. Perhaps enough has been said to make clear how unclear are some of the most fundamental suppositions and presuppositions of the social-scientific undertaking.

12

Applied Sociology as a Vocation

We generally reserve the term "vocation," I think, for a "high calling." A calling is deemed high when, by the judgment of ordinary men, the worldly standards, the demands or tasks to be performed, are very painful or exacting, and the returns, by the same standards of judgment, are correspondingly low. A priest or monk who lays his sexuality (and perhaps also his aggression) on the altar of service to God and man and who receives in return little, materially, but his sustenance has, by common consent, such a high calling. If, in the course of his career, he either diminishes the element of sacrifice or increases the return upon it (in other than a "spiritual" sense) he is said to be making a business out of his career, to have lost his vocation, to have betrayed his call. Similarly with the prophet in the wilderness, subsisting on locusts and wild honey while performing that most thankless of tasks, recalling a people to its destiny, or people severally to their own "higher" possibilities. The statement that something is a vocation or a calling is equivalent to saying that it makes no economc or common sense; indeed, that it is the inversion of these, the uncoerced furnishing, by the supplier, of more for less.

It is this contrariety to common sense that makes the term "vocation" appropriate, for such behavior would have to be explained away as madness (as it sometimes is explained) or accepted as a reproach (which cannot be long allowed) unless a quasicoercive explanatory element is introduced. The explanation cannot be in terms of raw coercion because that would obviously rob the behavior of its social significance and utility, but it must have a quasicoercive character lest the appearance of pure voluntary choice indicate too uncomfortably forcefully for everyone: "Go thou and do likewise."

The precisely right term is, then, the "call." The call is not a command backed by this-worldly sanctions, but neither is it a casual invitation to be accepted or declined at whim or will. It is a call from something or someone whose authority is moral—preferably, *purely* so. In the mixed case in which purely moral sanctions are joined to those of other kinds, we evoke, no doubt, the contempt expressed by Swinburne: ". . . And as for the Gods of your fashion, that take and that give, In their pity and passion, that scourge and forgive, They are worms that are bred in the bark that falls off, They shall die and not live."

The possible sources for such a call are, in the realm of the sacred, God or the highest of ideals (acting as "forces," but almost personalized), and in the realm of the secular, the inmost self, or some sufficiently great "cause." Note that where the inmost self is allowed as a legitimate source of "call," it has already been assimilated to the highest good (or to God: cf. the Quakers' "light that lighteth every man that cometh into the world"); and where a great cause is allowed, its imputed greatness is held to be in its relation to the same.

The difference between following a vocation and being under a spell does not lie, then, in either the externality of the commanding agency, or in its semi-coercive force, or in its being in the realm of morality. The difference lies in the polarity of that commanding or responded to in the dimension good and evil.

The notion of a call is commonly associated not only with an external source of call but with the notion of selective calling by the caller and selective capacity to hear (as well as follow) the call in the called. Many may be chosen, by one means or another, but only a few are called. Only relative to the number who both hear and follow are the called a considerable quantity. For the aspirant to priesthood (or the vocation of nun or monk) the quite agonizing, protracted first step is the assuring of oneself (and sometimes others) that the call was genuine and not something imagined on the basis of inner needs or low motives (or, indeed, high ones!).

Even when we quite secularize these explanatory principles we are left with a high something that is held somehow to have a differential claim on us (severally), a selective sensitivity to that claim, and a selective "willingness" to attend to what is intimated by the interaction of both. Thus a nurse, if held to have a vocation for nursing, will be presumed to have a differential attraction to the high aim of relieving certain kinds of human suffering (a high value) by nursing, and a differential willingness to respond to that attraction, at the cost of other possibilities in herself and for herself. If, per contra, she "uses" nursing as a leg-up to marriage to a doctor for reasons of economic and social race winning, we might say she had a talent, but hardly a calling.

It may be necessary to make the point, for a generation that has grown up since my own, that sociology in my day was a calling in these terms. (It may not be all that clear nowadays, since sociology has gained since then some modicum of deserved or undeserved respectability *and* reward.)

When I entered the profession a sociologist was a poor man, concerned with what were widely thought to be poor problems: problems that either few understood or everyone understood as well as he. They were men talking in a strange language about familiar objects, challenging comfortable views and preconceptions (when intelligible), and, in general, living a very laborious life with little income, deference, or safety—even when, as sometimes happened, they were not mixed up in the popular mind with socialists. The lack of safety, of "security," was of two quite different kinds, only one of them of the sort intended in Mr. Lasswell's triad. Of course, there was uncertainty or insecurity or lack of safety in terms of employment at all or employment that would at all substantially use one's talents, but this was true also in those days for other academic men of many different kinds. What was most insecure about sociology was its *inner* safety (and therewith its safety in relation to the other disciplines or vocations themselves). For whatever brave show sociologists might put on for others, and particularly for one another, doubts would not die down (and have not yet) as to what sociology "is," and—given some definition of what it is—as to whether such an enterprise is possible, and—given its possibility—of positive, zero, or negative utility. The endless discussions of methodology were similar in many ways to the Puritan's agonized self-examination on the question of his salvation, and the sorting and resorting of evidence bearing upon his "election."

The less modest probably talked in terms of a "science of man," and the very stridency of its archproponents (a Lundberg, for instance) served only to heighten the doubt as to how such a thing could be possible. No one doubted that sociologists could pick up formal glossaries of terms (von Wiese comes to mind) and make formidably fine distinctions where none had been seen to exist before. But that they could thus—or otherwise—talk fruitfully or illuminatingly about the life of mankind or the problems that beset us remained yet to be determined and was not encouraged of a positive answer by the performance of ourselves or our predecessors.

I must not exaggerate or make myself seem older than I am. I do not antedate Durkheim—or, for that matter, Park and Burgess, or the Lynds, or Reckless, or Zorbaugh, or Parsons.

These people were or had been; their products were there for perusal or their example was before us. But, with all due respect, for me—as for many others, inside and out—the most fundamental questions had not been settled or even, perhaps, well posed. We passed with terrifying casualness over the profoundest philosophical and intellectual precipices, glancing down perennially, but with a sort of blurred focus, lest we lose such seeming balance as we had and plunge into a pit from which we might rescue neither ourselves nor our discipline. We strung words together with all the satisfying complexities of the Athanasian creed, but with all the dubieties as to what it all really meant or whether indeed it had any ultimate referent in reality.

We talked of "social forces," and the people who used such terms could name examples of what they meant, but in what sense they were forces, in what medium, deriving from what, and impinging on what or whom, and whether "social" because of source, medium, or "sink" never became clear. The words gave an air of analogy with physical science (which was abandoning such anthropomorphisms very rapidly). But *was* there an analogy, and if so, in reference to what elements, and with what utility and effect? We talked of "society" and "the person," and of how the two were, or could be, related—we even came out with such comforting formulations as that the two were the "collective and distributive aspects of the same thing"—but I don't believe any critical mind believed we had really formulated something that retained the most important aspects of the experience that makes us speak of "I," "we," "they." We spoke of "social structure," and that tended to resolve into "social class," and that turned out to be susceptible of anthropological analysis in Newburyport, where patently people had a rating scheme of some sort that corresponded with life patterns, life chances, and so on. (Finally, it was concluded you could class-type a man by his housing, education, area of residence, and the like.) But what a class *is* was never settled (on the assumption, I assume, that you may define terms in any useful way), although almost everyone in a class society knows what class means, and that to be a member of a class is to take on a class-defined, class-approved, class-demanded set of behaviors, attitudes, loyalties, enmities, and value and idea standpoints.

I do not want to go on indefinitely like this, particularly since, as I make the contentions more detailed, I risk that we debate the details and overlook the force of the whole. My point was that from within and without, sociology appeared in a gel state rather than a sol state, if I may use such an analogy. Unlike a liquid, which invites very few to walk its surface, or a solid, which normally sustains all who do, a gel looks inviting but is incapable of furnishing firm footage. (I do not know how far the present state of our discipline departs from this image; I suspect, despite the multiplication of "middle-range" studies—or because of them—very little.)

The general way in which sociologists—or the ones I knew—coped with this situation was not too dissimilar from parallel behavior in other pariah groups. There was an air of great urgency to find true dogma, to show oneself scholarly (almost Talmudically scholarly) in linking current argument to prior high authority. There was disputatiousness and, in part growing out of it, the formation of "schools" and sects that recruited, rewarded, and penalized, scanned for evidence of the true faith, and demanded loyalty and forensic fire. What revealed the true meaning of the rather fierce rivalries within the group was the fact that differences of opinion were rather readily extended into differences in the imputation of intelligence (a not unnatural conclusion, perhaps) and hence into differences in imputed worth or, ultimately, goodness. This is the normal way of defining the heretic: a person worthless, or worse, because of unwilled or wilful blindness, but, in any case, "invincible ignorance."

Again, not atypically, despite these desperate dissensions within, all were expected to share, and largely did, in a common set of attitudes toward the outgroup: the barbarians without the gates, the Gentiles upon whom no light shone. And again, characteristically, the more nearly the outsider resembled, in some vital way, the insider, the stronger became the invective, the more developed the structure of reasoned contempt. The deviationist is more dangerous than the enemy, just as the apostate is worse than the pagan.

The humanists, like the Negroes, were, I believe, all right as long as they knew and stayed in their place. That place was to embroider and enliven life, not to explain it. Explaining human life was a task for the social scientists, but among them some were far and away more equal than others. The sociologists were clearly the most equal of all. Cultural anthropologists were tolerable, at least in the abstract, as were economists and political scientists, as long as they did not overassert their claims or overextend their dominions. The greatest unease was felt (within the "formal" disciplines) about psychologists, who seemed so wrongheaded as to attempt the explanation of virtually the same realm of phenomena by other means. Indeed, what was worse, they seemed to make sociology derivative from or conditional upon psychology, whereas it was plain to the faithful that the opposite was the case. But even so, all abstract disciplines were somehow within the pale: a church in heresy or schism is still a church, not an antichurch.

So low on the ladder of contempt as barely to deserve mention were the two groups to whom I later, much later, came to believe we were most nearly related: the social workers and the applied sociologists. (I preserve the distinction between the two, partly because the social workers were "applying" much else besides some sociology, and partly because such applied sociologists as there were had mostly at one time been "respectable," which social workers had not.) These two groups threatened the purity, and hence the existence, of the pariah people proper in two quite different ways.

The social workers themselves, then also largely pariahs, functioned like a "related people," whose whole way of life both competitively threatened ours and was likely to bring all of us into disrepute. The feeling was perhaps not unlike that between Bedouin and pastoral people popularly identified as belonging to the same stock as, for example, in Biblical Palestine. Indeed the relationship was held to exist only in the popular mind, while in our minds, differences exaggerated into antitheses were held clearly to override mere superficial resemblances popularly exaggerated into significant similarities.

It was not merely that they were less intelligent, which, given the recruitment problems of those times, may well have been true. It was that they were less intellectual, patently putting a lower value on thought itself, indeed rather regarding it as a means than as an end of action. They also used a rival, partly overlapping, jargon—like two variants of Yiddish—hence threatening all jargon. They were activists, interventionists, meliorists, and, perhaps worst of all, unwarranted optimists. There was a strong feeling that, by a sort of Gresham's law, their bad currency of discourse and *Weltanschauung* was driving out our good currency of talk and frame of reference. There was a worse feeling that while we patently waited to be called in as the only appropriate Grand Viziers to such Sultans as Hoover and F.D.R., the social workers, not content to be powers behind thrones, were insidiously filtering into the palace and its surroundings and beginning to occupy seats of power themselves. It was not even clear that once they had power *de facto* they would have the good sense to seek power *de jure*, to legitimize themselves belatedly, by calling in their self-evidently appropriate mentors, ourselves, who, equally patently, had what they lacked.

An additional, seemingly peripheral, but quite unforgivable crime was that they used the word "social" in their style and title as social workers, and invited confusion with social scientists: nearly as bad as the usage of Christian in "Christian Front" to cover a counter-Christian (as well as anti-Semitic) movement.

Given this major battle order, the major charge against the applied social scientist (beside the instrumental imputation of lower intelligence, lower intellectuality, and lower motives) was that he tended still further to confuse vital distinctions by his willingness to engage in or to influence action (openly), and by what was properly presumed to be his inferrable melioristic stance. It was not merely that he was led away into action (from theory) like going a-whoring after strange gods; it was not just that by permitting himself to be so led he acted as a potential decoy for others; it was also that he threatened thus further to confuse the already excessively confused popular mind as to what it was all about. Like a "working priest" he confused equally what it was to be a priest and what it was to be a worker. To engender and promote such confusion, when a beleaguered minority is striving to protect itself or at least establish a position of minimum safety, is to commit high treason at a very deep level.

I am sure that not everybody's experiences were the same as mine, and, even when they were, that identical conclusions, logical, social, and emotional, were not drawn. But I think I have made a fair sketch rather than a caricature.

What we now need to ask is who was called, and why, and with what consequences, into such a calling. My answer must be partly general and speculative and partly personal, autobiographical, and still speculative. (About himself each of us has also only an opinion!)

If I am going to generalize without fourfold tables and "hard" evidence, I had better allow myself the usual exit by saying now that I do not suppose that what I consider "typical" excludes the possibility of a small (or even a substantial) number of atypicals. It may be, for all I know, that some small number just happened into sociology and stayed there by accident, just as some people happen into pregnancy and stay on for motherhood. It may also be that for some, though I have never encountered any, their being and staying was a result of intellectual curiosity, pure and simple, and that it was sociology they stayed in, because society was just another fascinating object of attention. I doubt that the numbers of such were (or are) large.

For the greater part, I think we require a great deal of explanation of how and why they heard the sociological call, heeded it, and then went on deeper into the wilderness by recognizing and proclaiming themselves "applied sociologists." Let me deal with the two steps, separately.

Although sociology was perhaps the latest of the social sciences to arrive, I never met anyone "in" it who was there because it was *dernier cri*, like folk music at present. We did not think we were fashionable, or shortly about to become so, any more than the Christians in the catacombs had the feeling that they were fashionable or were there because of that. Indeed, the figure may be extended: there was an earnestness, an air of having the true gospel *not* likely soon to be accepted that made the association something more than accidental.

For only a very few, I think, was the major attraction the sort of interesting, not to say fascinating, facets of social life thrown up by the enterprises of Professor Park and his school: the intimate looks at gangs, taxi dance halls, lives of waitresses, juxtapositions of gold coasts with slums, stories of delinquent careers, distributions of mental conditions, glimpses into the lives of the hobo and the homeless, the Negro family or the family wrung in the wringer of depression. As material of interest in itself—apart from its bearing on a theory of society—I believe it held no primary place of interest. Largely gone already was the evident delight and excitement in the variety of the city and the variety of human behavior that clearly animates Park's writings and those of his nearest followers. Not that they were uninterested in scientific sociology, but they, much more than we, were evidently entranced at the sheer wonders that the traveling telescope of field work revealed readily to the even moderately steady eye.

We were, I believe, a different breed of cats. Something of the assurance, the urbanity, the gaiety almost, the detachment, the optimism and the spaciousness of Park and his time were wanting. For one thing, I do not think that we had the feeling that he—or Giddings, or Small—seemed to convey, that there was lots of time. The older of us had lived through the Great War (the "First World War," now), the collapse of societies with which we were identified and the sweeping away of ways of life for which we had been made ready, the wracking revolutionary and counterrevolutionary years that followed the Armistice, the disappearance of even such working certainties as the value of the currency in one or another of the great inflations, the general economic collapse of 1929, and the depression that followed. We were the children of catastrophe in a way quite different, I think, than were our immediate predecessors, or even those earlier notables, like Durkheim, whose work was in its way his response to the French Revolution.

I think many of us were unrevolutionary or antirevolutionary revolutionaries, and for us sociology held the promise of being—was—the continuation of revolution by other means (just as trade and diplomacy are the conduct of war by other means). When I say that we were nonrevolutionary or antirevolutionary I mean that we held the strongest preferences, conscious and unconscious, against disorder and violence. (Indeed, a utopian latent hope was that man's self-understanding out of sociology would make disorder and violence diminished or redundant.) When I say that we were revolutionaries, I mean that we looked to an altogether other society that might be brought into being (or at least assisted at birth)by our efforts. We were nonspecific revolutionaries, as we had to be, since we represented, so it seemed, *wertfrei*, value-free social science, a social science above and outside and beyond politics. We had, I believe, a revolutionary sense, but without a revolutionary aim. (When I say "we," I must concede there still were a substantial number of "reformers," or middle-range utopians.) We were then, I suppose, revolutionaries of process rather than product, men who might teach man to think about himself in ways so different as really to change the conditions of human action.

But even this could not be openly discussed, so that insofar as the ascription is at all true, we were covert revolutionaries. The high hopes we held of our discipline, that did appear to connect our professional performance with the concerns from which it sprang, bade us, in effect, be wise as serpents and gentle as doves: wise in maintaining the even tone of detachment and gentle even in presenting our findings deadpan in analogy with a good biologist's professional description of the flora and fauna. We spoke blandly *because* cumulatively we expected to have all the more radical ultimate effect.

We were able to do all this in good conscience, I believe, because momentarily the social scientific claim seemed credible—just as the Marxian ones once had to others with other canons or other creeds. It did *seem*—I cannot quite tell how, even today—that one could write from a position as if outside of society, representing a more general or higher interest, not specifically declared. Perhaps the sociology of knowledge was too new and recent for us to sense its full impact in its application to ourselves. Mannheim, in the *Ideology and Utopia*, while generalizing the term "ideology" to permit the unmasking of the partiality of perspective and specialty of position and interest in all social argument, seemed to have saved a special position, not open to the dissolving acids of his own attack, for the arguments of the sociologist. The position is not logically impossible: even the statement "all propositions are lies," if clearly seen to lie in the metalanguage about propositions, is not self-contradictory. Whether indeed the sociologist had a position so special should have been less a matter for logical argument and more a matter for honest and open-eyed inquiry.

Those who were drawn into sociology at that time were, in my memory and opinion, utopian, revolutionary in intent, and, of course, they concentrated on the diseases of society, their social etiology, and social remedy. Despite, or because of, what they had seen in Europe and indeed all over the world in the unchaining of the tremendous forces of the irrational, they retained a faith in the power of thought to affect or control events that was, to say the least, magnificent. Even as Freud was able to say and believe (in his optimistic moments) that "where id was, ego shall be," so were we able to believe that rational study of the irrational would be the taming force upon it—or, if not believe, act as though we assumed such to be the case. By another irony, although we believed with Max Lerner that "ideas are weapons," we thought of ourselves as simultaneously idea bearers (and idea makers) and men of peace. We were certainly not, as sociologists, *in* the battle in which ideas were weapons, perhaps ultimate weapons. Implicitly, I should think, we must have believed that our ideas were of a different order of weaponry, or that we could, like classic arms manufacturers, be indifferent to which of the contending parties used our weapons, for what purposes, and how. I think the "approved line" was closest to this last position: we could not be partisan politically; we could not prevent men in their wanton folly from misinterpreting and misusing ideas, including ours; our task was to furnish good ideas (valid, relevant, encompassing) and, I suppose, send them forth to take their chances in the idea market. There was, on the other hand, as I have indicated, an anything-but-laissez-faire attitude, an attitude of hope and desire for a better world in which our effort had meaning, a setting toward what I have called elsewhere the support of the generalized underdog (after George Herbert Mead), the utopian, revolutionary spirit of which I spoke.

Similarly unreconciled in our minds were, I believe, two strains of passionate belief, the one in holism, the other in piecemealism with reference to etiology, definition of the problem, and remedy. There was a strain toward isolating social problems—broken families, delinquency, mental disorder, poverty (barely mentioned), and so on—from each other, and to encourage the separate study of them, even if with similar concepts, on the obvious implicit assumption that the condition of society might be ameliorated by the mitigation or reduction in prevalence or cure of these problems, as though, to say the least, the state of society might be improved by improving the state of social subsystems. On the other hand, we were equally insistent on a view caught up by Lawrence K. Frank, in a different context, that society was the patient, and that these various manifestations of symptoms in subsystems were of interest only as indicative of deep-seated disease in the whole, which had to be addressed directly before any benefit could accrue to the subsystems (which might then also take care of themselves). We were thus again radical reconstructionists oriented in a whole-to-part direction, and moderate meliorists set in a part-to-whole posture. I must admit that this particular conflict lay not always unresolved within persons, but sometimes was a matter of dispute between them, so that there was a recognizable party that opposed and looked down upon the social problems and the social pathology boys as both in intellectual error and, to some degree, in social sin. But many or most of us carried around a both-and, rather than an either-or model. An observer might have said, kindly or unkindly, that we were latent opportunists, intending to base action or argument on either set of beliefs as need or opportunity might dictate. (This is, I believe, roughly what the British mean by "muddling through," and it seems to have served them well practically while leaving them with less apparent intellectual respectability than Continentals. I think we each wanted both practical successes and intellectual respectability, on American and German models respectively.)

Besides this *implicit* left-of-middle-left (the radical reconstructionist theorists) and right-of-middle-left (mild and moderate meliorists) dichotomy, I think there was another unacknowledged (and perhaps unconscious) split, to which Bremner has drawn attention in *The Politics of Sociology*. This amounted more nearly to a slightly-left-of-middle sympathetic inclination with a considerably-right-of-middle effect. The first represented our heritage from our essentially "liberal," intellectual ancestors in America, which, for example, led Burgess and his school into many productive small-scale-reform-potential studies (e.g., of marriage, probation, etc.). The other represented the unforeseen effects of intellectual tools more commonly derived from European preoccupations, or from other sciences, such as led to a focus on system, equilibrium, social order, mores, social structure, social control, system-stability—even, or particularly, our preoccupation with and preference for *Gemeinschaft* over *Gesellschaft*—that had patently supporting and comforting effects for a moderate or radical conservative ideology.

I am not saying, not even faintly suggesting, that we were stupid, unsubtle, or unperceptive. On the contrary, I am only saying that we came to sociology, itself a social product in a *given* state of social development, with social problems of one kind and not another, stemming both from the given state of society at the moment and from our own personal social development. I am also saying—I suppose, inferentially—that in addition to all the other qualities involved in the answering of the sociological call, there must have been a high capacity to welcome or sustain the strains implicit in holding, or attempting to hold, these difficult intellectual and social positions. In their nonresolution lay a role crisis for sociology, I believe, which it still has not worked out, and, for many sociologists, an identity crisis that is also still unresolved.

I think that by now many analogies between the vocation of the religious religious and the secular religious of sociology must have become clear—as well as some disanalogies, since few of us took vows of obedience and still fewer of chastity. The ascetic elements of great labor for little material return, of a special relation to the world such as to separate the sociologist in a sense from it (noninvolvement in one of its senses), the commitment to high ends and a hard discipline, the strain growing out of the complexity of explanation, the uncertainty of perception, the difficulty in catching *clearly* the object of attention, all gave us as students more analogies with seminarians than I would at the time have cared to admit. Disanalogically, we were not assisted either by Church (or an admitted one, at least), ritual, singleness of dogma, common discipline, long tradition, or explicit agreement on a creed that would give at worst the semblance, and at best the substance, of unity. Analogically again, we had focused our attention and our causal-ascriptive activities on (next to God or the Universe) the largest possible unit of explanation—Society—from which all originated and to which all returned. I believe a parallel modesty about individual man (even, perhaps, sometimes ourselves) was involved, since ultimately man was a whole and entire social creation, and his effect was, must be, upon and through society. (Again, quite inconsistently, we appeared to think that we, or men with our aid, could make over or reconstruct society, so perhaps we were inconsistent or held some covert reservations with reference at least to our professional selves and their merely social causation.) In any case, I mean to contend no more than that we were called out by and called into a rough analogue of a not-very-well-established, not likely soon-to-be-established, somewhat covert or curiously nonexplicit secular, utopian-revolutionary, sectlike movement that must have appealed to profound inner needs to keep its votaries in the way in the face of very high demands in relation to any this-worldly, common-sense returns.

Who in the society would be differentially likely to hear, attend to, and remain attentive to such a call, invites lines of social and psychodynamic explanation to which I invite speculation, each for himself, but to which I do not propose to, cannot, give adequate attention here. Certainly there should be food for reflection in a number of matters such as, for instance, our compresent beliefs in the power and ultimacy of the irrational and our belief in the power of thought, particularly scientific thought. What is the significance of our selection for causal ascription (and, occasionally, praise, but mostly blame) of the largest possible human system?

What may we infer from the indirection involved in the reformatory or revolutionary intent that counted on radically changing the going order without direct clash with it or without a clash in which we could be hurt (in contrast with the everyday revolutionary's or political reformer's commitment and risk)? Why the selection (or arrogation) to ourselves of a most peculiar role in the society, at once modest, like Simmel's stranger, simultaneously near and far, within and without, and much less modest, somehow outside and "above" or "in advance of" the society that gave us birth (a parent-analogue) and the society that surrounded us (an analogue for the sibship)? Whence and wherefore our high preoccupation with and practice of "unmasking," or tracing unanticipated consequences with reference respectively to the ideology and acts of others, while carefully preserving our own professional preserves from such probing?

Out of persons so selected—or many of them so selected—had yet to come a further selection for applied sociology. As I have indicated, that selection was rather against than with the professional grain, so that having once faced all the risks attendant on being called out of this world into the profession, one had to face the new set of risks involved in being called out of the core of the profession into a not highly esteemed, or even a highly disesteemed, variant.

There is great difficulty here in distinguishing what was meant by an interest in applied sociology. (Note parenthetically that at this career stage the problem was the problem of electing an interest and a definition, not of *becoming* an applied sociologist, which would have to happen, if it happened, largely following the apprenticeship and largely out in the world.) It certainly did not mean more closeness to living data, or starting from—or descriptively with—the problems some people claimed they had. Nearly all American sociologists believed in closeness to data, and, for many, the problems of others, as stated by them or others still, were at least data of high interest and perhaps beginning points for reflection.

It would be too easy to say that part of the difference, or the crucial one, between the applied and nonapplied (pure?) sociologist was a difference in belief, expressed in word or action, about which existed for the sake of which: theory to illuminate or alter social practices, or practices merely as matter for theory. Both sides might even then have conceded that something of a conversation took place in history between theory of society and social practice. And yet something of a difference, driven further into a distinction, did appear to animate the definition, as though the question were, "Which is the *ultimately* more important term in this conversation?" Something attended upon and imbued the discussion that was closely analogical to the view, on one side, derived from much of ancient Greek high culture, that thought and thinking (and the thinker) are high (and perhaps eternal) in relation to all other aspects of life, and the view—derived from much British empiricism culminating in American pragmatism—that act and action and actor (and life) are high, and that thought derives its value from its capacity to illuminate situations and alternatives and to direct an active process, in which it is only a phase, toward its own building up or enrichment in many dimensions other than, or additional to, thought itself. Substitute theory for thought and application for action, and you have some more or less close analogy with one of the arguments that was thought to point toward one of the distinctions.

But more than this was involved. Anyone interested in applied sociology had to be interested in application *now*. The antagonist or counterproponent had merely not to be interested in applied sociology *yet*, either for general reasons or for the very practical one that sociology was insufficiently developed theoretically so far to be of valid or practical use as a source of guidance in action at any important level. Those who differed on this point—i.e., believed in action now—had to believe that sociology was ready, or that necessity dictated, or that sociology never would be ready unless the effort were made. I think for most a combination of all three arguments was allowed to overbear doubt. (Necessity, be it noted, could be external or internal to the sociologist.)

There was at least one other dimension in which a difference had to lie. In the stage of social development of that day the intending applied sociologist would expect to work on, to test out application in reference to something below the level of ultimate or largest-scale social problems. He would not expect to be called in or admitted to the planning of a world society or the replanning of a national one. He might be given an arena for action with reference to standard textbook social problems—like delinquency, or neighborhood renewal, or housing, or race relations (meaning, I presume, diminution of violence, or discrimination or distaste between whites and Negroes or Jews and non-Jews *without* radical reconstruction of anything), or mental health or alcoholism or whatnot. Application, even as an interest, did thus imply a shift from global to partial problems, from revolutionary beginning to reform beginning, and in part from self-set problems to other-set problems (problems defined neither by oneself nor by other sociologists). Application, then, also implied a shift of attention to the "worthy poor" as the probable ultimate beneficiaries of success: those "underprivileged," but by no means the unworthy most underprivileged. The worthy poor are, of course, the clientele at any time of the most liberal of social agencies, who in turn largely determine (or did) what are (textbook) social problems, which in turn defined the applied sociologist's most likely field of operation. (The unworthy poor must, I presume, be the interest and concern only of others, like themselves, in some sense outlaws.)

Those who could and would accept such sizable constraints, particularly drawn from a fraternity that would view each constraint with alarm or disdain—and the yielding to it perhaps with contempt—had to be drawn or driven by strong attractions or forces. One of the strongest such drives was to secure reassurance, social and psychological, that one's discipline (and therefore, perhaps, oneself) had a bearing on practical affairs, could be of use in the practical activities of (ambivalently viewed) practical men. One of the strongest such drawings—analogical perhaps to what might draw a man out of biological theory into medical practice—was the appeal of common humanity from which withdrawal—even "in the short run for the sake of the long"—had been achieved with something short of enduring completeness, at least for some. This lack of an enduring and severe self-severance is not self-evidently to be praised or dispraised. How it is to be evaluated is not in abstract, but in reference to some judgment about actually available goods or avoidable evils in a concrete historical context. For those of us not driven by necessity, who made what is called a free choice, it must have appeared that, on balance, more was to be gained than lost (for society, for sociology, for us?) by an attempt to apply, with all its attendant risks and costs, than by refusal to engage on the actual terms available.

As I recall it, those who were willing to go on to application were not differentially distinguished by their sentimentality, though there may have been an element of that there. I think they may have been distinguished by what to one side would seem impatience and to their own side sensitivity to the pressing claims of those seriously interested in testing collaboratively what sociology could do for them on their small, particular, but no less excruciatingly urgent segment of the social front: the family, the school, the mental hospital, the probation service. . . . The appliers also had a different estimate of the pedagogical risks involved: over against the doubtlessly valid warnings of the nonappliers as to the risks of contamination, loss of perspective, desertion of grand theory, segmentalization, becoming labeled (with the name of the field of application, as, for example, educator or mental health specialist) the appliers set the possibility or likelihood that precisely in attempted application would new problems, new insights of the highest theoretic importance come into view, and thus their education, even as high-level theoreticians, would be quite probably differentially furthered. We also saw the possibility within large segments of our career, or even within the day-to-day activity itself, of shifting gaze rapidly from primary preoccupation with theory to primary preoccupation with practice, with probable, otherwise unattainable, net gains to each.

Again I invite speculation but I do not propose to treat either the social or psychological characteristics that would make for this second selection from among the previous select. Social origins, retained or looked-forward-to social connections, estimates of social possibilities, previous preoccupations with problems functioning in their own right or as symbols of other things (cf. Lasswell's *Psychopathology and Politics*), security needs of various kinds (and evaluation as to what was more or less secure), different attributions of importance, on rational and nonrational grounds, to "action" or "completion," different access to different opportunity systems, different life-chances estimates, different tolerances of different risks or certainties of alienation (from one's colleagues, from one's noncolleague contemporaries), different attractions from community as over society, all these and many more must have entered, in various weightings, into most such decisions.

Once the fundamental decision to risk application was made, a quite different process took over in which one became what one did become out of an interplay between theoretic considerations of the kind one had had in lively consideration in college and graduate school, and a practical *entraînement* in which career choices flowed more evidently and intimately out of previous career choices and decisions.

On looking back over my professional career I see that one may, by intent or inadvertance, be doing so many things at any one time, that it is only by "forcing the data" that one can classify one's activities, and perhaps by a further forcing have them make sense (or at least yield pattern) to oneself or others. For the sake of the reader, for mine, and for sociology's, I do not wish to do that much violence to the data.

Even those who may feel that in this career they have been always and only doing what looks like "one thing" would probably find, on adequate inspection and reflection, that in the complex play of motive, intention, effect (and the interplay between these) they were almost sure at any given moment to be really doing something different from what they had been doing the previous instant. And yet that is not quite right. In any case before one, one may in one light (to take motive alone for a moment) be struck with the immense and rapidly changing variation in motive, and in another light be struck with its almost unvarying fixity. One may, for instance, in a very simple case, believe that one sees in a given career a serving, in alternation, of affiliative, tender, or affectional needs and of needs for power accumulation, dominance, and so on. And one may be right. One may, however, taking a closer look (or a different one) see rightly that one motive was always, altogether, or largely in the service of the other, and thus conclude inexorable fixity of motive and virtual unalterability of purpose. Analysis may also run the other way, and reveal (in what looked like monolithic motivational unity) a vast flux of "real" or deeper or more ultimate motives masquerading under a single cloak. Tenderness, for instance, in our society, in our day, in certain social strata, is often thus concealed.

I am only saying so far that—even limiting oneself to one category, such as motive—it is very hard to tell in retrospect what others were doing, let alone what one was oneself doing, without introducing fictitious unities and simplicities. There is also the opposite, and perhaps equal, risk of failing to discover and report a real unity concealed under a factitious diversity. And what is true for motives is, I think, equally true for intentions, both those in the forefront and those on the margin of consciousness. And as for effect, one knows in any case very little. However, one does not have to talk frankly to many in one's ambit of acquaintance, or one-way or reciprocal influence, to discover that one has been many things to many people, both useful and useless in countless and often unforeseen and unforeseeable ways. Perhaps the elaboration and illustration by example of these complexities would be more instructive to you than an attempt to describe a pattern at a simpler level, but it is the latter that I shall have to do, if only because the time I had for self-searching and the time I have for presentation will not allow me to do more. I shall simplify chiefly by saying little about motive, by dealing with intentions in terms of dominant, conscious ones at a given time, and by restricting effects to those most obvious or most evident to me. I shall deal with the interplay of the three as well as I can.

I have, even now, an equal but different difficulty in drawing, except at the outset, even reasonably neat boundary lines around sociology-connected enterprises, that might be thought to be at least conceptually distinguishable.

I should have been inclined, in contrast—near the end of my student days, I believe—to recognize, legitimize, and sharply distinguish between three such major enterprises: sociography, sociology, and applied sociology.

I would have thought that there was a recognizable activity of sociologists that consists essentially in the *description* of social situations in acceptable, and (for the moment) established, sociological terminology. The formal purpose here is not to test hypotheses, to make generalizations, to seek new laws, or, indeed, anything else except to bring a social object (e.g., this gang, these gangs) fully into view in terms thought useful to or usable by sociologists or others. Such description, analogical to historical description, may have richness and interest of its own and may thus be justified, if justification is needed, or it may be raw material for sociologists sociologizing, although some, perhaps, would use it as an illustration of one thing and some of another (in the gang illustration, "subculture," "small-group behavior," or "deviation," or "counterlegal organization," for instance). It is evident that a man trained in biology can—without any special attention to the further development or the confirmation of biological theory—send in valuable accounts of the flora and fauna, and perhaps the particular ecology, of his *nova terra*, his new-found land. And since society is ever changing through time and is inexhaustible in objects of interest at any one time, sociography is an endless enterprise of never-diminishing justification. This sociology-connected enterprise is most clearly idiographic, though, I should hasten to add, it must assume universal terms to render particulars intelligible.

I should also have assumed, at the same time, that there was a distinct enterprise called "sociology" whose intent and achievement it was, in a phrase of Louis Wirth's, "To discover and describe the laws of human behavior insofar as it is affected by membership in groups." Since so little is *not* largely so affected (and particularly so little that is of interest) the mandate seemed virtually equivalent to a demand to develop the laws of human behavior, period. I not only assumed that this was not self-evidently (logically) impossible, but also that there was no practical bar to possibility, and, further, that our predecessors had already gone some considerable way toward such statements of significant invariances under the sign of eternity (which is the hallmark of the idea of science and the guide to its daily practice). I should have regarded this activity not only as possible, distinct, and justified, but as vested with highest eschatological hope: the vehicle, if there were any, of man's secular salvation, via self-comprehension, to such self-control as is possible and to serenity where it is not. The vision evidently makes full use of man's capacity and desires for activity and passivity, but distributes them rationally over the possible and the impossible respectively—chiefly by the continuing clarification of the difference.

Next, I should have assumed as possible, distinct, desirable, and open to immediate exploration, if not conquest, a realm of applied sociology, in which known general principles, applied to known particular cases, permitted (and humanely enjoined) partial remedies for part-ills, the sum of which might not be social perfection, but would at least not be inimical to more general improvement.

I was shortly to learn, as the issue will show, not only that these things were not all that distinct in practice, but—much later, and gradually—that, even conceptually, the distinctions could not be drawn without violence to the nature of society, of the sociologist, and of sociology. Over and above this, I certainly had not distinguished, as a part of or apart from applied sociology, the mere diffusion of the sociological attitude or set, sociological methods, and sociological knowledge, a diffusion we all further without much reflection on just what it is that we are doing or intending. I had also, then, not clearly set apart mere action on the basis of sociological knowledge, which is an inevitable aspect of the action of any sociologist, but is quite different generally in intent and always in effect from what I had separated as applied sociology initially. I was finally to be brought to a quite different standpoint, hardly connected in any way with my point of beginning except for the thread of a single experiencing self on which the beads of revision and re-revision were bindingly, if not brightly, strung. My personal pons asinorum was *Crestwood Heights.*

I should probably preface my statement about Crestwood Heights by saying (in case the fact should prove to have a significance that I do not attribute to it) that I had had about five formal encounters as a sociologist with "the world" before I came to "my community"—of study, not of membership. I had had a three-year experience in the Canadian Army at Army Headquarters in Ottawa and London, and in United States and Canadian training centers, in personnel sorting and officer selection, but primarily, at the highest level, acting as a kind of intellectual broker (and community organizer, in a sense) between psychologists, psychiatrists, social workers, and so on—the advocates and protectors, to a large degree, of the soldier as a human being rather than as a mere body. I do not know where this fits into my fivefold scheme, except that it was clearly neither sociology (I was building no theories, formally testing no hypotheses) nor sociography (I was *acting upon*, not reporting on, the Canadian Army, where I touched it). I was not primarily oriented to the diffusion of sociological knowledge or the sociological habitus. Nor was I merely quite "acting in the light of sociological knowledge," since it was quite clear that I looked upon things, spoke about things, and raised questions about things that cast them in a different light than that habitually shed upon them by common sense, by any of the represented disciplines, or by army habits of thought. I was there a puzzle, an annoyance—what people mean by "a stimulus"—an indigestible foreign body, but also somehow a bridge maker (if I may so mix my metaphors) to top brass, to those to whom I was "scientific advisor," and even upon occasion to the presidents of courts-martial (of other soldiers, not me) or directors of penal camps and "neurosis centers," as well as camp commandants. I still do not know quite how to define that role. It was a sort of combination of a generalized Socratic probative questioning and a role not unlike that of Simmel's stranger—or, better, in virtue of method and substance of things known, a representative of The Strange.

I had also had three briefer experiences, to none of which I should be inclined to attribute much significance: the gathering of some ecological-psychological data in Chicago for a doctoral dissertation (never written), a "mental-health survey" of an Ohio county, and a study of the structure of neighborhood disorganization around the University of Chicago for the University of Chicago.

The fifth experience prior to Crestwood Heights undoubtedly had significance. It began with mere friendliness and curiosity, went on to a sociographic study (with intent to report, but not to write), had strange aspects again of the sociologist as the stranger, and wound up with friendships and, for me, a rather profound initiation into the delinquent (and, to a lesser degree, the criminal) culture and society of a part of Chicago nearly twenty-five years ago. Something like William Foote Whyte—but more immersed, I believe, because I had no formal reporting responsibility—I was for two years a virtual member of street-corner society, a jacket- (or, in those days sweater-) wearing member of several gangs, their protégé and pupil, their highly participant questioner, only in small degree a representative of, and certainly not an ambassador from, the overworld or the incredible middle-class and University society with which, they knew, I was somehow mixed up—like a potentially good boy who has got into bad company. I became a true and somewhat more than honorary member when someone of loose tongue, influence, and fertile imagination put it about that I had a racket (blackmailing middle-class ladies, I believe) which made me at heart one with my delinquents, while also explaining my need to be circumspect with regard to V.D., robbery, and a few other matters. I did not disillusion them, since they needed to believe it and I needed them to define me as they wished. They spoke of it in my presence, but never asked me. Thus—to each other—"Don't ask him to do nuthin' like dat; 'e can't take no chances on dose mudder-jumpers findin' out an' holdin' it over *him*."

Whatever else I was doing here, it was not applied sociology. If anything was being made over it was the sociologist and not his new society. If I had any reform impact, it was not upon my slum world, but on the third world in which I lived, the company of the good social workers of the University of Chicago Settlement, who thought of themselves as subsociety rebuilders, and hence, perhaps, as applied sociologists of a sort. Though I could tell these good people very little in particular—the first law of the street was "Dem's social workers, see! Don't tell dem nuttin', you."—what I could tell them in general would tend rather to call into question and move toward reconstitution of the Settlement than the slum. But that was a side issue. The main issue was understanding so interfused with affection that to split them apart in retrospect into participant and observer elements is to make the experience retrospectively false. Within my limitations, and conscious that at best I could have only an extended visit, I *belonged* as far as I could, I made the initiation as genuine as possible, not on an "as if" basis, but because I *wanted* to belong—for its own sake—to so fine a company, beside which much company I had known and was yet to know would seem pallid—or corrupt. So, anyway, the prelude to *Crestwood.*

I had better abandon for a moment any attempt to be orderly in classifying activities, and (speaking in terms of conscious intents) set forth first the vast variety of activities that comprised the Crestwood Heights Project.

We had all of the following enterprises operating simultaneously:

(a) A community study: an attempt to describe the life and hard times of the relatively rich: the upper middle class in a suburb, self-consciously dedicated to "liberal" values and, self-consciously again, about half Jewish and half non-Jewish.

(b) An experimental study: an attempt to determine (and demonstrate) the effect on the feelings and behavior—the "mental health," of children of all ages from six to eighteen—of free discussion—in a sense to be later defined.

(c) An operation in and on the community's schools, by a variety of methods, to secure a new vision, a re-vision and a revision of the whole educational enterprise, of the meaning of "the child," "teaching," "the teacher," "the community"—as seen in heightened consciousness and depth in general and in the perspectives of psychoanalysis and sociology and social psychology in particular.

(d) An operation, not *in* but *on*, the school systems of the remaining Provinces of Canada, by organizing a new subprofession within the teaching profession, recruiting carefully for this profession, negotiating agreements for their proper employment, and then training them (a year each, a dozen at a time) for their new role.

(e) An operation in and on, finally, the community itself—or, more precisely, key officials, functionaries, and parents within it—in which we, or some of us, were counsellors, educators, questioners, psychologists (individual and social) acting "therapeutically," discussion leaders, redefiners of situations or issues, sometimes participant-*observers* but also frequently *participant*-observers.

(f) An operation in and on the Canadian *psychiatric* community (after all, I was a member of the University of Toronto's Department of Psychiatry, related primarily to psychiatric colleagues and partly responsible for teaching psychiatrists) in which it was my *minimum* aim to provide a better picture of the (statistically) normal lives their patients live to set against the standard psychiatric fantasies and projections. (I had so often, in the Army and in clinical case conferences at the hospital, heard explanations of behavior that was culturally normative in the patient's culture of orientation couched in terms of idiosyncratic psychopathology, largely because no one at the conference knew the cultural or social circumstances, or, sometimes, that *not* all North American subcultures are standard, lower middle class, modern, urban, Western.)

These at least were the principal overt intentions. What some of the covert intentions were, I only gradually realized. How serious a part the overt and covert intentions of the subjects of study would play both in illuminating and reshaping our intentions, and certainly in affecting our effects, was yet to be discovered in the particular situation and reflected upon in due time for its general implications for sociology or for sociology-connected activity.

If I may return now to my original scheme, we had one sociographic aim, the description of the community that was to eventuate in the book *Crestwood Heights*. We had one sociological or social-psychological aim in our "human relations classes" or "free discussion groups": to make a contribution to mental health or socialization theory by testing for the predicted effects of a far-reaching intervention. The remaining operations may be called applied sociology, or the application of sociology, though I would now reclassify a great deal of it as sociological diffusion (whether for its own sake or as designed, active, meliorative intervention), and mere action on the basis of sociological knowledge. We came to have one other aim, in very substantial conflict with all the other intentions, taken severally or together. Despite any thing we knew how to do and did to maintain distance and due detachment (or just because of these acts) we were drawn into genuine, profound, human, and affectional relations that gave, as a minimum additional aim, the preservation, so far as possible, of these priceless bonds and the protection and preservation of those with whom we were thus socially (morally and affectionately) bound up.

What came out of Crestwood Heights for me, however, was not primarily a book, or a series of papers, or new sociological knowledge (though these did issue). What came out of it was a shattering encounter whose consequences I have not yet by any means fully worked out. What was shattered beyond redemption, and is still in process of slow and laborious reassembly, was the connected series of "views" I held regarding myself, other sociologists, the nature of sociology, and its connected operations. Simplistic, false, and illusory views that may have had peculiar personal force, but that were the common heritage, reinforced by education and professional training, fell victim to the realities of the experience, which, by a self-chosen fate, we had made ourselves morally bound to look at.

I would like to forestall, by an aside at this point, a line of thought that is bound to arise in your mind: that whatever eventuated may have been largely caused by our having cast ourselves in a number of different, perhaps incompatible, and not sufficiently distinguished roles. We might reasonably be expected to have reaped confusion at the end if we had sown it at the beginning. I want to forestall this line—not in the sense of declaring it out of bounds, of course, but in warning against letting it blind you to other possibilities—because, naturally, it was the first line of explanation to occur to all of us, the most personally, professionally, and socially acceptable, the most obvious, and, as I finally concluded, the most misleading. The premises, for one thing, cannot be supported by the facts. We *did* sharply distinguish roles and, so far as such things are ever possible, got others to distinguish them progressively more sharply the same way. If I finally concluded that the distinctions were false and, like all major falsehoods, caused by obscure purposes, and all the more endowed of strongest affect, it was not because they were not made to begin with and sustained with skill by common desire and consent as long as they would hold up. If I may anticipate the end of the argument, I should say that I did not revise my opinion of sociology (as well as sociologists and myself) *because* I was doing so many things in its name, but rather the reverse, that I *was* doing so many things because all of them are and must be implicit in the very idea of sociology. (Surely I should have known, even as a student, that the very strength of certain professional denials was a probable pointer not only to a hidden truth—hence an assertion by negation—but to one of consequence and painfulness. That I did not note what I should have known—did "know"—points merely to the serviceability also in my personal economy, as of that time, of the shared madness, the common myth.) I do not know how much of this I can make clear, since much of it is not clear to me yet.

The views to which I was—by seeming inevitability—led

confounded the distinctions between kinds of enterprises that others had drawn for me and that I had accepted. I was led to the view that all sociology is applied sociology—if we mean by that an activity that alters the society by the activity of the sociologist acting as such—and, more particularly, that that activity is most applied that is most "theoretical." (A new theory of society *is* a social revolution; all that follows is mere acting out.) Inevitably, I came to see the sociologist as *mostly* an actor, more an actor in the society than the "actors" whom he observes and upon whom he reports. Value neutrality, insofar as it was not nonsense or fraud, was a value position with extraordinary practical effects as operating in society by the force of the sociologist's example. It is partly, in reality, impossible, but, insofar as it is actualized, it bathes all things in a new light, like the counterpart of a mystical experience, and, like that experience, makes all things new. I came to see judicial, legislative, and executive functions as central to the sociologist's acts qua sociologist, whether in research, in theorizing, or in educating (diffusing). I came to see elements of priestly and political roles, only best concealed and hence most potent in the classic sociological role definitions. I came, needless to say, to question the pose of the social scientist as one who is somehow, to a significant degree, outside history, outside society, outside culture, and I came to ask sociologically how that could be and where, then, he could be. I began to observe effects and gradually became convinced that they corresponded to intents, whether merely unconscious, undisclosed, or just hidden. I came to a focal interest in the psychology, and sociology, and "philosophy" of sociology (the metasociology) which seemed at least as integral to sociology as the history of philosophy is said to be to philosophy (i.e., philosophy, on this view, *is* its own unfolding; they cannot be, except illusorily, distinguished). I came to see the student of culture, particularly of his own culture, in many lights, with reference to both his effect and his intent. (If the culture is the womb, the common matrix with the siblings, what? If it is the mother's breast, the source of our common nourishment, the very substance of our psychological and social substance, what? If the culture is a set of constraints, even if also "liberating" directives, the echo and enlargement of the father's heavy constraining hand, what? If an edifice, a structure, an elaboration of towering levels, a superphallus over against nature, our mother, what? If the "culture bearers," our erstwhile sibs—from whose company and culture we must needs go out if we are to get "perspective"—are our subject or object of study and contemplation, as if from afar, what Joseph-in-Egypt-and-brethren-in-Israel relations have we not instituted between us, with what causes and consequences for us and for them?) In another view, the sociologist, most particularly the cultural anthropologist of his own culture, appears to have inherited the role of the singer, the minstrel, as Uhland sketches for Bertrand de Born:

> *Du der kamst mit Schwert und Liedern,*
> *Aufruhr trug von Ort zu Ort,*
> *Der die Kinder aufgewiegelt,*
> *Gegen ihres Vaters Wort . . .*

or, in *very* free translation:

> *You who came with sword and singing,*
> *Uproar bore from place to place,*
> *'Gainst their father's word upbringing*
> *E'en his children, out of grace . . .*

The "uproar" is the ferment of ideas and attitudes in the world, which flows from the operations of such persons as social and personality theorists, chiefly, in practice, sociological and psychoanalytical theorists, who pose in their products (and even more forcefully by their "sacrilegious" behavior, as examples) ever-new impossibilities of rest, ever-new demands for change, not at the trivial external level where we often think such problems to lie, but at the inmost level of individual and collective self-image, and hence of proximate attitude and ultimate set. The carrying of the unrest from place to place is the essence of and the reason for publication, ultimately popular publication (whether by self or others makes little difference; it is one integral act, invariably with that effect and commonly with that purpose). The sword is the body of sociological knowledge, and the song is the public lecture. The "father's word" against which the children are stirred up is of course the received culture, the conventional wisdom, which must be, is, the object of re-examination (read re-evaluation). Even when the intent is conservative (at least the conscious intent) as, for example, in Durkheim in reference to religion, the support that is given is the kiss of death, for a religion that is justified by social utility in terms of its power to create social solidarity is no longer a religion as such, but a social gimmick or instrument of social control. If religion as religion is necessary to society then surely the society that knows this (by the working of the sociologist) can no longer have religion, or at least not in the same sense. (If God is loved because it is good for one's health, mental or physical, the love of God dubiously has any longer any of its alleged curative or preventive properties.)

As I finally came to see and feel it, it was not sufficient for a responsible sociologist to have such insight as he could into what sociology is, in general, or how sociologists operate, in general. Of overwhelming importance—for him as for the psychoanalyst—is an understanding not alone of the play and the parts, but of his own particular, private, and personal version and variety of the play and the style of playing out the social part. For, as with the prototype of all symbol systems—as Norman Brown out of Sigmund Freud reminds us—the primitive first symbol and its successors function as play material, weapon, property, and gift. But which of these, in what proportions, combined how, why, and with what effects is what the practicing sociologist most needs to know and is, in the nature of things, both least likely to know and least desirous of knowing. The styles in sociology—shocking, mischievous, superior, snide, indulgent, falsely detached, asserting-by-negating, falsely committed, negating-by-affirming, remote, simplistic, overcomplex, turgid, spuriously transparent —all cry for understanding because they are of the essence, not the accidents, of what it is, and therefore of what the relation of society to sociology and sociologist can and should be. The anecdotalist is asserting to and pretending one thing, the systematizer another, the middle-range theorist a third. Even preferences among Stein's Trinity (history, system, drama) have more than their ostensible utilities to recommend them; they involve at the least as conditions of tenability, sizable shifts in the self-image (and the held-out other-image) of the sociologist who holds them, for somewhere within his preferred scheme or metaphor he must find a place for himself both as a sociologist and a self among (if that is the right word) selves.

Still later and last, I came to see in generalization from W. I. Thomas' "definition of the situation" that the greater part of social facts, and those the most important, are and forever will be constituted by their definition (brought into being, and so sustained, by faith); that a redefinition is no less, rather more, a definition; that the sociologist's profession is to initiate redefinitions of society or subsociety; and that hence he is in the business, necessarily, of the continuous reconstitution of society—whether he does it ill or well, effectively or ineffectively.

Thus this innocent abroad (like all innocents abroad, perhaps), this *rapporteur* merely or *raconteur*, this urbane student of the social scene, is a crucial actor within the play he purports merely to watch, only to record or enjoy. Even by his refusal so to see himself he decisively affects the drama, holds himself only from the consciousness of his history making, and deceives himself as to his place in the system.

The questioning of the actual set, posture, and effect of the sociologist in society led me to revise and re-examine not only what was involved in selecting particular objects (say gangs, communities, or suburbs) for attention, but what was, or could be, meant by the imputation of social causation where the canons that guide the nonhuman sciences—convenience for intervention—have no clear meaning, or have a radically different (political) one. I became interested in, or curious about, the actual social uses of sociology—a Vance Packard, seeking status and clad in the symbols of successful seeking, lecturing an audience on "the status seekers" as though the term referred to them, or to others, but not to him; or grade-school kids recasting ancient child disputes in our terminology. At a more vital level, I watched more intimately young college and old high school boys and girls explaining and explaining away their agency in acts which we had taught them how to attribute for causation to history, the social structure, the culture, or whatnot.

The whole matter comes to one beautiful, practical, but only illustrative sort of crux in the decisions over the last few years from the bench of the Superior Court of the District of Columbia, more particularly those of Judge David Bazelon. The record is there to read, and should be read. Suffice it to say here that, taking psychic determinism seriously, he has sought to extend and has extended, not into the mitigation of punishment or the assessment of extenuating circumstances, but into the determination of criminal responsibility and guilt (the central doctrine of *mens rea*) a much extended set of notions of how human acts come about without the intention (or negligence) of the principal actor. And similarly he has sought and is seeking the admission of what might be called sociological evidence to adult trials, so that, in principle, if a competent sociologist could convince a jury of the "social causation" of a given act, then clearly it would fall as far outside the realm of culpability and criminal responsibility as if it had been committed as a consequence of mental illness, or, in the older terminology, "while of unsound mind." Clearly, we are not much longer going to be able to have our causal arguments both ways, and we may well be required to come to some crucial decisions (or have others do so for us) in connection with the criminal law. The direction I see events taking is toward a much-diminished notion of individual responsibility for personal acts—the notion in turn then altering the facts—with a much increased individual responsibility for the collective acts (e.g., segregation), which furnish the conditions and limits (or causes) for personal acts. If, as seems entirely possible, such individual responsibility for collective acts cannot be borne or adequately responded to by individuals, the likeliest outcome seems to be highly increased centralization, no doubt benign in intent, going toward an iatrocratic sort of society, with still further consequences for the idea and possibility of personal potency and responsibility.

Some of these ideas may be assessed or debated on their merits, no doubt, in due season, but how did they come out of the experience in Crestwood Heights? They came out of Crestwood Heights because the circumstances, the nature of the enterprise, and my own and my colleagues' readiness (if you want to call it that) forced a collision between theory (or professional ideology) and the facts that, ostensibly, we were there to look at. I can touch only lightly and illustratively on what I mean.

First, it became evident that what we were actually doing at any moment, in any part of the enterprise, was a function not so much of our intentions and techniques, or of our definitions of what we were about, but of what others, individually or collectively, imputed to us as the motives and nature of the operation. Thus, to take a crude example, some people thought that the psychiatric clinic we installed was, despite our claims and disclaimers, altogether or primarily a research station, and they responded to it as such. Depending then on what they thought of research and therapy respectively, and, more covertly, on disposition to help, to be helped, or to enter into specific help-exchange bargains ("I'll tell you this if you tell me that"), the consequences might be therapeutic, countertherapeutic or therapeutically neutral not only for the client but for the aid-tendering professional. What people thought the clinic was, and hence what it practically came to be, was, of course, not just there, not a datum. Nor was it a result of our conscious defining activities. Any definition at any time—and, with the definition, the temporary, tentative operating reality—came out of an obscure conversation or transaction in which the overt and covert interests and needs of both parties to the transaction—the professionals no less than the clients—were of the essence of the outcome. And as to what either of these terms, research or therapy, meant to the participants at deepest levels, initially or sequentially, this too turned out to be ultrasignificantly affected by the initially unknown life experience which on the one view would be the subject of study, and on the other view would be the object of "helpful" intervention. Thus research might really mean something most like early-experienced (in reality or fantasy) parental investigation leading to guilt or punishment; or it might fall into a matrix of "ego-syntonic" experience of self or others, where investigation had been the prelude to reward, satisfaction, or coming to terms with reality. So not only which was the defining term, but what the definition "really" meant—and further depths are involved: "help" as something to be welcomed or feared, etc.—and, consequently, what the clinic was, and thus what we were doing from their viewpoint, and thus in consequence and by reaction what we were "really" doing in the clinic, was a shifting consequence of a social action initiated by both sides and controlled in any vital sense by neither, and only detectable in sketch or impression by listening with a most attentive "third ear" to our own nonexplicit expressions and theirs. And note the circularity: the desire to know what is actually going on is primarily, formally a research interest; but the discovery of such subtleties rests primarily on a therapeutic—or, at least, benevolent and mutual-aid—relationship and definition of the situation. No repeated set of forceful assertions, no education campaign or public relations program can more than touch these fundamental facts; for each of these in turn depends on the same set of complexities for what it is defined to be—and hence for its effects—and, ultimately, since we are not really totally blind, unless willfully, to our effects, for its motives.

I chose the clinic as an example because it was separately staffed and located, most easily recognized in conventional terms (in a psychiatrist-using and child-education and child-raising-centered community), most protected by established professional practices designed to safeguard professional definitions, and doing almost only one thing. For children, teachers, principals, school officials, parents, outside observers, professionals involved, as groups or severally, it was far from one and the same thing, and what it was operationally had small relation to what it was initially and officially defined to be. If this is true for the clinic, it is a fortiori true for all the other less conventional enterprises.

Again, and more generally, it turned out that the principal, most common, and most significant effect of what we were doing bore very little relation to what we were actually doing. For the project as a whole, for instance, one principal effect was the raising of morale since it was a point of pride that this community had been selected as a place for operation and a subject for research. Its inhabitants were evidently, by implication, even more interesting to people of a type they admired ("experts") than they had ever thought.

The point may bear driving home with a few other examples. In a "concession," whose politics I can leave you to guess, we conducted for several years a graduate seminar for women, not on Crestwood Heights or anything we were doing, but essentially on Culture and Personality, just as we would have done in our universities. The effect of this peripheral activity (peripheral, that is, to the project) went further, perhaps, than any one thing we officially did, in the direction of applied sociology. Our observers at P.T.A. meetings, or still more informal, but vital, meetings, could roughly trace the spread in this sophisticated, literate community, not only of a body of knowledge, but of a way of looking at problems, that was seriously to question previously received doctrine on which institutions (school, church, temple) were operating, as well as to cause practices previously accepted there (and in homes and families) to be seen in a different, unfamiliar, and action- or adjustment-requiring light. So here, where we were most abstract, theoretical, academic, we had the greatest practical shaking—almost society-reconstitutive—impact.

Similarly, clinical conferences with teachers and with guidance personnel, designed to secure consensus on the handling of a given child, turned out to have their principal effects not there, but on the social organization and status system and system of alliances within the school, in precipitating new individual and collective self-images, and, in many cases, in affording a therapeutic or cathartic outlet for the teachers who were ostensibly involved, not thus, but in their role as caretaker-educators.

The one most clearly labeled "scientific experiment"—the attempt to measure the effect psychologically and sociometrically of "free discussion"—turned out to furnish one of the most vital and detailed sources of information for the sociography, information we could have secured in no other way short of mass psychoanalysis. Before our very eyes and around our very ears there unfolded in dynamic fashion—a social analogue of personal free association—the concerns, worries, coping ways, of these children as embedded in their personality and social structure, inside and outside the school. We got living pictures—not undistorted, of course—first of the idiosyncratic and then, under discussion, of the communal experience of being a child in Crestwood Heights, as seen by children of the several sampled ages. (We could and did check later for objectivity, or—the best one can have, generally—on their subjectivities by comparison with the subjective certainties of their parents, teachers, and others.)

We got not only something other than we aimed at, in this fashion, but something additional in the experiment itself: mere serendipity, to use the current jargon. Our "experimental subjects" made not only very notable, "significant," and substantial gains in the (mental health or psychological) directions predicted but, quite unexpectedly, dramatic academic-grade gains too, even in subjects they had to "sacrifice" in order to permit time for the discussions. Also, unanticipatedly, not only the method but the underlying attitudes were brought home by children and adopted or imitated by some parents, quite a few teachers, and even some temple personnel with extraordinary results. Indeed, the method and more carried over into school staff meetings (nearly oversetting the structure of the one authoritarian school) and, believe it or not, into the youngsters' own, extralegal fraternity and sorority life.

Again some odd results. By coincidence or otherwise, about three years later when everyone had forgotten who had and who had not been in any experimental group, of five students winning major outside-awarded scholarships, four were experimental children (and one a newcomer) and none were controls, though there were four times as many controls as experimentals. Again, about the same time, one perceptive teacher said he could (and proved he could) pick out the experimentals in the entire three-times-reshuffled grade, by the way they went at a problem (in history, his subject) and by the feeling they communicated of how they saw him and his role as a teacher. Again, at about the same time, an outside and independent team of investigators interviewing the experimentals found (a) each believed he hadn't changed much as a result of the discussions but that all others had changed a great deal, (b) most felt it had been a vital experience but could hardly remember anything discussed, (c) strangely, a majority thought the object had been to "teach them how to *think*," though most referred to changes in feeling or sensitivity or perception of their social and especially peer world as illustrative. (The double distortion—that we aimed at thought, and that we were *teaching* them—gives food for thought about teaching!) Also, and coincidentally, we set off within the teaching staff inside the school passionate discussion and debate on the relation of the school to the pupil, the adult to youth, the place of ethical or other indoctrination in education, the teacher's private conscience vis-à-vis his public responsibility, and so on. Not only that, but among educators and others in the metropolitan area of Toronto and outside, a parallel agitation was set off as rumor or report (or observation) of what we were doing circulated and variously reached various targets. Observers spoke essentially of three things: (a) a tremendous positively toned emotional experience for them, (b) a shaking blow to their beliefs about what children could and would do with such a freedom, and how much they unsuspectedly knew, and how wise and responsible they seemed, and (c) a need to go away and carefully consider implications for educational theory and practice (or, sometimes, family theory and practice).

Again, I would be inclined to say either that the principal product lay outside our conscious intentions and designs, or that the by-products were so numerous, important, and various that they alter substantially what one means by the product. Certainly we had not aimed to illustrate for Crestwood Heights itself what acceptance, respect for others (chiefly children), attention to covert as well as overt message, and especially self-direction and, in essence, free association as against structured attack could do for participants and, evidently, observers. (If we had been able to have our way we would, I am sure, have insulated or isolated our precious experiment for the sake of scientific purity.) Certainly, we did not aim at altering the intellectual-emotional climate of the educational enterprise (parents, children, and teachers).

But, nearly more visibly than anything else, this, I believe, is what we unwittingly did.

Similarly, with other aspects of our operation—though I will not burden you with further detail. Even a public lecture in or near the community on some quite unconnected topic might turn out to be more a rite of solidarity, or an exercise in sociability, or a genuinely transference-attended situation than any of us, in our then naïveté, would have been inclined to believe.

You may have noticed that hitherto I have spoken with almost pedantic insistency on conscious motives and witting intents. I did so by design, because it was not borne in on me till much later that the actual upshots, where they were not wedded to conscious designs, were indeed the offspring of unconscious intents. Not inadvertency but indirection marked the route from motive to effect.

I must compress a great deal into a little space, and while I am sure the generalizations would be true for all members of the project and for all social scientists I have known, I must speak, from this point on, only for myself.

If I had to condense all I propose to say into a single generalization, it would run to the effect that a scientific career, like a dream, is a message telling in detail, for those who can interpret it, of a rich and quite different inner life, a compromise solution of an affect-laden conflict, an indication of some unfinished business in the social drama of infancy, a symbolic representation attended by condensation, displacement, reversal, and so on. Of course, just as in a dream, there are accidental factors and elements and traces of daylight purposes, but the significant and dramatic and illuminating connections are not there or there, but in the largely unconscious life which necessitates the second displacement. Sociological and psychological studies and careers are, beyond this public and ostensible character, partially but significantly returns of and fresh attempts at coping with the repressed.

I say "partially" because, like other art—to which they should be assimilated—there is a controlled and socialized element that makes for intelligibility on two planes, rather than one, as in the dream or somatic symptom.

It would not be proper for me, and indeed I should be reluctant, to burden you here with intimate detail. I should only say that gradually so fine-grained an appreciation of the connections between my childhood experiences, my present personality, and my scientific operations emerged, that one could see and become convinced of even very fine connections between particulars. Thus in retrospect, and comprehensible only at depth level (though I *can* give also surface-plausible explanations), virtually nothing seems accident—beginning with the basic turning away from any community of any kind I had ever known and toward delinquency (in Chicago) and the subsequent turning toward a community of about the socioeconomic level of that of my origin, with a special eye to the ideology and behavior of authority figures vis-à-vis the child, a very special eye to the unanticipated consequences (and hence the basic folly) of their acts, even when well motivated, and a particular sensitivity for and interest in emotional consequences. This is perhaps too general. It would perhaps be more convincingly particular to say that the free-discussion groups (or human relations classes) represented an experimental, point-for-point upending of my own most important experiences in a very Victorian (and otherwise very stormy, stressful) home. The scientific character of the experiment is, I think, unassailable or as nearly so as these things can be. But, at another level of language, what is one to hear but, "Look, if authority figures treat a child as I wished to be treated and was not, what good may not all come of it (and could have come for us) for them all." Even the serendipitous discovery of the tremendous academic gains after "wasting" all this time on discussion only adds with psychodynamic cogency, "And look, at no cost!" The whole also demonstrated another buried conviction of childhood: "Effective knowledge is assimilated only in affection."

One could go on thus piling up detail after detail from *Crestwood Heights*—or, with reference to one's friends, from other studies. But by now conviction will likely have set in—or it will not set in at all.

You will have several legitimate questions. Have my primary observations on myself been correct? I believe so. Am I correct in generalizing to others? I suggest you check in yourself and those to whom you have access *if* they have access to themselves. So what? This is more difficult.

So, I think, we certainly can, and probably should, and perhaps must view our own "scientific" conduct, personal and collective, under the same microscope as we viewed, or aimed to view, our subjects of study. I think that this microscope not only enlarges, but—forgive the mixed image—transforms. Therefore, on this second view, neither are they so simply doing what we thought they were doing, nor are we doing largely, or at all, what, on the first view, we so simply thought. Indeed, in this transforming vision we may see ourselves engaged with them in a common social life and struggle, much like the other poets, artists, seers, and nevertheless associates, speaking perhaps in a different idiom, moved perhaps by a different vision, but purveyors nevertheless of a gospel we should be at greater pains to make clear.

13

Phylogeny and Ontogeny of Applied Sociology

There is a dual social origin of such occupations and preoccupations as those of the applied sociologist.

On the one side lies some development in the impulses of actors to order their action by thought. On the other lies a development in the impulses of some thinkers to test this thought by action.

Let me put it again. When we come upon the human scene as an object of study we find some men preponderantly engaged in and oriented to social action. As these develop and utilize an examined—conscious and criticized—body of beliefs regarding human life, they are applied social theorists. Insofar as their theories are theories of the social, and insofar as these theories are tested by their mutual consistency *and* by the rejoinder of the world to which the theories refer, they are sociological theories, and those proceeding in this way are applied sociologists. Similarly and simultaneously, when we come upon the human scene as an object of study, we find others thinking about the social, striving to render their thought internally consistent, and to test its credibility by the rejoinder of the world to which it refers. Such are sociologists. As they become occupied in furthering or preoccupied by the action consequences of their thought they tend toward the applied sociological.

There is a fundamental difficulty about the definition

which I have noted before, will note again, and pass on. In all other "sciences" that which makes the rejoinder upon which men properly judge the conformity of the theory to the canons of utility is not within the compass of the theory itself. In the social sciences that which rejoins and that which renders judgment upon the rejoinder are alike human, the process is alike social, and the validating act is inside the set of enterprises that is the object of study.

In this sense, at least, the sociologizing is the subject also of the sociology; and neither analytically nor in actuality can the distinctions that hold in other subjects between the knower and the known, the separation between that which consents and that which is consented about (or *to*), the clean conceptual break between thought about action and action upon thought, be at all posited or in any fundamental sense sustained.

On this view sociology is merely a particular form of the very social action that is its subject matter, and social action is merely the active form of the sociology that it is the desire of the sociologist, by comprehension and abstraction, to put before the actors.

Since the sociology—no matter how much or how little applied—is itself a form of action, unlike the other sciences it cannot be freed of the ambiguities or agonies that attend upon action itself because there is nothing that is not itself social action so to free it.

Indeed, since it is a more complex form of action with the added imposition of mandates to more order, more self-consciousness, more asceticism than is commonly the case, it is to be expected as well as discovered, that it must be more agonized, more difficult, and more open to question than the first-order social action that is (was) its first-instance subject matter.

A second fundamental difficulty is that the sociology re-encounters itself in its own subject matter. Any society is acting upon, enacting (in both senses), and acting out a sociology, explicit or implicit. Only a literate society has an explicit sociology. But insofar as it has such a sociology, it is, in whole or in part, the background against which, or the body of principles upon or within which, men are or deem themselves to be acting. Hence the sociology is inside the social action which is itself the subject of study of the sociology. It is, in roughest analogy, as though macrophysics were the description of how relatively large objects act, but it was empirically observable and conceptually evident that such objects act (solely, largely, or significantly) upon principles alleged by the physicist to be physical principles. (Moreover, in the analogy the physicist would be centrally and relevantly, instead of peripherally and incidentally, a physical object.) There would be thus, at the very least, little or no independence between "the physical facts" and "what were said to be the physical facts," and there would have to be a different, attenuated, or altered test for truth. Indeed, so situated, it is anything but clear that the tests for "good" and "true" are in any wise independent, or hence that the obligation to believe the truth even against desire ("though the heavens fall") can be even analytically separated from the determination to establish heaven though what seems to be (first-order) truth suffer. Thus light and fire are not so readily or not at all separable from their matrix in incandescence.

* * *

To pass on after paying a tributary nod to these difficulties, instead of to start from them and to reformulate in the light of what they assert what our whole enterprise is and must be, is not merely to allow them less than their full force, but, probably, to ensure that we shall remain entrapped in countless contradictions and confusions quite additional to those we must encounter, given the paradoxical nature of thought's encounter with life itself.

But pass on we must, I suppose, if only because we cannot arrest thought, action, and talk while other and better foundations are sought and articulated for them.

If we take it for granted—as we must, I think—that everywhere, in all times and places, in every human society, there is an implicit and more or less explicit sociology, then it enters (like the psychology and the theology) into the social-psychological ontogeny of every child that is psychosocialized therein. Indeed, as itself only a refinement of the everyday and common-sense world, it enters into both as a constituent of that world first, and as a refinement upon it later. To put it another way: (a) no matter what else the sociology itself is, it cannot be other than an elaboration upon the common-sense formulation of the everyday social realities as encountered in experience by the child in his earlier *fons et origo* experiences; (b) the elaborated version enters (in part), in the next generation or the next, into the first-encountered forming system that is then the common-sense world, and (c) it enters subsequently into the refinement and reconstitution of that world that is the child's education, formal and informal. (d) This new and revised perceptive system is (will be, in time) the altered system of perceptive possibilities out of which an amended or altered sociology will arise, while (e) the new society that is even then and thus coming into being is the subject matter of a new sociology of which it cannot be predicted just what or how much of the old sociology will hold.

I have made the point so often that the purest sociology is thus (and otherwise), in a radical sense, applied, that I am bound to be asked whether I have left any ground at all for a pure-applied distinction, let alone antithesis.

If we judge, from the viewpoint of effect, how much sociology is pure and how much is applied, or how much a given sociologizing is applied or left pure, we are in the realm of general history and the history of sociology (or, possibly, in the realm of a second-order sociology or sociology of sociology). By "pure" I would mean here that which is left largely to reflect at most upon itself; by "applied" I would mean that which is used to affect action in any way, from the important manner I have outlined to the relatively trivial one of merely affecting its ostensible matter of study (e.g., recreation or "delinquency"). Note that the criterion here is use and not problem origin. Since history is at best only history-up-to-now, anything that could be said would have to run only to "applied up to this point" or "not applied (hence pure) so far." I cannot resist adding that any sociologizing or historicizing of this kind could, and quite likely would, alter its erstwhile matter of description by directing attention within the as-yet-pure to the potentially applicable and hence soon-applied.

If we judge from the viewpoint of intent—of the sociologist, I trust, not his employer, if any—we are, unless we wantonly restrict ourselves to the ostensible, in the mazes of psychological complexity. I say it is wanton to restrict ourselves to the ostensible because it is not here that action can be more than trivially illuminated by intelligence, nor here that the connections, if any, between interests and effects largely lie. I take it for granted that men do not declare their intentions to others ungoverned by some lively sense of social consequences (i.e., on the basis of an implicit sociology, sociography, and calculus of values). So declarations of intent are impure as sociological variables. Next I take it that, for most men, too great a discrepancy between other-declared intent and self-declared intent is a source of substantial strain, and hence that in most cases some substantial qualification is had of self-declared intent, so that, to say the least, the internal perception of intent is clouded or significantly deformed. I have to add that, beyond this, that which basically informs the intent—in a sense, basically *is* the intent—is ordinarily not known to the intender, or at least, is last and least to him. The intents we admit or know of are not mere random samples from real intents, but as it were feints, or movements designed to draw away attention—in discoverable but usually undiscovered ways—from the real line of movement.

Beyond that, any linkage of intent with effect presupposes a not insubstantial knowledge of the social order, i.e., an accurate and reliable sociology and sociography already in being. This is not to say of course that there cannot be such a linkage, but only that whereas say, in physics, what will be foreseen as applied depends on a knowledge of society (i.e., on a sociography and sociology) what is the case in sociology is that it depends on previous sociology and sociography.

The point is, if it is not already clear, that the sociology and the society are either like Mead's mind, self and society, coemergents (and, I would add, coconstituents), or, if we wish to inflate negligible time intervals to study the dynamics, society and sociology may be said to stand in a symmetrical, dialectical relation to each other, with the sociologist as the imperfect creator and creation, mediator and mediated, of the dialectic. In this conjuncture, human intents have generally as much or as little relation to effects as our general rough present knowledge of psychology and sociology would suggest. The real business—or one real business—of applied sociology would be, one might suppose, to permit a diminution in this looseness of fit (that is, in frustration) at least where we can approve, or do not radically disapprove, the ends aimed at. (Where we do, we might be glad for the discrepancy and the resultant frustration as a natural penalty on those whose values we do not share: "frustrate their knavish tricks, on Thee our hopes we fix" as the hymn has it, of the Queen's enemies.)

This brings me to the question of values. For it is patent that if one sees oneself in action in one's sociologizing, one is brought face to face with "the value problem," since action is conceptually inseparable from purpose, and purpose is nothing but the dynamic—"moving," in both senses—integration of a value system or some integral part thereof.

Now there is nothing, so far as I know, in the training of the sociologist, pure or impure, that prepares him to act *in loco parentis hominum*, or, in general, in the role of the moralist. He has, nevertheless, I believe, some peculiarities of role that permit his contribution to the conversation about values to be unique, indispensable, and, even if partial, ponderable.

Failing a better test of moral credibility, we must assess value pronouncements in a variety of ways. We may ask where they come from—assess the quality of the man who speaks for them or the class of men to which he belongs. We may ask what angle he speaks from, or what illumines or informs or is background to what he says. And we may ask in whose behalf he speaks: what is his affiliation, brotherhood, or company; in whose advocacy is he engaged. We may also ask questions "internal" to the position taken: its consistency, grasp, capacity to engage mind's respect and heart's commitment, its conciliability—if we trust that test—with what in some sense we already know. (Morality is, I believe, like mathematics in that it explicates with surprising consequences what in another sense we recognize as what we already know.) We may finally assess or attempt to evaluate foreseen or foreseeable consequences.

The problem of assessing the quality of the man who makes the moral pronouncement—and there is a triple test, of practiced intellectual competence and practiced moral sensitivity and integrity—is too complex to enter upon here. I only draw your attention to the fact that if we credit the capacity of men to make it (as I do) then we have further reason to assert that the sought value system is somehow latent, for men in general, in the existent.

Similarly, I shall not press the claims of sociologists as a class to a practiced high morality, though in virtue of their calling, their role as professionals, and their assimilation of some or all of the higher morality of science I think such claims have some not inconsiderable prima facie credibility.

I should be inclined to put great weight on a number of considerations that bear rather on the later tests, but in doing so I should like to be seen less as asserting claims, let alone claims against other participants, and more as recalling my fellow sociologists and myself to duties that I believe they cannot well escape.

We must remind ourselves that it is the professional duty of the sociologist to deal with—contemplate, enter into, empathically and intellectually, order, report, assess, criticize, and expound upon—the social order. The social order lies within, or encompasses, or is the moral order. (Even religion rests its case upon a bond, the constitutive element, I like to believe, in its etymology, as it certainly is in its nature. The bond derives its binding force from a relation, asymmetrical it is true, but essentially social.) The minimum, the most modest statement that can be made, is that the sociologist's object of study is that which embodies the actualized moral order and, simultaneously, that which is to embody such moral order as is ever to be actualized in the affairs of men. It is not that "value patterns" are somehow a factor in the affairs of men, but that they are a restatement in one language of what may be observed in another. So the sociologist *is* a student of that which is germane to the discussion.

There are, however, many such students. That which is distinctive about the sociologist is that he speaks with peculiar information (or preoccupation) from a peculiar perspective. The "peculiar information" which he has, or ought to have, not so much at his fingertips as in his blood and bones, is his knowledge of (not merely about) the vast variety of cultures (value embodiments) that are the human record now in space, and over the world, through time. Additional to this (in a sense) is his knowledge regarding the mores "that make everything right" collectively and the "rationalizations" that make everything right distributively, and the interplay and interpenetration of these. He is, therefore, a practiced penetrator of those human maneuvers whereby value growth is sold out for value maintenance, the essence abandoned for the accident, and becoming betrayed for being the *ex parte* masked as the judicial, the particular masked as, mistaken for, and masquerading as universal, the parochial misrepresented as the cosmopolitan, the ideological under the cover of the self-evident, the sectarian posing as the ecumenical, the merely uncontested passing as the consensual, the merely imperialist garbing itself as trancendental—all these are not merely the everyday coinage offered him as moral tender, but precisely that which he has to learn to discriminate if he is to discharge his function at all. No matter whose the coinage, and no matter how faint or obscure the image and superscription it bears, he is at least able to see whether the likeness is the likeness of Man and the superscription *in nomine hominum.*

Which brings me to his peculiar perspective.

Professionally detached from such parochialisms, particularisms, and peculiarisms, he has three possible choices: he may function essentially as an alienated man, a creature of and prey to *rassentiment;* he may call into being a new parochialism of his fellows; he may attach himself to the emergent, transcendent fellowship of mankind. The first and second occur and result respectively in lone *hommes du rassentiment* and mutual aid associations of technicians, value free but also free of value, or very nearly so. The third occurs too, though it seems to be a state secret. Clearly, innumerable social scientists, at least by their negative behavior, indicate the laws of their identification and the source of their criticism and protest. In its mildest form this disposition inclines them, wherever they are, to deal with each problem as an example of the next most general category of problems. In a more obvious form, this universalistic thrust is exhibited in refusal to deal with the segmental by itself, to accept without redefinition problems presented from parochial perspectives, by selective lack of interest in advancing limited interests even by indirection, particularly those of the paramount and powerful. Most positively, in what is too easily mistaken for cultural relativism, is the suspended moral judgment revealed whose underpinning and justification is the promotion and pushing forward of the most general ecumenical movement: not the mere compromising and conciliation of present value conflicts among men, but the search for the moral substance of one world in the only material sense in which the world may become one—and not merely one world of value, but, it is to be hoped, on that foundation, an expanding universe of value.

It is essentially this unacknowledged ecumenicism, I believe, that accounts for and in-so-far justifies what I have elsewhere called the advocacy of the generalized underdog. I praise it, less for sentimental reasons than because the prologue to ecumenicism is that all authentic voices be heard, and there is so far as I know no positive correlation between authenticity and privilege. Quite the contrary!

Such a morality cannot be discerned, let alone legislated, overnight. Rather, it lies at the end of a long chain of sociological and nonsociological thoughts and acts that are the matter of present and proximate decisions. The function of the foreseen end is to inspire and color, commend and contain, form and inform policy, strategy, and tactics, professional and personal. Even so, like any distant beacon, it may give a firm sense of direction, but shed faint light over the immediate darkness.

It is probably not good enough, although it is titanically tempting to stop here. All that I have made out is a special claim for the sociologist to be heard, and, implicitly, a principle of value judgment: that that is to be valued which allows enrichment of values, which expands or heightens the possibilities of value.

On such a principle, without one set of beliefs as to how values are, by their nature, related to each other, and without a further set of beliefs as to the methods and processes by which all values or any are enhanced or destroyed in human action, we have no guide except our several intuitions as to what is to be recommended or disrecommended on any given occasion. For intellectuals who, to an unusual extent, take the folklore not as a sufficient guide, but as an object of study or suspicion, the danger is very real that we are left guideless

—which may be the real source of modern man's terror, the real anomie below the seeming order, the sickness only faintly and quaintly pointed to in the Nietzschean assertion that since God is dead all things are possible. (And, be it noted, by the same token, impossible!) "Other-direction," which means the elevation by idolatry of the minutely local and temporal folklore into the unoccupied throne of the dismissed general folklore, is at least a defense against dissolution, although at bottom it amounts to no more than the mutual legitimation of whim. (Its philosophy is, "Well, isn't it all purely personal, after all?") Similarly intelligible, if not intelligent, is the "privatization" that Riesman has noted and commented upon as a general trend. And Shils' final formulation of the societal as, in essence, only the logistical and administrative matrix for a congeries of value-disjunct "primary groups," first recognizes and then legitimates the preference for *ad hoc*, accidental, working solutions over public, general, and systematic formulation.

It is surely a curiosity that sociologists (especially applied sociologists) who have everywhere noted a folklore as integral to society as breathing is to breath, have helped destroy the moral force of it by treating it as a quaint weakness from which one ought to wish to free oneself, whereas on their own showing it is the life in the living, and the problem, if there is any, is everywhere and anywhere to improve on it. Indeed, since it is not only the operative moral sysetm, but in its heart is the justification for the moral system, and, in its heart of hearts, the set of principles by which any moral system is to be justified, one might have thought it an object worthy of sustained and respectful, if not awed, attention; more particularly so since, as has been long since said, the moral order and the social order are as physics and the physical world to each other. (I will not repeat here at length the argument that it is precisely the folklore that the sociologist is tampering with in his purest activities, even as he pretends to be in some sense above or beyond it.)

The problem would rather seem to be, how, from within the folklore, to struggle forward *with* it, altering it without wantonly disrupting it as one goes.

It is, perhaps, credible that a necessary—though not sufficient—condition is the heightening of consciousness with regard to the folklore. Many sociologists are satisfied that this is what they do. Nevertheless, I think there is reason to think that their ministrations may be fatal, benighting rather than enlightening, because they lack any principles for differentiating between liberating and crippling manners of heightening consciousness.

For the heightening of consciousness to be other than maleficial it must itself proceed on principles of order, relevance, and value. As to order, it is patent that much that is knowable cannot be known for what it is until logically, structurally, psychologically, or otherwise vital knowings have been had. At best it is useless, and at worst it is bewildering (to the point perhaps of procuring paralysis in the beneficiary) to enhance awareness, say, of the fine properties of triangles before some general notions of figure and surface (say) have been had. A fortiori, so for matters that matter more. Similarly, for relevance it is not merely no service but a positive disservice to distract attention, affection, and awareness from the more relevant to the less, or, perhaps worse to move at random in the domain of relevance. Nothing short of exquisite unremitting attention to the relation between what is to be made conscious and the legitimate central purpose or essential desirable desires of those in whom it is to be made conscious is a tolerable strategic principle of responsible life enhancement. As for order and relevance, so for value, as I have implied by the words "legitimate" and "desirable" in the last sentence. (You may note, of course, that the whole argument presupposes, warrantedly and justly I believe, that a sufficient working value scheme exists to make possible the definition of meaningful principles by which it can be improved, *and* that these are free of fateful bias, i.e., bias that in the long run leads us into further error or value diminution.)

But the principle of heightening consciousness first (attending of course to order, and thereby defining relevance) of that which is most valuable, requires in and of itself that the value question be always focal, and, moreover, that attention be selectively directed upon those values (or conditions) upon which all other values depend, and hence, in some sense, upon value theory itself.

Perhaps this is little guide. Certainly it is insufficient, but it may be better than what we have, for what we have in effect is an analogue of a patient confronted by and invited to attend to some two to twenty thousand therapists—some interested in his leg, others in his psyche, and others in the fine morphology of his navel—all talking unrelatedly about different aspects of the same object, on different suppositions, from different sciences, and bearing different assumptions of his purposes and theirs, actual and desirable, all the way from an assumed centrality of his desire to survive to an assumed centrality of his desire to explode as brilliantly as possible with the maximum *éclat*. Some patient! Some therapy! Some doctors! Some discipline!

14

The Making and Taking of Problems

I have great respect for the folk wisdom that resides in words, and hence make no apology for seeking my first orientation to my topic from etymology, more particularly if it gives me ground for saying what I wanted to say anyway.

"Ethics," which looks one way (through the Greek ηθikós) to moral, and beyond that to ηθos, custom, looks the other way (through its Sanskirt cognate *svadhā*) to self-will and strength —from *sva,* the self, and *dhā,* to place.

There is almost, definitionally, nothing more to say: an ethic is a morality become, in its settled part, custom; it is self-willed, and the strength that makes possible that strenuous enactment lies in self-location, the appropriate placing of the self. The "placing of the self" is itself an act involving, actively and passively, knowledge, thought, activity—if you will, self-will. But in the beginning is the autolocative act.

But—as, again, the folk wisdom inherent in the dual meaning of "to take a position" indicates—it is not possible for an active agent to take a position without having, indicating, acquiring a dis-position: position and posture presuppose each other. Coordinate with the self-placing act is an explicit or implicit programmatic declaration; intentions are sub-stances to stances; stands imply movements; *status* (sociological word habits to the contrary, notwithstanding) implies *motus.*

Lest I be understood to say that morality becomes custom

and there is an end of it (or, worse, that morality is "merely custom"), or that a stand is merely an instant in a motion, let me clearly establish my belief that these terms are to be dialectically viewed. Going morality does indeed become mere custom, which, under civilized conditions, raises fresh, unforeseen moral questions, which restructure practice and then custom, which in turn raises fresh problems for morality. And a stand is no mere moment in a motion, but a gathering, on the ground of the motion and the vision it thus far permits, of select possibilities into a richer and more coherent set (again, observe the dual meaning!) with a view to reconstruction of the motion thenceforward.

Thus it seems to be, whether we have an eye to personal history or to general history, and whether we talk of the ethics of each of us, or the ethics that some of us share, hold jointly with others, whether because of our coprofessionality or otherwise.

Let me, since I have implicitly broached the subject, deal with the question of the relation between personal and professional ethics. The view seems to be gaining ground, ably assisted by eminent sociologists, that we all play many roles, that these are not and need not be mutually compatible (the only cost being role strain, perhaps, and even that can be lightened by redefinition), that we engage in these roles segmentally, involving only aspects or shells of our persons, and that occupational and professional roles engage only, or principally, the outermost shells of our personalities. I do not believe any of this. I think it is a perversion of the word "professional," upending the directions of high and low, confusing center and periphery. Outermost is in this sense to be read uttermost, and one's profession, one's calling, vocation, *Beruf*—if it calls at all and is therefore a profession—calls out and calls upon all else, organizes, dominates, structures, and gives point to all else. At the principle point of conjunction of the capacities for love and work, wherever topographically located in the imagination's image, it is the capital point, the high point of the gradient of commitment. Disjuncture, then, between professional and personal ethic bespeaks the institution of that alienation from the world, which would imply a poor professional and a poor profession, or alienation from the person, which entails an impoverished professional and an impoverished self.

Nor (though here again sociologists have almost necessarily set forth and furthered such views) may we view the process in the patient or passive mode without paying great penalties for such a conceptualization. When Bernard Barber cites [1] as one criterion of a profession "... a high degree of self-control of behavior through codes of ethics internalized in the process of work socialization ..." I am horrified by the direction of the thought as well as by the barbarity of the language. What is stated is neither a necessary nor a sufficient condition, for the achievement of professionality–indeed, I should think anyone so prepared to "internalize" an ethical code in the process of "work socialization" would be an unlikely professional candidate. The very beginning of the engagement, which is to lead, if anything ever will, to professionalization, is the active sorting over of what is with a view to what may be and had better be. Such code as is there is not to be internalized, but carefully kept external, struggled with, wrestled with, cross-examined upon its meaning and its relation to larger ends that it only feebly points to, and there–outside, not in–reconstructed and made over, or at least begun to be so reconstituted and reformed. A tinker's apprentice may well do what Mr. Barber says; an acolyte to a profession, a future traveling companion, has no business with such business. He is to be called, not programmed.

An ethic, then, marks a position in the present and a posture looking to the future; it is grounded in what is and is borne up by what is to be. It is a net cast about a future from a throw-point in a present. It represents a solution and a resolution, a solving of present problems in the form of a strategy for the future.

[1] *Daedalus,* Fall 1963, p. 672.

Such a strategy, like all grand strategies, has a structure, indeed a double structure. It has a temporal structure with reference to both order and duration. With reference to order it must specify what we ought to do now of what we can do now, and must distinguish what we ought to do later out of what we will be able to do later only if we have done before then what we ought to do now. And so, indefinitely—perhaps in declining specificity, but nevertheless, thus. And as for duration, clearly the structure of such imperatives is like that of the law itself; it consists of passing convenient practices changeable on almost any pressing provocation; statute law, not worth passing unless it endures more than a modicum of days; constitutional law meant to serve through long historical periods and withstand almost any foreseeable storm and strain; and finally legal principles that may be thought, at least for all practical purposes, eternal, i.e., not violable by any species of society that could be said to have historic link and cultural continuity with anything we would importantly call ours.

I hope no one envisions that I shall pronounce such principles or produce such a document here. The development of even a first draft requires at least the kind and quantity of labor committed to the Constitutional Convention, and entails the common labor of men of equal caliber collaborating, I should think, for at least an equal length of time. But the point at which an ethical construction begins is with the commitment to search it out and to continue so to do—perhaps the ethical first or principal principle. The most I can hope to do today is to begin to lay a groundwork for the work that is to be done. Even that is hard to do because before a beginning can be made a vast and laboriously erected structure of errors and self-deceits as to who we are and what we are doing—extending to almost all going definitions—and why, needs to be cleared up, cleared out, and cleared away, decisively and, one might hope, forever. This by itself bespeaks a book, and this is not the time or place for it. But let me begin. And let me begin where we are.

I suppose I must begin with what we *say* we are. We say we are social scientific students of social problems. I don't know quite what we mean by "social scientific" (or indeed whether the two terms are reconcilable) but by "students" we mean to put about, and perhaps be taken in by, the notion that, with regard to our subject, we look at what is to be looked at and see what is to be seen, something perhaps like a student of art, a student of history, a student of witchcraft, or of wines. What is the anticipated outcome? Connoisseurship (or some derivative of *connaître*) is what comes to mind.

And what, pray, are social problems? Social problems are, so it is said: ". . . breakdowns or deviations in social behavior, involving a considerable number of people, which are of serious concern to many members of the society in which the aberrations occur." [2]

Really?

Then the population problem of India—as long as nearly everybody is doing the same thing, and as long as not very many in Indian society are concerned (or not seriously so)—is no social problem and hence is not matter for a professional student of Indian social problems. But suppose that student does not know our definition and studies, persists, publishes, and does not perish. And suppose after a while, and as a consequence, a great number of people are seriously concerned and that a majority have reduced their fecundity, and that more and more are concerning and reducing every day. Only now—when victory is in sight—do we have a social problem, and only at this point should we begin its study!

By this token, German antisemitism and mass Jew and Gypsy burning never do become social problems. At first the problem does not qualify since, in the behavior that might be complained of, not "a considerable number of people are involved"—indeed only a small corps of specialists. And by the time enough are involved, directly or in sympathy, it does not qualify because not "many members of the society in which

[2] I have not chosen a definition carelessly or at random, but have drawn of that *fons fontis et origo originis*, Merton and Nisbet, *Contemporary Social Problems*, p. 11.

the aberrations occur" regard it as a matter of serious concern. Indeed, those "concerned" would soon be the "deviant" (by any of the standard definitions) and, if the butchers did not get them first, of enough concern to the others to constitute the social problem now worthy of study by the German sociologist!

Of course that is not what we meant, but it serves nicely, since it is typical, to pose the problem of why we pose so, and what it is that we are hiding.

We pose so for reasons of professional politics and personal psychology. Professionally it would be wise, prudent, we seem to think, to appear to *take* our problems rather than *make* our problems, to accept as constitutive of our "intake" what is held to be "deviant," in a way that concerns enough people in that society enough to give us primary protection. Thus Christians may be problematic in pre-Constantine Rome and non-Christians soon after. And so—up to a certain point—we do take the unwed mother rather than the unwed father, the delinquent boy or gang rather than the delinquishing society. And so saving—or sinking—ourselves politically, we save—or sink—ourselves psychologically. For so situate, at least formally, we need never confront alone or together our humanity, our tenderness, our concern, our decency, our agency or affect, our desire to intervene in history, and the actuality of that intervention, the grounds therefor, the motives thereof, the regulating principles on which we are in fact proceeding—all that redeems, justifies, and animates our efforts. Because we carry no vestments, we are not priests; since we wear no wigs, we are not judges; given that we carry no scepters, we are clearly not men of power; and since we have laid aside alike our likings and our prejudices, we are not "*as* social scientists" (as they say) agonists in the battle, "either pro or anti."

What palpable nonsense. If we say it, it is bad. If we believe it, it is worse. If others really believed it they might wish not to limit their bullets to verbal ones.

We have been taken in just enough by our own propaganda, I think, that the table of contents of almost any "social problems" text shows a notable bias in the predictable direction. The text I have momentarily at hand [3] lists, under "Deviant Behavior" only, crime, juvenile delinquency, mental disorders, drug addiction, suicide, and prostitution; and under "Social Disorganization" only population crisis, race and ethnic relations, family, work, military, community and traffic disorganization, and disaster. The presence of the military chapter is unusual and somewhat happenstantial, but otherwise this is pretty well the mix as usual, representing our studies of categories of persons sufficiently powerless to offer small resistance to violation by inquiry. (Even the charge is old, I guess.) On the social disorganization side also we have a more or less customary collection of relatively unresistant units that could be disorganized and could be inquired into. Note no business disorganization, religious disorganization, intellectual anomie, political breakdown, or disorganization, debasement, and degradation of the most eminent candidate: post-primary education.

Safe. Safe. Safe.

And yet this is not what we do at all. Even in this text so disguised, and a fortiori in the better monographs and articles, an operation goes on under cover of the approved definition (and only partly strait jacketed by it) that bears in a different direction and operates to an opposite effect. We do, in effect, study strikes and conclude to connections with the whole structure of business ostensibly controlled not by the strikers but by the managers; we do study delinquents and implicate the delinquescent; we do study prison unrest and portray the jailers, justly, as just accomplices.

Whether or not this is what we intend—and I faithfully, fully, and firmly believe we do—we appear, in effect, as attorneys for the defense. In principle, by taking and taking on the problem, we cause the behavior complained of ("deviant" is a moral as well as relational judgment) to appear in a natural

[3] *Ibid.*

light. And, be it noted, selectively so: Whatever is not in our "natural" spotlight is presumed to be in the area of responsible moral judgment, just matter for commendation or censure, praise, or blame. Thus, if we establish that children lie because they are uncontrollably terrified of terrifying parents, and if we stop there, palpably parents had better change or be made to change. And if we later establish that parents act terrifyingly because of economic insecurity, and stop there, likely the remedy for children's lying will be seen to lie in the taxable pockets of the economic elite. And so on.

Nor is that all. Since everything is, even proximately, connected with many things, we choose not merely how *far* we trace out the line of causation (leaving responsibility where we arbitrarily rest) but in which of countless different directions to do so. Thus while no one ought to question the justification—provided the analysis is valid as far as it goes—for our passing the buck thus far, the essentially arbitrary stopping points insure, as far as I can see, that one injustice (if only of blame ascription) is remedied, only to bring another into existence. And, may I add, we cannot go on indefinitely, partly because of practical considerations (the ramifying chains are endless) and partly because of moral ones (carried to totality, the procedure dissolves the moral world and the world of responsible persons-in-society altogether, and brings a new society into being). Perhaps the last statement is a little misleading because what it hypothesizes is impossible: by and large, responsibility, like energy, can be passed around but not made to disappear. (The trick of passing all causal force or responsibility attribution to "the social structure" is, of course, intellectually so much nonsense, though politically consequential. Taken generally, "the social structure" is equally implicated as effect with those behaviors which we are trying to explain by treating it as a cause; i.e., "the" social structure is a structure or outbuilding of social behavior.)

How we function, I think, is not merely as attorneys for the defense, but as attorneys for the defense of the relatively socially indigent. As far as we go, seems mostly to me to be in the direction of passing responsibility from those less able to bear it (or those less culpable, if culpability is conditioned by means at hand) to those better able so to do or more rewarded otherwise and thus more credibly taxable. But let it not be disguised that we are acting as publicans (and perhaps also, sinners). For, for want of a theory of these things, cognitive and evaluative, we distribute this negative largesse in a way that is not quite random but certainly not calculated, let alone judicious. There is a great deal to be said for "disjointed incrementalism" [4] where nothing better can be had (or had except at undue cost) but there is very little to be said for a casual disjuncture—especially among those, like ourselves, accustomed to undue insistence on the organic unity of culture or society or both.

If I am right so far, we do indeed "take" our problems rather than make them, but in a fashion we refashion or remake them, so that the outcome is not the expected consequence of naïve acceptance.

But while what we do does show the desire to do good—despite all denial—I do not think it is good, or not nearly good enough. Given what it is that we *are* doing, it is, I think, ill done. For we proceed—individually, let alone collectively—on no known plan, with no canons of relevance or criteria of effect, under no clear vision, in no defined history had and to be enacted, and with, as far as I can descry, no God-given or naturally emergent convergence of counsel.

Dismiss the nonsense embodied in the definition of a social problem. Acts committed by persons as few as our national presidents, of concern at first to almost no one, not the least bit un-American or deviant or evidently a breakdown, might, to a sociologist in the know, be not only a social problem but one worthy of great and urgent study.

But if you dismiss this view, as I do, and think *we* must, you are left with an awful responsibility: you become a

[4] Lindblom and Braybrook's happy phrase.

social critic, and moreover, to the degree that you thus make instead of take your problems, an unwelcome one, and one, therefore, open to unfriendly countercriticism or worse. So a sizable increase in prudence is well advised.

What is prudentially recommended is, moreover, morally mandated if we are to be other than captious or perhaps carping. For criticism that is anywise a professional performance is not only taken from a credible critical position, but conforms to canons that signify in effect a strategy insight. That implies that we know in acceptable fullness not only where we want to go—or want the society to go—but how we want it to get there, and how the criticism is to function in the getting of it there. Moreover, since we pride ourselves in being in some sense scientists, that we do in fact know something significant and reliable about the effects of our successive interventions.

All this brings me to a general aside, before I go on. An adequate ethic would specify not only what we ought to do but what we ought to know, and, even here, in what order. In a moderately well-established field such as medicine, obviously it is negligent (i.e., morally reprehensible as well as technically inept) to prescribe without knowledge of certain kinds, and in certain cases such lack of knowledge, far from functioning as an excuse, would establish the fact of criminality, legally, and the basis for professional penalties, socially, and justified serious adversion, morally.

Let me tell you what else I think we do, and do ill and unguided by more than vague hunches and social suppositions that—in others—we would label naïve.

In a society that, on our own showing, may be said to be a society in virtue of substantial unity of important beliefs and schemes of "evaluation," we intervene increasingly and quite decisively to alter beliefs, among them the core of crucial general beliefs and attitudes. On our own showing also, we must suppose that sufficient such shakes to the belief-system and jabs and jolts to the mores must, at the very least, carry with them the risk of that social sickness that we have ourselves designated as anomie. More particularly, we would expect such outcomes to ensue if we could create a Tower of Babel effect: everyone talking at once, in terms of a great variety of mutually incompatible schemes and models, about "problems" selected and attended to in no particular order or sequence, and then dropped or brushed into the corner on no rational dictation, as we are brushed by the waves of intellectual fashion or battered by considerations of extraprofessional funding. But this—like a collection of mad doctors—is what indeed we do do.[5]

What is worse, perhaps, such "intelligence" as we do secure—and, it should be so viewed as potential advantage-creating information for those who have it over those who do not—is, partly by inadvertence and partly by an inbuilt characteristic of the system, distributed in such ways as to further power disparities and diminish resistance possibilities in the already relatively powerless. Thus employers learn of projective tests and other armor-piercing paraphernalia, before employees do, partly because we do not take pains to the contrary, and partly since our publishing practices require time and literacy of a sort that employers can hire while, generally, their labor pool cannot.

I could go on drawing up a bill of particulars covering those things small and great that I believe we do and ought not to do, and do not do but ought to. But that—to draw an exhaustive indictment—is not my purpose here, nor is it within the compass of brief possibility anyway.

What, given these views, do I believe we ought to do? [6]

We should, I think, to begin with, gather out a company of

[5] I hope few will be able to kid themselves that society is protected well enough anyway, and that the babble is safe because the noise all cancels out. Both are, I think, unlikely social effects.

[6] I neglect altogether here—though I do not think trivial—such questions as have been widely dealt with: problems of whether we may or may not steal our students' work (for example) or may or may not rend the fabric of faith by lying to research subjects in reference to what we do clearly know ourselves to be doing.

those who believe at least that there is a prima facie warrant for concern, who believe we may do something, and who are willing to begin.

We might, next, actively, rapidly, but not superficially, explore for a common consent in those large principles that have seemed to many to be the meeting ground for all humane and reasonable men, and for others to have the nature and status of "natural law." We may thus be committing ourselves to an endless debate, but I believe even this, by its direct and indirect producings, justifies itself of its costs.

We should next, I think, establish more nearly where we are by a careful and critical examination and evaluation of what we have been doing and are doing. If we have one eye to theory—and I do not doubt that we shall—we should have the other and closer eye to society. What have we, even at first blush, done with, to, or for society? What society? What things have we not done that we ought to have done, and what things done that we ought not to have done, and what health is there in us?

We should, then, with utmost rapidity build up that almost utterly neglected body of knowledge without which it is, in my opinion, not possible to operate responsibly at all: a knowledge of the effects—first proximate, then more remote (in time and social space)—of our own actions and inactions.

We should, next, bring into the open, elaborate, discuss, debate, re-form, and reformulate those covert (and often vague) utopias, partial or total—or those "better states of affairs," general or particular—that all of us carry around in our hearts and heads, and that justify—and, I think, motivate—a great deal of the effort we expend anyway. Such discussion as is here suggested would lead back into and render vivid those more general principles spoken of earlier. It might also begin to give the general principles enough particularity to prepare the ground for a collision with actual and existent states-of-affairs-to-be-improved-or-made-over.

As we begin to bring these beginnings together we would

initiate, I should think, an appropriate endless dialectic in which the claims and cogencies of long and short perspectives, undying general principle and proximate practical proposal, present locations, desired future states and transition possibilities (in all their actual interpenetration), and the respective claims of knowing, doing, acting, and reflecting, could be brought into never-ending collision and cohabitation. We would then, I think, have the beginning of a profession.

You may ask, at the last, about "sanctions" (a good sociological term): rewards and penalties. Naïvely, perhaps, I do not think any are required or will be . If a profession related to society in moral and intellectual responsibility should come into being, and if an expanding body of knowledge to make that responsibility real and to reinforce and particularize and expand it should arise, I believe men will know us for what we are, and we shall not lack for the rewards we should properly wish, nor need sanctions to protect and defend us from those who do otherwise. In any case, if I have understood men aright, and the motives of professionals when they are not prey to fashionable deceits, the rewards and penalties are intrinsic to the practices, and in the power of no man to bestow or withhold, to offer or refuse.

Or so at this moment of our history and this stage of my life, with such light as I have, it seems to me.

III

Society in Psychodynamic Perspective

15

The Shaping of Human Nature

We are faced, almost the world over, with a sorry spectacle of massed hostility and hate. Group is set against group, man is set against man, and man is set against himself. This is a problem upon whose solution may well turn the survival of mankind.

Man is not born human, he becomes human in society. All his distinctively human characteristics—the gift of speech, the ability to reason, self-respect, self-control, his ability to put himself in the place of others, to sympathize, to love or hate in any human sense—all these and more are mediated to him by the society into which he is born, and they cannot be had without it. The supporting evidence for such a point of view comes not only from the instances of feral children—children not raised in a human society—and from the instances of children highly isolated in their upbringing, but, more weightily, from careful observation of the process of growing up in a number of societies. In short, in the view of the social psychologist, the little biological organism, the little mass of reactive protoplasm, the little animal that is only potentially human gets his human nature in and from the society into which he is born.

Out of the "buzzing, blooming confusion" that is the infant's world there emerges in the process of growing up in a human society, a more or less definitely structured and ordered view of the physical world, of the social world, and, most important, of that most marvelous world that is the person's self.

At the very beginning, the intimate family begins to pick out of the mass of his random activities those that have significance for them. By their responses to those so picked out, they either stamp those activities in or stamp them out (or permit them to suffer extinction by default). Out of the vague, random, and initially aimless host of syllables and noises that the infant provides, the parents pick out those that have some reasonable similarity—at least to them, if not to the family friends—to the first terms that the child will learn in that culture. (In ours, evidently, any vowel or grunt connected with "M" will do as a first step toward "Mother.")

By behavior that is essentially similar; by behavior that "defines the situation" for the child; by the response to a smile; by an activity such as suckling connected with one kind of cry and not with another; by providing the child with a stable, systematic set of responses to his unordered activities, he learns, largely by implication, the "meaning" of these activities. Without such a system of responses they will remain essentially meaningless, which is to say, subhuman. It is particularly to be noted that the meaning not only of *his* activities, but also of words like "Mother," "Father," "Brother" in a sense that is not given in mere animal experience, emerge together. That Mummy ceases to be merely a pattern of light, a pleasant smell, and a warm feeling, depends on her coming into communication with the child as a *person.*

In the course of time, and with the biology of the matter providing the necessary, but not the sufficient conditions, the child comes to the discovery of other persons as persons, and with himself as a person also. He comes first to these discoveries (when he is biologically and socially ready for them) essentially by way of the play activities that characterize every culture. In the course of his play, and doing at first nothing more than re-creating his previous experience with his family, he begins to try out various of the ordered systems of activity

—the roles—of those immediately around him. Anyone who has seen a small child playing with a doll, or a favorite rabbit, or a bear, must have been quite struck with the essential resemblance of his play to the normal course of interaction between members of the family—at least as he sees them. A child from a family much given to nagging, to violence, or to moralizing about "naughtiness" will tend to put an equal emphasis on these activities into its play.

What is important about this play, from the viewpoint of our discussion, is not, however, the content that is involved, but the form or essential nature of the process. It is in this process, and only in this process, that the child, by taking in his imagination the role of others—generally, the members of his immediate family—gets a picture of how he looks, what he "means" to others. By taking his mother's attitude in imagination to his doll or to himself, he not only enters into and begins to "understand" his mother, but, in the process, gets a notion of what he, himself, is. For the first time, in any intelligible sense, he has a "self"—or, rather, since the definitions that he gets from various members of the family may be quite conflicting, he has a number of selves—partly actual, and partly potential.

For quite some time there tends to be merely an increase in the number of such selves that the child has, rather than any evident organization among them. He may think of himself at one moment as a "baby," at the next moment as "Mummy's little man," and, at the next, as a bold and dauntless knight, fireman, cowboy, or pirate chief, if the society provides models of these for him to pattern himself upon. Much of the instability of childish conduct probably depends on this instability or lability of his notion of himself, rather than on many of the more esoteric grounds upon which it has been commonly supposed to rest.

In the normal course of events, however, since only some of these roles with their corresponding self-definitions are held up to the child with any constancy, and others of them are either ignored or more or less radically discounted and disvalued, the child tends to emerge with a relatively small bundle of roles and selves—or self-conceptions—among which he tends to wander rather loosely according to the exigencies of time, company, and place. He is not so likely now, perhaps, to think of and define himself as a rabbit one moment, and "the boss of the whole world" the next. But he is still quite likely to think of himself as a "tough guy" at one instant —and act accordingly—and to feel that he is a poor, defenseless little creature much in need of mothering when the consequences of being a tough guy are visited upon him.

It is quite conceivable—and indeed it sometimes happens—that an arrest of development should take place at this stage. We all know people who have nothing more than a series of selves, none of which appears any more important and dear to them than any other. We even know people arrested in the previous stage, where they still depend for their sense of self on whatever company they happen immediately to have. They have what Cooley has called "looking-glass selves," i.e., selves which are purely and simply a function of whatever image of them is held up to them by their companions.

But again, in the normal course of events, and as the child is caught up and implicated in the *organized* activities of his society, the various selves that he has had in imagination and actualized in conduct come under the necessity of being ordered and organized.

It is only in virtue of this achievement that he can participate in organized activities with others, is rendered independent of the passing, local and temporary judgment of others, becomes in some sense autonomous, and is, in the only intelligible meaning of the term, a "free" and hence a moral agent.

For the organization that is achieved is not limited to each of the *separate* organized activies of the society into which he is born—activities in connection with the economy, the government, or the manipulation or placation of the spirit world. To the degree that these are themselves interrelated, that is to say, organized parts of his society, the "generalized other" which it is possible and necessary for him to take, and which he does take (as he becomes implicated in the total organized activity), is ever more and more general. In a society with a written history, like our own, Aristotle may be his companion together with Dale Carnegie and St. Francis—or St. Marx—may be "nearer to him than breathing, closer than hands or feet."

It should not be necessary to add, I suppose, that it is only this capacity in socialized man to act in a social relationship with himself—to talk to himself, to take an attitude to himself, to "stimulate" himself just as he would another person—that permits him to *think* at all or to bring his own conduct under control. Out of the welter of stimuli, external and internal, that beset him from moment to moment, out of the disordered but constantly welling impulses that are his minute-to-minute experience, he must select those objects to which he will pay attention: those that are to be *permitted* to be stimuli for him, and those impulses that are compatible with his pattern of activity and intent. Man has been referred to as a political animal. He has been spoken of as a reasoning animal, as a playing animal, and as a making or manufacturing animal. He is all those things. But, centrally and a fortiori, he is a career-making animal—the only animal that spins forward in imagination and then follows in conduct a lifeline that he builds as he goes. Here is no simple "chain of reflexes" or stimulus-response scheme, but a caterpillar-tread-like laying down of the road as one goes, a virtual creation of the stimuli to which one will be responsive—the most important stimuli being those that one gives to oneself.

If what has been said so far is true—or a reasonable facsimile of the world of events—then it is at once apparent that without a clearly defined, well-organized self, compatible in all its aspects, conduct cannot be coherent, orderly or self-satisfying. Lack of clarity will render issues fuzzy and decision bumbling, lack of organization will render thinking disjointed and action uncertain or inept, and lack of compatibility will render the inner life conflictful, and the outer self-defeating and frustrating. And self-frustration leads to the hate of oneself, the hate of others, or both.

The second question to be answered is: how is it that highly individual lines of action can be so concerted or coordinated that *social* or corporate action is possible at all?

Such joint action is, in the run of cases, possible only because the individuals concerned are not so totally unique and individual as has been sometimes supposed. Convergence of individual lines of action may sometimes occur by chance, or on the basis of a common biological makeup. Two cricket fans will probably dodge a flying ball (if they cannot catch it) by simple reflex action, much more simply than they would if they sat down, analyzed the situation, and came to the agreement, "You duck right and I'll duck left." But ordinarily a common animal nature would provide but ill for concerted action as between human beings.

Cooperation—antagonistic or other—between human beings is ordinarily possible only on the basis of a shared world of common meanings. To behave "properly" in a professor-student relationship there must be between professor and student a common understanding of what a professor is—what he is and is not expected to do; and what a student is—what he is and what he is not expected to do; and what is to be the relation between them. This understanding runs from gross details, like the spatial distribution of the two in reference to a platform, through less gross matters like the respective amounts of material goods that each is entitled to possess himself of, right down to the very finest of refinements in respect to the kind of deference behavior that each is expected to show—or not show—to the other. Only if all these understandings are shared pretty well by all participants can the organized system of activities we call a university go on.

These understandings, these common definitions of situations, these systems of reciprocal rights and obligations, these shared meanings, these mutual expectations are what constitute an aggregate of human animals into a society—or community—and what make its individuals *members* of that society. That such common understandings and definitions come about neither by chance alone, nor because of anything that can be said about the biological nature of man alone, is almost too trite to state. The system of understandings is communicated to the infant in the way I have already described, and hence mind, self, and society are what the philosophers call *coemergents*—they emerge together—in the process that may be called the socialization of the child.

It must be clear, too, that the amount of interpersonal harmony, of peace, order and good government in any society is a function of the identity of understanding, on the part of all the people who may be implicated in any situation. It will be a source of conflict, and it often is, if the professor's view of what is a student, and the student's view of what is a student, are, in any important respects, dissimilar. It will be even more productive of conflict if the administration's view, and the student's view, and the professor's view of what is a professor, bear nothing but a fleeting and tentative resemblance.

It appears, therefore, that if the individual is not constantly to frustrate himself, to trip, as it were, constantly over his own psychological feet, he must be possessed of a self that is clearly defined, well-organized and self-compatible; and if he is not to be constantly frustrated by and frustrating to the other persons with whom he is in interaction, both he and they must share broadly a common system of understandings and expectations and definitions.

Unfortunately, however, in view of the very nature of our society, it is inordinately difficult to achieve either, let alone both, of these related conditions.

16

Society, Social Pathology, and Mental Ills

A friend of mine, a Judge of the Superior Court, a man of superior judgment and sensitivity, has noted a curious set of facts about the cases that come before him for judgment. Year in year out, 90 per cent of the cases represent crimes against the person, crimes of violence, and moreover a limited selection from among possible crimes of violence—if I may use the word, a highly stylized, or perhaps ritualized performance. And as for the perpetrators of these so-called "antisocial" acts, some 90 per cent of them come from a small area, a few blocks each way, perhaps a quarter square mile of city in all.

As he sits on his bench year by year—as one kind of population goes into the area, yields up its quota of "criminals," and goes out, only to be succeeded by another—as he watches one crop of babies grow into youth, turn out their percentage of defendants, and go on—as he keeps his court for the sake of justice, he begins to wonder. He begins to wonder in particular what the word "guilty" in this context means. He is a good lawyer. He would not abandon so vital a concept lightly. He—or a jury—must make some such determination. How?

He might not go so far in his conclusions as the Shah of Persia was alleged to have done when he accompanied King Edward to the races at Ascot. The King noticed his companion gazing at the gaily dressed women instead of the horses, then in a breathless heat upon the track. "Are you not interested in the race?" asked His Majesty. "Well," said the Shah, "in Persia everybody knows that one horse can run faster than another—and who cares which one?" So, with my judicial friend's criminals and delinquents, the first point at interest is that the neighborhood in question will—come good times or bad, this population or that—turn out its quota for his court—and which particular child or adult becomes his district's delegate to the court, his society's sacrificial lamb, is of quite subordinate concern. If twelve virgins are to be sacrificed annually to the dragon, I should initially be more interested in why we have dragons and why they need sacrifices than in the selection system that determines which are to be any particular year's twelve virgins.

As soon as some such facts as I have alleged are borne in upon reasonable and sympathetic and well-meaning people, as soon as the explanation of the criminal as the wholly willing author of his own fate has to be abandoned, a second line of defense is hastily thrown up. In form the defense line is a concession; in effect it is an evasion, an evasion that further confuses the issues.

The line of defense is to take the view, with seeming generosity, that there are situations in the society—sites or circumstances—that are just so tough that they must be taken into account in mitigation of whatever sentence is handed down—following upon, nevertheless, an adjudication of guilt. This *is* progress of a sort; a mitigation of barbarism, but hardly more.

Four major evasions are implicit in the position taken. In the first place, of course, if there is justification at all in the view that some sites or circumstances create different pressures to commit crime, the proper conclusion goes to the question of guilt, and not to the problem of mitigated penalties. It hardly makes sense to talk of personal guilt where the system turns out its breakdown products with statistical steadiness and seeming inevitability. The second evasion is that if this is the situation it follows immediately that we cannot hold up our heads to judge anyone in the name of justice so long as persons by no choice of their own (children, perhaps, particularly) are thrust into situations that we do not remedy even though we know they are bound to bring the victims into what we judicially determine to be the category of the guilty. The third evasion is the refusal to see the connection between the sites and circumstances in question, and the needs and desires of the large, supposedly saner or more respectable society that brings them into being and sustains them. The fourth evasion is a similar determination to ignore the connection between acts socially necessitated and acts socially (or, at least, legally) disapproved. Let me touch briefly on these points, one by one.

I do not think any amount of semantic juggling will allow us to separate the two determinations that are bound up with the single word "guilty." It is clearly not a mere objective judgment that an act did in fact (probably) occur—though, of course, it is that. If it were not something more also, however, we should not say "not guilty by reason of insanity" when the act occurred but what is called *mens rea* was presumably absent. That "something more also" is a moral judgment, a judgment as to culpability. But the notion of an act's being caused by causes external to the person—more specifically that the person had no power to avoid their impact and no part in their provenance—and the notion of culpability, simply will not lie down together. Our very idea of culpability is inseparable from the idea of choice: where the one is not, the other cannot be.

Second, it seems clear that where a set of circumstances has forced someone into evil or wrongdoing—or cajoled or seduced him beyond reasonable capacity to resist—judicial recourse should lie against those circumstances (or the persons who brought them into being) rather than against the victim of them. We do not prosecute the minor of whom someone has had carnal knowledge (even if consent was obtained by fraud or force or favor), but we bring our penal machinery to bear on the one who had knowledge of her. Or, if the postman breaks his leg on an object left carelessly in my driveway, the charge lies against me, not him, and the complaint is his, not mine. But where, as in my initial illustration, a situation is allowed to perpetuate itself in which, with certainty, every *n*th child is brought to fall foul of the law, the plaint lies against the child rather than those who maintain the stumbling block. It is a crime, I suppose, to bring up and maintain a youngster in a brothel or beer parlor—where there is no demonstrative, or even putative evidence that he will come to any harm—but it is no reproach to maintain for him, to bring him up in, and maintain (indeed restrain) him in a slum (which is just as sure as a slot machine to throw out its regular jackpot in the form of sentenced offenders). It is curious! No matter whether child or adult, the form of the procedure is identical: the society punishes those—perhaps always those and only those—whom it has previously offended. Their punishment is, in effect, the cause of their punishment. It is of God that it is said "Whom He loveth, He chastiseth, He loveth to chastise." I shall want to come back to this formula later; let us leave it here for now.

I now want to drive home the variety of vested interests that the nominally noncriminal segment of the society has in the criminal segment of it. There is in reality a triple investment: an investment in what might be called the criminogenic circumstances, an investment in the criminal activity, and an investment, a superinvestment, in the retributive process—extending the formula I used earlier from our punishment of those we have previously wronged, into a punishment of those who have served us well and been wronged into the bargain.

At a most superficial level, it is obvious that part of the respectable society has a direct economic interest in the slum and all that preserves it. The image you should have is not that of a few landlords, individuals accidentally or incidentally happening to own a slum tenement. The landlords are not usually lone individuals owning petty properties, but great institutions (banks, churches, and the like) owning great gobs of such land and dwellings, owning them because they are so profitable, owning them because, more than any other available and equally sure investment, they milk the most out of their tenant-victims per square inch or foot of soil brought into exploitation. They own the machine that grinds the faces of the poor because no other faces yield so much dividend per inch of derma. But all this is most respectable, anyway, widely acknowledged, and regarded as falling within the reasonable ethics of business discretion and ingenuity in investment. (In one of the several slum studies I did *on behalf* of a university that was worried about the places of prostitution, and worse, that the slum had brought to its door, my partner and I found after a great deal of labor that the same university, through its business office, owned a great deal of the property in question and, by restrictive covenants made with its neighbors against Negroes, had driven the properties into the still more profitable uses of prostitutes and paid perverts to prey upon their pupils.) But, as I say, all this is respectable.

I do not deny that slum dwellers also have investments in the slum. But they, and the landlords of whom I just spoke so highly, are the minor beneficiaries. The major beneficiaries are you and me, all of us, not seemingly at benefit: the whole overworld as against this underworld.

For whatever else our society may be, it is a competitive society. A competitive society is not—cannot be—a society that just awards prizes to everyone; it must, of its very nature, award prizes to some and not to others, and to work at all its nonawards must be dis-prizes, badges of failure, tokens of disgrace, markings little short of the clarity of the Stars of David foisted as stigmata on the Jews of Germany. A competitive society is of necessity a stigmatic one. And everyone who has an investment in a prize, anyone who has any commitment to the award system, anyone who has even a dream of success or hope of glory is committed to the retention of an adequate stigmatization system, failing which the value of his prize would disappear altogether, as would the value of his money if someone gave everyone all he wanted. Scarcity is the key to it: of money, goods, honor, the tokens of respectability—all things held to be good. (Just think of what would happen if diamonds became plentiful! They would cease to have any value only because they were many.) A competitive society is not then one in which one must merely hold one's place, but one in which one must hold one's place against some competitors. If there is no place to hold thus, one is *by definition* at the bottom and, in a profound sense, outside the society. It is no accident that links, in the folk-saying, the two terms "down" and "out." To this formula too I must return later.

In any case, there is thus not only a primary psychological investment in the existence of slums (and like conditions) by the successful, but there is a supervenient interest in keeping such purlieu populated. For if it is true that prizes must be rare in order to be valuable, it follows that most people not only must not have them, but must be properly labeled and, barring heroic effort, kept in their proper station. So we must have a bursting slum, burstingness being itself one of the stylized badges of shame.

Again, it is essential to the proper enjoyment of one's prerogatives that the disadvantaged be psychologically present but physically absent. Thus every proper plan for city—or a corporation or church hierarchy—must provide for the proper segregation of those who are to be disadvantaged in it. (Segregation here means generally not merely separation, but a one-way right to trespass: I may visit his territory, but he may not usually visit mine—as any study of a red-light district and a "better residential area" will show.) Indeed, the right to exclude is itself one of the highest prizes, and for many members it is the principal reward in a club or similar organization: some property rights amount to little more than the right to prevent trespass, that is, access to the unenobled. This formula too will bear another look.

It has been a frequent observation, of which much is now

made, that within any such large aggregate of unfortunates as we have been discussing, an elite of unfortunates—a small cadre of specialists in misery, the so-called hard core or multi-problem families—have achieved a concentration of bad luck for themselves: usually physical illness, plus mental illness, plus someone in prison, plus school troubles, plus sex troubles, plus economic dependency, plus overnumerous dependents, and so on.

This is partly caused, I am sure, by one trouble's "naturally" bringing on another, but it should be noted that in this case "naturally" means by the sheer operation of the social system, or, as it might seem, by neglect.

But it is not at all by neglect that such concentration of pains and penalties is a social law under conditions of competition. This is shown by the virtual identity of the mathematical distribution of the miseries with the pattern of distribution of rewards—and, for that matter, the distribution of charitable receipts intended to alleviate the misery. The curve of concentration of misery is the same shape as the curve of distribution of incomes—or, to be exact, the portion of the curve following the median incomes. It is what is called a J-shaped curve in which the first few items represent the bulk of the income in a very few hands (and the same with the misery); it takes a relatively immense number more to represent the next chunk of income, and so on. Note that I am *not* saying that misery is distributed according to deficiency of income: on top of that curve, which would yield millions of people moderately and about equally miserable, is imposed a further factor of misery concentration which allocates misery—like a reverse income—differentially among the miserable.

This distribution is, as I have indicated, the same distribution as one finds in any part of the award system: military medals, honorary degrees, number of papers published in any decade in reputable learned journals—and, as I observed before, gifts received by any major charity. I am not indicting the system, I am only trying to establish that it *is* systematic and consistent, also that it is a dual system of concentrated awards and concentrated penalties: a perfect (or nearly perfect) embodiment of the biblical saying that "To him that hath shall be given, while from him that hath not shall be taken away even that which he hath." And note that this applies not only to material goods but primarily to spiritual or nonmaterial goods: access to knowledge, music, laughter, flowers, truth, beauty, and the example of goodness. It follows the commandment: feed the fat, maim the halt, hold up the strong, blind the short-sighted, comfort the comfortable, and afflict the weak.

I must beg you not to shudder: this *is* our system and we cannot have a competitive system, with its emphasis on status and similar ethereal goods, without it. Besides, we may comfort ourselves that we have set up a countersystem of taxes and social services to deal with the worst of its excesses. I shall hope to do justice to that later.

The point I have just made is that the supersociety has a major investment in the subsociety's site and circumstances, something like the enjoyment to be derived from the contemplation of men hanging in chains at Tyburn. But this esthetic and morally edifying effect is not all that is to be had out of it. Dead criminals can do no more, but live ones can.

Live ones can perform services for live and lively noncriminals. I have no idea how many people in this country have any idea how vast an industry crime is—even neglecting the vaster volume of everyday, so-called white-collar crime performed in the best of business offices and the most respectable surroundings by the best of all possible people, little things like pipe-line speculation and drug-price rigging. Neglecting even this massive enterprise, the nonwhite, presumably blue-collar, work-a-day crime represents an empire at least as colossal as any of our major industries, perhaps as great as several of them taken together. These megathons live, like any other business, off income, cash money, and they certainly do *not* live off one another or they'd all grow broke together. They live—like Macy's or Gimbel's—off thousands of small sales to thousands of ordinary people, and a few not so ordinary, people ordinary enough to spend spendin' money on the luxuries or necessities they offer for free and open sale.

All major crime depends on a gigantic conspiracy which is as much a part of the social system as any other part—say, the school or university system. The conspiracy is to perpetuate a division of labor in which we delegate one body of people to pass a set of laws that our consciences approve but that are never intended for more than sporadic enforcement, while employing another set of officials (called criminals) to provide those things that we employed the first set to legislate against. I want to be perfectly clear: this is nothing like the familiar "failure to live up to our ideals" of everyday life. It is more like our paying both the Russians and the Americans to fight each other, or perhaps—as was the case—paying both the Coast Guard Patrol and the rum-runners.

The products provided—and thus made puritanically expensive—are, in North America, drink (dope on a smaller scale), sex (for males), gambling. The utmost care must be taken, and is taken, to see that the good guys, who are meant only to provide suitable harassment anyway, never win. This is achieved today by methods much less blatant than of yore: the essential mechanism, when the method is fully developed as in the United States, is to control and curtail the budget of such forces as the T-men, which takes only a few corrupt legislators per legislature, as against the buying of whole legislatures that had to take place before criminals learned Harvard Business School methods.

What has to be purchased at this seemingly high price is sanctity and sin, or sin with sanctity: the prohibition sanctifies and makes pious the enterprise, which is nevertheless designedly carried on in the face of it. What has to be paid is—in moralistic terms—the high price of hypocrisy.

Now let no one think that this is some sad or unfortunate

lack of virtue that preaching or citizenship courses will wash away, or that a better police force would render unworkable. Such hypocrisy is no more "natural" or, somehow just "there" than the virtue of punctuality into which children have to be arduously trained: the one requires as much molding, and is as much or as little against the grain, as the other. Into the child-raising methods by which such characteristics are nurtured I will not now go, but suffice it to say that it is done, it is as well done and is done in the same way and for the same reasons as indoctrination in loyalty to the flag (that is, it is just as much and just as little necessary to the operation of the society).

Nor will I go now into all the subordinate details that follow from this particular way of working a social system: the necessary corruption to a reasonable degree of the essential number of enforcement (that is nonenforcement) officers, the emergence of an orderly underworld (because all continuing activities have to be ordered within some world) and a certain amount of nonofficial violence since the underworld has to be policed to maintain order, and the courts will not support nor the regular police enforce the underworld's contracts and arrangements. All this is perhaps too familiar.

You will have noticed, perhaps, that I have concentrated on organized crime, and you may feel that by omitting white-collar crime and unorganized crime I have improperly favored my argument that crime is a socially necessary activity of our society in the same sense that carbon dioxide production is of our biology. But what I said for organized crime goes twice over for the bulk of white-collar crime also. The tragedy of the men convicted and imprisoned in connection with the massive decades-long price-fixing among the great electrical giants was that they had been acting not only according to perfectly normal business practices, but in ways necessary to make the economy run the way it is supposed to run. Only because we wish to retain the pretense of a free market, which pretense lulls the consumer into a false sense of security so that he can the better be mulcted—only because of this pretense, which has, over nearly all parts of the economy, ceased to have any resemblance to the facts, do these decent, upright citizens, who were only trying to *stabilize* production and profits, find themselves in jail. Again, we pay the antitrust people to protect us against the officers of corporations we employ to fleece us, again we ensure that the system cannot be policed, and we get the piety of election talk about a free economy together with the everyday convenience of a managed one. And then, as a bonus, we have the periodic mummery—like a Punch-and-Judy show—of seeing the police force cart off a few select victims from one side or the other. But we commission both, pay both, and commission and pay the rest to throw a few of each into the legal bonfire every now and then.

As for that part of crime not yet described—what might properly be called petty crime—the formula is basically the same, although the social payoff to the respectable is not so evident. At the very least, it furnishes the respectable—and the really big operators in crime, as well—something to be superior to, much as the best Negro in the American South does for even (or, rather, particularly) the lowliest white. It also furnishes grist—stuff to keep them busy—to policemen, magistrates, and sociologists, and, incidentally, manages to mislead most people about what crime is by concentrating attention on the play of its children in the mistaken belief that it is the same as the work of its adults.

It is time to turn now from crime—entertaining as it is as a subject, and profitable as it is as an occupation—to a direct confrontation with the "mental ills" which furnish the subject of this chapter. The point of the extended treatment I gave to the subject of crime in its relation to society was to give body to the statement I now propose: that the relation of mental ills to society is similar or identical. (I shall leave for another time and place my argument about two related beliefs: one, that crime and mental ills are generally alternative expressions of the same forces and serve the person and the society similarly; and, two, that there is little to choose, except for public relation values, between referring to them respectively as the outer-directed and inner-directed criminals, or the outer-directed and inner-directed sick.

But, before I go on, I had best assure myself that we are on the same ground with reference to what we mean by mental ills. I do *not* mean that minute fraction of a normal neuropsychiatric practice in which a discoverable or known physical or biological defect or disturbance has as one of its signs abnormal or disordered mental processes. Everyone knows that with a clout on the head, a neurological disease, a defective CNS structure, a hormonal imbalance, a spirochete invasion, or enough or too much of the right drugs, we are going to have some pretty weird mental experiences. (We sometimes induce some of them ourselves with an ethyl compound!)

The mental ills I refer to are those in which, despite years of research, *none* of the above—and indeed nothing to do with the physical world of matter and energy—have been found to be the effective etiological agent. (This is not, of course, the same as saying that material and energy exchanges nowhere come into it—which is unthinkable—but that they are not the causative agents.) I think we know, as surely as we know the neurological tricks, how to produce a depression—going even to the point of death—in otherwise perfectly healthy children, by just leaving them alone with all the ingredients for living except mother love at the right time. We know how to produce hallucinations in perfectly healthy adults just by depriving them for long enough of their accustomed flow of stimuli (*information* input, note, *not* energy). We know, in other words, how to produce the signs (and symptoms) by which we identify mental illness when we see it, by simple disturbances in social relations (or in what goes on in social relations) at any period in life, though most sensitively, early therein. Moreover, many of the consequences of such enterprises (for example, early, acute emotional deprivation) are, so far as we know, irreversible. (Note again that I am not saying that these disturbances in the message system have no physical consequences that subsequently themselves act as causes. Quite the contrary. We may watch the unloved child—or, worse, the unnoticed child—fade physically before our eyes as he shrinks psychically. What I am saying is that he changes, or sickens, in response to a message, and that what you may call his sickness is itself a message, a reply, as much as crying or laughing or a blow or a smile would be.)

Now I want to go beyond saying that we can do these things—which is not, I believe, in dispute—to two perhaps disputable statements: first, that what I said we can do is, in fact, what we largely do do; and second, that the vast bulk of what we now see as mental ills is the product of what we have done and are doing.

I think the place of psychotherapy in dealing with such disturbances makes my point. Various as are the theories, methods, and techniques of the vast variety of psychotherapeutic schools, they all have in common the establishment of a relation between at least two people, and the transmission or exchange of a set of messages within that relation. The patient is told or brought to see or allowed to see something new (to him) within a relation where he can hear or see it, for the first time, because he somehow missed getting the right (and, for many purposes,) indispensable message at the right time. In fact, of course, the relation and the message flow into and out of each other. The relation is a general message saying, "I love you," "I have faith in you," "I trust you," "I call you, as far as I can, to the human company to which I belong and the human enterprise in which I share." The messages particularize and clarify what that means in relation to where the patient is, what he is, and where he really wants to go.

Now I said that the *place*—not the fact of psychotherapy—

would make my point. If psychotherapy were *a* means to recovery in some mental afflictions, I should not regard the view I have taken as convincing. But I believe it is, in the class of cases I have referred to, not *a* means but *the* means. Those who had high hopes of the knife—the psychosurgeons (!)—did not find, I think, that they could do anything much less crude than we already knew we could by decorticating rats or pigeons, that is, destroy some functions by destroying some structures. The more shocking of the brethren who pinned their hopes to electricity found mainly, I believe, that they could thus *prepare* a patient for some other process. And the chemotherapists, despite their great achievements and the resultant battery of psycholeptic means, confronted the psychotherapists with great populations of "accessible" patients, patients who needed only to be rehumanized by humaneness in order to recover. All the interventions except psychotherapy are seen for what they are—mere preparation—like dressing to go to the play, and as little a substitute for the play's message!

The problem with which psychotherapy deals is the problem of alienation, the people with whom it deals are alienated, the therapist is truly an alienist. By alien I mean simply "foreign," with all its far-reaching implications. In the alien—or the alienated—we have people, still people, but they have left from following after us, their ways are not our ways, their gods are not our gods. To call them "sick" at all has the virtue of bringing them under pity instead of hate, care instead of punishment, doctors instead of policemen—even though for many it is a kind of hateful pity that they get, a kind of punitive care, and a pretty custodial or jailer-like medicine. Indeed, it is for the sake of these effects that society legitimized their status as "sick." But the label (as Szasz observes) is misleading. What kind of sickness is it the cure for which is to teach the patient your language instead of his (open anger, say, in place of facial tic), to recruit him from his loyalties to yours, to embroil him in the life game you are playing instead of the one he is playing. I do not need to deny that your language, loyalties, playing rules may be "better": the point is that what happens in recovery is more like what happens when we secure a Communist defection to the West than it is like a recovery from, say, an infection. What kind of "disease" is it that is a defection from the human enterprise from want of having been won over to it, and the "recovery" from which consists of being won back to the common task?

Note too that it is not simply a matter of winning the mentally afflicted *to* something; they must also be won *away* from something. It would be simple ignorance to suppose—any more than with the criminal—that because they are not engaged in our enterprise, bound by our loyalties, or participating in our game they are therefore not engaged in any enterprise, bound by any loyalties, playing in any game. They are, like the criminal, simply in another network, hearing another drummer, following another parade—and one, I might add, not so unlike our own as we might like to suppose, a variant, let us say, on our theme.

Now this kind of ill—or defection, or extrusion from the common life—is, I maintain, as much a function of the society that makes it necessary as I have made crime out to be.

This kind of "necessary" connection is somehow obscured because we do not carry out of the consulting room the perspectives we carefully preserve within it. If a patient perpetually encountered the same kind of disaster, we should ask ourselves how he operated to procure it, and why, in a most important sense, despite all his pious protests, he might properly be said to be getting what he wanted. Indeed, we should direct his attention to both the primary and secondary gains for him in the procedure he professed to view only as profitless or pernicious. If he alleged ignorance, we should wonder how he contrived to ignore facts generally so salient that most people feel they fairly leap upon one. Yet, for some reason, when we extend our regard to the patients' family of orientation, or his community or other social system, we sound, whether we so intend or not, as though the disaster they had engineered into the patient had no relation to *their* personal needs, and the requirements of their social systems. I find this puzzling. We produce engineers because and as we need engineers. We produce precisely as many competent swindlers as the necessities of our commerce require—"there's always room at the top!" Do we not, presumably, produce as many psychotraumatized as the operation of the system requires?

There are, I believe, many senses in which the system may be held to "require" what it gets. Let us try a minimum illustration. It is a commonplace in the treatment of alcoholics (and other types of cases, as well) that as the treated spouse reduces pathology in one way the untreated one increases pathology in another. Like A. A. Milne's bears of whom "one was good, and the other was not" we might say, "And then suddenly (just like Us) One got Better and the other got Wuss"—but not with Milne's air of whimsical mystery. For we should need to say, "One got Better *since* the other got Wuss" or, more exactly, "One worsened *because* the other bettered"—as though the "amount of health" they could afford between them was a constant. And indeed just that is the regulative norm between them, for they are a *system*, a symbiotic system psychologically, in which the well-being (of a sort!) of one is dependent directly on the ill-being (of a sort!) of the other. Or, put another way, the health of the whole is dependent on the illness of the parts. Or, at least, the stability of the system rests on the mutually supporting instabilities (illnesses) of the parts.

I do not think we have any difficulty either in recognizing, in a certain type of family, a kind of three-part system—a father, a mother, and one of the children—a triangle of neuroses, in which the neurosis of each supplies the need of the other two, and the interlocking neuroses furnish an entrenched and stable system. Norman Bell has well described the process in which the child is taught his role ("given his neurosis") out of the "needs" of the parents, who commonly cannot "communicate" with each other because they cannot use the language of direct aggression toward each other. In one vocabulary, we might say they "displace" their aggression upon the child, using him as a "scapegoat." Note that this procedure enables them to transcend their separateness, unifying their antagonism in a common pursuit, even if that pursuit is partly a struggle over, as well as a joint attack on, the child. But he is not only their common victim, he is also their battleground, and also, and more important, their communication center. They talk their real talk through him, and his necessary internalization of this conversation, his playing out of the roles made necessary for him, *is* his neurosis, his fitting into a shared and necessary part in a social system which, without his participation, would fall apart. Eventually, he needs them as they need him, and the social system *is* the interlocking organization of the complementary neuroses. If, to quote Dewey, "community exists in communication," that family's community "exists *in* neurosis"—which, in any case, is a name for a certain sort of communication, an indirect sort of cry for help (that is, for vital communication itself).

What has been observed in such rich detail in families has, I am sure, been observable by most of us in our experience in larger, more impersonal (supposedly), and more public organizations. I have also had occasion to study the process professionally, where I and my personal preferences and pathologies would be less directly and critically involved. Such organizations may or may not deliver socially useful products—automobiles, military defense, education, therapy, religious ceremony, or what not—and they will have greater or less degrees of seemly, orderly, predictable external behavior. But the very condition for this external rationality is the complex interweaving into a dynamically fairly stable system of the vast variety of psychologically pathological patterns that characterize its constituent elements. The "masoch-sadism" of "leaders" must be integrated with—stabilized upon—the sado-masochism of many followers. The oral exaggerations of sales departments are organizationally not just counterbalanced by, but are positively (interpersonally) interpenetrated by, the exaggerated analities of accounting, the sphincter functions of comptrollers and chartered accountants. The histrionics of the promoters are not only matched by, and balanced by, but engaged in a dynamic system with the obsessivenesses of the conservators: one cannot properly, profitably, or viably play his role without the other. The dependent depend and are depended on not by the independent, for there are few if any such, but by the counterdependent, that is, those who depend on the dependent to satisfy (their reaction formation to) their own dependency needs. The need, in a vast variety of senses and modalities, to invaginate is met by the need to be invaginated. Those whose fate it is to be used need those who so use them no less than the latter need the former. The system is, in fact, like any other ecological system, a system in which one element's waste product is, or contains, other's food; in which prey and predator, out of their antagonistic activities, cooperatively sustain the system; in which the blind search by each for his place of preference, in sun or shade, contributes to the conditions that permit the other the continuance of what he needs by way of nurturance in shade or sun. I will not go on, for the figure begins to fulfill itself: its entirety is prefigured in the sketch of it.

What is true for the kind of organization I have sketched is, I maintain, true for the nation-state or the comity of nations. The need of each to have particular, credible, and personified devils is met by the need of another to be and behave diabolically, and even while seeking to destroy the other, to sustain "constructively" and together the drama, the scheme, of destruction, destructiveness, and destructibility. My need responds to your necessity, but your necessities are also functions of my needs. And vice versa.

I have not yet really made my point that the social system needs the psychopathology of us all! I have only made the point that it effectively utilizes it. I have also not by any means made the point that the society has no similar use for what is not pathology, for what one might be pleased to call our strengths, or, in another vocabulary, virtues.

I have not made the second point because it is not wholly true. Indeed, the only view compatible with what I have been asserting about pathology is that the society has, and utilizes also, all the strengths, the nonpathologies, it wants and can use. The common ground for both propositions is that things are the way they are because we want them so; they are no better because we want them no better (we draw nourishment from our poisons, pleasures from our pains, profits from our losses, and no worse because we want them no worse (we draw also nourishment from good food, joy from the enjoyable, pleasure from the pleasant, and profit from that which is good). But if I have erred on the one side, I have —if that is balance!—also erred on the other. I have not limned in the sense in which we profit by the plentiful populations in our mental hospitals, as we do from those in our prisons, by deriving a just sense of our worth from the plight of those labeled patently unworthy. Such people fill in peacetime the role the enemy fills in wartime—cold war or hot—providing us with that essential class (essential for our peace of mind): the human nonhuman, that is, the person who can be hurt as only humans can be hurt, but who need not be respected as a common humanity would otherwise require.

When I said that I had *not* made the case that our society requires our psychopathology, but only that it uses it, I drew, perhaps, too fine a distinction. It does need it if things are to continue as they are. And they will continue as they are as long as we, with the psychopathology we have, are in the management of them—or, indeed, our successors whom we will train into their psychopathology to fit into it.

When, then, if from anywhere, hope?

Not, I believe, from any "natural process," some undesigned mechanism to bring good fortune, like Santa bringing toys. But, if not from fortune, what then from our own providence or provision? How can we hope to procure change if we assume, as I have said we should, that we have what we want, that our pathology is of our own provision, and that the stability of the system requires the persistence of what we like to label its evils together with what we like to denominate its goods?

I cannot answer such a legitimate question with warranted hope or fidelity to reality without breaking out of the sociological strait jacket. If men individually, or if society taken as a whole, were such a closed system as I have (necessarily as a sociologist) made out, we should have to accept that the system is what it is, and it would be futile to talk of changing it. (Indeed, under deterministic assumptions, it would be futile to talk, period!)

But we know better. We surely know better, in a sense that no set of intellectual constructs, no matter how useful for some purposes, can enduringly shatter or substantially shake. We know that it is of the essence of human systems to be unstable, that it is our business to unstabilize them, and that these are the grounds respectively of such freedom and responsibility as we have.

Within the limits imposed by the society such as it now is, and by ourselves such as we now are, two grand avenues of strategy open up. One of them—relatively well attended to, but insufficiently appreciated—is what might be called a generalized psychotherapy. I mean nothing more by that than the skilled process in which people are wooed from that woundedness, loved into life, and won into a companionship potentially higher and better than most of them have ever known.

The second process—for some reason less attended to, but essential if the first is to have any meaning—is the task of social reconstruction. (What, otherwise, are the redeemed or recovered or regenerate to do in a lost, sick, unregenerate, and essentially sickness-demanding world?) Curiously, it is perhaps the easier of the two processes. For it is far easier to vote for justice than to be just, to ensure that at least formally our social structures are not *organized* so as to exploit dependency and reward piracy, than it is to refrain from these in our immediate and interpersonal relations. There is no more mystery about this than there is about banking highways to prevent our tendencies to go off the road. Moreover, while banked highways will not make good drivers, just laws and democratic, egalitarian institutions do tend, in the long run, to call out in men, who are always largely mixed in their potential, that in them which is more just, more democratic, more egalitarian, more mature, more human, more humane.

If we do not want the pathology we have—or, to be more precise, if we dis-want it with that part of ourselves that is not itself pathological—we can with reasonable ease envision and then engineer those institutions, for others if not for ourselves, which do not by the very nature of their division of labor, their assignment of roles, require and reproduce the very pathology about which we complain. We shall still need decent people to run a decent social system, but we do not need to wait upon personal redemption to begin to build up the city in which the redeemed could find a breathing place. We do not need even to await our own redemption to begin on it. Indeed the very effort in behalf of the one might sufficiently free energies on behalf of the other that we should ourselves be fit—or almost so—for the city that we had builded.

17

Hostility in Modern Society

The most notable characteristic of our society—so noted now that it is almost trite to call attention to it—is that it is a society of rapid, and probably increasingly rapid, change.

It is instructive to contrast our society with that of the thirteenth or fourteenth century. In medieval society the words "sacred," "sanctified," "hallowed," not only still had meaning, but referred to matters of central concern. It was a society in which a term like "just" or "moral" had relevance to life, and a meaning not very different from "traditional" or "customary." It was a society of ordered and ancient ways—ways made accustomed and fitting by their existence "from time immemorial." It was a society of direct experiences and person-to-person ties. Such person-to-person relationships were matured over long periods, in profound intimacy, and taking the "whole person" into account. It was a society based on the family and familiarity, and the other relationships—of serf to lord, or man to God—were merely the same relationships writ large. It was a society of crescive institutions—the institutions that had merely grown, and that seemed right and natural because no man lived long enough to tell whence they had come or whiher they were tending: to every generation, what was seemed necessarily to have always been. It was substantially a homogeneous society—a society in which any two men on any one of its few levels were likely to have much the same "knowledge" and beliefs, the same judgments of what was true, worthy, and of good repute. It was a society in which the division of labor was simple, specialization rare, and money something that most people had never seen, and, some, never heard of. It was a society of little freedom, few alternatives and little necessity to make choice. It was a society in which there seemed to be some relation between virtue and reward, and where the few discrepancies could be credibly accounted for in terms of a still-believed-in life-to-come. It was a world in which man's view of the universe, of himself and his fellows, was unified, consistent, encouraging, and not patently contradicted by the brute facts of his daily experience. It had predominantly the character of the seamless web.

To that picture it is possible to oppose—though perhaps it is not necessary—a list of type-words that characterize our society, today. It is a society predominantly secular and "matter-of-fact." It is a society in which order is difficult to discern; and what is ancient is very nearly synonymous with what is discredited. It is a society of indirect and mediated experience, based largely on such local and temporary ties as cash and shifting interest afford. It is a society in which no relationship—even that of parents to children—typically endures more than a few years, where "contacts"—the very word reeks of the twentieth century—are shallow and superficial, and based, for the most part, on some one or other segment or facet of the personality. It is a society in which the family and the friendship, the primary groups, are disintegrating under the impact of secondary-group attitudes imported into them—the ulterior motive and the manipulative attitude. It is a society, very largely, of enacted institutions: institutions enacted so fast and so easily that wise is the man who keeps his lawyer at his elbow. It is outstandingly a heterogeneous society—a society indeed so heterogeneous that communication between its members is rendered nugatory by its difficulty where it has not already been poisoned by its purposes. What is true, worthy, or of good repute is not only *not* the subject of widespread agreement, but is the object of endless dispute; even the very canons by which it shall be recognized, and the possibility of achieving such recognition, are themselves in doubt. It is a society in which the division of labor is so elaborate as to have made of labor something altogether different from what it once was; a society of incredibly fine specialization; a society in which little that is important is done without the intervention and mediation of money. It is a society of—in one sense—much freedom, innumerable possibilities, and an abiding necessity to make choices of importance, without in any sensible degree being able to predict the consequences of choosing any one of the possibilities proffered. It is a society in which the connections between reward and luck, or chicane, or insensitivity, or greed, seem evident and spectacular; but where any connection between reward and virtue is widely believed, in the words of our current literature, to be "purely coincidental." It is a world in which the comforting belief of some sort of compensation for the unjust now in some just hereafter is increasingly difficult and, perhaps, increasingly necessary. It is a world in which man's view of the universe—if he has one—has little hope and less consolation; where his view of himself is disorganized and incoherent; and his view of his fellows jaundiced and malign. It has predominantly the character of chaos. In Walter Lippman's apt quotation, "Whirl is King" indeed.

In a stable society, a society such as ours approximated before the dawn of the modern period, or such as some preliterate societies approximate today, the rate of social change is, like the movement of a glacier, invisible to the unaided eye (and, since they are preliterate, and hence have no recorded history, invisible to *any* eye). A man's picture of himself, his fellows, the universe in which he lives, and the relations between these, is likely to be very much the same at the end of his life as it was near the beginning. The worst that can be said to happen is that, as the years go by, his picture of himself as a boy melts almost insensibly into his picture of what he was going to be like as a young man, and then as a mature adult and an elder. At most, there is a sense of unfolding, of getting to know himself better (just as one gets to know a spouse or friend better and better) as time goes by. There may even be ceremonial changes, *rites de passage*, to mark the dropping of one role and the assumption of a new; but these are changes in the outer shell of the personality, and do not call for radical revisions in one's notion of what man is, and what one is, or how one should properly feel.

In a society like our own, however, it is not merely the wise child who knows his own father, but a still wiser child who knows his own self. I say this neither facetiously nor with any desire to exaggerate an already sufficiently serious situation.

The second general characteristic of our society to which I should like to draw attention is what goes under the technical name of the "cultural lag." We might also want to add to our consideration the "social lag."

The impressive term "cultural lag" covers a rather commonplace, though very important, idea. It is obvious from a cursory inspection of our recent history (though it can be more beautifully documented by more elaborate methods) that not all parts of the culture change at the same rate. If this is true, it means that the culture is always, at any one time, in a state of relative disorganization; and the organization of the person and of the society in ways that minimize frustration and hostility turn on the culture's being itself a well-organized whole.

A typical instance of cultural lag may be seen in the present state of our rather pitiful attempts to control or order sex behavior in general, and particularly in the unmarried. The man who may be fairly said to have upset the standing and reasonably well-working arrangements in this regard was a Dearborn mechanic, recently deceased. In the days before he brought the dubious blessings of mobility at high speeds, and suicide by carbon monoxide or collision, the control of sex behavior rested with the good old horse. A courting couple, even with the aid of a relatively lively animal—which most, rather happily, were not—could hardly, between sunup and sundown, pass the boundary of an area which was neatly covered by a gossip web. They were likely to be recognized and known, and their family was likely to be known and gossiped *about* and gossiped *to*. (This is not to say that there were not occasional evasions of the net of surveillance and control, but it was exceedingly difficult and risky to find what Kinsey has now called by the devastatingly technical name of "outlets.") On the whole, the social controls via the gossip vine, and the inner controls via the common ideas of how a young man and a young woman ought to, and did, behave, tended to reinforce one another. Came the car. Came the wayside gasoline station, and the hot-dog stand, and the far hotel, and the lonely road—not lonely, necessarily, in the sense of untraveled, but in the sense of untraveled-by-anyone-that-is-likely-to-know-me—and the controls that had stood behind and enforced a code of behavior were, for all practical purposes, gone. Certainly the invention of the automobile made impossible the policing and enforcement of the code that had previously stood, and made possible a type of behavior that is in rather sharp distinction to it. Lagging a little behind the technological invention, the actual forms of sex behavior changed under its impact. But what of the realm of ideas? In the realm of ideas we have the typical phenomenon of a pathetic, hopeless-but-determined clinging to the old definitions and to all the ways of behavior and items of belief that accompanied them. Even the very persons who manifest the new behaviors in this area are frequently found to pay lip service to the old ideas. (I am *not* saying that we should, necessarily, change our ideas to conform to every new way of behaving; I am saying we cannot have organized persons in an organized society where lip service is paid to one set of values, while the run of behavior indicates adherence to a set altogether dissimilar. The one or the other, or both, must undergo change.)

If cultural lag is manifested in the area of sex behavior, its manifestation in the economic area has even more fascinating and fantastic results. The run of economic discussion and belief, and, most particularly, the generality of the propaganda put out, runs in terms of a set of conditions that characterized (to a very rough and approximate extent) nineteenth-century England. Only by a most ingenious stretching of terms and concepts—like the legal fiction that a corporation is a "person" —that is as difficult to learn as Chinese, and about as useful in the discussion of economic realities, only by the distortion of language in an Alice-in-Wonderland-like game of "let's pretend that this is that instead of this," only by such heroic *tours de force* are we able to keep our notions of how things ought to be (and what they once approximately were) in line with the realities of how they actually are.

This general phenomenon of cultural lag means necessarily that there are present in the culture, at any one time, all sorts of elements incompatible with one another or incompatible with the realities to be confronted, or both. Age-old superstitions, venerable for their antiquity, but for nothing else, dispute the field with the best knowledge of the day. And, most serious of all, it is unfortunately true that the greatest lags are found in precisely these matters that have the greatest importance in the guidance of conduct: notions respecting the nature of man and society, and the relations between man and the Universe at large.

I referred briefly above to "social lag," but I shall not discuss it here at length. Suffice it to say that there is in our society, at any given moment, a substantial lack of common understanding between those who are respectively near to, and far from, the centers from which new ideas diffuse—and I mean here by "near" and "far" not, of course, geographic distance, but social. Despite the wonders—and horrors—of modern mass communication, it is frequently possible to find within the geographic span of a few city blocks definable groups of our population whose central ideas about life, and whose lives, guided by those central ideas, are not much less different than those of a Chinese peasant and a modern apartment cliff-dweller.

I want to refer, briefly, to one more characteristic of modern social life that militates gravely against the possibility of establishing a stable, harmonious personality: the grave discrepancy between the attitudes and values expected in, and appropriate to, the secondary institutions in our society as against the primary. So characteristic is this, that James West has said that the process of growing up is very largely one of "finding out that the world is less like what mother said it was, and more like what the neighbors said it was."

This is not a matter, merely, of cultural lag. It is a matter of gross incompatibility, again in the central definitions and understandings, between the primary institutions—the family and playgroup—and the secondary institutions—commercial and industrial and professional—in our society.

To take a graphic illustration, let us call up a picture of a young adolescent. Let us assume that he has grown up in some relatively stable area and that he has come to be what we like to think of as the typical product of a good, happy, loving, Christian home. He has come to be, and has a picture of himself as being, an open, generous, considerate, treat-the-other-fellow-as-you-would-like-to-be-treated lad. He is now sixteen or eighteen and ready to enter the world of business—though I am not here impugning business in particular (teaching, medicine, or any other occupation would do).

He must now learn some, shall we say, "sophistication." He should still be "honest"—but the word has a substantially different and more limited connotation than his mother or Sunday-school teacher intended. (Shrewdness and that kind of honesty are a little difficult to reconcile.) Maybe one should "look after the other fellow"; but after all, number One is first (even if number One means the firm rather than the individual). Generosity is probably good, and so is frankness; but, again, a bargain is a bargain and only a fool wears his heart on his sleeve.

He must learn a great many new things. If he continues to think of people as people, he may be mighty uncomfortable. He must learn to think of them as "consumers" or "labor" and their relation to him as instrumental; they help make a profit or they don't, and are valued or disvalued accordingly. He must learn, above all, that success depends less than he had been led to believe on skill and knowledge, and much more on the ability to "sell oneself." He will learn that there is a new kind of skill called "public relations" or "personnel relations" whose essential technique, very often, is nothing more than the use of primary-group attitudes—or reasonable facsimiles thereof: love, the sharing of interests, etc.—for the manipulation of persons in a secondary-group situation. He will here get aid from all kinds of experts. He will read books like *How to Win Friends and Influence People* and discover that the word "Friends" has a substantially different meaning from what he had, naïvely, thought. If he had been raised on Machiavelli, the novelty of these views would be less striking; if he has been raised on St. Francis, a whole brave, new world is being opened up to him. He may reject such crass formulations as "It doesn't matter what you know, but whom you know." But he will need a gospel of reconciliation, and he may have to find it at the level of "After all, advertising is what makes the wheels of business hum" . . . and . . . "What is good for business is good for the nation."

But he will not attain to this happy estate where he has found the sophisms that will allow him to live precariously in two incompatible value worlds until he has passed through a difficult and painful transition period, and that transition period is really something to see. I speak here not from the comfort and distance of a study armchair, but from direct observation over a decade in the business world. I have experienced and watched the process of "change"—the mother in the case might call it "subversion"—that is involved, and I have talked intimately and long with people in various phases of that transition, both then and in the years since then. Some have felt keenly the process of making themselves over: I remember an office boy who had qualms about saying the boss was "out" to an unwanted visitor, when he was clearly and audibly in. Let's write him off as overscrupulous—perhaps an obsessive type. I remember well the director of a large corporation who had moral scruples (as well as reasonable fears) about the price-fixing arrangements, the "combination in restraint of trade," which was one of his responsibilities. He had the usual perfect rationalizations, but somehow he was not quite happy about them and would feel compelled to explain and re-explain how the situation *should* be viewed until I felt he was talking to himself rather than to me. Some come to despise themselves in the process of change: another Director said "Sure, I'm a son-of-a-bitch; but who isn't?" One man's theme was: "What else can I do; you can't change the system, can you?" And some, the successful, I suppose, successfully submerge and lose their earlier, "truer" selves and learn to exult in the new self they have latterly wrought. When they became men, they put away childish things—to good effect! But not without some wrenching, some pain, some scarring, and some loss. And, therewith, commonly no inconsiderable hostility.

I cannot at this time go further into the many important aspects of our society that are productive of unhappy, divided people and an unhappy, divided society in general, and of hostility within persons and hostility between persons in particular. One can only refer to the increasing bureaucratization of our society (not only on the part of the government!) which renders the individual so remote from the sources of power that a sense of apathy, indifference, impotence, and hostility is the inevitable outcome; to the increasing killing out of creativity and spontaneity, in the face of a demand for external conformity that is supposed to mask and hide our inner diversity; to the increasing preoccupation with the output of material goods so that economic considerations in the narrow sense have become paramount, and necessitated the subordination of all other aspects of living; to the subversion of communication itself—the very medium in which society exists and man becomes man—to the service of statecraft or "selling," under no matter what name or guise.

I am tempted to say, in summary, that it is my judgment that a society so constituted cannot long endure. A society that cannot give a child a reasonably coherent, self-consistent notion of himself and his fellows, that cannot tell him with some assurance what things are true, worthy, or of good repute, cannot expect to be a society in which there is a stable and abiding order within men or between them. A society that expresses—wherever, in little islands it is still coherent—one set of values in its primary institutions and a radically different set in all others, cannot expect that its members will be tolerably free of frustration and hostility. Such a society must expect, and will surely have, frequent and cataclysmic mass explosions wherever and whenever a person can be found who can mobilize and canalize the latent mass hostilities for whatever ends he deems worthwhile.

And the answer does not lie in the direction of executing enough war criminals, or, at least, not in that alone. We must address ourselves to other questions than the wickedness or psychopathology of this or that individual. The gravest danger is that we shall in our sense of insecurity take measures that in the long run will increase sevenfold the hostilities that we now have. "And the last state of that man shall be worse than the first. . . ."

There is no dearth of "answers" in this area as in so many others. There is only a dearth of answers that make any sense. One cannot list them all and examine them individually, but we should consider the three major "heresies."

The first major proposal (which I believe to be impossible,

rather than vicious) is that we should arrest the course of social change. The suggestion is that we should control the rate of invention, especially technical invention, so as to be able to slow the rate of change down to a more manageable pace. My judgment is that, in the process of getting control of the rate of invention, we shall have to sacrifice so many paramount values that the game would not be worth the candle.

The second major program maintains that we should "return" to the ancient values and the bygone ways. In the face of difficulty, the suggestion of regression falls ever on willing ears, but my feeling is that the recommendation is *both* vicious and impossible. It is impossible in a double sense. It is impossible because one cannot wash out the experience of mankind, the experience that has been *had* since those values and beliefs held sway, and, in their day, made sense. It is also impossible because men are not disposed to reattach themselves to a system they have firmly rejected, on the ground of what they have experienced. It is vicious in the sense that it is an invitation to man to deny his highest nature, his willingness to believe what is true rather than what is merely comforting, and his willingness to sacrifice a lower for a higher good.

The third major program maintains that since all social problems are conflicts about values, the answer is to make man value-free. This is very like the suggestion that we abolish crime by repealing the criminal code. Nevertheless, it is seriously put forward. My sense again is that *it* is both impossible and vicious. It is impossible because, it is safe to predict, no living body of men can be got to behave in this way. And it is vicious because if they did, they would destroy the possibility of any kind of society and any kind of person, in the process. It is an invitation to man to deny his moral nature, his capacity for choice, and therewith to save himself as a biological organism by destroying himself as a human and social one. I do not see any hope in any of these directions.

We have to accept a rapidly changing society as a datum, though we can do something, if we will, about our cultural lag and about the major incompatibility of the elements in our culture.

We *can* live in a society of rapid change, but only if we are organized and oriented in terms that may remain invariant, but still appropriate under changed conditions. This means that we must learn to be attached to an order of values and a system of understandings that is much more general, much less tied to the vagaries of time and place, than any ethical or knowledge system we have yet known. The only systems of value or of knowledge that have this order of generality are those that derive their authority from what is abiding and universal rather than transient and local: the nature of man on one side and the nature of things on the other. A rational ethic and a rational science have both some likelihood of surviving the vicissitudes of time and space, and a rational ethic is a derivative of a full-grown science of man.

That full-grown science of man we do not yet have, and are not perhaps likely to have, in the proximate future. What we do now have, however, is sufficient knowledge to indicate that many cherished notions, beliefs, and practices do not have the universal validity to which they once laid claim. We have sufficient positive knowledge of the nature of man to say with assurance that some things are good and other things are bad; meaning here, "*good for man*" and "*bad for man.*" Here and there, we may have to cover the gossamer-slender structure of knowledge with the web of faith—human faith, a sense of the true potentialities in men. But that it is possible to have an ethic that is derived from our knowledge of the nature of man in one part and is *not* in conflict with anything we now know about man in its other part, I do not doubt. Whether my hopes are ill- or well-founded, I submit that only so shall we steer between the Scylla of absolute relativism—which implies intrapersonal and interpersonal chaos—and the Charybdis of our present absolutisms, which imply the perpetuation of the conflicts, frustrations, and hostilities that we now face. In the face of such an achievement, the problems of cultural lag, and the conflict of incompatible elements in the culture, will either not arise or speedily find their resolution.

So, and only so, can the kind of society we have dreamed of, but never quite achieved, come to its birth, and man come to the fullness of his manhood. So, and only so, when man, with a more adequate knowledge of himself, comes, by that knowledge, into control of the conditions that make him what he is, will he reach to his full stature. So, and only so, will man, who has timelessly made his gods in his own image, remake himself in the image of his gods. This way lies Life—and the other way, Death.

18

Progress from Poverty?

No progress will be made in reference to the problem of poverty—or any other problem—without an appropriate perception of what the problem is.

Poverty is a lack of power to command events. Hence, existentially, we are all poor, poor almost beyond enduring. Part of that poverty may be irremediable. We may never be able to prevent or offset the cooling sun; we may never fully conquer death; we may never, perhaps, learn even to avoid self-defeat, self-stultification, or self-destruction. Hence we may always be poor in some sense.

But this is not the poverty that is pointed to in the scriptural statement "The poor you have always with you." Those poor are the *differentially* poor: those who have less command over events than others.

To have command over events requires schemes, skills, and command of means. Means, in this context, are persons and things. Perhaps—probably—command over persons is decisive. Command over things—either over goods to buy service or force to compel it—is largely a means to command, coerce, control, or cajole others—and, circularly, a product of so doing. Schemes and skills can be hired provided that control over persons is assured. In a fully developed scheme of command (developed fully, that is, as far as the technology permits) the slaves provide the means of their own enslavement: the food to be given or withheld, the whips to their own backs, even the "internal controls" to stabilize the system and to polish it with politeness. Finally, their own hands —under command—wield these self-fashioned weapons against themselves and their own.

Poverty, differential poverty, has the structure of slavery. There is the primary insult, with all that it entails, of lack of command over events, so that the children of the poor die when under a mere redistribution of means they need not. There is the secondary insult of involvement in a productive process that gives the nonpoor the means to increase, maintain, or very slowly diminish the existing relative poverty, i.e., to maintain command. There is the third and final insult that causes the poor to become willing poor—"happy slaves"—who support the system of poverty, whether or not any particular one tries to struggle out of it.

We need to distinguish sharply between three very different schemes for "improvement" in the existing state of affairs. One, the one on which we pride ourselves most, is the rendering of the system "open." We say we have "an open society," or a fairly open one that we aim to make more so. We point to the fact of "mobility." The progressive equalization of opportunity, the career open to talent. These are undoubted goods—relative, at least, to closed societies with similar advantage-disadvantage distributions. Perfected, the scheme resembles one in which it is possible (or easy) for slaves to become slave owners. In sharp contrast are schemes directed to the diminution or extirpation of slavery. And still different, of course, are schemes designed to give "comforts' to the slaves.

None of these schemes is wholly to be despised. Given a slave system, and given its perpetuation with reference to particular persons or categories—"once a slave, always a slave" —it is better that there be mitigating comforts, Bibles, and mouth organs, than not. Or, given a slave system, it is better it be open than closed. But if the necessity for a slave system is *not* given, then not only are these measures not good *enough*, they are not even good, since they militate against the abolition of slavery itself.

The need for a slave system—whether mediated by whips or by money—is not wholly a matter of wish, or at least not a matter of wish regarding slavery itself. It depends on the real world at a given time and place, and on other, seemingly unrelated wishes.

If what men wish—or what those who make public policy wish—in a given situation and state of the arts, *entails* that most men must mostly do what they do not want (and cannot reasonably be persuaded to want) to do, then the wishes must be forgone or the men must be enslaved. (Again, whether the means are "economic" or "politic," though important, is, relatively, mere detail.) We cannot, for instance, conquer the world (or police it, likely) without a slave society, and we may not be able to sate our limitless hunger for security or gadgets without it either. Even such esoteric desires as the wish to "conquer space" or land men on moons may entail such slavery.

Political democracy by itself is not a sufficient hedge against such enslavement. We may not wish to remember that Hitler *was* elected. But even failing such extreme examples, and assuming that the makers of public policy do reflect and act upon the wishes of the majority of their constituents, the tasks men so elect to impose on themselves, may well—indeed, commonly do—commit them to a perpetual program of doing what they must then be made to do, i.e., to a "voluntary" program of servitude. If force, naked, is not to enforce such a program, patently poverty must.

Political democracy, even conjoined with national affluence, could act to diminish or dissolve that kind of slavery only if the majority of voters were sufficiently educated with reference to means to see the connections between their choices, and sufficiently enlightened with respect to ends to know (and vote for) their true desires. But poverty itself—the problem!—entails, above all, insufficient knowledge and freedom for the informed votes necessary to poverty's abolition or sizable reduction.

"Poverty in the midst of affluence" is thus no puzzle, let alone a paradox. Even in the face of affluence, and even given political democracy, it is entailed, necessitated by the choices the poor in their poverty make or are caused to make.

Indeed–and perhaps here is the real paradox–if they can be persuaded to hunger after gadgets and to measure their progress from poverty by a census of such gadgets, and if they can then be persuaded to value the armaments that protect them against those who have still less, then they can be made accomplices in the systems of poverty, internal and external, that yield such dividends. Thus, the system of external poverty, i.e., the existence and perpetuation of relatively poor or "underdeveloped" nations, reinforces and necessitates the system of internal poverty that supplies the motive to produce the defense of the "developed" system. Absolutely, planes of living can move up, internally and externally–as they have–without any real attack on poverty and its problems, which are relative. To starve where there is no food for anyone is a malign fate to be suffered or accepted. To hunger where some are overfed, and there would otherwise be enough for all, is a human insult, an enslavement if suffered unwillingly, a self-enslavement if accepted. And even when the "base" shifts from starvation to poor medical care and poor housing and poor schooling, or from these to what is relatively poor later, the insult and the resultant psychological and social damage are the same or similar. Again, the shift in the base is not be be despised or deplored–it *is* better that no man go corporally starved. But if we develop secondary hungers–such that, for instance, a man needs corporal cleanliness to retain self-respect and being thought "decent" by others–and if the means to satisfy such hungers are withheld from some, then for nearly all purposes these "starve" no less, suffer no less cruel pangs, reap no less really the rewards of poverty.

Any serious attack on poverty, then, is an attack on the

discrepancies between the powers of men to command events, principally each other. A successful attempt, for instance, to increase everybody's real income by, say, one half, is at most a prologue to such an attack, and, most often, a way of avoiding it. For the operative problem of poverty—psychologically and socially—is like the problem of minority status in its form and consequences. It would help the Negro-white problem very little if we were twice as nice to each other: the problem—that which is intolerable, personally poisoning, and socially destructive—is the *difference*.

Clearly, the personal poisoning and social destruction have been borne—and are perhaps to be borne—where higher values are at stake. If pyramids are to be built there may be no other way. The more humane we become in the direction of disliking brute force, and the more ambitious we become in the direction of demanding mass effort (or its effects), and the more skilled we become in directing those efforts to ends ever more remote from the immediate wishes and needs of living men, the more do we need poverty as the only effective spur to secure men in such obediences and bind them in such bondage.

And, rather clearly, that is what we have hitherto done. Our "prosperity" has hence rested upon, and rests now upon, our poverty. Not without poverty could we have had our industrial revolution, except where (as in King Leopold's Congo, for instance) it was delivered at the rifle's mouth. Not without radically differential payoff (combined with the linking of advantageous payoff) to self-respect, could we have kept men at work—or, at least, at such work. Certainly no other scheme would have yielded such "happy slaves."

But by an ironic, unforeseen, and unforeseeable twist of history the scheme has yielded a successor scheme: industrialization has given birth to automation.

Whatever else automation means, it means the multiplication of power, at least over material things, into another order of magnitude, without an attendant increase in the burden of human labor to be borne. The problem in sight—under statable conditions—is no longer governed by the necessity to keep men at work, intrinsically meaningless work, like horses in harness. That particular ground for the perpetuation of poverty is, under the statable conditions, removed.

The statable conditions are essentially two. First, that equal and simultaneous attention be directed toward the external poverty system, so that what we gain does not go or get dissipated upon armaments to preserve what we (materially) have. And second, that we do not open up or expand essentially limitless schemes—like conquering the universe or the world or achieving absolute security—that consume the increase and indeed make it necessary to perpetuate the coercion that is needed to keep men at arduous and demeaning tasks. (It should be noted that these stable conditions point away at a 180-degree angle from our current course, which "keeps the economy going" by flinging the output at the moon and "the enemy.")

But if we assume the conditions can be assured, another temptation will open up that has something to do with a problem and the preference of men (not only the ostensible beneficiaries) for systems of slavery, anyway.

The new problem will be that once we no longer have, at least in recognizable form, the "problem of production," we shall still have the problem of order, public and private, and we may well have it in a form acute beyond anyone's imagining. One side of the problem—difficult, but still easier than the next—is that work itself, with its routines, formal and informal, has filled so much of the temporal space of life, that a great deal of order, private and public, has been provided just by its presence and pervasiveness. The second, the more difficult side, lies in the deeper "meaning" of work, at least in our "ascetic" cultures. Work is now virtually the only positively sanctioned outlet for those vast aggressions which, in so pleasure-denying a culture, run so deep and press so hard for release. It is difficult to imagine vividly enough what will be the situation once those outlets for aggression—now mediated by assaults on objects or by labor-management conflict (in the case of blue-collar workers) and by the piracy, conspiracy, fraud, and cheating that are the essence (or payoff) of a great deal of white-collar enterprise—are removed.

Men so situated may be glad of almost any "direction," and those less afraid of themselves than of others may, as at present, be only too glad to direct them. If the coercion is to be disguised, to appear "internalized," we may have to preserve—or reinstitute—differential poverty, so that the coercion may have the air, as now, of "voluntary" striving, the so-called "struggle to get ahead."

Any release from "the grip of poverty"—i.e., from the system by which we actively or passively engineer ourselves into the donkey-stick-carrot penal servitude that we have—will have to solve the problem of restraining aggression or channeling it so that it does not disrupt the psyche or the society or both, or we shall have to find methods that do not generate the same quanta of aggression. Restraint on this scale requires a police state or the threats of severe poverty or both. Channels, even though machines can readily cut canals and level mountains, are hard to come by. It looks as though the only way to abolish differential poverty, *especially* in the face of such general affluence as now faces us, is to reduce characterological aggression.

Thus, the problem of poverty is bound up with the problem of character change which is bound up with the problem of child raising. However, the problem of child raising does not exist in a vacuum. Children are raised in the way they are—ignorance and fashion apart—because of the way their parents were raised, modified to a considerable extent by those same parents' perception or vision of the future society into which the children are to "get." But since those parents, rich or poor, were nearly all raised in a world of poverty (where the question is to be "up" or "down" on the competitive ladder, slave holder or slave or a little of both) and since they have not even been brought to imagine a free (poverty-free) world, what else can they do but raise their children in poverty for poverty. By raising them "in poverty" I mean that the children learn under conditions of *conditional* non-deprivation; they are rewarded for doing—not being—and for doing only what is contrary to nature. By raising them "for poverty" I mean so structuring them that they cannot be comfortable under unlike circumstances, e.g., in the presence of free goods. Even when they are "retired," i.e., finally given a respite, a breather before death, they die before they have had the breather. They "cannot stand prosperity," or, more exactly, they are so poor they cannot bear escape from the goad of poverty. People—nearly all people—have the "minority problem" built into them in their minority: self-distrust, except under constraint and confinement—the boss or the balance sheet indifferently; self-hate and identification with the aggressor; anxiety about those who "pass," or escape the system; false pride in the miserable status occupied.

Is there a way out? Perhaps so, but it is very difficult. Just as punishment generates a need that cannot be slighted with impunity (to punish and be punished), so poverty, a variant of punishment, generates a need to continue in a poverty system (as rich man or poor), and, more radically, an inability to imagine any better workable system. The spurred horse comes to need the spur on his flank, if he continues to be a horse, on his heel if he becomes a jockey. Horse and jockey are more alike than anatomy indicates or zoology suggests.

Such self-sustaining systems of cripplement are hard to break into. A deprived child cannot accept a gift; he can seize a proffered object, but his deprivation does not permit him to receive it in its intended meaning; the giver appears as the bearer of ulterior designs or a sucker or both. To such a child the very threat of a gift may endanger his security system so strongly that he wards it off with more energy than he would a blow. The prospect of a workless world, or a world in which worth no longer depends on work, or in which plenty might descend, like the rain, on the working and workless, seems to generate, as a prospect, nothing but anxiety in the hearts of rich and poor alike.

For the deprived person, the first step out of the vicious circle of seeking to be depriver or deprived is the establishment of belief that another and better order is possible. The belief must be (a) that there *is* enough for all, and (b) that what is to be desired is enough for oneself, and not competitive moreness or lessness. The belief can be established only by repeated experiences of nondeprivation and nondepriving, accompanied by affection-warmed re-education, persuasion into faith, and trust in that better game.

What is true here for a person is not directly but analogically true for the social problem of poverty. There must be belief that another state of affairs is possible—and better—before it will be possible to perform those acts (especially in a political democracy) that will lead to that better stake. If what is wanted is the breaking of bondage—not merely the moving into a cozier bondage—then the faith in and the longing for an unbound stake must go before and accompany the breaking of the bonds. The fear that unbound we should be dangerous to ourselves or others, the belief that unspurred, unbitted, unbridled we should be worthless or pointless or worse, the fear of freedom for others or ourselves—these must precede and go out along with the progressive and rapid abandonment of the prison system that the current poverty-riches system permanently provides.

Unfortunately, as things stand at present, the pace in the two systems of events is not even loosely coordinated. The progress that will render us all soon workless (or nearly all nearly so) goes on apace. The radical re-education that would make such a potential state supportable—that would make thinkable the removal of poverty as spur and bit—is not well begun, perhaps hardly begun at all. Indeed, even at this instant, in virtually every last corner, cranny, and reach of the educational system, every last resource and effort is employed in bending as many as can be bent into the internalization of the poverty-system. (Indeed, the "educational system" with its credit-hours, degrees, and grades, simulates and incorporates the poverty system, using such symbols for counters—in place of the symbols such as money, carpeted offices, and parking places or club memberships of the "real world outside the academic environment.") The process that the educational system stamps and puts its seal upon is, of course, begun at the womb's mouth and well launched before ever the child is thrust through the school door.

The job we confront—most especially given the time we have to do it in—staggers the imagination and appalls the heart. For what is needed is a new national character (and, eventually, world character)—*and* a way of getting from here to there, i.e., of having the impoverished prepare the affluent-to-be. And not only nationally, but on a world scale. Incidentally, but not trivially, it means dealing with widespread, perhaps nearly endemic, masochism: the desire to be poor (or poorly) with all its attendant benefits by way of treasured resentments and grievances, and the agenda these bespeak, and the point, or seeming point, thus lent to life. Such investments—especially when they are institutionally dovetailed, as they now are, with opposite needs in the same or other person—are not lightly, or by simple act of will, renounced. But how are we thus to lift ourselves by our own bootstraps, as it seems?

If the "we" were a uniform and structureless we, the task would be, as the phrase suggests, impossible. Even an illiterate nation, so-called, is not uniformly illiterate, and each-one-teach-one programs have therefore been successful, while simultaneously the most literate have not ceased to become more so.

The problem of poverty is structurally similar while much more far-reaching and profound. It is a pity that the fine phrase "The War on Poverty" has become attached to what, with the greatest generosity, can be seen only as some preliminary stirrings and skirmishes. For a *war* on poverty is what is required, if "war" calls up the right images of life-and-death issues—for everyone—utter determination, limitless commitment, and the risk if not the certainty that all institutions and practices may be made over in the course of it. What the conquest of poverty requires is a national and world reorganization for the conquest of it, the necessary means and resources made available, and the needed time to wage so far-reaching and long-lasting a war taken and set aside from the other tasks of history on which we might otherwise wish to embark.

Given the fundamental set and determination, I think the task is not impossible, but let us make sure one last time that we know what the fundamental set is, what we are looking toward. We are looking toward a world in which everybody will be "rich," objectively and subjectively. By "rich subjectively" we mean that the goods of life can be accepted and enjoyed. And since we have specified "everybody," successful sibling rivalry cannot be a condition (let alone, as now, a principal ingredient as well) of enjoyment. Indeed, the opposite must be the case: enjoyment by others must be a condition of one's own (as in a good, and sufficiently common, suckling situation, or in a good, but sufficiently uncommon, sexual one). The whole present basis of the social order that induces guilt, and then mines for life the golden yield of it, must be overset. The associated hyperaggression that served so well to motivate and sustain the "attack upon the world" will find no further use. And with it must go its linked instrument for self-attack, the kind of "conscience" we have known, which has been hitherto not the warden of life (ours and others) but the driver to death, the father of the ulcer and mother of the coronary. We are, in a phrase, thinking of turning our backs on an anal and phallic world, to bring into being a reign of genitality—the like of which the eye of man hath not seen.

In one sense the situation contains the seeds of its own

solution, but seeds must be recognized for what they are and nurtured for what they can become. The seeds lie in the imminence of unemployment and boredom for everybody unless we find ways to turn our energies to the cultivation of men, viewed in all their severalty, and viewed as a society. But one cannot cultivate men—if one correctly appreciates what is involved in cultivation—without becoming oneself both more cultivated and more capable of more cultivation—of self and others. Therefore, the process is potentially benign and self-sustaining, but only potentially, for, as I indicated in hedging, "*if* one correctly appreciates what is involved in cultivation."

We have a suggestive model in good parenting—when it occurs. The relation is a relation in depth, mediated at every level from unconscious to unconscious, through touch, to speech or even to the force of example. It is a nearly total, certainly nonsegmental relation. It not only is not—in the words of the trade—a "zero-sum game," but it is a game in which losses to one are sharply felt losses to the other, and gains, likewise. It is a relation that transcends and embraces the parties to it, so that they may love not merely themselves and each other, but that which joins them, their love itself. (Here the true unity is the true Trinity: Father, Son, and Holy Spirit, each implicit in everyone.) It is a process of mutual evocation in which the more and better the parent assumes his role and nature, the more and better the child assumes his, thus providing the next succeeding better conditions (and rewards) for the parent . . . and so indefinitely. It is a condition that provides—again at every level from the "acquisition of skills" to the structuring of the unconscious—for its own succession, such that the best (virtually, only) way to provide better parents and parenting next, is to have better parenting (and childing) now.

In extending the essence of parenting to the whole society in rendering it imminent and transcendent—which is what is required for a poverty-free society—we must preserve what we want without carrying over the implications of profound and long-lasting inequality that normally inheres in the parent-child definition, and something of an air of patronage (in its worst sense) that attends it. It may be that if everyone is parenting someone no problem need arise, and children, real children, are always there as potential residuary legatees of anyone's need to bestow love lest he be shamed before the love he receives. As in so many vital processes, it seems that we cannot have a very clear idea of "steps" until we commitedly engage in it, and are borne along by our past commitments, even as at every stage new vistas open sufficient to illuminate what is the next succeeding necessary step.

In the realm of child rearing, this requires "only" the speeding up of a process now imminent, I believe, and requiring primarily for its acceleration the endowment of all parents with generous material means and a recognition of the unconstricted world within which their children and their children's children will "have to" exist. Let me not trivialize this task: it is an immense task, in principle, to discover new ways and new institutions to support parents in their fear-laden steps to the authentication, legitimation, and suitable expression of their generous imuplses.

However, if the task is difficult enough with regard to family, it is of overwhelming difficulty when we turn to the institutions of formal education, for what is required here is not an acceleration, and perhaps mild directional correction, but a turn of 180 degrees.

What educational institutions now do, in rough outline, is to take the child—warm, living flesh-and-spirit in the kindergarten and nursery school—and turn him into sinew, skeleton, scar tissue at the high school, college, or graduate school exit. He comes full of life and leaves full of schemes. He comes open and leaves closed. He comes in sensitive self-awareness and goes clad in clanking armor. He comes singing, skipping, and dancing and leaves carrying himself, presenting himself, "using himself," posing, and posturing. He comes to give and receive; he leaves to trade at the door of life. Not out of some inherent necessity of "growing up"—indeed this is growing down—but out of the very structrue and content of education designed to that end. And rightly so, for what we have needed hitherto were not human beings but skilled ants, and the institutions appropriate to their production, our schools and colleges, have been and are, mostly, ant hills.

Look at any high school today—close up. Then try to think of a process not patently punitive—which would secure a different effect—better calculated to produce empty meaning, value, sense, sensibility out of life—to produce pseudo robots ("free" enough to manage, but not free enough to ask "what for?"), to institute triviality as normative, to lead straight to the life of "kicks" as the only appropriate response, to "cool out," for life, the life that still presents itself not wholly chilled by the grade school lockup! College and university are not visibly worse or better. The educators speak of "educating the whole child," but unless the child checks pretty nearly everything that makes him a child and a human being at the door, they panic. Let him show, at the right time, the pervasive smoldering sexuality and love that holds the whole promise of the future, and they clip his hair and legislate the tightness of his trousers. Let him show even the faint and stibbled shadow of the aggressiveness he needs to hold out against his own castration, and they involve the already castrated on the "student council" in complicity in making "student rules" that elevate politeness and smoothness into arbiters against life. Let the "kids"—even at the age of Berkeley students—take seriously for a moment the pretensions of their own society, let them act for a moment to demand that we act as we *say*, and the whole state quakes, and firearms must be carried onto the campus in the hands of men to confront children who ask them to be men!

This is a falling away from a high calling by design and in essence, not by accidental defect. The "whole child" may not come to school at all; he is too frightening. What we will accept is a little simulacrum, a homunculus, a cheerful little idiot to be homogenized—except for what David Riesman calls "marginal differentiation"—like a Skinner pigeon. Indeed, more truly a "pigeon" in the underworld sense, since he is needed as a party to his own undoing. What the school wants and worships is "cooperation"—and that means collaboration in the task of self-constraint, self-constriction, and self-evisceration. (Not that the school is to be "blamed"; it is, first, immeasurably better than, but also necessarily "preparatory for," the institution that lies ahead, and that needs such fodder.)

What is wanting in the school is not a matter of defective educational theory—in the sense that we do not know how to do better—though what the school takes up (and distorts) out of such theory as there is, is clearly distorted and defective. But the child who goes to school is not suddenly and thereby another child, even when his capacity to grow up has been enhanced by the vast powers of visual-symbolic communication. He is not suddenly a thought-processing machine with a sad necessity to be relieved occasionally, to go to the bathroom, to whisper to his neighbor, or to be paraded down the *down* staircase. He is a living, sentient, and, unless distracted, vitally engaged little human being, *naturally* organizing the world around him, objectively and subjectively, in terms of his (growing) concerns. Good education takes him *in toto* and links, not artificially but naturally, his expansions and reviews to the concerns he has now. The difference between liberation and enslavement, education and training, parenting and manipulation, lies in the nature of the linkage effected. There is little to add to Dewey—except Freud—and little to add to that, as far as theory is concerned, except the new economics, and the new psychologies they carry with them.

But how is education in fact to be reformed, root and branch? It is hard to say. Patently, many things must be done together. It must be endowed, very heavily endowed, on a different scale of magnitude altogether. It must, "worthy" or not, be loved and respected in order that it may become lovable and respectable. It must be given, on the highest authority, a new and highly different mandate: to "humanize" its children, or help them humanize themselves, not mechanize or "program" them. It must be encouraged to let the children do the "work" (as they would, if we did not prevent them) for one another; four-fifths of the energy and "skill" needed is already there among them. Finally, teachers themselves—and, even more, "educators" and educational administrators—must themselves be helped to be less frightened of themselves and their charges, so that they act less like beleaguered burghers and more like—literally—Kinder-Gartners. Perhaps then they would welcome what they now hysterically resist, the implication of the to-be-educated in the government and control of the process wherein he is becoming educated.

It will be a long, slow, hard process and blood, sweat, toil, and tears will not be enough. We may be, in some way, too poor to be able to dispense with poverty. But perhaps we only need to realize how rich we are in order to become truly rich.

19

Crestwood Heights: A Transaction

It is the commonest of commonplaces in the social sciences to say that the meaning of an act observed is not immediately evident, that before we can begin to understand its significance we must have access to a great deal of the lifeway of the actor or actors concerned. That is one reason why we do community studies, or, if not a reason, a justification.

On a second view, the making of a community study, or, indeed, the performance of almost any sociological act viewed as a social act, is unintelligible without access to the lifeways of the participants: those studying and those studied. The original sociological product, the study itself, is an artifact—to use the jargon—and should be no more immune to examination than the activities it examined. Indeed, a case can be made, I think, that the understanding of the study, as against what the study studies, is a matter of paramount interest socially and sociologically.

The social interest in just what it is that the sociologist is doing should surely require no very extensive elaboration. From the viewpoint of the society, an active sociology has emerged as a new force, allied with God knows what among pre-existing interests. American sociology is no longer represented by some dear old men sitting in their offices classifying the "forms of association," or trying to illuminate themselves and confound each other by etymological or semantic analyses (not that even these enterprises were free of consequence). On the contrary, American sociology is represented by a multitude of not-so-old, not-so-dear men actively poking about, and, by a bias of the profession, poking about so far as they can in many places where they are wanted least.

I know it is fashionable to pretend—even though to do so has a spurious air of humility—that sociological inquiry is no great force, at the same time that motive and morale among sociologists are sustained by the belief that their work is a very great force indeed. It is mostly no professional secret since W. I. Thomas (if not before) that social facts are what they are defined to be. And what, pray, is the content of sociology except the redefinition, and hence the reconstitution, of social facts. Social facts for whom? Not, as may briefly have once been the case, social facts for the sociologists, but now, much, very much, social facts for the society. The sociologist substantially makes over the culture; not the professional subculture that has to be sought and broken into, but the culture proper that seeks one in one's formative stages and from which it is hardly possible to become disenmeshed.

It is hardly possible in the new, postsociological society, for a person even of the most modest literacy to avoid thinking in Weberian terms: not necessarily in Weber's words, but with his set toward the Puritan ethos, and his notions (roughly) as to the roots of work attitudes in a religious faith now largely inoperative in practice. It is not possible to be a youth in even middle-brow surroundings without struggling, almost in so many words, with the problems of "other-direction," named by Riesman and, therefore, in its current form, constituted as the experience of others by him. Warner's analysis is in the culture via *Life* magazine and Vance Packard. The Bethel Laboratory is in the school and is absorbed there directly and by indirection from Madison Avenue. We are not far from the point where what the social scientist said yesterday is part of today's mores (in Sumner's strict sense of unquestioned and unquestionable thoughtways). Who *can* think, talk, or write today without explicit or implicit use of terms like "mores, folkways, social structure, culture, role, self-conception, social status . . ."? (Some weeks ago, I saw two little boys, one nine, one ten, banging the front wheels of their bikes, one old, one new, together in a primitive attempt to settle who was to have the right of way. Said the owner of the older bicycle to the other boy "Whatcha tryin' to do? Pull yer social status on me?") How many college students have used Kinsey to justify what they otherwise might not have done? The transforming of the otherwise private to the public sphere by the public presentation of the sociological report may constitute a form of legitimation for the actions described: "If they can do it, why not me?" The effect may also be to illegitimize by rendering open what was previously legitimate only because it was a secret of common knowledge.

I do not think we can deny our defining role and sometimes our definitive ability to specify reality by the terms we introduce. That the wish among us to deny it should be so widespread itself invites sociological speculation and investigation. Detached sociological innocence is not possible as a defense for the practicing sociologist.

With the emergence of a new social force arises a legitimate social interest in the understanding of it, and, unless we are to have a new profession of metasociologists, that social understanding must come to society through sociologists.

But, independently of the social claim (which we may have to be the ones to press, *faute de mieux*, against ourselves) there is a vital sociological interest at stake. The metasociology is not some footnote or addendum to, some gloss upon or afterthought in reference to, the sociology of anything: once recognized and treated it alters and makes over the sociology itself, just as the sociology makes over and alters the society. Each next stage creates its own new reality.

Let me try to press my point all the way home or, at least, try to make the meaning of what I am maintaining crystal clear. The analogy with the psychoanalytic process will serve us rather well. The psychoanalytic profession rightly maintains that it is not possible to practice psychoanalysis without both having been psychoanalyzed and virtually reanalyzing oneself in every analysis of another. Note both points. It is not possible, on this view, to perform an analysis in virtue of any amount of knowledge about analysis; the learning about analysis is, in its major aspect, a consequence of the undergoing of it, and the virtual reanalysis with every fresh analysis is a tribute to recognition of the fact that neither patient nor practitioner, analyst or analyzed, is left the same after as before the analytic act. A set of "bad" practitioners can be imagined in an ordered series (a real Guttman scale?): those who thought they could practice by mother wit[1] and in the light of nature; those who thought they could practice by merely adding knowledge about psychodynamic theory and consulting-room practice; and those who thought that all that had to be added to that was their own once-and-for-all analysis.

We have a corresponding series in sociology. Very few, I suppose, hold that they can adequately analyze or describe society by mother wit and in the light of nature; nevertheless, even this is evidently a non-null class. The vast bulk of our fraternity not only has been indoctrinated into the second position, but stands there and indoctrinates its students therein: the position that it is possible, meaningful, and satisfactory to do sociology, to pursue social analysis in virtue of knowledge *about* social theory, sociological method, and social status and dynamics. The very sophisticated save themselves from the most obviously self-damnatory implications of this position by some slight and informal apprenticeship procedures plus some formal exposure to the sociology of knowledge. The first is too trivial to speak about. The second is analogical to telling the would-be analyst, the psychoanalytic candidate,

[1] By mother wit, I mean what others mean by God-given wit, the natural wit with which we came into the world. The transposition is interesting!

about what happens in analysis, about the epistemological status or psychological roots and implications of the communication events in the consulting room. It is surely strange that we should say insistently that the meaning of what is learned depends substantially on the social context in which it is learned, and then turn away from our analytic eye and hush our didactic voice in reference to both what our students are learning and what we ourselves have learned and reported upon. I do not believe that sociology can be so taught any more, or any less, than psychoanalysis can be so taught. Becoming a sociologist must be a matter of self-consciously entering a special society (in one sense a subsociety, in another a super- or extrasociety). At the beginning self-consciousness must be at a minimum, but at every point in the subsequent social relation, the normal, uncritical or unsociological perspective is increasingly made over.

It is true that a little of the latter goes on. When a Warner or a Hughes lectures to a class or has lunch with a student, a little of the significant matter is allowed to show forth. One knows when the matter *is* significant by seeing how the students come alive. It is not only that the instructor's heightened color and brightened eye communicate some mere undifferentiated excitement that the students cannot find in the text. It is much more. He reveals by his emotional involvement and commitment what the text and the formalities *conceal*, his involvement as a human being, as a whole human being, not merely setting out to solve some intellectual problem or to see something interesting, but a man with a personal and social agenda, manifest and latent, overt and covert, praiseworthy and reprehensible, kind and malicious, in recognizable mix: an intelligible human object. Without too much effort one can see the meaning for the sometime minister's son in treating dead pan, in academese sociologese, the time-honored sacred objects: "religious affiliation," "cult," "hierarchy," "table showing relation of religious denomination to class level," "The Church in the Power Structure of the Community," "The Parish as Social Unit," sect, and church. What appears in these momentary flashes is that the speaker is not "objective" (whatever that could mean in reference to human affairs), not neutral, not detached, not unbiased, not "scientific," not disinterested, not nonpolitical, not noninterventory, not disengaged from or "above" the battle he purports to describe. Even in the most rigid "scientist" total repression is happily never achieved.

But note that I say these leakages of involvement are momentary flashes, and the didactic status they have is not only unsystematic but largely that of the smoking-car story. They are, in the first instance, breaches of a conventional order of silence. In the second place they meet in most places explicit denial or, more generally, explicit assertion of their contraries. In the third place, where the silence is broken and the facts given partial acknowledgment, they are rendered *déclassés* by being confessed as lamentable weaknesses attributable to personality quirks that it is the business of more or better training to counteract. The subjective basis of all sociology is thus distorted out of all recognition to the point where objectivity has become a cardinal canon, a dogma not to be questioned by the pious.

At least so my experience ran, and not for want of exposure to the best minds at Chicago, in the Sociology Department in the College, and elsewhere. It was an exposure more than formal, and. indeed, unusually sociable and protracted and profound. There was no want either for discussion with peers. True, in class and out we kicked around the classic chestnuts: "Is sociology a generalizing or nomothetic science?" But despite the maturity of that postwar year's students, we might as well have been prepubescents discussing the joys or fatigues of defloration. We might know in a lexicographical sense what the terms meant, but that's about all. What was communicated to all was the sense of ongoing intellective process in reference to society of the same kind essentially as the process of the sociologist's natural science counterpart in reference to pendulums or amoebas. When the metatheory that ought to have raised disturbing questions about this stance *was* discussed, it too had the aseptic tone as of gods discussing their godhead—to be reviewed but never to be altered, hurt, let alone made or unmade by their discussion. No one, to my memory, asked or faced the question, "How does my role differ, if at all, from that of minister, social worker, or politician?" In fact, in headlong flight from just such possible dangerous identifications, those who spoke at all showed directly and by a stylized, ritualized expression of contempt that they regarded what now appear to me to be minor distinctions as total antitheses. There were sects and heresies *inside* the established sociological church, but no act comparable to the heinous one of an apostasy in which the apostate asserted that that which divided the faithful from the pagan was less and other than the faithful thought.

I have so far accounted for the blindness in myself to the logical and operational status of my discipline in terms of a social system composed of my peers, my teachers, and myself. Surely, this is legitimate enough, and, on a superficial view, sufficient. But a minimum degree of honesty should drive me to ask myself how it was when I had so easily, so often in the past, seen through so much; how was it that I was not able to penetrate this most penetrable of pretences. I had but to look inward to see what I was doing and experiencing. I had but to look around at what my professors were actually dealing and revealing in their flashes.[2] I had but to use on

[2] I should not overexaggerate the ease of unmasking. One professor with whom I was intimate and to whom I was deeply attached was himself a supremely skilled participant-observer in the higher echelons of Chicago's underworld. He was moreover a man who let passion show. We even did field research together. But he left me with the impression—designedly, I think—that his passionate espousal of the criminal was for the sake of *intellectual* honesty, i.e., for the sake of scientific exactitude, for the sake of sociology. All his subsequent career—at this distance—denies that view. The sociology is (was) an intermediate term, not an ultimate. He was and is essentially a reformer, not of the type of the Christers and do-gooders for whom he had so much contempt (because they were incompetent), but a reformer of a much more revoluntionary type. His sociology func-

"us" the analytic methods we learned to use on "them," and the analytic methods that, in a two-year participant-observership in the slum that I was taking part in concurrently with university study, and stripped away easily the conventional nonsense about crime, delinquency, and such. Why did I look here and see, and look there and *not* see?

Contributing to that inability to see the obvious (if not sufficient by itself to account for it) was the existence of a known but not at all adequately appreciated massive investment in the illusion. The investment was personal and social. On the social side were the same set of weights that bore so heavily on my professors: the need to distinguish a distinct profession, with all the returns in income, deference, and safety that that entails; the need to leave, therefore, the core of the professional creed unquestioned; the need to separate oneself from previously discredited professional interveners by further discrediting them (by homily and by "studying" them, if need be); the need to retain academic and intellectual respectability by claiming the posture of the disinterested scholar; the need to invoke the sacred name of science to cover the new magic, to sanctify the new ju-ju; the need to define a social role not dirtied by direct or close involvement in a too obviously dirty world of action. The tremendous force of an essentially Enlightenment outlook with regard to the value and consequences of the pursuit of "truth," as necessary or sufficient to other goods, made permissible intellectually what was profitable socially: the stance of "science" in reference to the social. The "great day coming," if one allowed oneself even that much involvement, would occur when man understood himself sufficiently to enter (largely) into the control of himself and his destiny. Even bare *logical* analysis should have raised doubts about what intelligible meaning could be given to *that* slogan. The capacity for pro-

tioned as an attack on conventional justice for the sake of a higher justice. The function was the same as the motive. He had been like that even as a boy. I do not think he knew it then; he may not know it now. At bottom, he was an intellectual, and a more effective, Robin Hood.

fessional self-deception is proportional precisely to professional necessity.

Even given these odds on an initial entertainment of the conventional view of social science, it takes, I think, a further line of explanation to make intelligible why it was penetrated (in my own case) so little and so late.[3] The supplementary line of explanation must be personal. I had quite special reasons to believe in the value of thought, in the efficacy of knowledge, more particularly of "scientific knowledge." I had the catastrophic childhood that seems to be the fairly common lot, so no special tears are called for here. What is germane is that the childhood was, for the greater part, so insane as to defy comprehension without one of two lines of "explanation": that the significant figures therein were monsters of malice of an unconfrontable order; or that they didn't "understand," i.e., that they lacked the knowledge and skill that were or would be somewhere available. (The middle position, that they might have been slightly or severely mad, did not occur to me as a real possibility till much later, and

[3] Throughout the period of intense participant observation in the delinquent and other youth groups "Back of the Yards," I was able to preserve somehow some strange duality of perspective. When I was with them, I knew that what I knew was in their service; when away, I was able to believe that these friendships were primarily instrumental, prices paid (albeit pleasant paying) for enlarged sociological mastery. How passionately I was on their side, or the side of what they stood for, so that the carefully "scientific" sociology was partly preparation for advocacy and partly an advocacy in itself. Not only the direction of my interest, not only the sharpness of my probes, not only the selectivity of my (in themselves perhaps accurate) observations, was governed by my growing perception that the social workers functioned by and large as confusers of issues and blunters of the edge of social discontent, Meddlesome Marys who, in the act, "done no one no good." I did not, therefore, turn an uncritical eye on labor union or church leadership, which had much the same effect but much less; but I had my hidden hierarchy of villains and the social workers headed it. I don't want to write a subchapter here, but (a) they were so much more pious, and (b) they were women. What might one infer that pious, meddlesome women who prevented justified rebellion from becoming self-conscious and open, would be likely to represent to a male "lover of truth and justice," himself not a decade away, even chronologically, from adolescent rebellion? The conscientious sociologist I aimed to be would not on this ground admit any untrue facts to his reports; but who can control selective vision of what is clearly there to see?

when it did it seemed like a certainty.) The "malice" theory yielded to the "misinformation" theory, if only because what would have had to have an accounting under the former, taxed even a child's lively capacity to imagine human evil. The belief in the susceptibility of atrocious behavior to education thus received a heavy charge of plausibility from wish and need. The prototype of what my quasiparents had seemed not to know was precisely the kind of view that the social sciences were delivering as their product. Hence there existed in me a *need*, whose presence I recognized but whose distorting force I failed to assess, to see in the beloved, the Social Sciences, those matchless virtues which her professional protagonists said she possessed, but which a second glance should have told me she did not, and a moment's free thought that she *could not*. For me, social science was not just mildly cathected, it was libidinized.

Even so, with this much more than the usual told, what was going on is not really intelligible. The same "weapon," social science, that was in one sense supposed to "legitimate" the quasiparents (and thereby me) by demonstrating that they were *merely* "ignorant," was also supposed to serve to discredit them by demonstrating (compatibly but quite inconsistently) that they *were* ignorant, and moreover, ignorant of knowledge easily come by, i.e., negligent, i.e., wicked.

To this barest sketch I must add what almost goes without saying, that in a trivial sense I knew these things, but in any meaningful sense I did not. The sense in which I knew them was that had I asked myself or been asked the right questions I should undoubtedly have given the right abstract answers. But this necessarily meant I knew nothing of detailed interconnections (which are of the essence) nor the force of the forces that animated me and, as far as I know, animate us all.

The point of all this is not meant to be idiosyncratic or autobiographic (except incidentally). It is rather, as a matter of fact, that every sociologist I have met before or since is recognizably playing out in his science a very complex play, intimately related to, if not ultimately governed by, the original drama experienced and played out by him in his "family of orientation." The second point is, surely, that on the showing of our sciences themselves it cannot be otherwise. The third point is that it is strange, passing wondrous, that we should ever seriously have "thought" otherwise.

A third play in which the social scientist is clearly enmeshed, but which has received too little attention, is the play that he shares with his colleagues in his own discipline, surely, for him a major "reference group." The nature of that play will also not be unaffected by the primitive drama just referred to, but it will also have a very important determinative effect of its own on what he does. We point with pride very often, in public to the disciplinary effect of the scientific group, and we are inclined, perhaps justly, to see this social bond as constituting or underlying the very discipline of science itself. But so powerful and significant a society can no more be productive of purely beneficent results, for science or the scientist, than the similarly powerful family group can be productive of discipline without damage. Here again there is a scuttlebutt of such things, but no well-articulated intrafraternity knowledge or culture, let alone an open, public, and daylight understanding. The high premium set upon distinction, for instance—not meaning here work that is distinguished, but only distinct—in a field where almost anything may be said with credibility, clearly puts a premium on the observed constant shifting of attention from one field, topic, or aspect to another, if only to find a relatively noncompetitive niche. (This centripetal force, rather than alleged theoretic difficulties, may well account for the fragmentary, noncumulative nature of sociological knowledge.) A better way to preferment is to become distinguished (distinct) by achieving the dramatic, which, given the earlier-alluded-to bias of the profession, invariably means the scandalous. Two such avenues to notoriety through scandal offer themselves: social scandal and sociological social scandal are typically achieved by demonstrating, for instance, that incest is for some enduring group a stable way of life; sociological scandal is produced by upending a cherished sociological theory or by oversetting a widely believed fact.

I am not saying that these things are good or bad in and of themselves. I suppose I am saying that I find it odd that we refuse the social medicine we prescribe: a sociology of the profession finally integrated with and incorporated in the professional training. We (not only I, but, I believe, also my colleagues) were innocent of all this when we came to Crestwood Heights.

The enterprise in Crestwood Heights was not, of course, any simple community study to begin with, even at the ostensible level. I cannot find any simple term, not even "operations research," to describe it. There are many reports on what we intended to do, and did do, and did not, and there is no point in repeating these except summarily here.[4] I am still, in retrospect, not a little frightened at our temerity, though I was not so at the time.

Briefly, we had as part of the Crestwood Heights enterprise:

(a) A set of "clinical services" for "disturbed" children and their parents. This was intended partly as direct service to the community, partly as both demonstration and education source to Crestwood teachers and educational administrators, partly as a research tool (a source of information) for the community study, partly as a demonstration for other educational systems, and partly as a testing and training ground for psychiatry.

(b) Also for the children, we had the extended series of free discussions ("human relations classes") that were intended primarily to be a directly beneficial mental health intervention (my "venture in eupaedics"), but also designed to provide a rigorous test of the efficacies, emotional and educational, of the intervention; to demonstrate to teachers and educators inside and outside the Crestwood Heights system what children could do and would say; to train an intended

[4] See, e.g., John R. Seeley, R. Alexander Sim, and Elizabeth Loosley, *Crestwood Heights* (New York: Basic Books, 1956).

new profession of "liaison officers" (personnel "between" psychiatry and education), and, perhaps as important as anything, to provide massive inside dope on the children's lives as perceived by them, in very considerable content and in great depth.

(c) For the parents of school children we had or participated in a program of parent education, sometimes extensive, sometimes intensive, partly functioning as an explanation system of what we were doing otherwise, partly Socratic, partly indoctrinatory, above all functioning, like the special classes for the children, as a massive source of material on how the parents saw life, school, children, the entire range of matters discussed. Incidentally, without original intent on our part, this "parent education effort" yielded a corps of researchers ("participant-observers") about as good as one could hope to train in a graduate program.

(d) For the Crestwood Heights teachers, we had a formal program lasting several years; we took part at policy and operation levels in the schools' inservice training program, we counseled counsellors, we collaborated with the guidance system and drew the teachers deeply in, and again, of course, we listened, recorded, and made use of the material for the community study.

(e) For the teachers from all over Canada whom we brought into our university for the equivalent of a full year's full-time retraining, we provided an intellectually stimulating exposure to the social sciences as they bear on education, an apprenticeship in the psychological and "human relations" services, a group experience, and formal and informal "therapy," group and individual, as necessitated or recommended by the impact of our operations on their lives.

(f) We particpiated in the semiformal community life in matters from "interfaith relations" to "teenage dances," as opportunity offered or diplomacy required.

(g) We provided incidental services ranging from short researches into some correlates of success in learning Latin to running a rather unexpectedly extensive psychiatric referral agency for all kinds of people who somehow just thought we would know who was who and what was what in this connection.

(h) For students in many departments of our university, we provided a research field, research opportunity, supervision, training, and the usual aids to academic progress.

One could go on describing functions. Suffice it to say we were busy and our lives complex and our lines of communication highly intertwined, if not tangled. It is important to distinguish between mere tangling and conceptual confusion. At the time, the various supposed roles were held clear enough in administration, in everyone's mind, in practical arrangements. Whatever my subsequent views developed from, it was not an antecedent confounding of the therapeutic, teaching, scientific research, administrative, and political subenterprises of which the whole project was composed. It may have been helpful to participate in all these enterprises personally so that the distinctions between them, if invalid, would be continuously hammered at by experience; but even that is uncertain, since in the different roles, supported by different associates, I was also supported by the normal conventions that we were doing very distinct things in each, and that these distinct things were governed by distinct and statable professional canons of performance.

What forced into recognition against all self-interest [5] a new definition of what we were doing lay largely in the logic of the process, the nature of the data, and the presenting situation.[6] Let me deal with the last first.

Crestwood Heights, it will be recalled, had among its

[5] At least against self-interest in any obvious sense. The pretenses of the podium, the consulting room, the "social science laboratory" are *protections*, internal and external, primarily for the teacher, therapist, researcher. To abandon them is to expose oneself to dangers: from within, in terms of stability of image and level of self-esteem; from without, with reference alike to client and colleague.

[6] I say "largely" because it is not possible abstractly, or in the given case, to exclude mere masochism as an explanation, but I suspect it is a necessary rather than a sufficient one, and it permeates much, if not most, social science.

extraordinary characteristics its self-conscious "ethnic composition" (roughly, half Jewish, half non-Jewish), its dedication (or the dedication of some large part of it) to values similar to those of the researchers, its high degree of literacy, its degree of participation in "the high culture," and its long historic exposure to "experts" not very different from ourselves. The bearing of the first of these facts may be least and the bearing of the last of them, most obvious.

The polarities thus present in the situation were for both sides unusually heightened, unusually conscious, and unusually ambivalent. Our "subjects" wanted, sometimes passionately, to be regarded as virtually part of the research team itself, as also highly "educated" professionals in human affairs, as, at least, semiexperts. They also wanted to retain a sharp distinction in the same realm, a distinction so sharp and so "morally" loaded that it almost amounted to an antithesis between secular-sacred, lay-religious, disciple-leader, acolyte-priest. The ambivalences of at least some of us were equal and complementary. We too wished to be of them and not of them, to redefine ourselves now as in and now as out, to accept and to reject the counterposed definitions offered. We oscillated, as they did, between the detachment or pseudo detachment in which we had been trained, the stance or substance of lofty leadership, and the kind of encounter that, shattering in its intimacy, sweeps away conventional pretense in its preconditions and its consequences.

We walked the brink of a crisis or a succession of crises of identity, individually and collectively, and we led and were led in so doing. The crisis focused on the operation and its aims, the nature of the "team" (or whether indeed it was a team), the division of labor, the intended product, the nature of our sciences "pure" and "applied," and actually, for some, who we were and what we were doing here. Interpersonal conflict, overt and covert, increased, and so did intrapersonal stress, for some of us, to the point of threatening or breaching habitual defenses. Hardly one of the senior personnel involved failed to show a sharp career break, objectively visible as well as subjectively palpable. Two of the senior authors ceased to be practicing social scientists, and one retained the definition but played a then largely anomalous or unconventional role.

Indeed, for at least one of us, all the conventional poses and postures became untenable, and ethically intolerable: "teacher," "detached observer," "lecturer," "reformer," "community organizer." Precisely what had been best defined became most problematic. Problems of possibility as well as problems of legitimacy presented themselves in a new light and had to be faced at precisely the moment when all the normal supports for facing such shattering questions were wanting. The shaken psyche could be repaired, but the world in which it had lived could not be re-entered. The man who coined the term *Entzauberung der Welt* retained nevertheless the aura of the wizard and created a wonderland of his own; but we had deglamorized the glamorous-deglamorized, and could not reinvest our world with any available magic.

One upshot for this author was a necessary formal turning to the exploration of his own inner world. What might have been desirable in any event became psychologically, socially, and intellectually mandatory. This is not the place for a "story of my analyses" except as it bears on the present topic. What emerged, as far as that is concerned, was a recasting of point of view with reference to the whole drama in which we were acting, *including* the supposed formal observation of the drama that we call social science.

This "professional activity" as much as or more than recognized "projective" material such as dreams or TAT responses, became visible with increasing clarity as the playing out of a drama of the same sort, complete with replicates of, or surrogates for, the earliest infantile dramatic figures. First for myself, and then for others, social science appeared as a palimpsest, with interesting enough depiction of a sort on the topmost layer, but a much more interesting, highly colored, and significant message underneath. Indeed, the figure of the palimpsest breaks down, for in the case before us, unlike the analogy, the surface script can be only superficially understood without access to the layer or layers underneath.

By a perhaps necessary, but certainly destructive, courtesy, such recognition is commonly barred. It is permissible for a Freud to explain the life of a Leonardo da Vinci in terms that render his acts clear as functions of his unconscious needs or drives; but it is usually regarded as unnecessary or immodest in a Freud (or impertinent in a colleague) for a similar explanation to be supplied of the analyst's analysis as itself an expressive, projective, and symbolic gesture. The "rational" or polite reasons why a Freud might turn to a da Vinci and place him in just that light are acknowledged; but that he may, indeed must, be playing out for himself a much more complicated and covert play in so doing, is either unacknowledged or passed over (suppressed) with a mere "Why, of course. . . ," followed by rejection of the obviously necessary implication.

We have good reason as well as bad for refusing to follow this lead. For one thing, it poses serious problems for self-relation, and social relation (but then so did psychoanalysis in the first instance). More seriously, perhaps, it opens up upon an infinite regress (but then we have never let that stop us, in any practical matter, from going as far and stopping as soon as we wished).

We have also good reason as well as bad for following that earlier lead deeper. Social science so seen is not impoverished but enriched. We continue to ask questions about adequacy of description, accuracy of observation, validity, reliability, the usual "reality checks," but if we choose we may also hear —in any serious piece of social science writing, as in any poem —the cry of a soul calling attention, obliquely but obstinately, to who he is, what he wants, what he suffers, where he is, who is with him and against, what is struggling and reaching for dramatic recognition, in the existential flux that neither he nor the poet can fly over or escape from. It is not enough to to say that even though we are social scientists we are still people talking to each other, even if we could recognize the ambiguities of every word in the sentence. The contention is rather that the formalization of social science misleadingly inclines us to believe we are doing something much different from singing love songs to each other. A fine distinction (not to be denied, but not to be overstated) is thus exaggerated into a false antithesis, and under its cover a drama that need not be covert, and should not be if social science is to be useful, is smuggled in and played out. It would be better to overrate the identity. If we could see ourselves as fighting similarly in our lectures, on grounds equally obscure, for the things we fight for in our families or our politics we should be closer to the truth. We could then afford to *inquire* about how the scientific element in social sciences affords a marginal safeguard for "substantive rationality," rather than take for granted what we ought most to question. We might still see in every topic chosen, in every word used in its treatment, in every turning of differential interest on this aspect rather than that, a retracing of paths early laid down for us (or an attempt to run counter to those groovings), but we should be less certain, less simplistic, less likely to "take in" ourselves or each other or our publics. The cost would be, is, great; but the gains would be, are, incalculable. We might find ourselves without firm foundations if we renounced false firmities. But that is, I think, worth daring.

Even as such complexities drove me into Crestwood Heights as a community and as an enterprise, that community and that enterprise drove me into these complexities. With an eager reluctance I rejectingly embraced what I had unwillingly sought; a clarification, even if clouded, of the I-we that is presumably the basis of sociology.

20

"Lex Salutis, Salus Legis..."

In principle, "mental health legislation" covers at least as wide and important a province as "criminal law." Indeed, the distinction between the two bodies must be very fine. The second, the more familiar, regulates roughly what is to be done when someone *will* not do what is (somehow) required, and the first, and less familiar, regulates what is to be done when he *cannot*. No matter what metaphysical position is ultimately taken, the borderline between these two classes of events has to be drawn on an empirical basis: we conclude that someone *cannot* do a given thing if he does not (or would not) respond the way we want after or in the face of the maximum sanctions we are willing to apply. The provision "or would not" allows us to use our heads, for prediction on the basis of experience with others "like" him, so that we are not forced in every case to exhaust sanctions before concluding disability: so that we need not actually (though we frequently do) punish psychotics for their behavior before we conclude that, in certain respects, they cannot help themselves, and hence, in those respects at least, are not criminally accountable. "Not criminally accountable" means exempt from (because, presumably, unfit for) the normal reward-punishment game that the criminal law dramatizes and epitomizes and the civil law fills in, in detail.

On the view taken, we must deal, to begin with, with the whole set of provisions governing what is to be done when someone does not do what is (somehow) required. Changes in what is required (legislation) bring into existence by human acts (or Acts) new classes of persons who will not or cannot meet the legislatively imposed tests upon which freedom of the person rests as a right (in the legal, rather than the moral, sense that a court will enforce it). Changes in what we are willing to use as sanctions alter the boundaries between (legal and effective) "will not" and "cannot," and hence shift classes of persons in and out of the categories of "criminal" and "sick," "reprehensible" and "pitiable," "prisoner" and "patient," "to be reformed" and "to recover," to be punished and (if the actual facilities were not in so many cases so God-awful) to be compensated, to be taken from, respectively, and to be given to.

Ours is a society that is (seemingly inevitably) growing more complex. We would like to think—or most of us would, most of the time—that it is simultaneously growing more humane. Unless we can find by eugenic or educational procedures radically different new ways to compensate, increased complexity means, surely, that the proportion of persons who *do* not do what is required must increase beyond anything most of us have ever imagined. And, in the face of increasing humaneness, which implies at least decreasing severity of sanctions, the proportion of those who "cannot" among those who "do not" must sharply increase also. So we must look forward to "mental health legislation" (or something equivalent to it) as governing a very large fraction, if not a majority, of any population in the future in any of the developed and affluent societies at least. What the social effect would be when indeed a minority were regulated by laws for the "normal," and a majority by the laws for those "exceptional" (in a pejorative or even charitable sense) is hard to imagine, but needs to be thought about—now.

I say "now" because I am not sure that the state of affairs I portray for the future is not the state we are already, unrecognizedly, in at present. If not, the future portrayed is so proximate as to be almost upon us, and what we have thought through so far, in relation to what we certainly have as the current state of affairs, is pitifully inadequate and confused.

For, in fact, the distinction I have drawn in order to make a point has no sooner been drawn than it has to be fudged. What little we have discovered in the social sciences for certain (or "beyond a reasonable doubt," as they say) has gone to reinforce long-standing common-sense perceptions: at least to the effect that neither persons nor acts can be neatly divided into "cannot" and "will not" categories. It is simply that we outsiders (judges and juries or persons acting as such) do not know or find it difficult to decide when to take the "he could not" and when to take the "he would not" point of view. It is rather that people and their behavior are not subsumable under such gross distinctions, even for the crude purposes for which law is required to function. It is not only that "the person" is, like the corporation, a "legal fiction," so that his continuity is only partial and what he may be "unwilling" to do one day or hour he may be "unable" to do the next; it is also that in his every act there is a complex entanglement of free and bound elements and forces that make it difficult (or meaningless?) for anyone, or anyone less intimate with him than his psychoanalyst, to say what freedom, and therefore responsibility, he might properly be said to have in a given respect at a given instant.

But it is more complex than that. For the view that has been taken and the view that will be taken—or, rather, his view of these things—of what he could not (and would not) do, enters as an element into what "actually" he can and cannot do, that is, the public suppositions enter into what is privately supposed to be supposed, and hence into the context of action, and hence, importantly, into action itself. Reciprocally, what we see in action itself furnishes the data from which we draw our suppositions, and hence our laws, and hence the context for future action, public and private.

Hence, "criminal" and "mental health" law (or their equivalents) can, do, should, and must "infect," if not interpenetrate each other.

21

The Law of the Retardate and the Retardation of the Law

We expect the law now to lead (as in the desegregation decision), now to lag (as in the case of capital punishment). Perhaps, in general, we must expect it to be more laggard than not, but we hardly expect the law's delays to extend so far as to confront the facts of this century with the presuppositions of the middle ages. Much law is retarded, but little is so absolutely retarded as the law regarding the relatively retarded themselves.

I hope it does not sound callous to say that, from the viewpoint of law reform and the consequent improvement of human life, the retarded seem as if sent by God. For, as the retardate confronts the law, he poses—unless Justice gives a strange new meaning to her blindfold—the problems of all mankind in a form only more highly visible and only more purely pathetic. To deal with him seriously we may have to reconstitute society. If so, he may well be a hero of history, just as the little chimney boys, the little mine and factory slaves of England were the heroic figures who broke the iron logic of the "economics" that would shortly have made of all men everywhere mere commodities if it had been permitted to endure. There is a straight line from the law's taking count of the factory children's moans to the vast network of protective and social services of today. There may be a similar straight line from the present plight of the retardate, once legally taken count of, to a more generous, reasonable, and noble society altogether.

For the retardate, as he faces the law, raises clearly (bless him!) a number of vital issues that all men raise, indeed, but none so clearly and unambiguously; and the clarity of the retardate's case makes more difficult the evasion of the lawman's duty.

The retardate poses the first issue by what he is. A retardate is merely (a) a person classified as belonging to that per cent of the population who (b) *do certain defined things* worst, because (c) they *cannot* do them any better. I put the matter so because I want it to be clear (a) that it is a social classification we are dealing with, and not a "natural fact" like, say, the taste of salt; (b) that the percentage is or can be, 1, 2, 5, or 25 per cent, according to social convenience; (c) that the social test depends on what things are socially defined (like schoolwork, say) to be peculiarly important; and (d) that the test that distinguishes those who *cannot* from those who *will not* is itself a very subtle social test. I want to be clear on these points because they are important to seeing clearly what is at stake. The whole question of who is or is not "retarded" depends on social desire (or "need") to classify in this way at all; it depends on the percentage arbitrarily chosen, on the tasks held to be sufficiently vital to justify the discrimination, and on the techniques accredited for distinguishing between "will nots" and "cannots."

These points may seem primarily philosophical but, as with all well-taken points, they are preeminently practical. For retardation cannot be "wiped out," because it is defined in relative terms. If all those now defined as retarded were whisked out of sight tomorrow, then society would simply turn its attention to a new group to whom it would give the same label, the same worry, the same treatment—or neglect.

We must recognize the damage that is done by the defining process itself, in which a human being becomes very largely what he is said to be as a consequence of what is said about him. We must also recognize that as society becomes more complex the tasks it uses for the retarded-unretarded test become ever more complex, abstract, and difficult, so that the proportion of the "effectively retarded" becomes continuously greater. As affluence arises, permitting us to be more "merciful" to more people, and as automation increases, making more and more people productively irrelevant, the class of the "functionally retarded" that comes into sight is some very sizable fraction of the population. The retardate functions thus, at least, as a forecast case for us all; all of us in most respects, and most of us in all respects, are going to be confronted with problems identical with or nearly analogical to his. So whatever we do or fail to do for the retardate now will speak one way or the other for the greater part of the population soon.

But indeed we need not wait so long. For the retardate raises in his proper person—without any further social changes —questions that are proximate and pressing for every person even now.

If the retardate raises, as he must in his confrontation with the law, questions about even justice in relation to uneven capacity, he raises the question for all of us. Whether the issue is to "know right from wrong," to foresee the remoter consequences of present acts, to understand the law's own complexities, to read and write "adequately," to dress or express ourselves appropriately, either with social competence or to meet the law's demands, we all of us fall on a continuum that can only by a strained and useless legal fiction be separated into discontinuous classes: "retardate" and "nonretardate." Just as the United States Supreme Court doctrine that State Court *must* provide counsel in felony cases only under "special circumstances" had to be stretched and stretched (illiteracy, to mental defect, to complexity of the case, to virtually anything), so the meaning of "retardation" will have to be stretched and stretched as the obvious and intractable facts require. Just as this doctrine had recently to be reversed (in the Gideon case), so that all defendants under felony charges must have counsel (i.e., all circumstances are special), so will the law finally have to concede *for all*, what is so obviously true for the retarded—that capacities affect cases. When that day comes, the retarded will have led us into a new and humane law, as children are said to lead us into the Kingdom of Heaven.

But as in criminal cases, so in civil. The same logic will similarly force us to revise our doctrines of "fair trade," taking advantage, false representation, fraudulence, and fraud. If we raise a question of capacity to make a contract for *some*, said to be of lesser capacity to understand the tricks of trade and the force of technical language, we are only a step away from raising the relevant question for *all*, depending on the relation of their defensive capacity to the trickiness and complexity of the contract or contractor. The gross principle is admitted that contracts are void that rest upon gross inequality in the contracting capacities of the parties. The fine principle cannot be far off that "fair" (and enforceable) is defined by a similar decency. (Actually the Gideon case goes in that direction; no layman, necessarily legally incompetent, may any longer be pitted against a trained public prosecutor.) When that day comes, the retarded will have led us openly and on principle into a state of law and human relations that we had been approaching piecemeal and pusilanimously anyway via pure-food laws, security-exchange regulations, and other disability-equalizing measures in unconnected matters and bits and pieces.

But even as with the central principles of civil and criminal law, so with such "special law" as appears to be written for the peculiar protection of the retarded; from the laws of guardianship, to proper hearings in the assessment of "competence" (particular or general), to the particular provisions it is appropriate for the general educational system to make for those who do not so readily fit its overprocrustean bed. Every one of these questions is only in the crudest first instance a question for a special class of people; it is almost instantly a question for all. It concerns the proper care of children or those anyhow handicapped ("all sorts and conditions of men," but especially "all those in any ways afflicted or distressed," as the Prayer Book rightly has it); it concerns the adjustment generally of social resources to *all* differences, whether of "capacity" or desire. So may the retarded lead us into that "to everyone according to his need" which must precede the hoped-for "from everyone according to his capacity."

Lastly, the retarded pose for us generally another problem. So vast a proportion of them are (in an opinion which I share) wholly and solely the product of cultural (and emotional) deprivation that they cry aloud to Heaven, in their needless misery, that such systematic blighting cease. But the deprivation is itself the fruit of concentrated poverty, based on unpardonable neglect. The relief of retardation thus calls, at least in an era of affluence, for the wiping out of every such pocket of poverty, every such focus of social infection of childhood, everywhere in the world, now and forever. That, too, is a task for the law. So perhaps may the retarded lead us from a shameful night of otherhood into at least a prologue of a dawn of brotherhood.

And who will do these things? Perhaps the parents of the retarded who have done so much, together with those professionals who realize what they are about. Not for nothing, do I believe, are these children given into their care; at least, not for nothing if they care enough!

22

Parents—The Last Proletariat?

A proletarian is, by etymology, if not by current usage, someone who has nothing to give (to the State) but his children), the proletarian is the last fine product of the divi-
of its attendant responsibilities and rewards, having as his sole business to have no business (except the bringing forth of children), the proletarian is the last fine product of the division of labor and the specialization of skills. A jest among parent educators—"There's nothing to child raising if we could just get rid of the parents"—is suggestive of a strain of thought that may not be wholly absent in the parent-education movement. That it is not wholly jest may be readily inferred from the quite genuine annoyance frequently voiced by all the professionals concerned—camp directors, counselors, teachers, child-behavior experts—annoyance at the ignorance and perversity of parents, manifested in their tendency either to interfere or to proffer well-meant but inexpert and unwanted help. The problem with the mothers' auxiliary, or parents' club, is almost always, from the viewpoint of such experts, how it is to be kept under control, kept happy and busy, without getting in the way of the real workers, the experts, who have a serious job to do. The answer, frequently, is busywork for the parents—fund raising (in a situation where economic fund raising is really a task for other experts) or curtain making (where it is diseconomic

to make rather than buy them) or food activities, or transport. Where such busywork is likely to be refused as irrelevant (which it is) or menial (which it may be) a carefully controlled study course will serve the same effect; it will keep the parent both busy and in the right posture of subordination! It is notable, perhaps, that this is only the logical transfer to the parent body of the attitudes found so productive of peace and order in the face of the problem posed by the fractious child. There may be at times—perhaps justifiably—a faint suggestion of sober child and sober expert wisely managing a well-intended, but essentially capricious and misguided parent.

This is an example only, and by no means the most important aspect of a general process of proletarianizing the parent, which is going forward on a vast scale in our society. That the mediators of that process carry it forward in the name of "helping the parent" is as irrelevant to the consequence as was, historically, the taking over from the worker of the sad necessity of providing himself with the means of production. In a series of such helpful steps our society has successfully alienated mass-man from all such onerous responsibilities, setting him free to become a soldier in the army of production and a cipher in the process of decision. In deadly parallel, we may well now, having alienated the means of production, be on the way to alienating men from the fruits of production.

The first step in emancipating the property owner from the burdens of his property, or the parent from his function as parent, is the establishment, on a sufficiently wide scale and with sufficient force and depth, of a pervading conviction of sin. In a rationalistic society the ultimate sin is incompetence—not the evil will, but the will inadequate to the ends intended.

This particular, vital first step is easily taken, since it is not difficult to demonstrate a nearly black and white discrepancy between child-raising intent and child-raising event. The more literate the parent, the more accessible to these animadversions, and the more imaginative and sensitive, the more likely is the parent to possess those high ideals that are the condition of his intimidation and that responsiveness to censure that sensitivity, detachment, and uncertainty provide. This makes the middle classes—people who share middle-class views, preferences, and aspirations—the ideal targets, by natural election, since the lower classes are illiterate (to "professional" literature, at least) and the upper classes are immune on the ground of insufficient uncertainty about what they want. Both tend—for different reasons—to dismiss such wisdom as nonsense, "unnecessary frills" to the lower class, and positive folly to the upper. That, empirically, the major "beneficiaries" of parent education are middle-class people or middle-class aspirants can hardly be doubted, but remains to be proved.

In any case, armed with a vocabulary of sufficient vagueness and menacing mien, it is not difficult to harness the guilt of parents who have grounds for guilt, both rational and irrational. The statistics are particularly impressive. In spite of our best efforts—or because of them—a given percentage of our children wind up in mental hospitals, jails, reformatories, divorce courts, or other hospices of failure. Why not, then, surrender? Why not admit the bankruptcy that patently exists waiting only to be declared? Why not go into receivership? Why not appoint as receivers the possessors of the new and astonishing vocabularies the new technicians who, whether or not they want for knowledge, rarely or never want for certainty? If we can maximize uncertainty on the other side—which is again easy in view of the necessary indeterminacy of the outcome of the best-informed acts in the present state of knowledge—the invitation to abdicate is particularly inviting. It can be rendered more attractive and is rendered more attractive by a formula in which the parent "still has an important role to play." Only sovereignty has been yielded, and, under tutelage, the previous monarch may retain the symbols and the seeming of his reign.

The second step is not much harder than the first, and is a parallel to one of the more refined inventions of totalitarian government. The step consists essentially in *Gleichschaltung*, the incorporation of the occupied in the machinery of occupation, so that his fate is bound up with its success or failure. Once the parent is thoroughly incorporated in the designs the child-training institution has upon the child (whether the conspiracy is in his best interest or against it, and who knows?), guilt and interest alike seal the alliance with the seal of permanence.

The third step is to render outward and visible signs of the new-found inward and spiritual grace. Those signs are made manifest by a proper attitude of awe toward the new vocabulary and its bearers, a proper regard for titles and other certificates of the new ordination, and a proper participation in the ceremonies and celebration of the symbols appropriate to the new way of life. The most appropriate ceremony—the secular equivalent, perhaps, of the worship service—consists in sitting for extended periods under the spigot whence flows the new wisdom, or in the earnest perusal and discussion of the approved printed products.

But all these do not themselves constitute the state of grace, though they are evidence of it. The state of grace itself is constituted of a combination of the conviction of one's own powerlessness and frailty (in the matter of child raising, but also, more generally, in philosophy-finding or thought or action) together with a lively faith in and gratitude for the power and ability of the expert, who can guide toward salvation.

If the process is anything like that described, then the evidence of it ought to appear in the product, the "new parent," freshly risen from the foam. To the degree that that parent differs from the expectations properly aroused, what has been said is more nearly caricature than portrait. But does she—and it is, mostly, *she* and not *he*—differ from expectation? I doubt it.

In increasing numbers, I believe, in communities that have most fully had the benefits of the longest and broadest exposure to the blessings of parent education, one finds parents convinced of their impotence, clinging to doctrine in the face of confronting fact-at-hand, robbed of spontaneity (or, equivalently, forcing themselves as a routine to "be spontaneous"), guilt ridden, dubious about their own discriminatory capacity, in double tutelage—to the child himself and to his agent, the "expert"—penetrable, defenseless, credulous, and sure only that, while it doth not yet appear, the day of salvation is at hand.

Some exception must be made for a differentiation of parents into two ranks—the mere learners and the assistant proselytizers. The latter, the noncommissioned officers in the parent educational army (frequently much sterner than the officers), having, usually, raised their children for good or ill, can now devote themselves undividedly to ensuring that the experience of others shall be at least as harrowing as their own.

But—noting the exception, and a second exception for those unregenerates who somehow will not accept the gospel freely, or not so freely offered—my impression of what is fast becoming general corresponds roughly to the foregoing. (That I only have impression to set against the equally tenuous impression of unalloyed bliss is no indictment, but an indication of the need for further study.)

The lengths to which such permeability and defenselessness can go is attested, I think, by the incredibly self-punitive and logically untenable frame of reference with regard to human conduct that many of these parents have been brought to accept and, for long years, to retain. What might be called "the bifocal fallacy," an extraordinarily audacious piece of special pleading, consists of the unspoken assumption that the child's conduct is to be viewed in a natural-causal frame of reference while the parent's reaction or action is to be evaluated as a moral act. If Billy pulls the cat's tail or smites his sister in the fifth rib, it is a consequence of needs that need to be understood just as the cause of a flat tire is understood; if his Mother flies into a temper under this natural sequence of events she is to be judged inadequate or immature, which are not less value-judgment words because they are made to seem scientific. She *should* do better; at least, she should take another course in child raising. Whether this is ever said or intended by parent educators is a question; but that parents so understand the analysis of conduct, after their ministrations, is, empirically, a fact.

There is a similar masochistic flavor to the rather careful statements about the conditions under which children's conduct can be expected to be satisfactory—love, consistency, and all the other similar sets of "need"—and the unconditional requirement that parents create those conditions. I have never seen a list of parents' "needs," or a parents' "Bill of Rights," or an estimate of the consequences for parents of various methods of child raising (or parent raising, for that matter, either). What income, how many servants, relief from what other responsibilities, what sort of history, what supplies of affection does a parent need to comply with the injunctions of the texts in all their bill-on-Santa-Claus-like ingenuousness and multiformity? What income, material or social, to produce this output?

Perhaps I should not have touched on material income since it complicates the expected picture. As far as my observation goes, the amount paid for the advice is nicely proportioned to the submission with which it is accepted, so that free advice will generally be taken under advisement, moderately expensive advice will be accepted if not too immoderately unacceptable, and very expensive advice will be slavishly followed regardless of consequence. (In the matter of chastisement, for instance, devotees of nonviolence for the child in the home will largely refrain from it themselves, will permit its moderate and hedged-about use in their tax-paid schools, and will welcome its enthusiastic utilization in the more expensive of their private schools.)

It is in such surroundings, too, that one finds most markedly the prolongation of infancy to the border of second infancy via the preservation (or resurrection) in the parent of those attitudes which characterize the willing pupil. The business of education is never finished—do we not put "continuing ability to learn" among the criteria for maturity?—and an inference seems to be drawn from this that the teacher-pupil relationship of the earliest grades must be preserved or re-instituted in the parent. (Even this turns on a misconception of the role of a good teacher, but let it pass).

One could continue particularizing, but the upshot in general is the emergence of a new group of "laymen"—which is polite language, not merely for the uninstructed, but for those who will not ever be instructed—accustomed to and willing to accept the lesser status of permanent tutors. The expression of this relationship, whether it takes the form of firm no-nonsense treatment of layman by expert, or the form of high but tolerant good humor at the expense of his faults, foibles, and fallibilities, is remarkably similar to the atmosphere of the nursery school, with the one minor exception that experience with the nursery-school child seems to have generated a more marked measure of genuine respect for him as a person also to be taken into account, rather than merely material for a process.

It is one thing to make some observations on the orientation of experts in general, and some other observations of the orientations of their devotees, disciples, or students, and quite another thing to say that one is the cause, let alone the sole cause of the other; or that one is the effect or the only effect of the other.

Even if the observations themselves are well founded—and I think they are, though we need a great deal more observation—it is possible to believe either that this is coincidence, the result of some common factor, or that the attitudes described are what have in fact called out parent-education activities as a middle-class movement.

Probably all these interpretations explain a part of what is going on. The diminishing family, the increasing demands for in-service training throughout many careers, the increasing body of knowledge, the enlarging of cities and therewith the shrinking day, the general spread of confusion and uncertainty are undoubtedly the matrix in which helpless parent and eager educator find their reciprocal role. It is even likely that first the feeling of diminished competence in the parent—together with the soaring of money-winged ambition—called out a class of professionals to whom these tasks could be delegated. But it is also not impossible, given this situation, that the parent educator has forged a new silver cord between him and the parent in exchange for the one between parent and child which he now bids the mother unloose.

The degree to which the latter is true could be assessed by the measure—if we had it—in which the parent educator may be said to practice the liberative arts. It is liberating to be relieved of irrational guilts; it is enslaving to be made or allowed to feel guilty for what one cannot help. Which practice do parent educators predominantly follow? It is liberating to discover one's potentialities in reference to a given situation; it is enslaving to be deceived, in either direction, about self or situation or both. What does parent education do? It is liberating to find out how little I know, provided I simultaneously find out (a) how I can know more, (b) how very little more the "expert" knows, and (c) how he got and how I can get some of that incremental difference. It is liberating to know that the expert, in spite of his knowledge or because of it, has not much less difficulty in raising his own children or managing his own family (if any) than the layman. Is the parent allowed to know this or just that *other laymen* are likewise mortal? It is liberating to know that psychological fashions come and go, that this year's wisdom is frequently next year's folly, that we experts have been frequently taken in, are likely to be taken in again, have helped others to be taken in, and are in general but very fallible guides. Do we let parents know this, or must they find out in the evening of life and the aftermath of dashed hopes? It is helpful to understand that the "experts," most experts—and this chapter is affected by it—have a tendency to overgeneralize, to go beyond their data, to extend a finding into a system, a system into a philosophy, and a philosophy into a cosmology. Do we teach them to look to us in awe to ask critically though with interest "Who are these like stars appearing?" Do we invite them to be critics, not idly (by furnishing no straw of knowledge or analytic skill wherewith to manufacture the critical brick) but seriously, as equal partners in a common enterprise? Do we so proceed that their independence is steadily asserted, their potency increased, and our own necessity diminished? Do we point to the divisions within and between us, that no incense may be burned before our feet of clay? Do we—on the whole—liberate or enslave, work for autonomous persons and operating families or clients and counselees?

Perhaps the answers to these questions would portray a profession oriented truly to the closing rather than the widening of the professional-layman gap. If so, I shall still be glad to have asked the questions. If not, I must ask if one unintended consequence of our unquestioned desire to do good has not been, and is not likely to be, the ultimate proletarization of the parent as a person and the ultimate evisceration of the family as a functionally meaningful group.

23

Education, What For?

To the unwary, the question "Education, what for?" may suggest that we are free to choose educational aims according to whim. Nothing could be farther from the truth. The very nature of the universe sets some limits. These, likely enough, we all accept; as a wag once observed, we'd better! The nature of human nature sets other limits, and these we sometimes disregard at our peril. The minimum conditions that will preserve a society—any society—set still further limits. And we have to recognize the limits set by the nature of a particular child who is fitting himself to live in a particular society.

If these limitations seem obvious, let us recall that it is only a few years since G. Brock Chisholm published "Can Man Survive?" In this article he proposed in essence that, since all mental ills stem from the moral certitudes inculcated in youth, we should cease teaching children about "values." [1] Apart from the probable impossibility of so teaching children at all, for want of possible teachers or methods, the upshot of following Dr. Chisholm's proposal would surely be no society (since society rests upon shared values) and hence, shortly, no children—or, at least, no human children. Dr. Chisholm's

[1] G. Brock Chisholm, "Can Man Survive?" *ETC.*, Vol. 4, Winter, 1947, pp. 106-111. For a rejoinder, see John R. Seeley, "Can Man-in-Society Survive?" *ETC.*, Vol. 5, Autumn, 1948, pp. 38-42.

point may have been well taken psychologically, but more conditions than the psychological must be satisfied by an educational system, including some necessity to preserve the society that supports the educational system and nurtures, while it limits, the child.

The minimum condition for survival as an independent human being is coherence. The child moves—as he grows up, or if he grows up—from the chaos of infancy, through the clamor of childhood and the confusion of adolescence, to the relative coherence of adult life. The fact that even adult coherence is partial and precarious does not detract from the point. Indeed, this melancholy recognition reinforces the point by informing us of what we already know: that few adults have been allowed, to any sensible degree, to grow up.

It is the business of education in the largest sense—all the child's learning experience—to achieve in him, and to help him achieve, that coherence. It is the business of education in the narrower sense—the task of the school—to share that labor of love and life and learning appropriately with other social institutions, particularly the home, and with the child's own peer group.

But before the school can share in the task at all, there must be an understanding of what coherence involves. In its barest sense it means a belonging together in the same sense that the elements of a good picture or the notes of a satisfying chord or the themes of a great symphony belong together. A child, however, must cohere on many more levels than a picture. He has a body and a physical inheritance and a physical organization; he has a mind and an intellectual organization; he has feelings and an emotional organization; and, at any one moment, he has a set of attitudes or preferences and a moral organization. If he is coherent, if he is one and whole, his coherence is manifest, not only at each "level," but between levels, so that feeling informs thought and thought reforms feeling and neither outruns nor lags far behind physical capacity and skill. Moreover, since he has memory and foresight (which enable him to transcend time and contemplate the future—making tomorrow, by that act, different from what it otherwise would have been) his self of today must be in organic relation to the self of yesterday and to the likely self, or one of the likely selves, of tomorrow.

Since every child is in some sense unique, and since that uniqueness is the very principle of his unity and the very ground of his value, the notion of educating for coherence implies "recognizing individual differences," a phrase that puts the matter most ineptly. It is not difference, as such, that we should be interested in: it is uniqueness. When we express the matter in terms of "recognizing individual differences," we tend to be led off toward mass psychological testing of children, "typing" each one by a number (an intelligence quotient or sociometric score or what not) until finally he becomes virtually a statistic in a complex calculation of "how to manage a classroom." We have thus come, by way of individual differences, to depersonalization and mass management. A school organized on such principles may be a "reflection," but it is also, we hope, a caricature of the workaday world outside.

What is involved in approaching a child as a unique being is very difficult to put clearly. We have difficulty not because (in the ordinary sense) we do not know what we are talking about, but rather because, for many important things, our capacity to define analytically is often in inverse ratio to our genuine experience of them. Where we cannot define, however, we may help by pointing to what we have in mind.

Anyone who has profoundly loved or been loved will be aware of the direction in which the argument so far points. That in the beloved which evokes love is neither the undifferentiated clutter of behaviors and characteristics (which, in one sense, is "what she is") nor some teased-out set of "individual differences" (red hair, blue eyes, dimple, cute pout) that one could put on a list in a guidance department's file folder. What love homes in upon, without analysis and weighing, is the perceived or sensed or felt principle of coherence or pattern, the unifying principle that, for each person separately, makes him, in the most important sense, distinctively what he is. It is this ordering principle that constitutes his uniqueness; it is this that is the source of his value; and it is this that calls for, and calls out, "understanding" and appreciation—as against, say, knowledge about, or analysis of, the child's characteristics or differences. One might safely say that love springs up only where such understanding furnishes the soil; that love is the seedbed for learning or any other creative activity. Good learning thus turns upon good teaching; good teaching, upon love; love, upon understanding; and understanding, on a set in the teacher toward discovering in and with the child his uniqueness, the basis of his unity, or the pattern of his coherence—indeed, his inmost self.

So much for the matter from the child's side; his coherence as a unique human being should be the end or aim of his education. Indeed, the induction into coherence *is* his education, the only question being whether his schooling gives him one or not. If it does, he may "find himself" with the aid of the school; if not, the school may have served only to divert him from what, successful or not, must be his life's quest.

Just as there is a minimum condition for the survival of the person as a person, so there is a minimum condition for the survival of a society as a society. That condition is cohesion, also a principle of belonging together, but now as between people rather than within one person. It is just as easy—and twice as dangerous—to interpret the principle of needed social cohesion mechanically, so that it is held to mean that to achieve "social solidarity" everyone must be taught or brought to think alike to a degree of particularity that would require a propaganda mill instead of a school to achieve and a totalitarian dictatorship to sustain.

But in our eagerness to throw out the totalitarian bath, there is every danger that we also toss out the democratic baby or, at least, the conditions for its survival, if one may mix a metaphor. It is necessary to the very notion of democracy, strange as it may sound, that everybody (or nearly everybody) think alike—in a limited number of vital respects. The emphasis must fall with about equal weight on two words: "limited" and "vital." As we move away from the demand or expectation that persons must agree in only a limited number of ways, we move toward a blatant dictatorship of power or toward a more subtle dictatorship of a conformist mass society. As we move away from vital—we could say vigorous, committed, dedicated—support for these few overarching universal agreements, democracy ceases to survive because its undoubted strains are not compensated by perceived and deeply felt rewards.

It is only when we take these views of the child and society together that the seeming conflict between the principles of coherence and cohesion, between the interests of person and group, of the one and the many, can be at all resolved, for it is only this kind of society that can give a place to the principle of coherence, and it is only on the basis of coherence that the kind of society that permits and encourages it—that requires limited but devoted agreement—can be duly appreciated.

If whatever we mean by that overworked word "democracy" has itself a unique and distinctive value as against other ways of life—and many of us passionately believe it has—that value lies precisely in this: What is to be valued in democracy is not a set of practices or forms—campaigns, ballots, parliaments, committees, debates—but its spirit. The spirit of democracy is manifest, from the side of the person, in its capacity to sustain, nurture, and value (not tolerate!) him in all his particularity. The genius of democracy, from the outsider's, or public, viewpoint, lies in its capacity to prosper the more its citizens are individualized, differentiated, and encouraged in the development and free expression of that which makes each a person, unique, irreplaceable, something quite other than an entry in somebody's "table of organization" or an item on someone's "list of personnel."

This is not the place to describe in great detail the nature of the limited agreement underlying a "democratic" society. Obviously, however, the consensus has to do with "the rules of the game" rather than with any particular outcome—indeed, more exactly, with the rules by which the rules of the game may be changed in such ways that the vitality of the game itself is preserved. Older children understand the idea and embody it readily in their play; only adult political philosophers have difficulty with the thought. What makes it elusive—as elusive as the principle of coherence—is that democracy is so much more a matter of the spirit in which something is done than of the legalities by which it is explained that it is difficult to capture in words what most people, children included, can recognize when they see it.

If this view of education is accepted, we are led, I think, to a process as unlike the whim-ridden schooling of the twenties and thirties as anything can be. As any experienced teacher knows, the minute a child discovers (and the majority, it must be admitted, never do discover) that his education is a search or quest for himself and therefore for the limits of himself—in that moment an enterprise that was all sicklied o'er with the cast of unreality suddenly becomes vital, alive, "challenging," worthy of commitment. Suddenly we have a "student" and prospective colleague instead of a "pupil" and prospective sheep.

This set toward self-discovery also detemines what is relevant and important, and justifies—if, and only if, it is genuine—the act of faith required of the young child, the beginning student, to make him study earnestly what at first must seem remote from his concerns but will finally be central. The value orientation involved furnishes the only ground on which one may legitimately distinguish between "frills" and "fundamentals." The fundamentals are those activities and experiences that, for this child—and for that one and that one—will most fully enable him to come into possession of himself as a member also of a society that will seek little more from him, except that he further the same quest in others. And education—as against, say, recreation—is the earnest pursuit of those fundamentals.

It hardly needs saying, perhaps, to so sophisticated a readership, that such views are neither an ideology to be thought about nor a sermon to be preached to the children (or the school staff) but a way of life to be embodied and exemplified in the school. Such orientations—to self and others—are caught, not taught, and they cannot be caught except from those themselves so infected.

Here not all rests on the school, for the child learns a great deal more than he learns in school and, for better or for worse, a great deal that is different from what he learns in school. The school only damages itself by overestimating (or underestimating) its own importance vis-à-vis the home, by making itself a cultural factotum, or by confusing its role with that of other institutions.

If the school does its share of the educational task, that should be sufficient and challenge enough for any institution! That share cannot be distinguished in a book or a short chapter, let alone a sentence. But we shall be pointing in the right direction if we say that the school is most notably the custodian of the reality system—as against, say, the wish system—the mediator to the child of those realities and that realism that may in due time enable him to become what he and we now dream of his becoming.

This, I think, is our task.

24

The Facts of Life: A Plea for Their Place in School

Time out of mind, in season and out, I have been asking educators and teachers, "How is it that the school does everything well—except tell its pupils the most elementary, basic truths about the world in which they live?" When I have been asked what the schools should do that they are not doing, I have constantly returned one simple answer: "Level with the kids."

It is not that these views appear to have been rejected—quite the contrary, they have usually, with abundant kindness, been "enthusiastically received." But nothing happens. I can only conclude that despite the repetition of a simple message, I have not been understood, perhaps because I have not spoken plainly enough. Rejection for good cause is to be bravely borne; lack of understanding demands a new attempt.

It is not that I do not love the modern school. One, the one my younger sons attend, is clearly visible from my window as I write; indeed, without a break of fence or boundary, its play yard abuts a strip of greenbelt which in turn abuts the home lawn. This is no accident, but a powerful symbol of a significant reality. No longer is there the sharp, designed break between the soft, warm protections and illusions of home, and the harsh, cold practicalities and "realities" of school. No longer does home represent the glad way the world ought to be, and the school, the sad way it is. In very fact, emotionally as well as physically, each child moves, almost insensibly as he grows, across that undivided greensward, from "his" lawn, to "our" greenbelt, to "their" school. It is hardly a weaning; the break, if there is one, is so minuscule, what has to be given up so slight, in relation to what is palpably gained.

And what he encounters when he gets there is as decent a society as he is ever likely again to encounter: as good and decent a society as his home, if he comes from a good one; far better, if he comes from a bad. The world he meets is largely scaled to his size, tailored to fit him, tolerant within reasonable limits of his odd angles and corners, impunitive, warm and bright, unconstrictive (as far as any mass operation can be), a place fit for a child to live.

The best witness to what the school is doing and has done is the child himself, more especially in his playground and going-home behavior. Bullying—the response to having been bullied, secondarily by schoolmates but primarily by the school—is almost a thing of the past, like cannibalism, sporadic rather than endemic. Expressions of meanness, the answer to having been meanly treated, are so rare as to leap out at one like a single flat note in an otherwise finished piano performance. Laughter rings glad and free; between boys and girls there are no great gulfs fixed; reasonable room for restlessness has been allowed; and aggression and affection are no longer resolutely stamped down or stamped out. The school has come a long way.

And it has come that long way out of the labors, the bitter sweat of the teachers and educators there present, and those just precedent to them. These were not raised by the methods they now practice, or, by and large, in the nurturant atmosphere they now foster. And nothing is so hard as to give what one has not received, to break a chain of cruelty (no matter how "well intentioned"), to fail to pay back life in kind, and in the very coinage of one's own endowment. For a generation or two of teachers to have carried the school so far—from a Puritan prison to a humane home—is not just magnificent, it is magnanimous, heroic.

I should not regard it as a charge against the school either that the work is only well begun, that the drive has not been driven to a conclusion, that elements of thought and practice based on the dark ages still coexist with the bulk that moves toward warmth and light. We are undoubtedly at a halfway point, and voices, a minority I believe, can, it is true, be heard calling us back: back to practices based on views of the child, the world, the teaching-learning process that may have been the best the age of Calvin could know, but that nothing in the light of present knowledge would remotely warrant our believing. But the wonder is that we are even half way. It is regrettably true, I admit, that as we go up the school grades the infusion of humanity and decency steadily diminishes, so that in the higher reaches we are not much more than medieval; but I am consoled that further changes are largely a matter of time—the kindergarten gradually, happily, infects grade one, and grade one, grade two, and so on—and that, in any case, as we rise in the grade system the obstacles to enlightenment increase in precise proportion as proximity to a darkened world is reached. It may be that nothing much more can be done about the higher grades until the world with which they are unavoidably in touch is changed—though perhaps that world will be changed largely by the agency of education.

With all the qualifications and exceptions that might be made, with all the pointings to the margin between intent and performance, it is my judgment that teachers and administrators of education together have built an institution better and more enlightened and humane for its day than any other in the society—without exception, unless the family qualifies as such. If there is a catholic church in the world today—a general fellowship of decently related people committed, largely in fact and almost altogether in intention, to ideal ends—that church is clearly the school, the likely last repository of such dedications and brotherhoods.

How then can a body so praised be open also to devastating criticism, especially from a single and the same source? For I shall have to say in what follows that what I regard as the best of institutions is the worst of *educational* institutions—if education is in any way sizably involved with what is formally communicated. What the school *does* is, to a large and highly creditable extent, based on the twentieth century; what the school *says* is lost somewhere in the mists of the sixteenth century—or the twelfth. (The university reverses the pattern, providing rather up-to-date "content" by very medieval method.) The school, as I see it, is a good society, or as nearly so as the surrounding society will permit. It is only that its central function has been somehow sacrificed, altogether or very nearly so. Its central function is, I believe, to tell the child the way the world is. All else it does with distinction; this only it fails to do.

Note that this is no repetition of Hilda Neatby's[1] cry for some sort of return to material or methods held to be in some intrinsic way good for "the mind." I am not even saying—though there may be more than a little foundation for saying so—that the school does not favor intellectual as against other types or forms of performance. I am not, here, joining in the cry for excellence, though I do not doubt, if we do not overdo it, that excellence is excellent. I am only saying in the simplest way that the school fails formally to teach the child which end is up, what are the facts he needs to know about the world in which he lives. If that is not a function, the central function, of the school, of course the charge fails.

The indictment is that with respect to all major matters, all matters that matter, the school stands today where it (and the family) stood with reference to the matter of sex a generation

[1] Hilda Neatby, *So Little For the Mind* (Toronto: Clarke, Irwin & Co., Ltd., 1953).

or two ago. In that most material matter, home and school, and indeed the whole adult world, as far as possible maintained a conspiracy of silence toward the child. Where the silence could not be maintained, they, the adults, largely lied to him or misled him, sometimes by intention, sometimes by inadvertence. As far as possible he was told nothing. Failing that he was told what was not so; and carefully not told what was so (and what everybody or almost everybody knew to be so). If he came at all, which often he did not, to any sane appreciation of the leading facts, his sources of information were largely informal and essentially bootleg. Companions not much older, in an atmosphere necessarily furtive and from a perspective necessarily juvenile; books, inadequate, allusive, as much mystifying as enlightening, disapproved and dangerous; servants, counterofficial and nonrespectable adults; fumbling and unguided experience, out of the light and away from the air of open and accepting communication—these were the dominant teachers of the truth, as over against the "line," as far as the average child was concerned. It is a tribute to the force of natural endowment that a juvenile society so situated did in fact manage later to reproduce itself.

The costs of this now largely abandoned procedure we surely know, and many of them we are paying yet. Knowledge that is bootleg in origin retains its bootleg character in its utilization, so that that to which it refers retains forever some considerable coloration of the darkness or twilight out of which it came. But that era is now—regardless of jurisdictional disputes as to who is to teach whom, what, how, when —largely over. No one who needs to be taken seriously, seriously disputes, I believe, that children should be told the facts about sex as fully and decently as their growing understandings—individually—will permit. We have had here something of a revolution.[2] Sex is really no longer a state secret, but

[2] Regrettably, I cannot say more than "*something* of a revolution," for no matter who does the teaching, even in this revolutionized matter of sex education, quite generally *the* vital fact is concealed from the child: that

matters coordinate with it in importance—some, maybe superordinate—still are.

The facts that are suppressed are, by and large, now even more than then, the key "facts of life": the facts about the nature of human nature, the facts about the nature of society generally and the state of ours in particular: the facts about power, wealth, the state of ethics and philosophy in our age, the facts about themselves, even the facts about the school and the educational enterprise. (Of course, it is *only* the key facts of life that are suppressed. And it is a fact that every society suppresses these. But who tells the children *that?*)

Let it not be said—it is all too easy—that we do not teach these things because the children are incapable of comprehending them. Nor because the facts are "still in dispute" or too uncertainly founded. Nor because we do not know the facts ourselves. As to the first, not only do the children easily understand such things, but they are the stuff of life that they want to learn about and discuss; here as elsewhere just *how* to introduce them to the truth is merely a technical pedagogical matter; the commitment to do so is a moral decision. As to the second, if the school taught only facts certain or beyond dispute it would teach nothing at all; the very geometry we taught yesterday is seen today to have been placed on a false foundation logically, and the same is true for calculus; and, notoriously, yesterday's fundamental physics is contradicted by today's. As to not knowing the facts ourselves, we should of course learn them if we were at all committed to communicating what they are. No, the reason they are not taught has inferentially already been given: they are not taught because they *do* matter; they are not taught because there is a vested interest in ignorance about them; they are not taught because, like most truths worth hearing, they are uncomfort-

---

sex is beyond compare pleasurable (and, in our society, pursued for the sake of its quite proper pleasure). Other vital matters—such as variations in taste—are also concealed, so that only one pattern is (falsely) legitimated. The distortion is thus still shocking, but the change since, say, 1890 is measurable.

able; they are not taught because they ruffle false composures; they are not taught because in favoring freedom and a better life they threaten order and a safe and easy hegemony for those who already have the most of whatever there is to get.

Does anyone think they *are* taught? How and where does the child learn the brute facts about power? How it is seized, and maintained? How it is served by institutions ostensibly designed to stand against it? When do they read Machiavelli, Mosca, Lasswell, Marx . . . ? How does the child learn the brute facts about money? How it is made—not, of course in the niggling amounts that represent pay or salary for work done, but in the really large chunks that come out of pipe-lines (for "owners," speculators, and Ministers of the Crown), or large electrical combines, or cartels or trusts or oligopolies? How and when does he learn how business, big business, is actually done as over against some image based on a seventeenth-century Hanseatic merchant, and the rewards of care, thrift, prudence, hard work, foresight, and all that? When does he learn how prices are set (as against the myth of the market); how "marketing" (successful marketing) is really done; how business and government interpenetrate; what kinds of conduct (not found in copybooks) do and do not have what kinds of "payoff"; how business decisions are actually made?

Where and when do children learn the actual nature of their own natures and what is now known about these? Who in any formal way helps them understand and cope with—and by shared experience socialize—the deeper more inaccessible (to casual inspection) aspects of the human personality, the profounder motives, the more hidden drives? When do they encounter Freud, Piaget, George Herbert Mead . . . even, relatively innocuous, surely, Gesell or the developmental psychologists?

How do they learn, and from whom, about social class—without which knowledge a great deal else that they learn is misleading or unintelligible? About the function of myth in society generally and about the leading myths of their own? About "interests," social conflict, about the mores that in any society make *everything* right? Why, if they can read stupid travelogues in the lower grades that merely make strange folk seem quaint, can they not have then or soon after, translated into language within their grasp, the deliverances of modern anthropology? Who tells them so vital a fact as this: that there is hardly a course of action or a form of behavior recommended in one culture that is not regarded as horrendous in another? Can they really grow up into the world as we know it as if Boas, Malinowski, Ruth Benedict, Margaret Mead, Robert Redfield had never existed?

Why go on? Why keep elaborating a point that is by now either obvious—or lost. The point is only that what we have learned about men and society since, say, the seventeenth century, is either withheld from the child, or mediated to him in an expurgated, misleading, and essentially false fashion.

The obvious answer is the "He gets all this when he gets to college, doesn't he?" And the answer to that is "Perhaps. But it is by then too late." The reason one has to say "perhaps" is that it is still quite possible to get through a good American university untouched by any nontechnical learning, and hence with the primary disorientation to the world that the school has induced, at the end, magnificently intact and untouched.

The reason why university is too late (apart from the fact that in America not everyone gets there) is that the kind of knowledge I have been speaking of is fundamental not superstructural. It is the kind of knowledge that transforms *life* as it is experienced—and should transform it early. It is the kind of knowledge that transforms all other *knowledge*—the plays of Shakespeare, the secrets of history, the meaning of what is done or taught in "guidance," the role of thought in human life, hence the day-by-day meaning of the educational experience in general and every particular part of it as well. Such knowledge is not properly a coping stone, but a foundation block. It can no more properly or profitably be added as a finishing gesture than the notions of number or order could be left for introduction in grade thirteen.

Which brings me back to the beginning of this chapter about not being understood. In season and out, I have been pleading with teachers to tell students the facts of life, the crucial facts for living, and in many cases I have specified the classes of facts. In this chapter I have tried to specify some of them more particularly, and to divorce this one criticism from all other criticisms.

But what all this may well break upon is a view of child raising that was attacked—and he was widely misunderstood—by Dr. G. Brock Chisholm many years ago. In a speech the real point of which was lost in a spate of public clamor almost before it was in print, Canada's great psychiatrist and the future head of the World Health Organization, protested the Santa Claus legend—not in itself but as a prototype of what we do. No more than I, did he care about this legend in particular, or one legend more or less. His real message was "Do not lie to children"—certainly not beyond necessity. More particularly, he intended that we should not designedly give children a false account (as against a necessarily simplified account) of major aspects of life, and then have to let them in on the truth subsequently as bit by bit we acknowledged the falsity of one part after another of the "explanation." The ethics are, I submit with him, as bad as the pedagogics. But that is just what we do in reference to the matters I have been speaking about. We do not give the children a simplified account of government and gradually fill it out; we give them a *false* one and finally have to withdraw it and make a fresh start—if we ever formally and officially get around to it at all. That perhaps is why 90 per cent of the first year in the social sciences in any university consists in "unlearning the student what he knows that ain't so."

Why not, may I ask, why not tell our pupils and students the facts of life—from the beginning?

I may seem to have provided my own answer. Every society, I alleged, suppresses (or attempts to) the key facts of life. How can I now ask that our society do other? I have to believe, obviously—and I do—that ours is, actually or potentially, a different society, in at least this one respect. Of course it is. This is not, perhaps, the first society in history with self-conscious, powerfully organized professional educators—though it is at least different in degree in that respect also. But it is the first society in history with a busy, self-conscious, dedicated cadre of social scientists whose business it is, in part, to report social reality, *what is* rather than *what we should like to be*. Their presence makes it more difficult to bury heads in the sand, because they keep drawing attention to what is not visible from that position. So educators who wish to know may know—indeed, may not be able to avoid knowing—what it is that they are joining with powerful interests to suppress. And, once they know these things, they are brought into conflict with their own powerful, professional goals. They can no longer be unwitting conspirators for ignorance. They may not be willing long to be witting ones.

There seems but one answer compatible with duty—and it goes far beyond tinkering with the curriculum to get in more science or mathematics earlier or better. The answer is to redesign the school experience so that what is most important to all—an adequate orientation to the human world in which the children live—has not only a place, but, without question or qualification, the place of priority—the first place—that it deserves.

25

Mental Health and the Secondary School

Everyone agrees that adolescence is a crucial, if not an excruciating, time of life. Everyone also appears to agree that the school that deals with the adolescent is a crucial institution. Most people, thereupon, promptly proceed to crucify the school and its personnel by expecting it, in view of its crucial position, to "solve" the adolescents' crucial problems. Poor school people! Poor adolescents! Poor public! To expect too much is to guarantee that too little will be got. To lay upon anyone too heavy a burden is to ensure that not even what could have been carried will be borne.

The broadest banner under which the school is to march is that of "mental health," the full-tilt "pursuit of excellence" not being thereby, presumably, interrupted. The minimum task-performance that the public will accept is that the school not make its students mentally ill beyond necessity. The next demand is that it early find those whom others have made ill, and either heal them or cooperate with those who will. The third expectation is that the school somehow act as an effective agent for positive mental health, and as a counteragent to whatever noxious influences coming from any direction impinge on the student detrimentally to his emotional well-being. More modest requirements require only that the school do these things "in cooperation with home and church," but since only the school among the triad is a public and vulnerable body, the chief burden is believed to, and effectively does, fall upon it anyway.

I hesitate to add my voice to those clamoring for busy school people to do more, but I cannot help myself for I see little hope elsewhere. Indeed, the school by its goodness invites such further demands.

If any one group more than another is to blame for this state of being overburdened, it is the teachers themselves, who have made the mistake of caring for and caring about their students as people. It is quite possible to teach (in an accepted sense of the word) caring principally about one's subject. It is quite possible to teach caring only or largely about the learners *as* learners of subject matter—or "good behavior" or "manners" or what not. And, in pathological cases, it is possible to teach caring for little more than oneself or one's performance. But to permit oneself to see a human being before one, to care and to take responsibility—to involve oneself at all—is, intended or unintended, to saddle oneself with "the problem of mental health." And this American teachers in large numbers, for whatever reasons, have done: they dared to care, and the weighty implications, like those of parenthood, are upon them.

For care is the key word in mental health. Barring those relatively rare conditions (really physical health problems) in which a physical disturbance leads directly to psychological malfunction, all else that we see in consulting room and clinic, in our everyday lives and those of others, is the result of (the expression of) lack of care, carelessness, bad care. To care greatly, to care for oneself and permit oneself to be cared about and cared for—sometimes to care enough to be careless—these are the touchstones of mental health. And the way back from any mental distress or disturbance is via care—which is what "cure" means—and being cared for. To be sure and constant, unshakable, in each other's care suggests at once the model of a good society, and a "sane" (i.e., healthy) person, and the wider and deeper the caring and the capacity for it, the more so. The so-called "anxiety of our times" follows upon diminution of belief that God cares, disappearance of any evidence that "the Universe" cares, and growing difficulty in believing that people care—or, even if they do, that they can make this care effective. We are afraid because effectively we have become orphans in a world cold and pitiless, not even—it were far better—the poor children of malign parents.

But caring—much as I have made of it!—is a necessary rather than a sufficient condition for mental health. The care must be, as we say, "intelligent care." Thus, quite in addition to our incapacity to love and be loved, to take and to give, we confront, inevitably and at every stage, limitations in our knowledge, and even more in our wisdom, without which, like the old woman who lived in the shoe, we simply do not know what to do—for them, with them, or about them. Not that the loving and knowing are independent altogether: love precedes knowledge of the kind we seek, and knowledge multiplies love (as well as gives it appropriate direction). But our principal practical problem is to know what to do next, particularly in reference to the school.

The school has essentially two quite different tasks, as do we all in our private lives. The first task is, given its given conditions, to make the most of its possibilities. The second task is so to make over the conditions that the school that follows—in a decade, or a century—has more possibilities within which to operate. (Incidentally, these seem also to be the critical tasks of adolescence: to live richly within the context while preparing an assault in favor of a richer future context.) The first task is the one we customarily concentrate upon; the second is almost invariably slighted.

As far as the first is concerned, it is difficult to praise highly enough what has been done without underemphasizing what also needs to be said: that a bare beginning has been made. Compared with any previous large-scale educational enterprise, the American high school is so decent and humane a society as to put itself on a plane well above any historic example. Violence, ridicule, the exploitation of shame, guilt, and anxiety—all important elements of traditional pedagogy—are all but gone except at odd moments in rare places. We have slain, or all but slain, the dragons, and our decisive danger no longer lies in that direction. Our danger now lies—as in all large-scale organizations—in detachment, apathy, bureaucracy, the perils of the stamping mill and the man factory, be the process itself never so smooth, psychological, and kind. We have unmade the school as a battleground; we are no longer afraid of the children (because we no longer treat them so badly) and hence we no longer need to overwhelm them. But we have hardly yet found ways of taking them in, shepherding them in and into a good, a careful, and caring society. Clinics, special classes, remedial this and that, school psychologists, guidance, recreation, what have you . . . all these are good, as good as food to the child if it is the sign, the embodiment, and the expression of the intelligent love and loving intelligence that underlies it—and not otherwise. And the test, in the school as in the family, would be the tender and informed understanding and the free action based thereon between student and student, student and teacher, and, even ramifying beyond the school, child and parent. All this can be done, I am confident—I have seen it done in large part—in a situation where teachers are also properly cared for by one another, by those they are responsible to, and by the community around them.

The force of such a school is dual: it is a model society that is exemplary in the sense that the child can hold it up against the world as a model of what human association can be, and it is a society to live, experience, grow, and grow strong in, in preparation for the day when one will wish to battle to make the rest of the society more like it: more decent, more human, more nurturing of life and health, more giving.

And if and only if it performs this task of exemplifying and strengthening does the school have the right (and obligation) to go on to its second task: to tell the child about reality, the bitter truth about the world, and to teach him what he needs to know if he is to help make it over. Some day he has to be told the facts of life about his society; and adolescence (if he can be made secure) is about the latest time suitable. The facts he rarely gets in school, except in fairy-tale version or distorted form, are the basic political, economic, social, and psychological facts, which nearly every teacher has garnered from his reading and experience and will tell his sons at need, but not his students. This is the vital content of adult-making education, which the student will gather otherwise if he does not learn it from his teachers.

Strengthened thus by the school (as a good society) and informed within it about the things that really matter because *it* matters, he can, then, with justification care about himself and his fellows, adult and adolescent. He is moving simultaneously into the discovery of the things of the mind, the self, and the society.

And if that is not what we *mean* by mental health, it is the foundation for and expression of it.

26

Education for Mental Health: An Experiment

with J. D. Griffin, M.D.
Medical Director, Canadian Mental Health Association, Toronto, Ontario

We are now in the middle of another cycle of heightened interest, concern, and doubt about education. Have the Freudians taken over our schools? Have the "progressivists" seduced our teachers and our educational planners? Have we now established a system of teaching which, in an effort to make the child happy and reasonably free from the effects of internal conflict, has actually made him illiterate, uncritical, and, in all important essentials, uneducated? This is not the first time that the searching spotlight of criticism has been turned on education and especially on the "frills" of education. Similar complaints were heard in the 1870's, again in the 1900's, in 1913, and so on. Some of the remarks of irritated university professors on the ignorance and illiteracy of the freshmen uttered fifty years ago sound as though they were clipped from yesterday's newspaper.

By and large, these cycles of action and reaction serve a useful purpose. They make it necessary for the social scientist and the research educationist to check even more carefully his basic premises, his observations, his methods of evaluation. On the other hand, there is always a risk that the pioneering teacher may be intimidated by such a reactionary movement and withdraw from the frontier of careful experiment to the safety of traditional, tried and true educational ideas. Thus development and progress may come to a halt.

Maintaining a balance between careful research and what is generally conceived to be good common sense is seldom easy. It always requires a breadth and maturity of professional perspective that challenges the most gifted.

If there has been a new note in the current critical comments about education, it has been the attention paid to those psychological, psychiatric, and sociological ideas which have been influencing educational theory and practice recently. It is a fact that the educational philosophy of John Dewey (for example) has colored the thinking and practice of teachers just as surely as the ideas of Freud have influenced the thinking and practice of psychiatrists. Occasionally this has resulted in a teacher's adopting a point of view and a method of teaching so extreme and bizarre that it is greeted with astonishment and indignation. (The same thing certainly has happened in clinical psychiatry.) We can expect such ferment to occur at the active growing edge of any vigorous living social process; and education today is certainly a social process that is very much alive. It is alive because its leaders and its planners are alert to the importance of research in determining which ideas are useful and practical in attaining a given set of goals. It is alive because it has realized the possibilities of the contributions from other scientific fields and methods in determining the answers to practical pedagogical problems and—more important—in deciding which goals in education are compatible with values that are believed to be really fundamental and worthwhile. Indeed, it is chiefly in the educational field that this melding of the various professional and scientific disciplines has occurred—the so-called "multidiscipline" approach to problems of human growth and change.

Typical of the way in which education is reflecting the impact of these other scientific fields—particularly psychiatry, clinical psychology, and the social sciences—is the increasing emphasis being placed on the development of personality (good mental health), citizenship (responsible living in a democracy), and character (an acceptable system of social and ethical values). These have become educational goals in themselves. They have not replaced the three R's or eliminated the interest in content, but they have provided an essential balance. They have highlighted the fact that proficiency in skills and knowledge without stability, responsibility, and character are without value either to the individual or to society.

Formerly, of course, this aspect of development was supervised almost entirely by the home and the church. There is no doubt but that these institutions play an important part still in this regard. But since the child cannot be divided into virtually exclusive facets relating to the home, the church, the neighborhood, the school, and so on, each of these in turn and simultaneously plays a part in his total growth. Thus the school *cannot help* influencing the psychological, emotional, and moral development of the child. In accepting these as legitimate interests, the educator is merely acknowledging the fact that the school should do something helpful about them, and in this sense they become "goals."

Like education, the field of mental health has learned to depend on the contributions of many different scientific points of view and methods. It is no longer a medical monopoly. Even the diagnosis and treatment of the mentally ill, to an increasing extent, is a matter of teamwork. The psychiatrist, the clinical psychologist, the social worker, the nurse, the educator, the clergyman cooperate closely to help the patient who has suffered a breakdown in living. In the field of preventive psychiatry or "mental hygiene" the need for a many-sided participation of professions is even more marked. This has always been so since the mental health movement began over forty years ago.

The search for worthwhile methods and opportunities to do preventive work has continued unceasingly. Increasing knowledge about the social and psychological roots of mental and emotional breakdown has drawn attention to *the child.* There is now substantial evidence to support the idea that that child is most likely to achieve good mental health (and to avoid mental illness) who is able to move from the passive dependent security of early life in the family to the mature security of mutual dependency in adult society. No one seriously denies the fundamental importance of the parents as determiners of the basic living patterns and the foundations of good mental health. And here parent education for mental hygiene is of primary importance. At the same time, it is a fact that only in the schools do we have an opportunity to provide for *all* children the kind of emotional and social climate most likely to help the child develop a healthy personality and character.

At this point, of course, education and mental health come together—the goals are identical and the methods are of interest to both. The possibility of studying what happens to children in school, how they develop their habits of thinking and feeling, their values (professed and actual), their social relations with each other and with adults—the effect of the teacher on children, his personality, his attitudes, his methods of teaching—all this is of primary interest to the mental hygienist as it is to the educationist.

THE FOREST HILL VILLAGE EXPERIMENT

In 1948, Forest Hill Village[1] embarked on a bold experimental demonstration. That experiment had the support and leadership of the Board of Education, the school staff and administration, and the Home and School Association. It had the indispensable cooperation of the student body itself. It had behind it the staff and financial resources of the Canadian Mental Health Association and the University of Toronto—particularly the Department of Psychology, the Department of Psychiatry, the College of Education, and the School of Social Work. It used funds provided by the Department of National Health and Welfare of the Canadian Government.

[1] An independent municipality (population about 15,000 at the time of the study) partially surrounded by the City of Toronto.

It was observed by the provincial Department of Education, the provincial Department of Health, and numerous representatives of other institutions in Toronto and far afield. The experience was shared by a group of teachers drawn from all provinces. The preliminary thinking, the process, and the product have all been discussed at length with many professional groups from coast to coast.

There were three major aspects to this experimental program: a *service* aspect, a *training* aspect, and a *research* aspect. The service and training parts of the project are described in this chapter. The first data were made public in 1952.[2]

The *service* aspect was designed to meet the expressed needs of the school system in connection with professional mental health services, both therapeutic and preventive in nature. To begin with, this meant the provision of a formal mental health or child guidance clinic comprising the traditional team of psychiatrist, clinical psychologist, psychiatric social worker, and secretary. This was made available on a full time basis for work in the schools through the Department of Psychiatry of the University of Toronto.[3] In a school system in which there were only about 2,000 children one might well ask whether a full-time clinic of this nature was justifiable. It must be remembered, however, that this is an experiment to see what would happen if an attempt were made to provide relatively generous mental health services according to our present state of knowledge. It is interesting that this clinic had hitherto had no difficulty in keeping fully occupied, providing therapy for those children showing the early signs of breakdown—in most cases well before the breakdown became too serious.

However, by the time a child shows sufficient deviation in behavior to warrant the attention of the child guidance team,

[2] A report "A Controlled Experiment in Group-Directed Discussions with Children" by J. R. Seeley and T. Mallinson was read at the annual meeting of the American Psychiatric Association in Atlantic City, May, 1952.

[3] The Forest Hill Board of Education provided space, facilities, and an additional secretary.

the breakdown in living, while perhaps not yet serious, has at least begun. A really "preventive" approach must begin before the signs of breakdown are sufficient to warrant referral to the clinic. To provide a service that would function somewhere between the classroom teacher and principal on the one hand, and the clinic on the other, the "counseling team" was established. This was a very informal group made up of the classroom teacher, the principal, the director of guidance for the schools, representatives from the special teacher training group (described below), and, from time to time, representatives from the university or the Canadian Mental Health Association who acted as consultants. These counseling teams met whenever a teacher or a principal felt that he needed help (beyond that ordinarily available in the solution of a classroom mental health problem) in deciding on a suitable course to follow in the case of a child who was presenting some difficulties.

Usually, the counseling team followed a conference type of procedure. The classroom teacher presented the problem as it was observed in the school situation; various other members of the team presented additional information from school and health records, other observations, and so forth. The principal was often able to add important information because of his knowledge of the home and family. Whenever possible, the teachers who had taught the child in previous years were invited to sit in on these conferences to add further background material. As a result of this pooling of all known facts and information about the situation or the child, it was usually possible to come to a conclusion concerning the appropriate measures to take in the school, the classroom, and in contact with the home. Sometimes this involved a change in emphasis in the academic school work. Often it involved the need for the teacher himself to establish a closer contact with, or different relation to, the child. Occasionally, the counseling team decided that the situation was beyond it completely and referred the problem to the child guidance clinic. While this was not the only source of cases for the clinic, it was certainly one of the most important.

An element of the service program looking toward prevention was the "Human Relations Classes," which seem to have aroused a great deal of interest on the part of children, teachers, and parents. This is not because the methods employed are mysterious or hard to understand. On the contrary, they are the soul of simplicity. They are methods that have been used since time immemorial by "good" teachers and "good" parents—and even by not-so-good ones in their better moments. The technique is only this: when a child has a problem or a group of children have a common problem, or something they feel is "problematic," it is talked through with them in free and honest discussion. All that is new in the experiment is the provision for regular and systematic discussion—instead of a catch-as-catch-can treatment—and a spelling out of the requirements that the discussion be (a) *free*, (b) *honest*, and (c) centered on what is problematic *to the students*.

These classes for free discussion were not intended to be thinly disguised Sunday School lessons. Indeed, the very essence of their nature is that neither the teacher nor the school had a previously determined objective or goal which they wanted the class to achieve by the end of the teaching period. In order to understand the nature of these classes, something of the background of the thinking that went on in shaping their design should be made clear. This background thinking is well exemplified in a report of a panel discussion (by students, parents, and teachers) which hammered out the following statement some time after the experiment began.

To begin with, there were three moral judgments accepted as basic assumptions. First, that "democracy"—as against some totalitarian system—is worth having and working for. Second, that "mental health" is worth having and working for. Third, that "good character" is worth having and working for (and is one of the chief ends of education).

Examining these three "goods," three conclusions were reached on the basis of logic and evidence. First, that a democracy implies, necessarily, free and responsible citizens. Second, that the hallmark of mental health is freedom and autonomy—freedom from irrational compulsions from within or without; and, therewith, the capacity to be oneself and to govern oneself. Third, that "good character" is evidenced only in free choice; and that personal commitment to good ends must, if it is to be good, be a free (i.e., an uncoerced) commitment. To summarize: ethics demand freedom if there is to be virtue; democracy requires freedom if there is to be responsibility; and human nature requires freedom if there is to be autonomy, which is the very seal and sign-manual of "mental health."

These moral judgments and basic assumptions were carefully thought through not only by the members of the interprofessional group who were guiding the experimental and research programs, but also by the parents themselves at various sessions of the Home and School Association.

In general, the following conclusions seem to follow from these basic assumptions:

1. What was said above "in general" applies no less, and probably more, to children whose characters, personalities, and political attitudes are being formed, than it does to adults.
2. None of these "goods" can be brought forth under coercion —including more subtle coercions, such as "selling" a point of view instead of imposing it. There must be really free choice after honest consideration.
3. It is bad education and bad child training if the child is made to accept views that rest on anything other than his own experience (direct and vicarious) helped out by rational authority. (A rational authority is one that (a) rests on competence, (b) tends toward the child's ultimate independence, and (c) operates in his interest.)
4. The only or principal method then must be the encouragement of the attitudes and practices of inquiry in whatever fields are important to the child. We must encourage the child to inquire—"prove all things, hold fast to that which is good"—and we must therefore teach the skills of inquiry, and particularly how to pursue a cooperative inquiry.
5. Such inquiry cannot be a threat to rational authority. It can only threaten authority that rests on power rather than competence; that seeks to increase dependence instead of independence; that operates to the detriment of, instead of in

the interest of, inquirers. Neither, similarly, can such an inquiry be a threat to rational faith or respect.

6. There are therefore no areas—economic, political, ethical, or religious—in which reflection or evidence are out of place.
7. The indicated procedure, then, is to: (a) give *all* children, (b) in *all* matters in which they are interested, (c) *up to the limit* of their capacity, (d) opportunities for *free inquiry*, (e) followed by *free decisions* as to personal commitment, if not always as to action, (f) and therefore, and only so, by *responsibility*.
8. The pooling of the experience of one's agemates is particularly vital to such a process (including, of course, their experience and one's own of the "inherited wisdom of mankind" as mediated by parents and others.)
9. The best place for such experience is the school (because of the presence of agemates). The home is probably most vital for the exchange between the generations.
10. So much is problematic about life today that such discussion needs to be provided for; it cannot be left to chance occasions.
11. The school is probably ready for such an undertaking; it requires, chiefly, attitudes and skills that teachers already have: fairness, objectivity, kindliness, and sufficient detachment and security that they will not feel attacked and respond with sarcasm, countercriticism, or *any* veiled or open counterattack.
12. Far from creating disrespect for the teacher, other teachers, or authorities, since the method is directed to "understanding," it can only increase respect where repect is due.
13. Taking seriously a student's (or child's) opinion, far from making him opinionated, is probably the only condition on which he may be led to reconsider it, if it is "wrong." Under pressure, particularly of contempt, opinion tends to harden, especially if the person wants to keep his self-respect.
14. The reaction of the home to the use of this technique in the school cannot be determined in advance. Everything probably turns on whether the particular home really wants mental health, wants a democratic citizenry, and wants real (as opposed to spurious) character in its children. It has been assumed that most homes do. Those that have actually tried the technique in the home report remarkable improvements in the family atmosphere and family solidarity.

15. Subsidiary goals like good English, good posture, good manners, need not suffer in such discussion, but they must remain subsidiary and not central if they are not to impede the air of free discussion.

This, then, was the thinking that lay behind these special classes in Human Relations. During the four years that the experimental program was in effect many children in the Village had an experience of this kind. The procedure, as has been implied, was simplicity itself. The classes simply had a regular time to discuss freely whatever they wanted, in whatever way they wanted and for as long as they wanted. As the class gained skill in thinking out and discussing its problems, the teacher as a controlling and guiding influence became less and less significant. For the periods of these classes, then, the experience can be regarded as a group-directed one. In short, it can be said that there is evidence now that seems to support the conclusions reached on purely hypothetical bases and detailed above.

It is also true, however, that some visitors who witnessed these classes during their Human Relations sessions were at first somewhat dismayed by the seemingly chaotic nature of some of the discussions. If they stayed through two or three sessions, however, they were usually impressed by the way clear, critical thinking began to emerge in shaping decisions. It is also true that in many instances emotional tensions became manifest and the children concerned seemed to be greatly reassured and relieved by the realization that such worries and fears are, after all, common coin in the business of living. Fears that so many children have of being different from their agemates in an unhealthy sort of way began to disappear. The morale of the children seemed to improve. In fact the procedure has been compared with group psychotherapy, with group social work, and with group dynamics sessions, depending on the particular orientation of the observer. There is no denying that aspects of all of these various techniques and approaches to groups of individuals appeared in these classes.

And there is no denying that the evidence, both qualitative and quantitative, now strongly suggests mental health value in this experience.

As still a fourth aspect of the service part of the experimental program, adult or parent education, which was already well organized throughout the community in close relationship with the schools, was assisted in some ways. For the most part such parent education takes place through the Home and School Associations and forms something of a parallel, in parent groups, with the Human Relations sessions in the classroom. The parents, as well as the teaching staff of the schools, were for the most part greatly interested in what was going on in these Human Relations sessions. Many parents reported that the discussions begun in school often continued in the family group at home. Some of the parent education activities were carried on in seminar form, led by members of the university research team. Other groups involved teachers and parents together, in regular meetings for discussion and study. Once again, the teachers from the special teacher training group were active as resource persons in these groups.

The *training* aspect of the experimental program came about in the first instance through the profound conviction on the part of the interprofessional scientific group that an experiment and opportunity of this magnitude must be shared *right from the beginning* with as many teachers as possible. The teachers and staff of the Forest Hill Village schools would undoubtedly learn a great deal as they became involved in the project (in exactly the same way as the researchers hoped to learn), as well as teach the research team what they, as teachers, already knew better, i.e., many of the realities of the teaching situation. But was there any way, it was asked, in which the experience of exploring the mental health opportunities and challenges in the schools could be shared with teachers outside Forest Hill Village? Naturally, it was hoped that the story of the project both in its general descriptive form and in its more technical scientific aspects would come to the attention of teachers through professional journals. But the value of *experiencing* the problems of *research in action* would, of course, then be lost until another similar project was established somewhere else.

For these and other reasons, an effort was made to secure a small but carefully selected group of teachers who would be prepared to spend an academic year in Toronto working closely with the research staff and utilizing the Forest Hill Village schools as a field for practical experience in school mental health work. For lack of a better title these teachers were referred to as "Liaison Officers." It was hoped that they would return to their own school communities to establish a liaison between the school and the various mental health agencies and resources, including, of course, the home.

By 1951, twenty-five teachers had completed this training experience; another ten teachers finished their training at the end of the 1951-1952 school year. These thirty-five teachers came from every province in Canada. The influence had on their own schools is the subject of further important research. From the informal reports received from them, and through occasional but systematic field visits, it can be said that these teachers are filling a role in the schools and are being utilized with increasing enthusiasm by directors of education to coordinate and round out the mental health services in the schools and to take increasing responsibility for the in-service training of other teachers.

The program of training is directed by a Working Committee representing departments of the university interested in the experiment and the Canadian Mental Health Association. For convenience, and in order to give the teachers the status of graduate students at the university, they were registered at the College of Education. While a large part of their work was actually in the schools, working on the counseling teams, Human Relations classes, and Home and School activities, there were, in addition, carefully planned lectures and seminars designed to help them understand normal children, their personality growth and change, the various mental health techniques useful in helping children with special problems, and some basic orientation in sociology, psychology, and educational philosophy.

Time was allowed for special reading, for auditing case conferences in a variety of mental health agencies, and for assisting in the overall research program as the opportunities arose. An increasing amount of interest is now being shown by these teachers in the possibilities for close cooperation between parents and the schools–largely through Home and School Association activities and parent-teacher study groups.

Whether the methods used in Forest Hill Village, or some refinement of them, provide an adequate or partial answer to the problem of helping children achieve good mental health, good character,and citizenship can be determined only by trying them. The trying–*and its evaluation*–is the Forest Hill Village Experiment. Let no one say, "We achieved nothing because we dared too little!"

27

The Forest Hill Village "Human Relations Classes"

The actual procedure in the human relations classes involved, like all simplicities, a complex and difficult discipline in the achievement.

Into each of several classrooms, from grade 4 to grade 12 in Forest Hill Village, and down to grade 1 elsewhere, went a staff member of the Project or a specially trained teacher with the following message:

We talk about many things in school, and I'm sure some of them interest you a lot and some don't. We thought it would be a wonderful idea if you kids had one hour every week in which you could talk about anything you felt like, and Mr. ——— and Miss ——— [their Principal and teacher] say we could have this hour every week to do so. Would you like that or . . .

The exact wording of course would vary appropriately to age, but the content of the message was the same. It would hardly be completed before the questions arose: "*Anything* we want?" "For the whole school year?" "Could we talk about . . .?" and so on. Actually, in effect, the first discussion was already launched, although in form this was a preliminary: did they or didn't they want such an hour? With the sole exception of one class, all classes that had an opportunity eagerly embraced the offer.

The following week, the same teacher would appear with a gentle reminder: "Well, this is our hour to talk about anything we like. What shall we talk about?" The kids took it from there. In subsequent weeks, the mere appearance of the teacher was usually enough to set things going, although some teachers preferred something like, "Where were we when we stopped last week?" or, less implicative of any expectation of continuity, "Well, where shall we begin . . .?"

After that, the role of the teacher or staff member lay largely in listening, no matter whether the remark was ostensibly addressed from child to teacher or from child to child. Rare interventions would occur if one child's statement needed clarifying for another or if a summary of what had been said seemed to be necessary to dispel confusion. Sometimes, acting upon the expressed or implied desire of the children, the teacher would note on the blackboard points that had been made. Otherwise, the teacher was to be as much as possible a warm and living presence, but interested only in watching a good game—a "good game" being one in which everybody got a chance to say whatever he wanted. One teacher, with an incredible facial vocabulary, opened and closed sessions and kept the verbal traffic from snarling with nothing but a smile that moved like a warm beam from one child to another. Ocassionally she said "Billy?" as a child moved to speak, or, very gently, "Jane?" as another seemed to want to, but needed "permission" to begin. In three months she said little more in a class of energy-bursting grade fivers. Under no circumstances was approval or disapproval of an act reported or a statement made to be shown.[1] The children's judgments on one another—part of the material—per contra, had to be accepted with warmth and interest on a level with everything else.[2]

[1] One leader (not a trainee) who had accepted the idea intellectually but was unable to cope with it emotionally received the children's statements with blandness or differential frowns. He could not keep his preaching out of his face. The result was what might have been expected: children pussyfooting around a temporarily naughty—hence also puzzling and frightening—Sunday School teacher.

[2] Any psychoanalyst who has tried his procedure away from the safety point at the head of the couch will readily realize the difficulty involved, the tendency for performance to fail of perfection, and the uselessness of a

What might have most struck a reasonably well-oriented observer, present at a sufficient number [3] of such class sessions? Or, since all kinds of observers did come at various times, what did appear to some or all?

An observation, striking for some, was that "the problem of classroom control" or "discipline" disappeared. This is not quite accurate but, apart from occasional difficulty in stopping the kids for dismissal at the end of the hour or for the next class, virtually no representation of adult rules or authority was required.

An observation, striking for nearly all onlookers, was the degree of emotional engagement of the children. Expressed at every level—sometimes flushed faces and altered breathing, the "ring" of voice, the body squirming in discomfort or wriggling with the pleasure of discovery or rigid or tense with struggle, at other times expressed as well or instead by the language in which communication was garbed, sometimes represented only by the unusual content of a statement or story—however expressed, it was difficult not to recognize very serious emotional engagement (for most children) in a very serious enterprise.[4] Such inferences were strengthened by the rather difficult to deal with requests to extend the length of the periods [5] or increase their frequency or (essentially both) to supplement them with further periods in the evening at the children's homes.

For many other observers the most striking effect was caught in the statement "I didn't know kids *could* talk like that" or "I wouldn't have thought kids *their age* thought

---

poker-face mask attempting to hide approbative or disapprobative thoughts and feelings. The test searched souls—especially given the fact that our trainees were "educationally" (i.e., preaching and teaching) oriented, rather than medically or scientifically disposed.

[3] "A sufficient number" because an isolated session might appear incomprehensible, like three words torn from a message the remainder of which had been lost.

[4] Serious enough, at least, to rank in terms of involvement with, instead of well below, play at one age, athletics at another, rating-and-dating enterprises at a third.

[5] An hour in the higher grades, a half-hour in the lower.

about those things." In some cases, the speaker referred to the emotional depth and range or quality commented upon in the preceding paragraph. In other cases, what seemed to be a "revelation" was the intellectual grasp of the children, the surprising amount of direct or indirect knowledge they could bring relevantly to bear or the analytic facility they showed in ordering it. In still other cases, what astounded the observer was the dominant "ethical preoccupation," the sometimes manifest but otherwise clearly latent, homing upon good or bad, better or worse, right or wrong, wise or unwise. Even their own shared behavior in the discussion itself came in for critical review. In one grade 12 class, first one student noted and then many commented upon—not so much harshly as in sad wonder—their tendency to "evasion" as he called it—evasion of an issue by looking elsewhere, or, once present, evasion of a stand upon it as against "talking about it." "Every time we really get close to something," he said, "we quick shift to something else." The animus of the discussion that followed showed both a desire to "understand" their own evasiveness—a psychological enterprise in both meanings of that term—and to avoid or reduce it—a practical and ethical pursuit.

For still others, negative impressions predominated. Evident was the enormous waste of time [6] in coming to a point; a conclusion that a good teacher could have quitely "demonstrated" in 10 minutes might take hours and the outpouring of considerable passion to reach. Uncomfortable also for many watchers was the amount of "unfinished business," from a pedagogical viewpoint, in the air at any one time: unfinished sentences, topics touched upon and abandoned, matters brought up but not "disposed of"—the near-opposite of a neat, well-rounded lesson. For still others, most difficult to view with equanimity or sympathy was the emotive expression itself, more particularly the exposure in word, tone, or

[6] Productive waste, as we saw it, and probably indispensable, i.e., waste only in a mistaken or irrelevant frame of reference.

manner of hostility or aggression, most particularly in the form of sudden breakthrough in normally unusually mild and pleasant children.[7] Others again were more impressed by the opposite of "ethical preoccupation" (as they saw it): the matter-of-factness, especially among children in the lower grades, with which they spoke of events in which adults would have expected them to have strong investments of guilt, shame, or disapproval.[8] Lastly, some could only register a deep unease, as the children's discussion stirred in them that of which, for various reasons, they could not be aware. But, positive or negative, few observers failed to be profoundly stirred, one or two bewildered,[9] one or two angry,[10] a few dazed, some enthusiastic.[11]

So much for form, but what of content? What did the children talk *about?*

A full account of what any one classroom talked about would fill a small book. The most that can be done here is to indicate by a couple of summary "case histories" something of level and general direction.

A grade 6 classroom, for instance, said at the beginning that they wanted "to talk about the atom bomb." The initial discussion was rather technical, rather well informed, but with some science-fiction rather than factual overtones. The dis-

[7] Not that anyone observed what could be seen almost any day in any therapist's consulting room, but something between that and the stereotyped behavior, "polite" or "impolite," which marks the range of everyday academic life.

[8] E.g., cheating in examinations or everyday classroom routines.

[9] One eminent cleric said he would rather not discuss the (children's) discussion "right now"; he wanted to "rethink his whole position" on educating children. One highly-placed educational administrator, wiping sweat from his forehead on a cool day, used almost identical words.

[10] One enormously competent, normally very smooth, rather authoritarian school administrator was angered to the point of near incoherence, and, where coherent, patent self-contradiction—very much "out of character."

[11] Perhaps the most eloquent testimony to impact lies not in words but in behavior. Those adults and students who adopted or adapted what they saw (or thought they saw) to home, to religious school, to academic staff meeting, to adult education ventures, to their own student-fraternity or other enterprises, were surely "saying" something thereby, even if they had said nothing else.

cussion passed from "the weapon" in its technical complexity and awesome magic to its destructive potential, its annihilating possibilities even if it "fell downtown," i.e., home and community could no longer provide protection against what might be about to happen in the big, public world outside. From this —and we must remember that these are weeks, not minutes, that separate stages in the discussion—the possibilities, or rather the impossibilities, of defense were canvassed, the feelings of and about "defenselessness" ever more plainly exposed. There was a relatively short excursion to talk about "the Russians"— the "enemy," the other, the alien, the dangerous nonego. From here, the talk turned insensibly to other "disasters," actual or potential—first cosmic, then closer to home. At some early stage in this, someone suggested that they do what they had been doing anyway: "Let's talk about things we fear." Without formal motion or approval, that's what "we" did—now looking through the other end of the telescope, nearest and most intimate things first. "Falling," "failing," "my Dad's belt," adult criticism, explosions, "fights" (verbal and at home), "my older brother—boy, what he can do to *you* . . . [trailing off] . . .," "my kid sister . . . when I think of what I'd like to do to her. She . . .," own emotions ". . . sometimes, my own temper!" and so on. Finally, one child adds what one might think an odd and specific instance: "Being on a stage. You have that funny feeling. Everybody [grown-up] is talking, and you know they're talking about you. You don't think you can do it." Others, first, add detail to these actual and concrete experiences.[12] The whispered conversation in the audience—what *must be* said when you cannot hear—various other aspects of the staged performance, the being under scrutiny, the mixed feelings in being the focus of mass attention. Elaboration goes on till the "on the stage" topic is nearly flogged to death, but still they hang on to it. Suddenly, another child creates another shift to another level of abstrac-

[12] Frequent in a community where children are much encouraged first to acquire skills and then to exhibit them in formal performance.

tion. "Isn't it *always* like that?" she asks, meaning life-for-the-child-in-the-presence-of-adults generally. Quickly (and with a seeming mixture of anxiety and relief) the correspondences between the specific and general situation are filled in. "They're *always* looking at you," "You know they talk about you when you're not there," their talk is invariably or mostly critical, "You don't know what they expect . . .," "They expect too much . . .," "Kids can't do [or be] the way they want . . .," "You can't tell them what it feels like . . .," and so on. Again elaboration—indeed overdrawing—to the point of exhaustion. Then another shift, occasioned by the remark of a child for a long time silent: "How do you know what they talk about when you're not there?" There follows a long review—first strongly defensive, then worriedly curious—of what they have just constructed as an account of "what life is really like." Points are tested for credibility. "Why do we think they're always criticizing?" "Well, when they whisper . . .," "They *must* be . . .," "Couldn't they be saying . . .," [Flatly:] "No." Assertion and counterassertion. Increasing doubt. A sudden turning of attention from their several homes and the vague communal adult "they" to their common teacher. "She expects . . .," "She thinks . . .," "She tells you . . .,"—no one emotion in evidence, but a great deal of the mixture there is. Again, piling up of detail; again, the return of doubt: "Does she really . . .?" "How do you know?" "Did she ever *say?*" Finally, a bold spirit: "Couldn't we *ask* her [what she expects]?" Some enthusiastic, some skeptical, some sure such matters can't be discussed between child and adult. Finally, a decision to ask *her* (instead of the special teacher) to have a session like this with them . . . tell her what they feel . . . what kids their age can and can't do . . . see what she really does expect.[13] Huge relief all round; wonder at how like and how different they all are; a set toward reality testing and action as against "worrying" and "adjusting"; perhaps other consequences, good or bad, which observation failed to catch.

[13] Some such session with "her" was finally had.

One grade 6 Human Relations Class has come to the end of the year.

Grade 10? Very much different, very much the same. Different in mode of expression, level of abstraction, amount of private material wittingly introduced or revealed, frequency of passionate outburst, elaboration of "defenses." Very much the same in the duality between the ostensible and the "real" (or, certainly, significant) matter of communication, the "circling" about difficult points, the sudden shifts in topic as the real meaning of what has been said becomes clear, if not explicit.

They begin by wanting "to talk about corporal punishment." [14] The subject is almost immediately limited to "corporal punishment for teenagers" (useless and bad) as against the same thing for children the age of their kid brothers and sisters (probably necessary and, likely, effective, though not for *them* at that age, either). The discussion again generalizes —from home, to school, to society generally; from corporal punishment to capital punishment to punishment in general. For three weeks there is nothing resembling orderly discussion, merely heated opinion with one dogmatic statement counterposed to another. Interpersonal anger and generalized irritation with the process mount. Someone finally draws attention to what is happening, suggests they look at evidence already in their possession. They look at what they know of English history (which they are currently studying) and other anthropological bits they have. At least doubt succeeds dogmatism. They ask themselves who "believes in it" and why, who doesn't and why. They conclude they don't know but could find out. They decide to "interview" some parents, some kids in other classes, a scattering of teachers, the principals of their own school system, and then, in a burst of insight, some of the private-school principals "who believe in it so much" and some principals of schools in poor districts. Re-

[14] Supposedly an "accident," since they have just been reading David Copperfield and have shown disturbance at the scene in which Mr. Murdstone beats David, and also at Mr. Creakle's free use of pedagogical prerogative in this direction at Falem House.

ports of and discussion upon these interviews consume several weeks. Insensibly the discussion is shifting from corporal punishment to the whole problem of control and authority, more particularly the relation of the adolescent to the adults and their institutions. There is a beginning tendency to empathize, to review with sympathetic imagination the problems of and possibilities in the role of "the other," the grown-up, the accredited representative of society.

In one of the last interviews to be reported a boy begins, "I went to see Mr. . . . [a key teacher] and first he asked if he would be quoted. . . ." He reports some thin material. Silence.

Noting his postural and tonal expression of weariness and discouragement, the "special teacher" [15] makes a rare—and clumsy—direct intervention: "His asking whether he'd be quoted bothered you?" Emphatically: "No." "What did it mean?" "Why, that if he wouldn't be quoted maybe he'd say what he really thought, and otherwise what he thought the school board wanted him to say. . . ." "And that didn't bother you?" "No." General excitement: many talking at once, many more wanting to.

The class was off on a "wholly new" track—"telling the truth." Emphatic, predominant, and well defended was the view that "you tell people what they want to hear." Personal anecdotes go on for weeks: "When my mother asks me what I think . . . ," "When people ask for your opinion . . ."—all voices in the same direction: the dominant consideration in communication is not truth value but effect. Some put the case in terms of achieving their ends (impossible by other methods), some in terms of "kindness" (the questioner only wants to be reassured and confirmed anyway; it would only be "cruel" to say what you really think). With the odd exception, there is near-unanimity: Dale Carnegie is justified of all his children. Suddenly one of the loudest protagonists of this viewpoint sees a new bearing and, without withdrawing any-

[15] In this case, the writer.

thing he said, makes an impassioned statement that if they (his classmates) are all behaving this way, it's useless to talk to them. *He* wants independent views, not mere confirmation of his own. He picks up things only just said in the locker-room: "Did you really mean . . . ?" The class is momentarily stunned. They begin to make concrete exceptions to their "general rule." They extend these. Finally they seem to be saying that truth is relational, something you owe your friends but nobody else (least of all, adults), certainly not your "enemies." The counterimplication dawns on them: if we're saying you can and should treat friends thus but enemies so, we must feel most people, including "well-loved" parents and teachers, are enemies. But students are already bringing in new evidence. They have tried being direct and honest, here with a parent, there with a peer; and the results, far from being catastrophic, were heart-warming or exciting or "just the opposite of what you'd expect" (i.e., friendship-increasing rather than threatening). No abstract resolution upon the dilemma is reached, but an air of reconsideration and trying out behavior founded on other principles is obtained. By now they tire of the subject: "We can't settle it here, right now."

What do they want to talk of next? A large list of topics is compiled and put on the board. At its first mention, one topic dominates all others (Jewish-Gentile dating) and a forest of hands and chorus of voices make clear that this is "it." The discussion, much too long to report here, continued with unabated interest for the rest of the school year. Again, in the beginning: simplicities, dogmatic statements of opinion, charges of hypocrisy leveled against adults who seemingly preach integration on the basis of personality value while practicing and ensuring segregation on the basis of different considerations. Then attention to the complexities involved—for society generally, for these living, concrete adults, for themselves, the "new generation." Finally, in the last two sessions of the year, they leave themselves with two troublesome questions for reflection. What kind of person would you have to be to change all this (the irrationalities and counterrationalities of the social order?) And, as revealed in this whole year's discussion, what kind of people are *we* (in relation to the previous question)?

A disordered year's discussion? Only superficially. More profoundly, who could have devised a better (more logical or psychological) order:

Punishment, as a lead in to

The Adolescent in Relation to Authority, as preparation for

To Whom Can You Tell What Truths?, before discussing the most vexed and double-talk laden community problem:

Jewish-Gentile Relations, to a realistic finale *What Do You Have to Be If You Want to Reform the World*—or even your corner of it?

The results of the experience upon the children could be evaluated "by naked eye," but then we should be relying on an unknown observer's reliability and credibility. There was a wealth of evidence on this point, some of it more convincing to me than the scientifically measured results—evidence from children's reports on their own feelings or altered behavior, reports from parents and teachers and the Director of Education. But, passing up the vividness of immediate perception for the safety of scientific procedure, what do we get?

In order to answer that question, the control aspect of the experiment must be briefly described. Before we did anything else in the Village, we subjected all the children to a battery of "measures": a personality test, a "health inventory," a "sociometric" test, and a teacher's rating-scale (in reference to the child's "mental health"). We then selected at several grade levels one classroom for the "Human Relations Classes." From the remaining pool of children at that grade level we selected as a "control" one child who was matched with each of the experimental children simultaneously for sex, ethnicity, IQ, etc. While these "control" children remained in their classes and were exposed to the regular routines of home and school, the "experimentals" had six to nine months of "Human Relations Classes." About a year and a half later, all children were retested on the identical tests they had originally undergone. Using careful statistical methods[16] we were able to estimate the net result of the experience (on the average) on the children who had undergone it.[17] We had started with 13 connected hypotheses of what the results would be.[18] The chief of these, of course, was to the effect that the experimental groups would show differential gains when compared with the controls in the three kinds of tests employed. If these are probes into mental health, then this is equivalent to saying we believed the experimental children would show differential mental health gains.

The analysis was actually confined to two grade levels: grade 6 and grade 10. For these two grades, the hypotheses were all or mostly all borne out, with varying degrees of statistical reliability. One hypothesis—that younger children would, because of greater flexibility, "profit" more than older ones—was contradicted by the evidence. They were much more "variable," but it was impossible to say reliably that they profited more. Another hypothesis was added later and tested only for grade 10 children: that experimental children, despite substantial loss of time for Human Relations Classes, would show differential gain over the control children in their school subject marks! This hypothesis—an unlooked-for by-product benefit—was dramatically confirmed for marks-in-all-subjects-taken-together, for—curiously—history, and—incredibly—for English, the subject in which the experimentals had had to sacrifice half their time to make room for the Human Relations Classes at all.

[16] Principally, an "analysis of variance and covariance."

[17] Detailed results are reported in Part II of a series of articles on Mental Health and the Schools in *Personnel and Guidance Journal.*

[18] See Chapter 28.

28

A Controlled Experiment

with THOMAS MALLINSON, M.A.
Toronto

From the present preoccupations and funded wisdom of psychiatrists the experimenters at Forest Hill Village drew a number of clues in posing their problem. The general view of mental illness as "a breakdown in living" permitted us to view pathology as a continuum between psychosis and the "psychopathology of everyday life," and also as an aspect of a dynamic process of organization, disorganization, reorganization. Clinical practice, as well as theory flowing from it, suggested the utility of experiment with a warm, supportive relationship maximally divested of authoritarian elements. Clinical insight suggested the central importance of "readiness" for problem discussion, and the critical necessity to begin with the patient's problem rather than the therapist's. From practitioners in this field also we drew some of our concerns with the "unorganized" (as against the "disorganized") character, and also our focus on a preventive (or, at least, antipathic) orientation.

From social theory and social psychological theory we drew our view of the crucial role of "the self" as the regulatory agency in behavior, and of organized social activity as the nexus in which the self emerges, and is made and continuingly remade. From the same sources—jointly with psychology—we drew our views about the relations between institution—in this case the school—and personality. From the material on group structure, on group "climate," and on the relative durability or bindingness of group-reached decisions we drew clues to the structuring of the group experience.

From ethical theory and research into the process of "character building" we derived suggestions about the nonutility, not to say disutility, of the traditional methods of coercion, injunction, and cajolery, and about the relation between the internalization of or commitment to norms and the essentially egalitarian, dominance-free social situation in which possibilities for its occurrence conclusively seem to lie. From similar sources derived our concern with the engendered split between "theory" and "practice," "realism" and "idealism" that is said to (and, in our belief, does) confound much behavior and operate as cause and consequence in much confusion and tension.

From education theory derived our views about the place of thought in action, most particularly the view that thought arises when one *has* a problem (not when one is given a problem), i.e., when habitual modes of behaving fail of their desired effects. From similar sources we drew the view that learning is (roughly) proportional to emotional involvement, and that, therefore, the only problems worth discussing are contentious—or, more exactly, contendable—problems.

Lastly, from political theory (and the problems of its practice) came our concern with the reciprocal effects of authoritarian personality and authoritarian social order, with the pressing problem of developing means and methods for reaching consensus if democracy is to survive, and with the plausibly indicated relation between political (and general) apathy and the situation of the middle-class child at the focus of the media of mass communication, of the processes of "other-direction" and of the multiple means of manipulation. These concerns relate on one side to the maintenance or restoration of the vitality of the small group and on the other to the creation of situations or occasions in which relative autonomy might be maximally preserved or minimally endangered.

This is a large paternity for so small and experimental a child, but it is, perhaps, sound to acknowledge it.

The form of the experiment was that of the classic agricultural experiments, *mutatis mutandis*, of "treated and untreated plots," with careful matching beforehand of children on test-relevant criteria,[1] before-and-after "measurement," and the assessment of differences in "gain" between "untreated" and "treated" plots.[2]

The experiment was guided by a number of hypotheses:

1. That the students would "seize" the given opportunity, i.e., become readily, willingly, and deeply involved.
2. That they would discuss social or common and communicable problems rather than merely idiosyncratic, bizarre, or ineffable aspects of experience.
3. That they would, in the process, alter opinions, attitudes, and "feelings."
4. That such altered opinions, attitudes, and feelings would extend to areas other than the topics directly discussed, and to areas more general.
5. That the alterations would predominantly be in the directions thought by mental hygienists to be desirable, i.e., "healthier" rather than "unhealthier."
6. That this (5) would be significantly more so in the experimental groups than in the controls.
7. That discussion skill would increase differentially in the experimental group.
8. That group cohesiveness would increase differentially in the experimental group.[3]

[1] Children in experimental and control groups were matched individually for sex, IQ, and ethnicity—simultaneously—all of which were known to affect test scores. In addition, the influences of these characteristics were "factored out" of the differences actually analyzed.

[2] The relevant difference is given by (E_0 minus E_1) minus (C_0 minus C_1) where E_0 E_1 C_0 C_1 are the before-and-after scores of the experimental and control groups respectively.

[3] Hypotheses 8, 9, and 12 were added after the experiment began, but before results were evaluated, and do not have, therefore, the same predictive status as the other hypotheses.

9. That differences would be noted (though not necessarily ascribed to the experience) by people (children and adults) related to the children but not related to the experiment.
10. That the differences found would relate very closely to selected mental health concerns, most especially "nervousness" (behavior expressive of generalized tension) and "withdrawal." [4]
11. That, in general, differential gains would be larger in tests bearing on "self-relation" than "other-relation."
12. That differential gains would be more notable in younger (as against older) children.
13. That the differences would be discoverable eighteen months or more after the experiment.

The hypotheses about involvement, about type of topic, and about discussion skill were to be "tested" by the observations of experimenters and outsiders. The other hypotheses were to be tested by the statistical evaluation of a battery of instruments ranging from a personality test,[5] through an adaptation of the "Guess-Who Game," [6] and a Teacher's Rating Form,[7] to a "Physical Health Inventory." [8]

Space and time will not permit development here of the full content of discussions. A mere naming of topics will only suggest the type of material discussed. A grade 10 class, for example, began by discussing "Corporal Punishment," did its own local opinion research on the issue, moved insensibly into a discussion of authority and the adolescent, passed thence to

[4] The experiment was based, in part, on previous work by J. D. Griffin, M.D., M.A., and W. Line, Ph.D., OBE, with "shy" and "withdrawn" children.

[5] The California Test of Personality, Elementary Form, Grade 6; Secondary Form, Grade 10 (see footnote 11).

[6] A Study of Social Definitions, adapted from Donald L. Grumman, and Eunice L. Fineberg.

[7] Teacher's Rating Form.

[8] Physical Health Inventory copied directly from Jack Hertzman to make comparisons possible. (See Jack Hertzman's "High School Mental Hygiene Survey," *American Journal of Orthopsychiatry*, Vol. 18, 1948, pp. 238-256.)

a discussion of the obligation (or its absence) to tell the truth or say what one really thinks in various relationship situations —and then, having "cleared" the problem of where they stood as adolescents and about what one could "afford" to speak honestly to whom, came to a pressing, practical problem—for them—interethnic dating, courtship, and marriage. The last topic occupied the last six weeks of the whole six-months' discussion.

Discussions in other classes were similar as to topics, with perhaps a tendency to briefer duration, more "concreteness," and more personal involvement at lower levels of ego (and/or intelligence) and longer duration, more abstraction, more "detachment" (and "intellectual defenses") at higher levels.[9]

The first two hypotheses respecting involvement and topic type were rendered more plausible by the behavior observed by the experimenters and others, and by the record of the discussions itself.[10]

Hypothesis 3—that opinions, attitudes, and feelings would be altered—was too ambiguously stated to be capable of testing. Both groups, experimental and control, did show radical changes, but if the hypothesis was intended to imply that the experimental group would show more, or more radical, changes, the result data will not support the hypothesis. The results show an equal number of opinion changes in experimental and control groups. It is *direction* of change, rather than volume of change, that differentiates experimental from control groups.

Hypothesis 4 is amply supported. Attitudes—or at least "responses" to questions purporting to tap attitudes—altered with respect to questions of wide generality and to questions of great specificity. Examples of the former are: "Do you

[9] These are only impressions—reconsidered and checked with the impressions of others, of course—but, by no means, demonstrated.

[10] What is reported here is the result of examining only grade 6 and grade 10 data, separately and together, since only at those two levels was it possible to create and maintain the experimental conditions. At three other levels either too-brief exposure of the experimentals, or too-early extension of the "treatment" to controls destroyed the test-retest possibility.

find it difficult to overcome the feeling that you are inferior to others?" [11] or "Do you prefer to keep your feelings to yourself when things go wrong?" [12] Examples of the latter, "Do you often have bad dreams?" [13] or "Do you frequently have choking spells?" [14]

Hypotheses 5 and 6—to the effect that changes in the experimental groups would not only occur (chiefly) in the "healthier" direction, but that they would do so with significantly greater frequency than in the control groups—are borne out by the data, sharply and definitely in grade 10, less sharply but with probable significance in grade 6. An analysis of the variance[15] of results in the former grade, for all personality tests taken together shows a result such that there is less than one chance in a thousand of its having occurred by chance. Similar methods applied to the grade 6 data show results favoring the experimental group, but not so significantly as to permit Hypothesis 6 to be accepted for the younger children.[16] Hypothesis 7, referring to increased discussion skill was supported by the later observations of outsiders with reference to the grade 10 group, as was Hypothesis 8, referring to the increase of social cohesiveness. The latter, moreover, was further strengthened by the behavior of the students in the experimental and subsequent year.

Hypothesis 9 was confirmed for the older group alike by the informal remarks of some parents and teachers, and by the two-year-later rating behavior of teachers and social imputations of peers in the formal "tests" already referred to.

Hypothesis 10, that greatest differences would show in tests

[11] California Personality Test, Secondary Form, Question 71.

[12] Ibid., Question 12.

[13] Ibid., Elementary Form, Question 62.

[14] "Physical Health Inventory."

[15] Actually an "analysis of variance and covariance" such that the influences of sex, nature of test, intelligence, and original performance were allowed for in assessing the significance of net change.

[16] Differences such as those noted could have occurred more than once in twenty times by "chance," i.e., in the absence of a real difference attributable to the process. This raises some interesting questions not explored by the study, about the role of the "maturation factor" in the process.

for "nervousness" and "withdrawal" is supported markedly in grade 10 with respect to the former and in grade 6 with respect to the latter. Hypothesis 11, that greatest gains would show in "self-relation" tests rather than "social relation"[17] tests is confirmed in both grades.

Hypothesis 12, that younger children would show greater gains, is not borne out by the scores, and, as far as the evidence goes, is contradicted. The evidence, however, is not such as to permit us to assert the contrary.

Confirmation of Hypothesis 13—that differential gains would still show eighteen or more months later—was embodied in the structure of the experiment since no retest was conducted within a shorter interval.

The weight of the evidence, qualitative and quantitative, makes it difficult to doubt that something of consequence, and something desirable, occurred. History itself added a footnote. In the graduating year of the grade 10 group (i.e., three years later) five students were awarded major scholarships on the basis of competitive examinations by the University of Toronto. Four of these came from the experimental group, one was a new arrival from outside the school system, none was a member of the four-times-as-numerous nonexperimental group. Perhaps, the long arm of coincidence . . . but enough to give one pause, I should think, for reflection.

We would like to see the experiment first reported and then repeated. Until then, we are left with a very strong feeling of promising possibilities and warranted hope.

REFERENCES

1. Committee on Preventive Psychiatry of the Group for the Advancement of Psychiatry. *Report No. 18* (Topeka, Kansas, 1951).
2. Mallinson, T., *An Experimental Investigation of Group-*

[17] The questionable vocabulary is a function of the tests used, and a concession rather to uncritical classification than to the authors' analytic preferences.

Directed Discussion in the Classroom. Unpublished doctoral dissertation, University of Toronto, 1954.

3. Seeley, J. R., A. Sim, and E. W. Loosley, *Crestwood Heights* (Toronto: University of Toronto Press, 1956).

29

Guidance and the Youth Culture

It is the beginning of wisdom to realize that every analogy involves a disanalogy. It is the middle of wisdom to understand where one stops and the other begins. It is also a part of wisdom to realize that the limitation of analogy by disanalogy reduces the heuristic value of neither. If we are to go beyond "A rose is a rose is a rose," we must say that a rose is like an apple blossom (or a cactus), and both statements are true in some respects and untrue in others.

Accordingly, while I shall seek to emphasize what is new—and, I believe, significant—in the situation of youth today, it is always open to anyone to quote back to me Thucydides or Herodotus speaking similarly (in some ways) of the youth of their times, or to clinch their argument from Ecclesiastes ". . . and there is no new thing under the sun."

To argue such points—and much argument is of this sort—is rather pointless. For even when we speak of change we must presuppose some "thing" unchanged to which the change refers, else we should not be able to speak of change at all. When you say "this child has matured" or "my mother has aged" you neither deny that something has changed nor that something has not. There *are* eternal verities, and there *is* eternal flux; and in any change there is that which changes not, as well as that which changes. Upon which of these you direct attention depends on your purpose. My purpose is to direct attention upon change, because I feel that change is most talked of and least appreciated. And how should it be otherwise? For custom is comforting, and change is strenuous in the confrontation, and few there be that prefer strain to comfort—except always for the masochists. So I shall point to what is novel, leaving to you the rejoinder " 'Twas ever thus." (Though it wasn't!)

I believe that youth, as we confront it, has undergone in our lifetimes transformations so tremendous that as guides we are largely without guidance, since they are not as we were, their situation is not any situation we know, and those means by which we were socialized have little relevance for their situation as they are now newly circumstanced.

Let me first define a little more clearly what category of people I am referring to as "youth." (The danger in America, which worships youngness, is always that an audience will include itself up to the "be young at seventy" in the glamorous term.) By youth, I mean simply people in that chrysalis period extending roughly from 14 to 25 years of age (or, roughly, physically, from puberty to full physical peak). These, I take it, are the young adults—or old children—with whom guidance people are most centrally concerned. It is of these young people—and those like them to follow, if we do not have too many Christmas Island tests, that I wish to speak.

As an oblique way of speaking about them, let me speak first of the social world in which, objectively and subjectively, they live. I do so because it seems evident that we can only hope to guide youth by *altering* the world in which it lives (again objectively or subjectively), or by understanding that world, relating ourselves to it, and in some sense entering upon it. In either case, we must first appreciate it.

Among the most significant transformations that the world has undergone in the single generation marked by our lifespan is the change caught up in Mr. Galbraith's phrase "The Affluent Society." The phrase, taken by itself, is a pallid description of what has actually occurred: we now live in not just a society that is affluent, but a society in which the flow of "products" is such that we are likely to suffocate economically, to drown in our own production, unless we can constantly invent new ways to "consume" or use up "the surplus."

It is difficult to imagine a more radical change. The whole creation up to this point has subsisted in an economics of scarcity. The industrious bee and the conservative squirrel function as you and I were brought up to function: creatively, to bring new goods, as far as possible, into being; and conservatively, to maintain them in being as long as possible. This orientation exerted a discipline, an ordering principle, over our whole lives, individual and collective. Since the discipline was completely general and common—except for the few people, like the nobility, hired to exhibit the opposite principle of conspicuous waste—it acted to order both individual behavior and social life, and both of these, moreover, in almost every respect.

The premium that we set on effort stems from this source. We in the West (in the era just dying) are so used to thinking of effortfulness as virtuous that we are almost disposed to treat the view as though it reported a fact of nature. I assure you that is not so: it is a fact of culture, depending closely on a cultural maintenance of a perspective of scarcity. Our words of highest praise—"accomplishment," "achievement," "fulfillment," "completion"—are all keyed to this cult of effort; and our next highest praises are keyed to the cult of conservation. Note particularly that the orientation does not apply only to "work," but to what is designated as "play," and to what lies in between by way of poetry, worship, or self-cultivation. Western men in their leisure characteristically do not contemplate, or even just happily consume: they *actively* play, or passionately *pursue* "hobbies." Hobbies are essentially ways of working without appearing to work, shifting not the work orientation, which is commonly heightened, but the material worked upon or the means employed, or both. (Even our language of love is largely couched in activistic terms or terms that assume scarcity: conquest, possession, accomplishment; capturing, cultivating, retaining; proving, straining, panting. . . .)

The premium set on order, on rationality, on the control of emotion (on control itself), on exact observation and meticulous observance, whether of forms of conduct or clauses of contracts, all stem from the same source. The very notion of discipline, as we know it, is underpinned by belief in scarcity. Not only the ends of behavior (the implicit worship of the strenuous and effortful) but the means of its collective control are traditionally, customarily, scarcity-based. The normal adult disciplinary force has been the economic sanction, operating in two ways. In one direction, it held out very scarce rewards for which very deep hungers had been cannily created in the preparatory period of youth. In the other, it extended the threat of very severe sanctions, going originally to the point of starvation, and later to loss of status, i.e., to public disgrace, followed by the inner collapse attendant on basic loss of self-approval, the feeling of "uselessness" equivalent to psychological death. Not only material reward and punishment, note, but nonmaterial, "spiritual" goods even more (honors, status symbols, access to all or most of the true goods of life, even to decency or natural beauty), fell within the economics of scarcity, and hence exerted profound and pervasive disciplinary effects. The goods that fed the body, but more important the goods that gladdened the heart, even the means of self-improvement in art, poetry, high religion, the inspiration that inspires the spirit, all were carefully rationed and meticulously metered, distributed according to "desert" (that is, imputed productivity) and allocated so that the means of grace and the hope of glory alike forced the hearts and hands of men to the unrelenting pursuit of those enterprises thought to accrue to the common weal (i.e., most commonly to private profit).

These things are no longer so; those ends are no longer at

all—or if at all, very little—relevant. The standing sanctions for self- and other-control are becoming of marginal, of slight significance. The perplexing problems of pervasive plenty are upon us—or at least upon our progeny.

It is not yet *quite* the case, but try to imagine for the sake of vividness a transition from a stage in which even needed food can be given and withheld as a means of control of the young, through one in which only such luxuries as candy are allowed to function so, to one in which even custom-made clothes and convertibles are to be "naturally" around one, like air, regardless of relation to duty, desert, utility, productivity, or any such norms or notions. They are there to be used, to be "consumed," regardless, because failing such consumption the economy will grind to a halt, and that which gives point and direction to our lives will be seen to be undirected and pointless. Which, as the kids say, "Perish forbid!"

Indeed, we see a reversal, a genuine inversion of values put upon functions, going much further than this. A new system of rewards, in more than sketch, in form more full than initial outline, may with no need for nice discrimination be detected as it exhibits itself rather blatantly even now in our daily lives. The successors to the former captains of industry, the persons at the apex of the pyramid of honor, monopolizing its material perquisites are now—in Vance Packard's telling phrase—the waste-makers. The waste-makers are the high priests on Madison Avenue and the holy kings in the engineering offices of the new order: it is they who keep our world going, just as formerly the priests assured the orderly precession of the equinoxes, and the kings ensured that the gods be sufficiently pleased and pleasured to preserve the civil order. These be they who see that a sufficient coefficient of planned obsolescence, of efficient wastefulness is built into things. These be they who, by a forceful fraud to which we are all in some sense and due degree party, maintain the fitful dissatisfaction with things as they are in favor of things that are no better, which goes by the name of Fashion. These are the people necessary to infuse sufficient appearance of meaning or value into events so that we do not come to the catastrophe of resting content in what we *have* got, or happy in a bounty too bounteous, even now, to absorb. These are the functionaries, highly paid to keep "calling the turns"; not to better turns, but only to turns different, so that motion and movement may be maintained even when both have been emptied of meaning. These are the salary-sanctioned slayers of the once-god, now-devil, Satisfaction. It is their task to ensure—what was formerly regarded as a regrettable aspect of the human condition—that "Man never is, but always to be blest." They are paid to perpetuate a now indispensable perversion.

The new deal has implications of the most far-reaching sort for "guidance" of others with reference equally to ends and means. As far as ends are concerned, it is evidently idle to guide your charges toward a world that has ceased to exist and that, in my opinion, can never be recreated or restored. But beyond this, you no longer have at your disposal—or insofar as you do they are rapidly slipping from your grasp—the aids to discipline (or, as you may prefer to call them, the means of motivation) that were formerly all too readily available to you. You no longer have—or, shortly, no longer will have—hungry little characters whose hungers are your capital assets: the very handles whereby you might expect to handle and hold them.

I want to deal next with another and perhaps more fateful, if not fatal, form of affluence: an increase, paralleling the material as far as magnitude is concerned, in the contents of consciousness, more especially self-consciousness.

I suppose that, time out of mind, self-consciousness has in one sense been regarded as a good; although everyday experience for most of us serves at least to raise a question as to its undiluted beneficence. Indeed, as I said on another occasion, self-consciousness is a burden not lightly to be borne. My own history and the history of the decade and a half since I wrote that confirm me rather than disconfirm me in the view. In any case, since then self-consciousness has vastly increased. I have an uneasy feeling that goods are good only when they *are* scarce; but in saying this I may again only be reflecting the attitude to scarcity in which (even though in the midst of wealth) I was brought up. Perhaps, philosophically, a good *is* a something of which one does not have enough; and perhaps we are now passing the point of insufficient self-awareness.

Be that as it may. What is certain is that, concurrently with the emerging affluent society of Galbraith we have the emerging "self-conscious society" of Eric Larrabee. (I have used his phrase, but I cannot claim to speak in terms of his views.)

The self-conscious society, perhaps necessarily, perhaps only as a transitional phenomenon, is a society of persons cut off from themselves in one way in order to be in communication or touch with themselves in another. It is hard to know now whether the link dissevered for the sake of the new link made is the link to the nutrient cord of life. But we shall doubtless shortly know.

The source of the new self-consciousness lies largely, as I have argued elsewhere, with the immensely burgeoning social sciences. They have secured to man some no doubt very precious understandings. But we need to appreciate better not only what was bought, but at what cost. Let me spell out a little the first, *first.*

What has been achieved as a new form of affluence is a rich flow of information, for the person as person, and the society as society, amounting virtually to a constant reflection of the individual and collective "state of the nation"—in certain respects. Perhaps the image of "a rich flow" is misleading; I should have said "a flood tide," for it is immense, forceful, not to be channeled, controlled, directed or—much as we may sometimes desire so—escaped.

The source of the flow—or tide—is as stated in the social

sciences, but more particularly in psychology and sociology. These, to alter the image, bathe us in a light that leaves us no shade to shadow ourselves in; they reflect us in a mirror from which we may not with impunity avert our gaze. Nor may we take refuge, as I indicated earlier, in our art, our literature, our poetry; for these are largely now (in more plastic appearance) still psychology and sociology—or drenched in their viewpoint, when they are not literally represented in psychologese or sociologese. A James Joyce is high art, I do not deny, and a rich and rewarding, if sometimes riotous, experience; but that toward which it opens (as well as that toward which it opens *us*) is not very different from what would be involved in the full-scale analysis of one of our own dreams. Abstract art takes, as I understand it, for its premise what the new sciences take for their conclusions: the new nature of man as envisioned in the conspectus the social sciences have of him.

Now, for better or for worse, a science that begins by taking man as an *object* cannot deal in deliverances that later take another view of him. So that the self-consciousness of modern man, or that sort of self-consciousness that is in process of limitless increase, is precisely that recognition of self (and society) as a sort of natural object. It has never been generally true, of course, that an actor acting has been completely unaware of himself as an actor acting; quite the contrary, with proper dual vision he has always acted within the play proper, and also, in his mind's eye (or heart's ear) in a second play in which he and the audience are in dramatic interaction also—the play without the play, as it were. But what we have now is rather different: man and men explaining themselves (and explaining themselves away) not by the method of unfolding purpose to render action teleologically intelligible, but by the method of establishing correlations *a tergo* to render movements scientifically accounted for. If purposes enter discourse at all they are themselves accounted for by the antecedence of prior events. The tendency of such "knowledge about" the self (or the society) is, I think, to extend itself at the inevitable expense of the other sort of knowledge, the knowledge of "acquaintance with" the object known. The relation to self or society as natural object first attenuates and then precludes a relation of mutual involvement or implication that is (or was) the characteristically human relation—a relation that in other eras was extended from men to gods and natural objects rather than from natural objects to gods and men. As we "naturalize" our world we de-nature it; it is no longer a natural home.

For reasons that are, I think, not far to seek, it is not possible "really" to believe in (let alone viably to inhabit) this kind of world. As with an alleged belief in "determinism," what is asserted is *necessarily* contradicted in the assertion of it! But it is possible to pretend to believe, and hence it is possible to live in that world a great part of the time, just as it is possible to live in the world of dreams—intermittently—for limited purposes.

This is indeed what men now largely do; though, as with those who do not distinguish the dream language from the reality language, there results considerable disturbance and distortion. By and large, the strategic possibilities inherent in a definition of man as a producing product are exploited to their limit for polemical purposes, most especially in the age-old battles between the young and the old. The young can and do, in that conflict, with much greater credibility than heretofore, account for their own vices and the virtues of their significant adults in *naturalistic* terms, thereby escaping for themselves the onus of culpability, while simultaneously rejecting the emotional appeal and moral claim that any perceived goodness in others might otherwise thrust upon them. This position is reinforced rather than weakened by making a strategic shift when they come to their own virtues and the adults' vices, which are seen in *dramatic* terms, as achievements deserving, if not blame and praise respectively, at least contempt for parents and appreciation for peers.

The convenience of this argument rather precludes the

emergence into consciousness of some sharp sense of its strategic unfairness. Indeed, unfortunately, it can hardly be successfully or sharply challenged, since the greater part of the adults upon whom it is directed do themselves share in its ambiguities, and would merely like to reverse or otherwise alter the direction of its application. It is not only because their peers support, but because adults permit (indeed, really teach) an argument that defines the defects of the young in terms of being "beat" or "shook" or "sick," but the adult behavior as the product of adult wickedness, voluntary wrongdoing, that the play is so effective and that to some considerable extent the young are themselves taken in by it.

I now want to turn to one more—although already implicit—characteristic of youth's "social surround," before turning to some observations on the youth social organization and culture.

What is already inferential in what I have said about the world in which we want our youth to grow up is the presence of a plenitude of means together with a dearth of ends. We have more matter, more power, more technique, more know-how at our disposal with less sense of what to do with it or about it, I believe, than ever before in history. We can almost literally reach the stars, but no longer have any fixed points of navigation. We are *all* by way of becoming "poor little rich boys." The very phrasing of the folk-term points to the stressful character of open possibilities in the absence of purposes of sufficient precision to permit pursuit.

The felt or perceived lack of purpose derives from a number of the changes to which I have pointed. (Perhaps no one has more sensitively and clearly sketched the situation and explored its consequences than has Paul Goodman, in, for example, *Growing Up Absurd.*)

In the first place, of course, the traditional cosmologies, the total dramatizations of the universe, that animated the whole with purpose, that guided our parents and substantially informed some of us, have been, except in eddies and back waters of the culture, largely cut away or wholly cut down.

The church census statistics—a turn to religiosity rather than a return to religion—notwithstanding, one may hear again the echo of "Not a roof is left the god, no roof, no cover; In his hand the prophet-laurel flowers no more"; and, if the resultant world is not "cold as a winter wave, in the wind from a wide-mouthed grave," it has an air of deathly chill about it.

In the second place, the scientistic view, and more particularly the acids of ideological analysis, have made the search for new purposes virtually impossible, by demoralizing the searchers before they are embarked on their search. It is one thing to discredit the high and holy purposes of one age in favor of a successor set; but it is quite another to have a general theory that discredits every one of the terms in *any* possible meaning that can be given to them *before* that meaning is even advanced for them. The conclusion that the world is *essentially* absurd—the proper existentialist conclusion—is of a quite different order from prior conclusions in previous ages about the absurdity of any particular assertion or assertion system about it.

The solution so far (except for such rare dramatic interludes as are provided by the Peace Corps, the response to which indicates the purpose-hunger of youth) has been, by and large, among young adults, youth's models, the privatization (in David Riesman's term) and the pettifying (in mine) of purposing life. Affect is withdrawn from what is public and what is political and focused—with brief success—on the purely private. It is also withdrawn from the great, the grand, the sweeping—and focused on the petty. It seems to be a time—to conjoin both figures—to cultivate one's own little garden. Except that it is not really possible to have joy even of that, as the strontium-90 seeps down, and the computers assess from second to second the changing probabilities of imminent universal death.

Substantially, but not wholly to be accounted for in these terms—forces as powerful but petty as sheer commercial exploitation have substantially entered into developing it—

there has grown up around the young a "youth culture" of a sort never quite seen before. Coextensive with it and coordinate is a youth society, or social organization of the young, of a kind that counselors who want to counsel or guide the young would do well to take into account.

The ways of youth have never, of course, been the ways of age, and everywhere to some extent there may be said to have been a "youth society." But the key words are "to some extent," and the key questions have to do with the new relation of the new youth society to the present society of "the old." ("Old" is over 30; or, in some places, over 26!) What is novel is the extent of the new society, the degree of participation it demands (indeed makes mandatory), its agenda and credenda, its place and powers vis-à-vis the adult world.

The new world, which is self-conscious enough to have a name—"youth" or "teenagers"—and to think of itself almost as though a distinct biological species with no relation either to "kids" or "grownups," is primarily a Universal State. No longer is it a matter of a gang or group, or even a linkage of groups on a circumscribed territory, but something much more like a People to which one belongs, and of which the persons actually present are only local exemplars. "American youth"—as exemplified in *Life* or *Look* or wailed over in *The Saturday Evening Post* or *The Ladies' Home Journal*, or celebrated and glorified in their "own" magazines—is probably the narrowest "reference group" to which the young relate; their more common felt bond is to Youth as such—everywhere.

A reference group of this magnitude, sensed as "the whole of youth" (except for a few "nuts") gives a sense of legitimation, of sure and certain right (forty million youngsters can't be wrong) beyond anything previously known. It almost makes of a judgment a self-evident truth; and the contrary opinion of the younger and the older confirms the judgment, since by definition they speak from another, and hence improperly biased, perspective.

The "we" of youth, to the extent that it existed, has always been a we of difference, but it is now rather (or as well) a we of antagonism: not the brittle antagonism of anger, or the delicate distinction of romanticism, but the quiet opposition, the sturdy and settled stance of the labor union versus management. And for good reason: the function of the two is more similar than meets the eye. Both think of themselves primarily as *defensive* organizations, as *minority* organizations, and as organizations whose best tactic is the slowdown (or "production-rate control" system), combined with something of the Negro's response to white domination: a polite evasion and systematic misleading of the "majority." The program against which the defense is erected, the imputed program of the adult world for the world of youth, refers to both aim and method, ends and means. What appears as youth's "slowdown" (as always, conceived as a defense against "speedup") is actually an acted-out refusal to accept such adult views as "Anything worth doing is worth doing well," and a defense against adult intensification, to the point of frenzy, of activity in the face of clouding or disappearing aim. The acted-out answer says "Nothing is worth doing well if it cannot be shown to be worthwhile," and "The only way to clarify aim is to stop jittering," to disaffiliate from wrong aims and their associated activities, to "cool it" until new intuition sheds new light. The "coolness" is directed especially toward large enterprises which, they suspect, are attractive to adults simply because they are large enough to fill large gaps in lives that are meaningless without them—and not likely to be much more meaningful with them. In a sense, the "cool" directive is only an intensification of the privatization and pettification in adult life: the old have constricted the area of affective investment to the local and familiar; the young constrict it still further to the personal (especially the sensational, in its original sense) and the immediately interpersonal (especially the sexual-affectional).

The new generation is a generation that does not intend, in either sense of the term, to be "taken in": either assimilated or deceived—which in their vocabulary are necessarily equated. That we see them victimized in other ways—commercially exploited; in thrall to the heroes they cast up each month to reign over them since nonreign is unbearable; exercising a vigilance over one another more tyrannical and deeper-reaching than any we knew—is only to be expected. Every counter-autocracy—sadly for democracy—must itself be an autocracy, although as long as it is emotionally invested in certain ways, libidinized, it will not much be seen or felt as such. And it will be so libidinized as long as the autocracy, against which it is aimed, is so ardently countercathected.

It may seem ironic—indeed, it is—to say that this most understanding, most easy-going, most permissive generation of adults appears as an autocracy in the sight of the young. Indeed, the impossibility of fastening on the generality of adults the ancient insignia of the autocrat is what gives youth's protective movement its force and lends to it certain touches of excess: for it is not protection against attack, but protection against seduction that they need and have, and, moreover, protection against a seduction they more than half desire. As always, that into which anyone is to be seduced appears inviting, overwhelmingly inviting, and dangerous, fatally dangerous—in a word, fascinating. What the young defend themselves against is our perceived intent to bring them into our world of comfort, content, aimlessness, smallness of compass, emptiness of significance—and absurdity. It is a world that seems to them absurd, if only because it is not able to credit, let alone accredit, itself. It is unbelievable, and by the greater part of the better of the grown, not believed in. It speaks, even of itself, in its bitterer and better moments, in terms of "the fur-lined rat-race," and "the split-level trap." And note that it is not now the unfortunate by-products of an otherwise decent way of life, or the pockets of disadvantage in a but-for-that decent and desirable order, which are thus brought by the better of us under direct attack; it is rather the very essence and principle, the very flower and most characteristic manifestation of the society.

What is puzzling to many of the good middle-echelon

people, middle-class oriented guides to and would-be helpers of youth, is that the youth culture that they confront has a "delinquent" overtone. This is true. The very language—and many of the practices—derive in a traceable chain either from lower-class culture "moving upward," or from such marginal and self-consciously marginal groups as American Negro jazz musicians. What this adoption ought to tell us, prima facie, is that youth, especially middle-class youth, has redefined itself, perhaps not consciously, as both exploited (the lower-class tone) and marginal or disaffiliated (the "hip" content and attitude). The "delinquent" overtone is accounted for, as Paul Goodman has so well observed, by the essential identity, in a society such as ours, of attitude, feeling, and practices in their inner meaning, between the delinquents technically defined and the other delinquents—those to whom society gives its highest rewards in money and glamour for making an inoperable system operable a little longer, and a meaningless activity seem temporarily to have a little excitement, if not significance. Madison Avenue, Hollywood, and the quite genuine delinquents I knew in the forties in Back-of-the-Yards Chicago have more than their presence in one nation in common: they are from my viewpoint, as from Goodman's, consubstantial. They are both responses—themselves absurd, perhaps—to the absurd.

One would come to know the social organization and culture of youth far better only if he were in some sense close to it or in it or intimately related to it instead of in mere formal relation to "students." Failing access to this social organization and culture, even less can be done by way of "individual guidance" by anyone, than was ever the case before. We face essentially now, for *all* children very nearly, what had to be faced for lower-class children in reference to delinquency a generation ago: the fact that, without access to the all-coercing, and all-rewarding structure of the gang, the likelihood of securing any sensible change in delinquent attitudes and activities is as close to zero as anyone could desire.

One would, moreover, face many of the same problems in securing such access to your children now as we had in trying to have communication with those children then. (As the Back-of-the-Yards kids instructed each other: "See, dere's de new social worker"—or teacher, or whatever. "Don't tell him nuttin'.") And for the same reasons—I do not know with what justification, but justly or unjustly—guidance people have a definition in the youth culture as emissaries of the adult culture more dangerous even than parents and teachers, veritable Greeks bearing gifts, of whom it is wise to beware. They are the ones, the kids say, who want to weaken you by defining resistance to assimilation as *your* psychological problem instead of *their* social one. They, the guidance people, are the ones, the youngsters say, who want to rehabilitate authority and adult practice in the eyes of youth by methods doubly dangerous because they are so insidious, because they come gentle and loving in the guise of "helping you," hiding their dedication to "saving them."

I am horrified and distressed. I hope the young are unjust, and that guidance people have only to make it clear. I trust that everywhere guidance people and such do think of themselves as a counterbureaucracy, a counteradministration, the Lenins in behalf of the young amid the Czarist regime of the old, the agents, attorneys, and agitators of and for youth, enjoining it only to find itself in its very proper battle, warning it against its all-too-present temptation to find comfort in compromise, in terms that promise it what is most destructive: a peace without honor, and a plenty without sense.

I hope that this is so, not simply because thus my sympathies incline, but because otherwise I believe there is no chance of your guiding youth. And even if there were a chance, there would quite certainly be no warrant.

30

Guidance: A Plea for Abandonment

Of the many meanings its practitioners give to "Guidance," I am interested in the one that intends it to be a *source of general aid or counsel for the child in the decision-making process.* I wish to argue that that function cannot be discharged under modern conditions by any process that carries with it the etymological overtones of the word *guidance.*[1] I wish to say why I so believe, and I want to offer an alternative conception.

The plea for abandonment of the very notion of guidance is based upon moral considerations—upon a judgment as to the centrality of human dignity—as well as upon the appraisal of the situation of guide and the person guided.

It goes without saying that if I am to speak of morals at all I must postulate human choice. In a deterministic philosophy both choice and morality must be absent or illusory. I should like to go further. If choice is not a first good—and it may not only not be a first good or supreme value, but experientially a bad or evil—it is an indispensable condition for all other (moral) goods. There is significance in neither ethics nor esthetics without choice—indeed the proper bound of these is the realm of human choice, actual or potential (i.e.,

[1] Guidance is the activity of a guide. A guide, according to the Oxford English Dictionary, is "one who leads or shows the way" . . . "one who directs another in his ways or conduct."

choosable). Whatever, therefore, needlessly limits choice, limits good. That this contention must be taken within the context of the entire human condition is also obvious. A limitation of choice (e.g., the choice to avoid armed service) in the defense of a good (i.e., generally choice-maximizing) society may be a positive good.

Given this view of the central or pivotal character of choice, I am led to regard those communication or educational processes as "best" that, in the long run, maximize choice for the parties concerned. These are what may be called the *liberative processes* or *arts*. Essentially they entail coming into power over that which constricts choice or, in the long run, would tend to do so. The child who learns to speak comes into possession of the power to stimulate himself, to cause himself shame or pride, a power, until then, which lay only in the hands of others. The child who comes to some understanding of how he has been and is being "educated" or "led" or "guided" or "developed" is in part in possession of some further possibility of autonomy or choice. The child who is barred from the greatest measure of understanding with which he can cope is to that degree crippled or retarded.

I have stated what I believe to be right, but, right or wrong, I think it can be asserted that the deceit of the child in these matters is now much more difficult than it once was.

I submit that the teacher's role has changed from that of an unconscious transmitter of generally accepted values to one where he is expected to "shape the child's character." I argue, therefore, that since there is no general value model, and since the child's situation or problem cannot be foreseen in any detail, teachers are thrown back on quite other techniques and obligations. I shall contend that *your* differential access to psychological knowledge and *your* peculiar position both enable you and obligate you to engage in a vastly different enterprise. And lastly, I shall attempt to sketch what I believe to be the general nature of that enterprise.

Time was when the lot of the schoolteacher was simpler

and happier, though he struggled manfully against it to his present unhappy destiny and onerous load. Time was—and not so long ago at that—when, working, essentially as a servant under direction, his task was to "pass on" as much of a clearly defined and widely agreed culture as the relatively feeble resistance of his pupils would permit. Like all but a very few in his day, his information came to him hallmarked, his morality certified, and, whether or not he had also internalized the going beliefs, he had effectively to serve them or cease to be a teacher.

Today's teacher is not so situated. No longer is there an attested and acceptable morality. No longer is there a world of blacks and whites, with nice firm borders around fields of knowledge or moral problems similar to those the teachers of the day caused the children to put around their "art" productions ("A good, firm outline is the first thing"). No longer for any but the wholly bemused or intensely unintelligent or the willfully blind are there clear and certain answers to any important question: the nature of man, the "best" social or political or economic arrangements, the destiny of the individual or the society or the species. No longer for the honest man are the certitudes certain or the philosophic or ethical boundaries secure. The rules that in an easier and perhaps happier day seemed to carry their justification for all eternity written upon their faces now carry with equal plainness their provisionality, their local and temporal limits, their *ad hoc* character, stamped upon them. Is it a plain principle of common sense, for instance, that no man shall be tried under legislation made to apply retroactively? Then what of Nürnberg? Is it a plain principle of international diplomacy and the peace and concord that rests upon it that interference by one State in the internal affairs of another is intolerable? Then what of Soviet propaganda? of the "Voice of America"? of permitting the atrocities of the Hitler years in Germany—or those of the Stalinist years in the Soviet Union?

The truth is that there are no longer any plain answers, or, where there seem to be, they are not enduring. If there are eternal verities—other than propositions in logic or mere tautologies—they clearly lie at so high a level of abstraction as to be virtually useless guides to conduct. We are all, in the image of a great American, "against sin"; it is only that we no longer know with any precision what is or is not "sin."

How indeed should it be otherwise? The world in which we grew up is so altered, so changed and made over by events that any resemblance between it and the world of our students is virtually nil. Why should we think, when events move more rapidly, crises are more cataclysmic, revolutions cut deeper, that we by some special dispensation are enabled to know much about the world in which the young are growing up. We have not gone with them, we have ceased from following after them, their people are not our people nor their gods our gods. What we have is the bond of our common humanity, little more.

We all know—do we not?—that we have precious little advice to give, that we are sure of few things, that those are of doubtful relevance. Where *are* we going? What it is *for?* What sense does it make? What things shall a man hold fast to? What things are good?

For what *do* we know? Only, I submit, that virtually every known answer to every important question is trivial or specious or both. This is valid knowledge, and a catalogue of all the exploded theories that have once been held to order the realms of fact or value together with an account of the dogmatism and certitude with which they were held to be true would be a useful though not edifying legacy to pass on to the young.

Indeed, it is possible that we are, in general, more bewildered than the young because we are better educated. They too will be bewildered in their time: a little less, perhaps, if we help them; considerably more, if we pass on to them at this late date as credible so many of the things we had to spend the best parts of our lives unlearning. They are now less bewildered because they rest temporarily on the false certainties that sheltered, rural, or otherwise parochial parents have been able to salvage for them. They are sure not because they have overcome the world, but because they have not yet encountered it.

Many of us attempt to cover the yawning chasms of our deepest uncertainties with high-sounding phrases of dubious meaning: "the good life," "maturity," "responsibility," "good citizenship," "the greatest good of the greatest number," "the welfare of the whole," and so on. If these terms are used as pointers, faint, feeble attempts to give form to our vague and troubled aspirations, well and good. If we pretend, as often we seem to, that they have a content that we know and that they define a program we pursue, we do but deceive ourselves.

Let us ask now from this vantage point what intelligible sense and what not undignified meaning we can give to the process we have been calling the guidance of the young. Let us examine first the situation of the counselor, then that of the counselee.

First let us recall that we have two priceless—and painful—professional privileges: the privilege of differential access to psychological theory, and therefore to knowledge of ourselves and others; and the privilege of a quite distinctive position and role in the information-dispensing hierarchy.

To those who have eaten the fruit of the tree of psychological knowledge the world can never be the same again. Even if the new knowledge is encapsulated so that it is "in the mind" without deeply affecting the life directly, the presence of the capsule as an irritant foreign body is a potent reminder that all is not as it once was. Gone is any simple view of man's nature; gone are the pretty fairy-tale-book colors of hallowed sentiment and memory; gone are the nice, clean forms and fair proportions that were once thought to describe alike man's dream and man's reality. Gone are the simple issues, gone are the ready rules, gone the sharp bounds and neat distinctions.

Access to the new psychology carries with it by implication the necessity of a new kind of knowledge as far reaching as it is narrowly focused, as penetrating as it is painful, as disenchanting and destructive of an old dream world as it is promising and potentially productive of a new. It carries with it not only a new knowledge, but a new focus on experience, and a call, inescapably tied to the new knowledge, for a new locus for loyalty. It *is* true that the Greeks said "know thyself"; it is true that Elizabethans could already repeat Polonius' "Above all this, to thine own self be true . . ."; but it is only in our own day that reasonably reliable methods of knowing the self have become available, and it is only in our own day that a profession dedicated relatively undividedly to such self-discovery has come to birth, if not yet to maturity.

This localization of loyalty in the self in the context of other selves, the new focus on feeling in the context of intelligence, these shift the meaning of morality, the character of relationship, the status of rules and the whole "grammar of motives." This is a Protestantism with a vengeance beside which the Protestantism of the Reformation pales. That protest against a priest-mediated morality drove man back upon his own "conscience" as a control in crisis, aided still however by a dubious legacy of rules for ordinary occasions. It was only when man discovered that, far from escaping the priest, he had merely succeeded in internalizing him, via his mother, in his "conscience," and that that highly prized function was no less irrational, demanding, arbitrary, and destructive than the old external enemy—it was only when he realized this, that a new Protestantism became a possibility and a necessity! For the new protest made it possible for man to take responsibility for his own conscience. What had been a guide, a support, something on which to unload responsibility became a charge, a drain, something to be faced as a problem, taken responsibility for, made over, re-formed and reformed—and so integrated and made human. This is the Revolution of our times—or at least half of it—and this is the Reformation that, witless or witting, willing or unwilling, we are now in.

We are thus privileged (and penalized) I submit, in the face of confusion on one side and rigor on the other, in having access to new methods and new moralities: methods that render us more intelligible or less opaque to ourselves; moralities that depend on such self-access, since self-loyalty is focal. This is the privilege of psychologists. But there is a second privilege inherent in their peculiar position in the information-dispensing hierarchy.

Next to the preacher and the publisher, perhaps no man has been under clearer mandate to be dishonest than the teacher. The young have for some reason been thought to be particularly aptly cast for the role of consuming the falsehoods that the old can no longer stomach. And the teacher, having differential contact with them, has been watched with special care to make sure he carried a pure variety of the current line. The higher the official in the hierarchy, in general the more is he under the necessity of deceit.

Guidance people are twice exempt from this institutionalized necessity for self-betrayal. Few of them are so highly placed that people think of them generally as policy makers, people who make a difference. (This is their present fortune, as it is the fortune of all professions before they "arrive" or of all who are at any time held lightly or in contempt.)

But by a further special dispensation, in virtue of their "mystery" or craft, they are exempt from some of the standard requirements to fabrication which weigh so heavily upon their colleagues. No one knows much about them or greatly cares so long as they fulfill their formal function: the task of adapting the young to the manner of life to which society would like them to become accustomed. This is such a desperate necessity—all other institutions having patently failed, the home and the church most notably—that the parents and school trustees are almost willing to give those so charged a free hand. Counselors have, hence, the "privilege of the confessional," and for much the same reasons: the hope is that they will somehow save the individual without really upsetting any of the arrangements that make perennial salvage necessary. In contradistinction to the classroom teacher with his covert preacher's permit or mandate, counselors have a substantial exemption from the necessity of bearing false witness.

Peculiarly, then, guidance people have differential and advantageous access to truth, and differential and advantageous license to make use of their own experience, and, indeed, to permit others the use of it. These are rare gifts—in our day or any other.

Let me now turn to the situation of the students.

The young are in our day under threat of a triple tyranny: the tyranny of impulse, the tyranny of power, the tyranny of number. The first is age-old. The second weighs with peculiar force, since submission to it—to the voice of the powerful adult—no longer yields even those secondary gains with which it was once invested. The third is new—new, at least, in its pervasiveness and force and the depths to which it penetrates.

As we all know and have long taught—though we may not have fully learned—the child can only escape the tyranny of impulse as he is caught up and given form and function in the social activities in which he participates. He becomes a person, a self, an organized being as and to the degree that, by direct or vicarious methods, he takes part in the common, collective, or shared enterprise. He is liberated—from impulse—as he is "socialized."

But this is only a primitive first step. Indeed it is difficult to understand why in a country in which "socialism" is such an evidently bad word, "socialization" should be such an evidently good one, unless we are really more tender of property than person. For the price paid for release from the bondage of impulse has been until recently, for the vast majority, very high. The price was either continued dependency on some powerful parental figure—or, in the jargon, "surrogate"—or the internalization of that figure in all its infantile oversimplification, within the personality. It was this situation that caused the "pangs of conscience" to have their peculiar poignancy. Whatever threatened this primitive control system threatened the return of the otherwise undomesticated and understandably feared impulses: forbidden because feared, and hence feared because forbidden. Men so situated are notably controlled, and in some sense self-controlled, but only in the sense that the self has been in part cuckolded: part of the self is not *ego* but *alter*.

In our day when powerful parental figures are hard come by, and where "Life with Father" seems a comedy rather than a report, the principle of organization—for the child must organize or, psychologically, die—is around a vague and shadowy "they" rather than a sharp and overpresent "he" or "she." It is not merely that parents have largely abdicated because life has undermined their position from without while we have weakened it from within—it is that two groups, both no doubt from the best motives, have rushed into the vacuum thus created, and have sought to give the child a place to lay his head—or, rather, his heart, for this is a matter of loyalty.

The first group includes the now vast array of quasi parents: the teachers, guides, counselors, advisers, scoutmasters, psychologists, children's hour specialists, social workers, group organizers, recreation directors, playground operators, librarians, storytellers, nursery-school workers. These new welcome operators of a gigantic child-raising industry do to a considerable degree fill the void, conferring on the child the dubious opportunity of organizing himself around their mistakes instead of his own parents. This may be a gain because the mistakes are likely to be more common than idiosyncratic, and thus more bearable.

In any case, this beachhead could not be held and consolidated without the aid of a second group: the child's own peers. After all, none of us in these new professions can be more than a collective parent to the children we deal with, in spite of all our attention to "individual differences." We are group parents and in the exertion of our quasi-parental function we call the group as a psychological reality into existence and consolidate its power over the individual. In fact, our ghosts now return to haunt parents who now pay us to exorcise them: they probably worry more about the child's lack of "integration into the group" than ever they did in the days when that might have been a problem. The child is now "helped" in that "integration" virtually from nursery-school days on by parent and quasi parent alike.

Children so naturally alive—both cruelly and cooperatively and sometimes both at once—to one another's necessities are quick to help one another out and to establish official or unofficial, conscious or unconscious group norms. The child knows the parents want him to "get along"; he knows the kind teacher wants to help him get along and that, unlike the parent, she knows how; he knows the kids themselves want him to get along. How should one resist so much kindness?

It is exceedingly difficult for a child so circumstanced—and the most privileged middle-class child is quite generally so circumstanced—to come to any clear picture of either himself or his world. He is not faced by an enemy or comforted by a friend; he fights or embraces a wraith. "People think . . .," "they say . . .," "it is generally agreed . . .," "the consensus was . . . ." All the points that ought to be jumping-off points for inquiry or foci for resistance are terminal points for discussion and resolving points for action. Popularity was never so hard sought, and perhaps never so dearly bought.

The outcome of this new "mode of production" tends to be of a character type that Fromm first described as the "market personality" and that Riesman was later to pin down more fully and clearly for America in what he well calls the "other-directed" character. This character, with its sensitive radarscope trained to instant reaction to any social "blip," he contrasts with the "inner-directed" character of recent days with his gyroscope-like conscience and with the "tradition-directed" character of still earlier days and simpler times.

I think with Riesman that there is, even in a generally other-directed society, a possibility of what he calls "autonomy," a chance of avoiding the death of "adjustment" (which has been until recently part of our stock-in-trade). In such a society, moreover, autonomy might well be a good so precious as to make other values puny beside it—and so difficult of achievement, unless we now institutionalize the means thereto, that it might come to border upon bare contingency—a limiting case rather than a type-event. How can a place for the nurture of autonomy be provided? What space can be cleared within which the care and feeding of the idiosyncratic self may be carried on, within which a "decent degree of insubordination" can be restored, within which cultural and group patterns may have less overwhelming weight and depatterning effect?

This will call, I believe, for the exercise of every known liberative art and perhaps the invention of new. What was formerly a luxury for the few—liberation from the accidents of time and space, from the parochialism of this culture and that family, this work-shift and that club—will become a necessity for the many. There will be a demand, more pitiable if unspoken, for the services of those who can help in this quest.

For the only flight possible for those who are not to flee freedom is a flight, *via self-discovery*, into the daylight of a self-conscious and responsible relation of oneself to oneself, and hence to others. As a mass task this is new necessity.

What do we know of the liberative arts?

We know surely that every liberative art rests on a limited number of complex simplicities: simplicities of relation, focus, value, process, and product.

The relation is one that joins the parties to it in, perhaps, the greatest intimacy combined with the greatest distance that is within the compass of human experience. The would-be liberator must be like the epitome of the friend and the epitome of the stranger, and the better in each role as he fulfills adequately the other. So also must the would-be liberatee.

The focus is always on making the unconscious conscious. This too is a two-way street, a process of mutual education. What each counselee discovers of himself to his counselor is part of his contribution; what he discovers to his counselor of his counselor is the other half.

The paramount and only necessary joining value on both sides is the pursuit of truth, ardent, relentless, unflinching—more accurately, self-rekindling when ardor flags, self-restarting when relentlessness weakens, self-recovering when flinching demands its brief day or hour.

The process is a continuous examination of the world as it is mirrored and distorted in the self, and of the self as it is projected in and distorted in the world—including the world of the liberative relationship—and again this involves both sides, or it is truncated and meaningless.

The product is, at a minimum, two people who know more about each other, each about the world, and each about himself. That is all. Perhaps, it is enough.

These simplicities, though characteristic of the "psychotherapeutic" enterprise, do not find themselves limited thereto. A good friendship, marriage, or education requires them if it is to have enduring value.

So much for the fundamental conception.

I think then that under present circumstances the proper purpose of the psychologically enlightened is to call a halt to the epidemic process of adjustment; to interrupt it as well and as radically as they may, both in themselves and in others who will permit and accept this use. As a sociologist, I am not unaware of the necessities of "maintaining the structure," "preserving the continuities," "keeping the culture intact." But because I recognize the necessity of toilets, it does not follow that everyone must wish to be a plumber. I think there need be no fear in an era of TV, radio, and powerful mass media that the loss of some supporting voice to the banalities will effectively weaken the chorus. Counselors have, I think, a special role: the role of maintaining in themselves, and in those whom they are permitted to affect, a tension to the limit of capacity against these subtle, pervasive, adaptive, and adjustive influences. One must adapt to live; but every adaptation is a little death, and while no physician may refuse death as a reality, neither may he welcome it—except when it has effectively arrived—as an ally.

The tension so created and sustained has as its function the continuous prevention of closure, the uninterrupted interruption of habit and custom formation, the unceasing war against the comforts of unconsciousness. It is an operation against the psychological and social grain; its stock-in-trade is the creation of sufficient unease to affect the ease from which all psychological disease is born.

If the guiding conception is not to be "guidance" but discovery—of a world and especially of the collaborating selves who are its focus; and if the purpose is the interruption of adjustment for the sake of consciousness, it is tempting to say that the whole pyramid of traditional "guidance" preoccupations should be up-ended: that jobs and intelligence ratings and interest and capacity assessments and the smoothing-over of "disciplinary" situations are trivial in that order. Perhaps "practical" people, and today's prematurely practical children, force such beginning points anyway. (Whatever "practical" may mean in theory, in practice it means flight into that which does not matter—even from the viewpoint of the claimant—as against that which does. When we use "practical" as a term of praise we should react emotionally as we do toward a crutch or a beautifully healed scar: it is admirable—but sad.) Perhaps such *beginning-points* are even praiseworthy: there is evidence, I think, that in many matters psychological there is an economy of waste. (Group therapy, for instance, goes farther, faster in groups that spend enough time on "irrelevancies.") But waste that does not move on to something else is—just waste.

If the resulting "conversations" are to have utility, from the viewpoint set forth here, they must serve to raise questions rather than answer them, must facilitate the joint and mutual exploration of the quadratic relations of "counselor," "counselee," and each of their worlds, and must do this *with reference to matters that matter.*

I insist upon the question-raising function because, in psychology as in the life of society, it is under and around either (or both) the questions closed (tabu) or the questions never asked that the darkness lies and the dangers multiply.

I insist upon jointness and mutuality for reasons I have already made clear, both moral and technical: I deem the deceit involved in alternative practices wrong, and I find the results abortive in the sense that the process comes to a stultified close at what should be the inception of its most rewarding portion. I insist upon the discussion of matters that matter here because they will, generally, be discussed nowhere else: every other institution of the society may not unfairly be viewed as having as its major object the provision of an agenda in the pursuit of which the important may be avoided. The school also has its agenda—and a very heavy one—to prevent the child from coming to grips with reality, but it may have more moral space in such interstices as counselors occupy than have other, and now more confessedly bankrupt, bodies. It is in the hope that this is so and that counselors can exploit their interstitial advantage that these remarks were set forth.

But this brings us to method. The method that can have any tenable hope of moving toward such high ends must be a method of exploration, essentially of discussion. But at this point a semantic shudder seizes me. It is symbolic of the world in which we live that such a term must be explicitly defined, since almost as many atrocities are committed in its name as are now committed in the name of "democracy"—and not all on one side of any ideological or political fence!

I find I have to say that it is *not* discussion (in the sense I want) if the outcome is predetermined, or even substantially biased. (The warning may be thought unnecessary but at the present time just such a pseudo discussion series is being used and advocated in the classrooms of several states under the rubric of Human Relations Classes.) It is not discussion if the range is restricted by overt—or, worse, covert—understandings of where it cannot go. It is not discussion if it demands restriction of the forms of expression—polite language, no emotionality, pseudo "reasonableness." It is not discussion if there is a hidden agenda; or rather, more reasonably, since we all have hidden agenda, it is not discussion unless progressively the hidden agenda of each of us is, of design, and as far as it can be, revealed and reintegrated. It is, of course, not discussion if other manipulative or covert-coercive devices are substituted for these. I say all these things because the notion seems widespread that discussion is a new and more efficient method for achieving the objectives of one party to it. In my lexicon that is fraud—and, if it claims exemption because it operates to the "real advantage" of the victim—it is fraud with arrogance and self-deception added.

It is also not discussion, of course, if it "takes the desires and necessities of the other party into account." Unless he is very sick or defective this is an ignoble nobility; it is also an assault, since by its pseudo generosity it makes of the victim less than he need or could be. That also is not mutuality.

It is only discussion when and if and to the limit of capacity of all participants it centers around what is genuinely doubtable—as to those who have eyes to see, what is not?—and moves, by whatever ways are mutually acceptable and productive, to its own properly undeterminable (and perhaps indeterminate) conclusion. It is not even, in Mr. Stuart Chase's phrase, a "road to agreement" unless agreement includes the agreement to disagree. Consensus and agreement, like peace, are currently overvalued goods, and to make agreement an object of discussion is again to trivialize it by imposing a sometimes relevant minor means as a distorting final end. Any lesser object for discussion than "mere clarification" vitiates discussion, just as any object for play but "mere pleasure" vitiates play.

I have argued on moral and technical grounds for the abandonment of what I took as the essential meaning of "guidance." I have pleaded instead for a joint exploration by young and old of each other and their worlds. This, it seems to me, substitutes for the relatively trivial problem of "passing on the culture" the one of making that culture over in transmission so that the generations may benefit from the exchange. This, as far as I can see, is a process without definable limit or diminishing return.

31

"Planning for Mental Health" —Paradise Stormed

There is a beautiful ring, a quality of siren-singing, about the title "Planning for Mental Health" that makes it attractive and almost fatally easy to plunge into some activity under that head without undue reflection about what we are doing or what it is all about.

Caught up in the phrase—and, even more, in the underlying proposal, if we are to go beyond speech—is so much of the belief, attitude, and hope of modern man, that its meaning is worth examination in its own right as a "diagnostic of our time." If planning begins, as I presume it does, with an assessment of where we are, then this is an excellent place to begin.

In form, the title names an activity, "planning," for the sake of a state, "health," qualified by a restriction—or perhaps an extension—"mental." In fact, it evokes a series of images that, in their properly appreciated poetic overtones, give the program an almost irresistible appeal. What permits the appeal to a modern mind is the concealment of these poetic meanings and intents under the guise of a "scientific" or "hard" vocabulary, preserving and protecting the paramount pretense of unsentimentality, factuality, the essentially "engineering" stance. "Health" is surely a scientific concept, and a proper object of concern even for sanitationists and politicians; the qualification "mental" only shifts our gaze to the "scientifically established" other-than-physical "factors"; and "planning" is a term straight out of the no-nonsense vocabulary, indeed the reason or *terminus ad quem* for having such a vocabulary at all. This is what it all appears to mean, and is meant to appear to mean. The danger here, as always, is that we should be taken in by or held to, in another context, a set of meanings that we had constructed or adhered to for a very special purpose. What is it that the slogan really evokes?

It evokes, I believe, a beautiful, powerful triple image. "Health" has for us that singing sound that places it properly with "Truth" and "Beauty" as fellow images, and with wholeness, wholesomeness, integrity as positive cognate terms. At its lowest, barest negative minimum it evokes an image of a state in which we (or those other "we's," our children, our loved ones, our successors) are, were, or will be free: free of the pains, dis-orders, dis-eases, deformities, and deformations that at present affect us, and, even more, for the future affright us. A state in which (to borrow two terms from Vickers) what is awry will be aright. A state in which hearts beat as they were meant to beat, blood courses as it was meant to course, those bodily humors have that harmony and balance that makes of the corporeal human habitation a mansion —indeed so disposes it that the liver and the lived-in are barely capable of distinction from each other. A state in which form is so fitted to function, and function so informed with fitness, that the only appropriate anticipation is that of free and continuous, essentially effortless and unbroken, physical *joy*.

I said "anticipation," but, of course, since all such words always mean their opposites, I meant "restrospect." What we look forward to is the past, the past approximated in reality and smoothed and warmed over in imagination, the past that is everyone's past, his childhood, his era of innocence, his paradise among his peers. And if not his childhood as it actually and literally was, that period as it nearly was and readily (but for genetic misfortune or grown-up mismanagement) might have been.

That is the world that the word "health" evokes, and that

is what is to be brought, or brought again, or brought for more, or brought for all, into being; what is to be brought from a time of brief morning to the duration of a full day; from contingency to certainty; from a gift of grace to an achievement by control; from a Paradise shortly held and long lost to a Paradise, not merely regained, but *wrested* from the very grasp of adverse circumstance in an alien and indifferent world, by the very strength that is the measure or promise of health itself.

So it is—is it not?—that we may envision ourselves, or our other selves, others like us, even in "maturity" and beyond: still green in the heyday of our youth, still golden and glowing, clear-eyed, supple and straight of limb, with "energy to burn," running free, singing in the sun, joy for our portion and joy the very coinage we scatter about us for the delight and delectation of those others who are also our brothers, our objects and sources of heightened pleasure, our reflected and recreated and multiplied and joy-returning selves.

And if that, or something like it, is the image that "health" brings into carefully blurred focus, what of "mental health"? Here also, the word "mental" functions partly as a pale ghost of what we mean, partly as a designed disguise, intended, like a neurotic symptom, to represent and remind us of our (disappointed) dreams and hopes, while preventing their emergence in all their force and vividness that, if adequately represented, might threaten, in one way or another, to overwhelm us.

For "mental," which appears to have reference to that cold thing called "mind," refers functionally and in reality to that more treasured totality called the self, that whole which renders us humane and human, appreciable and valuable (not just recognizable and discriminable) to others and ourselves. By the term "mental" we point one way and look another. We point to a supposed object of science, something that we believe, in our wilder moments, can somehow be adequately simulated by a computer; but we look at, and covertly "have in mind," that much richer set of objects of experience, ourselves and the treasured other selves, who are at one and the same time the ground of our several selves' existence, the creatures of our creation and continuous re-endowment, the medium in which, in one another, as human and social beings, we exist and have our being.

The "mental health" to which we point by pointing away from it, combines what seemed to be a datum of childhood with what, while it was only a dream of childhood, seemed a dream so close to reality, so possible, as to tremble continually on the very verge of realization. (Perhaps, indeed, even the childhood dream is a representation of an earlier memory, of something really given, even if only briefly, in reality, a genuine datum.)

The reality and dream—or twin realities—to which we thus point back are also wholenesses, healths, of a different but not unconnected kind: the undivided self in the undivided society. The undivided self dreamed of—whatever may have been the original generating reality—is *not* the undifferentiated self in all its infantile poverty, but the full, rich, differentiated, complex, complicated, interesting, sensitive self, simply not divided *against* itself. The undivided society dreamed of—whatever may have been the matrix of its origin—is not the society simply undivided because "you" has not yet been set off from "me" as an entity or object of experience or locus of agency, but the society simply not divided against itself in the sense that separable pleasures or separable profits for separate members would be even thinkable or intelligible.

It is this self not set over and divided against itself in a context not merely of similar selves, but of selves in some profound sense inseparable from each other, because the "we" is at least as real and cogent as the "I" (indeed each is the very life, ground, and justification of the other)—it is such a self, and set of selves, in such a state that is the image that is evoked and that ought to be evoked, that lends its warmth and force and urgency to the cold abstraction, the iron-plate-sounding hardness of "mental health."

What the term asserts by negation is again a proper Paradise. It is the state before (or after) our present guilt beyond bearing, shame past enduring, loneliness unfaceable, responsibility unmanageable, disunity and inner contradiction beyond resolution or acceptance—and, in general, not relief merely from burdens incapable of being borne, but escape into or back to a genuine state of "innocence," neither suffering harm, nor, by default of will or wit, doing it.

In the child dream (or reality) to which the term harks back, also, as in the most sophisticated statement of the most sophisticated psychosomaticist or mental health expert, "the mind" is not yet separated from (let alone, morally, set against) "the body"; I am my body (I neither have it nor live in it); the life that animates both is a common life, and the joy or grief that informs both is one joy or grief in origin, significance, and expression.

So that to which "mental health" refers "really" is to that undivided—or rather reunited—state, in which the distinctions we have made, then encountered as differences, then exaggerated into antitheses and antagonisms, are re-solved and resolved in some looked-for trandscendent unity that is not at the same time the undifferentiated uniformity of death. So stated, we may well see the reason for its tremendous animating force, for it is a statement in the grey vocabulary apt for our day of the roseate and undying human dream, the eternal, inextinguishable human hope.

Now as to "planning," it too is one of those words that, if it intends itself, intends also its opposite. The image it is designed to conjure up is, at the least, the image of knowing, orderly deliberation, of justified foresight, of the adaptation of means to ends, of control over intermediate events for the sake of successful subsequent outcomes. It too is a hard word in the vocabulary of the hard-headed, the "practical," the masters of materials, events, and—very often—of men.

Hidden behind it, at least as soon as we move from the mere engineering of things to designs in reference to men (and sometimes upon them), is a quite different set of intents and their corresponding vocabularies and procedures. It turns out that, while we plan production plants, or cities as physical objects, or housing developments, or business processes, if we are men and not monsters we do not plan men or societies, but, if we plan at all, we plan *with* them or *for* them. And the introduction of those little prepositions marks a distance of light years morally in the meaning and nature of the process. To plan with or among men is to live with and among them—in a particular way, it is true, with a particular "contribution," but nevertheless pursuing or enjoying with them a shared life in which their continuous participation is alike the ground and measure of whatever planning gets done or planned.

This second, and true—operative *and* "good"—meaning is not, however, what is heard in the slogan of the title. What is heard—and what exerts a fatal seductive appeal, or threatens to—is a conjuncture of the true and covert meaning of "mental health" with the false and overt one of planning. Thus the false dream—false because foreclosed by the nature of human reality—that the slogan summarizes is the achievement (or reachievement) of the good, the undivided life, by the division *against* all other methods and motives of externality and rationality. The picture that comes to mind is a picture of "engineering," in its narrowest sense, human "good," in its broadest sense. What is thought to be offered is a short cut via the methods that have given us mastery over nature, presumptively, to mastery over ourselves or one another—it is not clear which. It is also not clear which would be worse if either or both were possible.

What the image of "planning for mental health" invites as a conclusion is one particular answer to a long-standing problem that Western man has faced perennially, in another terminology, as a question: What is—or is to be—the relation between faith and reason, dream and reality, "value" and "fact"? The particular variant, of all the possible answers, that the title suggests is: reason *over* faith, reality *over* dream, fact *over* value. (This itself is a long-standing dream of mankind, and, typically, the assertion thus "contains it own negation.") So stated or conceived, the structure of action is assumed to be the realization or actualization by a rational process of intimations of desires that come to us through quite another—not necessarily irrational, but certainly nonrational—process. This pattern of belief is so important and far-reaching that it deserves examination for credibility as possible, and, if found possible, for desirability. More particularly, perhaps, does it merit such examination because to so many, brought up as most of us have been on just such assumptions, the stance seems so self-evidently the only proper one, that it is properly the substance of all our subsequent behavior, internal and external. It is, in truth, a substantial consideration.

First, let me say that it is characteristic of the thoughtways of Western man, but not necessarily of all human thoughtways, to divide the unity of human experience, and then to spend the remainder of history worrying about, if not fighting about, the nature of the relation between the elements that analysis, itself a "rational" procedure, has alone divided. Thus, to take an obvious and related instance, as between "thought" and "feeling," once divided analytically, the question that "arises" immediately—seemingly "naturally" in a power-oriented culture—is which rules which, "actually" or "ideally" (another such dichotomy!)? Does "heart" rule "head" or vice versa? Should it? In attempting to answer that question, the question of which is the more basic—or important or valuable—is sure to be next. It is not long before we have schools founded on all the different answers—romantics to promote and plug the claims of the heart, and naturalists or realists to advertise and advance those of the head—and presently we have men fighting, with actual blows or the worse weapons of exclusion and contempt, for *romanticism* or *realism*, each of which is anathema to those who cherish the other. A moment's reflection on the behavior exhibited in such a conflict ought to cut out the ground from any feeling of warrantability in conducting the fight at all; in order to "justify" the rule of the head the worst and most violent passions of the heart are spurred and given free rein in a most romantic manner by the "realists"; and in order to advance the claims of the heart a tremendous, reasoned structure is erected by the "romantics," and put about by all the devices that only the most unfeeling and calculating of minds could justify or condone. The romantics prove romance by behaving realistically; the realists further theirs by the most romantic of claims and stratagems. Moreover, the issue is never concluded, simply because, I suppose, a conclusion to a false question is inherently impossible as long as men have sufficient vitality not to be wholly taken in by the products of their own capacity to make puzzles, problems, and paradoxes out of experience, which does not come to them in any immediacy in that form.

For the form in which experience does come to us first is flux: formlessness if you will, but if not that, interfusion. Indeed, experience is, in reality and seeming, the seamless garment, until in inexperience we turn and rend it. I do not know anyone who has or has had a thought *or* a feeling, who thinks *or* feels. I know that I and those I know have feelingful thoughts and thoughtful feelings—excuse the new dichotomy, which I do not really intend!—but of pure thought or feeling I know nary an instance. Indeed, I am not happy with my dichotomy: what I recognize is a single process of relating to the world as an "I," a person, in which from moment to moment, foreground and background, thought and feeling (inseparable since each exists only on the ground of, is constituted by, the other) seem to change places in the sense of which is focal, which peripheral at a given instant. (Indeed, so leery of such dichotomies am I, that the one I had to use—distinguishing myself from "the world"—is, I should have to say, itself false: my experience is not of a self and a world, but of a simultaneous self-in-the-world and world-in-the-self that has the same structure as the thought-feeling complex that I was trying to analyze.)

We have, indeed, done worse than sunder reality into first distinct, then opposed, then counterposed, then warring terms.

We have, as far as possible, embodied those terms in institutions that utter or outer the intellectual and emotional confusion in social space (which we have, incidentally, also neatly severed somehow from individual space). As bearer and champion of the claims of faith we have then, naturally enough, a reasonless and unreasoning and unreasonable church; and as the standard-bearer of reason, a faithfully faithless, routinized, mechanized, bureaucratized embodiment of what is—without even a sense of irony—called "rationality," in the state. We then have, of course, in addition to the problem of the relation of faith and reason, a political problem of church-state relations to keep us busy. We pursue the same policy over another dichotomy, the realms respectively of "the public" and "the private," and so for an endless series of dichotomies, each in a different dimension—until we have no longer a living semblance of life, but instead an infinite and expanding series of nagging but insoluble problems.

I have not, I hope, taken you on this long excursion for nothing, or merely for the sake of exposing you to some of my perplexities and confusions in the name of furthering our general education. I have gone so seemingly about the bush because here, as so often, I believe that the longest way round is the shortest way home: more especially if the shortest way should prove to lead not home at all, but to a dwelling both alien and uninhabitable. I have taken this route because many people I know think thus: here is this desirable state called "mental health," and here is this wonderful procedure called "planning," and our problem is to use the second to secure the first. I think this about as idle a hope as the much-touted program that animates much of the modern "religious" revival: to seek grace with a view to increased profit. Only a childish notion of both grace and profit would permit so childish a proposal to be put about. And only a childish notion of "mental health" and "planning" can sustain the customary perspective.

I have, I believe, already made the point that "mental health" (at least in its maximum and motivating meaning) refers to the goodness of the life of the person in the world, more particularly that goodness as it is felt and reflected on, "evaluated," not analytically or intellectually or emotionally, but holistically, totally, *aus ganz Natur*. By historical accident, and by terminological misfortune, the problem has come to be seen as somehow located in the "individual," an individual somehow separated from the living of both his life, and the shared or common life from which "his" life is abstracted. If we are not very careful, we come to think of mental health as a property of a person, like eye color, which, unlike eye color, it is our duty and intent in some way to affect for the better. By necessity, as I see things, the term must refer to the goodness of the life in the person and the goodness of the person in the life. Hence a scheme to improve mental health is a scheme for a better health for men-in-society and society-in-men, though it is not the kind of scheme that can be schemed or schematized. If it happens at all it will be a something that will arise in and out of the common life, outered into a personal utterance by uncommon participants in that common life, only to re-enter the common life, transforming it as it goes. The nearest word that calls out for me what I want, look to, hope, and foresee is a "new spirit." But a new spirit is not to be caught in a schema or netted in a "plan." It is not to be set over against action, which in one sense it informs, but which is in another sense the source of its genesis and the renewal which is the sign and actuality of its life.

What is the new spirit which in fact already shows itself in the Mental Health movement, which draws men, many of them the best of men, to it, and which holds them and others not so much by its manifest performance—though by that too—as by its latent promise?

A spirit is not to be caught in words (any more than in a plan) and anything said about it is bound to be allusive rather than descriptive, evocative rather than defining. Let me evoke a little—or attempt to.

Let me begin by sketching the image of man that the movement rests upon, discovers as it goes, and presupposes in each new move. What the associated arts and sciences have discovered to man about men—to "individuals" about themselves severally, to man generally about men generally—constitutes a new universe wherein man may adventure more freely, with more wonder, and certainly with more economy and import, than any universe open to his everyday or outer eye.

What the associated arts and sciences of man have achieved and accomplished in the brief period of about fifty years that marks off the social scientific and psychological revolution is the collapse of the linear and cardboard-figure images of the official culture of the West with reference to man, society, and the nature of nature. The knowledge stemming from psychiatry and psychology, sociology and anthropology, linguistics and philosophy, modern political science, or the study of actual so-called "economic" behavior, makes look like pitiful, nursery-rhyme nonsense the simplistic beliefs that passed for explanations in the previous century—beliefs which, unfortunately, are still embedded in the underpinnings of most of our present major institutions.

All the beautiful dichotomies, to begin with, upon which so much of our certainty and security rested or rest, go dizzyingly down to dusty deaths. Mind and body, rational and nonrational, I and we, individual and social, economic and politic, good and evil, defense and attack, love and hate, reality and fantasy, inner and outer, figure and ground, past and future, thought and feeling, cause and effect, existence and life, being and becoming, freedom and control, personality and culture, reason and passion, infant and adult—lose their distinctness of reference and their usefulness as counterposed and antithetical explanatory terms. They still, undoubtedly, catch in an allusive way at aspects of life into which they yield fleeting glimpses, but none of them, and no combination of them, actual or hoped for, furnishes or is likely to furnish any key to the lock of life, any conceptual net in which to catch the free fish of experience. Indeed, the attempt so to contain the evidently uncontainable is soon seen as one more curious aspect of the life that was to be contained! The clear conceptual separations and the beautiful linear logic that yielded us the equation $e=mc^2$ and the atom bomb, hybrid wheat, and milk-fed children, turn out when applied to man not only to fail because they violate the essential nature of the subject but, if taken seriously, to violate as well the essential nature of the object—man. The whole instrumental posture, when man takes it with reference to himself, is, intended or not, a transformation of his nature that involves finally the abandonment of his highest function: to live as the only conscious creative and art-realizing force in the cosmos.

What we have, instead of these "linear" models, at the momentary ends of long and complex chains of sensitive and never-ending inquiry, are "configurational" visions, of a kind but not of a complexity, such as children see on looking into a kaleidoscope, or adults hear-feel-see on listening to Bach or Beethoven or Baez or Seegar.[1] For time sequences we have compresences; for cause-and-effect relations, mutual constitution; for linear evolutions, esthetic dialectic; for mutually exclusive categories, sets that reciprocally include each other, without identity; for fixity, flux; for singularity of meaning, the caught-at "family resemblance" that belongs to words by virtue of their shared history and long but loose association. For fixity of "knowledge" in social matters we have relationism, or perspectivism, requiring less attributions of right and wrong in the school-teacher's sense, and more "right for . . ." or "wrong for . . ." in the artist's or art critic's. Such familiar pairs as structure and function emerge rather as stroboscopic or durational pictorizations of the same set of events abstracted in different ways for different purposes, than as entities whose relation to each other requires a fresh explanation. Even "reality" and "projection" melt into each other as reflection makes evident that, for the greater part, social real-

[1] I owe the linear-configurational distinction to Marshall McLuhan, though he explains our changed perceptions in a different way than I.

ity is precisely the (shared) projection, and that in this sense the Queen of Hearts in *Alice in Wonderland* ("Words mean what I say they mean") is closer to the truth than otherwise. Similarly, we find nothing but irrationality underlying the radical belief in rationality; and rationality has led us to reluctant recognition of the play, if not the pre-eminence, of irrationality in every vital process; indeed the problem is to find a reasonable, rather than a reasoned, place for reason.

All formulas fail, for the force of life is precisely its formula-transcendent character: indeed, this is the sign by which we recognize it. The old hope of a social science of "prediction" and "control" is seen to be a chimera—or, if not chimerical, nightmarish: the ideological substrate of *1984*.

Gone are such comforting beliefs as St. Paul's "When I was a child I thought as a child . . . but when I became a man I put away childish things." As everyone knows now, the infant and the child are present, lively, struggling and kicking, crying for the satisfaction of their infantile and childish needs even—or particularly—in the best of men; and the only sense in which childish things have been "put away" in the psyche is the sense in which the child has swept the cookie crumbs under the radiator in the vain hope of unnotice and forgetting. And, symmetrically and similarly, in the erstwhile innocent preserve of infancy we see a man-sized drama playing itself out, complete with a for-adults-only cast of characters and plot, and a full-scale panoply of well-developed passions.

Gone too are the neatly counterposed "individual" and "society" that formed the basis alike for Adam Smith's theory of the market and for the thinking of the writers of the American Constitution. Only the American Medical Association and the writers of Khrushchev's monologue do not seem to have heard the news. There is no "individual," and no dignity of the person or soul apart from the society that brings them into being, gives them suck, nourishes them "spiritually" as well as materially into strength and use, indeed continuously creates and recreates them. And similarly and symmetrically, there is no society that does these things, except as individuals, so constituted out of the shared (and differentiated by and out of the social process) in their activity and passivity, are and constitute the society. Arguments about the priority of either genetically, or their primacy morally, are about as useful (and dated) as the very similar arguments about "mind" and "body" that have plagued the West and left in their wake perhaps as great a residue of misery as all plagues, persecutions, and pillagings combined. For such questions are not questions in reality about reality at all, but only about what shall be realized—or recognized, or legitimated. About as well argue about which of two spouses makes of their union the marriage!

I have probably already said too much without bringing into anything like sharp perspective the view of man-in-society and society-in-man that is the emerging picture from what I have called, in reference to him, the associated arts and sciences. I hope I have said enough, however, to indicate that what emerges is a subject capable of indefinite and infinite appreciation; like a well-loved person *not* capable of reduction to a system or systems, to capture by categorization, to any scientific strategy, technique, or ploy, without the destruction precisely of what makes "it" interesting and loveworthy. And the method that permits that expanding, limitless appreciation is a method of understanding—analysis only in a most synthetic sense—not very different except in the orderliness of its poetry and the poesy of its order from that which the best among the dramatists and celebrators of man have always used in their effort to understand and universalize him —and them. Indeed, the understanding of the human drama not only comes out of participation in the drama, but *is* participation in the drama—and, incidentally, playwriting, casting, and personnel production, all together.

"Mental health" as a social object then emerges as some something, some fitness or fittedness between the actors, given the limits and potencies of their body-minds and the play they are playing out and creating and recreating themselves in and by. Whatever militates against that fitness—that appropriateness, that design-adequacy in its largest sense—militates against mental health. Ugliness, undue distance, physical or social—or undue proximity—disjunct ideas, frozen feelings whether in persons or institutions, lack of human scale or excess of it, processes, procedures and ideals that alienate men from themselves, from each other, or from their matrix in nature, all that minimizes joy or fails to give it the place of primacy as the test and sign of human and humane achievement, all these militate against mental health. Injustice—and that kind of justice that is not bathed in and founded upon mercy; carelessness, lack of care and that excess of it that is really and essentially uncaring; mechanization, routinization, the flat graying-out of human life in the service of production or efficiency or rationalization, or any other idolatry; the segmentation of society by institutions, and the fragmentation of institutions by roles, bounded and limited in rules and regulation; the whole orientation of mastery unmastered by any object going beyond itself—all these militate against mental health.

It would be hard enough, I should think, to plan against the things that are against mental health; to plan *for* mental health is something that tugs at and taxes the limits of my imagination. For the second is to plan life, and I doubt if that can be done without squeezing it to death. But perhaps we can at least plan against what is against life.

Even that is hard enough. For when we attack problems piecemeal we discover so often that the wanted and the unwanted in life are so interrelated and interdependent that the solution or resolution of one problem gives rise (or place) to a host of others no less pressing and painful than the preexistent ones. And if we try a large-scale revolutionary approach, or far-reaching reform, we discover the overwhelming capacity of the unintended, unforeseen—and perhaps unforeseeable—consequences of such action to confound alike our outcomes and our aims. So perhaps we cannot advance. But neither can we stand still. We cannot believe that intelligence cannot better order our lives, but neither is there warrant for believing that, in and of itself, it can. Indeed, in so posing the question we have once again fallen into the trap of abstracting what is not to be abstracted, and then facing inevitably the problem of how to "integrate" it with that from which it cannot in reality at all be segregated. And such a word as "planning," at least in its ordinary and ostensible meaning, aids and abets just such false model making or pseudo representation. Planning thus appears as something over against—if not hostile to—the "natural" process, as though the elements of foresightedness, calculation, and the like were alien to human nature, or "natural human nature" as exemplified in those less intelligent, I suppose, than ourselves. I think it is a wrong model because it tends to bring about what it assumes: a separation of sense and sensibility, intelligence and wholehearted action, foresight and commitment, calculation and experience, commitment and control. This may look like an economic division of labor, but it involves, I believe, a wedge driven into the unity of life sufficient to make its survival doubtful as fact—or value.

If mental health as I have adumbrated or sketched it is our aim, I suggest a different procedure as our model. Indispensable, fundamental is a detached and passionate commitment to a joint search in association with all good men everywhere for the meaning and embodiment of a good life, or a variety of good and sufficient lives. Such questions cannot be answered, I believe, for any long run of time, let alone forever, because part of the goodness of life (as well as its difficulty) lies in the discovery that discovery makes possible only the delights of further discovery.

I emphasize detached commitment because aims must be sufficiently general and capable of reinterpretation to bar fanaticism, parochialism, premature focus, and narrowness of vision, but sufficiently particular to draw together (within and between them) the like-minded and like-hearted. I emphasize the con-sociation because the very bringing into being of such a fraternity is not so much a *means* to solve the problem as it is itself a solution to the problem (and hence a continuous working test of whether or in how far the problem can be solved). I emphasize continuous joint search because again this is less a means and more a part of the solution, but also partly because this view puts planning in its proper place as a phase in the process of examined action and tested inquiry. Planning then becomes not something set over against and separated from the action of man in history, it becomes not a "special function" with its own archdiaconate and a new set of priests, but a name for the thrust of intelligence within the human enterprise, as it actually naturally occurs, immanent and transcendent, interfusing all acts of all persons, though undoubtedly more dominant for all people only some of the time and some people nearly all of the time. Planning thus becomes inseparable from "education," which is also not something we can properly do to or for people, but again precisely a name for the diffusion and interfusion of what cannot be concentrated without rent to the fabric of human life and threat to the future of mankind. Planning also becomes properly inseparable from action, not only because more clearly and intimately it flows out of and back into action, but because it is just that which transforms action by expanding consciousness, more particularly the consciousness of centrally relevant consequences. And, in such a process, I should hope and expect that the meaning of "planning" would itself be transformed, moderating its engineering overtones, blurring its boundaries with dreaming and like imaginative and creative processes, diminishing its narrow rationalistic and executive connotations, its alliance with politics as usually practiced and decision making as usually defined, bringing it into closer relation to that poetry and art which has been at one and the same time the portal to man's joy and the record of his partial and intermittent enjoyment.

On some such lines—neither dividing men further from each other, nor exacerbating the already too deep divisions within them—I see some alliance proceeding between those who came to their preoccupations by "mental health" and those who came by the route of "planning." Out of such a meeting and melting might come a new vision that would better justify the high hopes that somehow we all feel to be latent in our enterprises and caught at but not caught in our favorite banner words.

32

Adolescence: The Management of Emancipation in History and Life History

Canst thou say in thine heart
  Thou hast seen with thine eyes
With what cunning of art
  Thou wast wrought in what wise,
By what force of what stuff thou wast
  shapen,
  and shown on my breast to the skies?
(from *Hertha*)

I am often amazed by the degree to which I am put off and put down by the greater part of what I read about adolescence. And the degree of my distress is not generally greatly different whether I read the scientific or the lay press, whether I read in my own narrower field or in those of the allied and associated professions. For wanting from all, to a substantially distorting degree, it seems to me, is a sense of society and a sense of history. The desire for some proper feeling for these is not at all dogmatic. Indeed, the plea for their place is almost purely pragmatic. For a consequence of their slighting is that, cognitively, I can barely recognize, within a great part of these writings, the adolescents I know; and, affectively, I find myself alienated, restive, and uncomfortable in the face of the prevailing posture taken toward them. The wrong—if I am right—is dual: an error in the realm of knowledge, and an offense—if that term is allowable—in the realm of value.

Fundamental to my feeling, I am sure, is the evident self-location of the majority of the authors. Some radically transforming and distorting separation of "themselves" from "the phenomena" has occurred, such as to ensure the virtual disappearance of the appropriate we-perspective—surely the most obvious and self-evident presenting social fact. Even where, as commonly, the treatment is empathic and kindly, what is steadily maintained is an essentially oppositional or counter-positional, narrowed "we" cast over against a similarly contracted "them." At its caricatural extreme we may get the bug-on-a-pin effect, with an object of inspection at one end, and a taken-for-granted, detached, and competent observer-judge at the other.

But "we" know, and "they," the adolescents, know, that affairs are not thus. Whatever else adolescents are, they are *people*—like us. And not only people like us, but people with whom we are most vitally engaged. And not only engaged, but interpenetrated. Not only are they "ours," they are by us and of us: of us in the sense that we sensibly constitute them what they are, even as they simultaneously constitute us what we are. And this is so as far as the relation goes at all, and hence as far as "adolescent" and "adult," as terms, have any operative human or social meaning. It is we (if we must narrow the sense) who call out in them the responses to which in turn we respond, and vice versa. And it is in that conversation of word and act, gesture and realized relation, that the fact and meaning of adulthood and adolescence emerge together and find their reciprocal significance. Within, and only within, that enlarged and inclusive we, thus engaged, do adult and adolescent appear properly—as coemergents and coconstituents. And the matrix—as well as the upshot—of that coemergence and coconstituency is one, single and singular, collaborative, shared history, formation, and fate. It is not that we simply *live with* each other; we *achieve* each other. We are not just, in the going jargon, one "system." We are one we of one substance, one most intimate, society, body corporate, fellowship, community, companionship, and company.

The sense of this overarching membership of one another affects not only the tone and manner of communication, but the very substance of things seen. Any want of an enhanced and lively feel for it will inform and infect reports that get back to the adolescents described, and will thus alter the relation between "us" and "them," and, indeed, so constitute the problems of them-ness and alienation that we shall presently be compelled to deal with. In that next phase our own deliverances, and those of other adults, appreciated and acted upon, will return to us as puzzles and problems whose origins we may then not even or no longer know.

Even neglecting the fatal alteration of affective and affectional realities consequent upon this stance—adults as students taking adolescents as objects of study—there is, in my opinion, a further, fateful distortion in that which the stand was taken to help secure: a balanced, appropriate, reliable, useful appreciation of what is going on and what is likely to occur. For as the most obvious aspect of reality—the overarching unity, our common creation and captivity—is played down or deserted, the adult participants enter with the adolescent into characteristic, shared, neurotic and neuroticizing, alternating fantasies. Adult and adolescent begin to see each other, falsely, in the sadistic mode of victimizers, or the masochistic one of victims. And as both do so, they drive the reality toward the fantasy, so that finally in fact, freedom and agency (that were initially not so distributed) may effectively lie differentially and destructively, decisively more on one "side" than another. If adults do enter into such a pact in irreality with adolescents, both are of course jointly responsible; but, here as elsewhere, some are more jointly responsible, as well as more equal, than others.

Not only are the growing and the grown one we, but we are all engaged together and almost altogether, in one enterprise: the making of history. And outside that recognized historical context, as little of what we are doing is intelligible as would be the case if we tried to understand a person without attending to the fact that he is not merely living out, but *building up*, a life, something that has also its own history: an irreversible, meaningful, patterned, large-scale action in and upon the world, transforming actor, act, and acted-upon, simultaneously and alike.

Once properly appreciated—as caught and caught up in one us, engaged together in the enterprise that is history—the adolescent appears rather differently, and "adolescence" assumes additional and altered meaning. For we now see it as a crucial articulation point or period in the historic as well as the ontogenetic process. At that point, supremely, the new, not only as further biologic fodder or *matériel* for social role playing, but as personal culture changer and pathbreaker, is in preparation and emergence. Adolescence *is* thus what spans the stage of the acted-upon-by-history (the child) and the actor in and upon history (the adult); adolescence is (roughly) what bridges between man as made and man as maker—maker of mind, self, history, culture, society-to-be And the reference is always exquisitely and excruciatingly dual: to the life history and the common history, each of which is context and container for the other. And of that intercept of history and biography, crucial for our understanding of the adolescent and critical for his comprehension also, few speak—so few that we have not even gone through the formality of giving it a name.

Failing such appreciation, adolescence appears variously as a stage or phase, as problem or puzzle or parapathology, as presumed pre-Paradise on the way to an adulthood of a predefined kind in a society of a previsioned character. Given, by contrast, a correct location of each adolescent as at the unique intercept of his history with world history, what is exposed is what is there: an intersecting set of constraints, tasks, and opportunities, additional to, coordinate with, and translatory of the tasks set by the life history, or by the needs of growing up, generically. These constraints, tasks, and possibilities, seen in their general and particular intersections, help make much intelligible that must otherwise appear accidental or remain obscure.

Those who do see thus may see, ostensibly, the same adolescents as others see, in the same numbers, and with, presumably, the same intimacy and similar loving curiosity, but they will see them in a rather different light. So far as I am able, I see them so, though not consistently or adequately. Thus, what I see them doing, thinking, feeling, saying—from Carnaby Street costume to the Berkeley sit-ins, from acute and angry argument with parents to rejection of the educational lockstep and the atomic-competitive ethic—appears to me, for the most part, to be the relatively rather reasonable response of relatively rather reasonable persons to the problems actually presented to them. *We* are part of those presenting problems; but what we present is not the whole problem. History, too, presents its problems and presses its claims.

When, sometimes angrily, they say that some or all adults are, in the going vocabulary, "square," "not with it," "out of it," they mean, as I hear them, that by providing false contexts, those not clued in read out wrong motives, put the young on with feigned understanding, put them off with phony explanations, or put them down with ill-founded criticism. These, thus misled, divide what should not be divided, and juxtapose what does not belong together.

Thus, they see separately and in disconnection good rebellion and bad rebellion, or, as someone said recently, "the constructive and positive" versus "the negative and passive." In the former category, the speaker evidently encompassed activities from Peace Corps participation to civil disobedience directed to the enfranchisement of Negroes, even over to student struggles to free their universities from the toils of the essentially colonialist regimes that do indeed dominate the most of them. By "negative" and "nonconstructive," he meant to impugn the whole of the drug culture, part of the sex practices, the new language, the redistribution of hair lengths between girls and boys, and so on. Where he would have located the repudiation of ideology, the rejection of the standard materialist package, the abandonment of a rule-oriented modality of judgment, I find it hard to say. What he overlooked entirely is that all of these are parts of wholes that have profound organic connections with each other—even if isolable elements, such as certain varieties of drug use, have far-reaching and different consequences for particular users and parts of the society.

By a similar *tour de force*, "liberals"—and the term is now very nearly a swearword, at least among later adolescents—attempted to separate (or missed the connection between) elements in the nationally celebrated struggles at the University of California at Berkeley in the 1965 academic year. I can no more reconstitute here the entire train of events for those who do not know them than I could hope to tell in brief compass the history of the Vietnam war. But it too was, in the United States, a matter, for a considerable time, of national attention. And it was perhaps the most important sequence of events in American higher education in a decade.

At the height of the controversy—essentially a battle over the status of students, their civil and moral rights, and the nature and morality of the government of the academic community—liberals in numbers were "sympathetic," for a time, with the embattled students. Sympathetic, that is, largely as long as the fight was fought in terms of standard oratorical appeals to unassailable constitutional rights.

But when, toward the "end," a poet sat cross-legged on a plot of grass holding aloft a sign that said simply "Fuck"—and when the leadership of the student movement was drawn into his defense because university administrators falsely implicated them as cause, with his action as consequence—sympathizers in their thousands opted out of even that thin but badly needed support.

I do not here question their right to do—let alone feel—as

they please. But their amazement and dismay rested largely upon serious disorientation with reference both to contemporary social connections and to relatively recent historic events. What was really embedded in a rich and intelligible context thus appeared as mere excess or *bizarrerie*. Many who took the poet's act as revelatory—which it was—took it to be "revealing" only in a denigrating sense: the whole prior contest was teleologically reduced to a "dirty word controversy," its original "inner meaning" finally shown forth.

For few, did word and act link up with another, then current, less collapsed, popular slogan, "Make love, not war," even though the poet partly explained his action in such terms. "If I had sat there" he said, "with a sign saying 'Bomb!' or 'Kill!' nobody would have bothered me." No one attended to his wry comment (looking both ways, to the war in Vietnam and the recent horrors on campus): "It's a panacea for all the world's ills." For few, did his act link up with the then recent obscene trial on obscenity charges of a youthful culture hero (Lenny Bruce), who had used (in a night club, and for adults only) "obscene" images to make shockingly alive great and far-reaching social issues. For few again did it link, as an expectable second act, with the stripping in the preceding months from the Berkeley students' University—by its own claim and their concession, acting always *in loco parentis*—of every shard of moral dignity. And hardly any saw it as a protest against the misuse of words—to divide, confuse, mislead, and defend the indefensible—that had characterized press and administration pronouncements in the period immediately past. None saw it as an overterse, overcondensed, overdetermined reply, in some sense, to the excessively polished, rounded periods of the Greek Theatre performance (whose real meaning was also in a sense "revealed," when carefully concealed campus police rushed from the wings to protect the podium against a student leader who wished to make a rather routine announcement).

The principal object of analyzing this event thus—even

though the analysis, incidentally, shows its own bias—is neither to indict nor to praise any of the parties concerned. The poet may have his pathology. Even more tragically, his pathology may have peculiarly cast him for his role, as well as provided him with his insights, prophetic and profane. And so may the officials involved have had their problems and their hangups, their incapacitations, paramount perhaps over good intentions. My purpose is not, here, to judge, but only to insist that the keeping in view of social and historic contexts is vital to the understanding and evaluation of living events, and is evidently much underpracticed.

In a similar fashion, but on a grander scale, a disconnection has, in going lines of explanation, been found or forced, between the "good" activities of Northern white students "laying their bodies on the line" to found freedom schools in Mississippi or to register Negro voters in Alabama, and the "bad" activities involved in the widespread adoption of "hip" language and posture (physical and psychological), the adoption of the uniform of denims and sweatshirts, the elevation of "keeping one's cool" into a major desideratum, and the somewhat successful sabotage of the standard high schools' manpower-procurement schemes and outlooks.

Indeed, one gets the feeling that while the "integration" of American society—across "racial," ethnic, age, sex, class, and other barriers—is, abstractly, widely desired, it is regarded, in its concrete outworkings, as horrific. And it is held horrific because what was originaly had in mind by its most vocal liberal proponents was not so much integration as *absorption* —actually the assimilation of all into the subculture of the speaker. (That this is to be desired is no more self-evident than that all forms and varieties of British speech should be lost to pound-note English.) Surely, a genuine integration *must* be preceded by a vast mutual migration of forms, fashions, fads, and values across the pre-existent boundaries, so that, in their collision, recombination, and mutual modification, a culturally creative and fructifying process may freely occur. This presupposes what we see: the migration of practices, views, schemes, and styles from socially below up, instead of merely, as formerly, only from up, down. Hence adolescents, properly about their history's business, will now exhibit, even in well-off Northern white communities, some elements of a culture originating with marginal, Southern Negro jazz musicians, even perhaps in still raw (i.e., unassimilated or unintegrated) form. So the noble freedom schools and the "ignoble" hippy walk may well be aspects of a single movement, an entirely proper response to an entirely urgent historic need.

So also for the very evident *rapprochement* between the sexes. The transforming conquests of technology, the avalanche of affluence resulting, and the emergence into dominance of large-scale ventures based more and more on cooperation, make less and less adaptive and aesthetic the virile Roman virtues. And so, similarly, the overdrawn, overemphasized, too sharply counterposed masculine and feminine role systems, and their corresponding supporting attitude sets, become ever less serviceable. The resultant response of the young is all too visible. But again, critics apparently desire to disjoin what is organically conjoined. They appear to approve the husband who shares with his wife the laundering, dishwashing, and diapering, but to disapprove the appropriate *attendrissement* of the young males. Hence, the critics frown on what is equally relevant and dramatically appropriate, the young males' turning away from mayhem sports, not to mention military exploit, their long hair and generally softened and gentled facial conformation, their cultivation of the inner life at some expense to "achievement," their abandonment of a hard calculus of entitlements in favor of an enlarged sympathy, and their preferential attention, *modo materno,* to need over desert.

Similarly, in the extension of the same sympathy over geographically and socially distant populations. Again the historic need. And again the disallowance of part of a single, a unitary, response. The same sentiment that recoils—and leads to most vocal protest—in reference to the Negro in Birmingham who is mauled by police dogs, trained by police for the purpose, extends of its own nature to the Vietnamese peasant, napalmed or personnel-mined for some unbelievable public benefit. And even those few critics who do follow thus far so often cry violent halt when the same interested and unalienated tolerance extends to those whom the establishment designates as criminal—most especially to those who illegally comfort themselves in their permanent deprivation with such means as are, for them, at hand. The common core of youthful sentiment—again a response to a kind of ecumenicism that history suddenly demands—is a reluctance to legislate for others, even in the heart and mind, particularly beyond necessity. What is involved is not indifference, for each adolescent readily finds and retains his own resonating *entourage*. But there is involved centrally a more humane readiness to accredit (in Polanyi's terms) the hazardous commitment of another, as, at least prima facie, likely to be appropriate to *his* distinct position and possibility.

And so, lastly, for a new union or wedding between *eros* and *agapé*. Nothing seems so visible among the young as a happy heightening and extension and enrichment of the erotic. And nothing is next most visible except the widening and deepening of the empire of goodwill. And nothing, after that, is more obvious, I believe, as one moves around among them, than the way in which these forms of love sustain, feed, and heighten each the other. Thus, typically, the energy for the weary picket line and the strength for the long-drawn sit-in emerge not so much from sexual renunciation and "sublimation," as from the extension and enlargement of a rich and early genitality. Indeed, what is oil to flame, and what flame to oil is a matter for discovery and rediscovery from moment to flowing moment.

Let nothing herein now be taken to detract from what has been elsewhere said and well said. Of course, adolescence is a peculiarly poignant phase in a search for identity. It is only that identity is more than merely the discovery of self; it is self-discovery in relation to what is thus simultaneously made vital and given its meaning: most particularly, in relation to the massive act we call history and the massive "we" that is society. Of course, there is in adolescence pathology and pseudo pathology; but even pathology is often called out by, responds to, and is reinforced by the general history that is container and contained to the personal one. Of course, there is in adolescence much rebellion that would, doubtless, seek some permissible form of expression even in a time that did not so insistently call for the rupture of old forms—from nationalist states that represent clear and present danger to infantilizing schools that prepare for them. These forms, the young feel—and feel, I think, rightly—cannot contain the valuable and vital forces we have ourselves happily set free.

What I plead for, then, in the realm of theory, is the development and recognition of a study: the study of what is to be seen in the simultaneous dual perspective of history and life history. What it calls for practically—as adjunctive to the self-exploration we call psychotherapy and the world exploration we call education—is an enterprise in which we, jointly with them, as one interactive we, explore and explain what is for each of us and each of them the unique intercept of my life with our life, my history with the common history of all of us. For *that* is, I think, peculiarly the locus of large action, the matrix of culture, the growth point of society, and the ground upon which—in adolescence only particularly—personality forms and figures, even as it is figured and formed. Were I speaking to them I would plead for a similar extension and elevation of sight and sympathy. But I should in so doing like to come to them saying that we had seen and sensed them so, cradled in a common concern that is not only paternally ours for them, but properly ours for that us that includes them in a vision appropriate to the principal presenting facts.

IV

Epilogue

The Beneficial Encounter

Many persons, I am sure, will see threads of unity and disunity, consistency and inconsistency, in the materials of this book. It would be strange if it were otherwise, for that is how, irremediably, we are all made. The book has been designed so as *not* to obscure such human evidences, for they may of themselves be more illuminating than the smoothed-out versions usually connected with our "presentation of the self in professional life."

From the author's viewpoint, the constancy in inconsistency and the unity in diversity is represented by two preoccupations. The first has to do with the relation between two "theories," or two habitual ways of looking at the world. The second has to do with the subtle relations between theory and action, more particularly beneficial, or at least meliorative action.

The two "theories," or orientational schemes, are represented respectively in a very rough sense by "sociology" and "psychology," chiefly psychoanalytical psychology. Each has immense explanatory power. Each illuminates and makes intelligible a vast range of otherwise disjointed and seemingly unrelated events. Each, moreover, addresses itself not simply to such "random" events, but to events most crucial for the view man has of himself, and most critical for any rational hope of human betterment. Each asserts, points to, or takes for granted, a set of limits to action which it is theoretical folly and practical waste not to recognize. And each, at least at first blush, points to a different line of action (apart from accepting either theory as paramount) in the improvement of affairs, insofar as they can at all by thoughtful act be improved. Each has developed a massive set of mappings—a psychography, and a sociography—which allows access to a gripping, rich, intimate picture of how things human are and how they work, each in a way quite different from naïve sense or, even otherwise quite sophisticated sense, supposes.

Both include most convincing theoretical accounts and practical demonstrations of how we come to think the way we think, especially with reference to ourselves and other human beings and the relations between them. Preference for one particular social theory or type of theory over another can be shown in almost any concrete case to be so deeply imbued with a person's life history, more particularly its most intimate, early, and least conscious aspects, that the seeming intellectual preference may be best regarded as an expressive gesture, not wholly unlike a dream or a story elicited by a projective test card. Similarly, preference for any particular psychological theory or type of theory is so deeply affected by "social conditions" generally, and the social situation and interest of the theorist, that the theory assumes, at least prima facie, the character of an ideology: a view representative of and so far as possible protective of the interest and line of social action of a distinct social class in a distinct society at a distinct stage of its development.

If either account is substantially neglected, we are clearly condemned to timeless continuation of the misery, destruction, and folly that is the record of history and life history. Anyone who has had the good or ill fortune to "look within" must have been appalled by how much of what he thought was evident was need-driven and need-dictated, at the mercy of most primitive and distorted needs, particularly his most general views, where the check of reality is so difficult to bring to bear, because least is evident and most is supposed. Anyone who has had the good or ill fortune really to "look abroad" should have been fatally shaken by the recognition of how much of what before was self-evident is part of a construction of the cosmos deeply and peculiarly bound up with his culture—a particular, limited, and purpose-peculiar mode of observation, construction, and analysis, which cuts out the "facts" from the limitless flux of events.

In both cases, the recognition that we have been profoundly wrong while thinking ourselves right beyond reasonable doubt carries with it, or should carry with it, the certainty that we shall continue so to be wrong, though perhaps less grossly if we bear it in mind. The most complete and perfect psychoanalysis, the most extended and adequate anthropo-analysis, will leave us at best with a lively sense of how we distort, misperceive, and part-perceive the world, with some of our prior errors corrected but with a massive and ineradicable disposition to make new ones. We can call to our aid the tremendous and impressive apparatus of "science," insofar as it has any application to human behavior, only to discover that while it protected us against one class of error, it led us further through false confidence into another. We find in the end, as in the beginning, that our purposes, which we could not or would not acknowledge, have outwitted our precautions.[1]

But if neither account is to be neglected, neither can it be driven to the point of totality. For if everything we say and think is either fully need-determined or socially determined, then discussion is pointless. Indeed, there is no discussion, only predetermined noises, and the question of what we *should* do or believe is meaningless. But a sustained belief that there is no question of what is credible, or what is to be believed, *is*

[1] The most dramatic illustration of the past few years was the coverage by some of the nation's top social scientists, who had unprecedented opportunity for access and were present on the spot from beginning to end, of the events of 1964-5 at the University of California at Berkeley. What each "saw" and "inferred" and reported bore very little relation to what each of the others perceived or concluded. An older, though still current, illustration is the much-referred-to matter on "delinquency."

not in the human repertory. Those who affect such beliefs in verbal statements invariably demonstrate, by their other asserted beliefs and by all their actions, that they passionately believe the contrary and confidently act on that contrary.

Nor is all this, as the book has perhaps laboriously been at pains to express, merely a matter of theory, with merely theoretic consequences. The theory held, or the holding of the theory, is probably the most consequential of all human acts. The beliefs about man are *in* the culture, and are the most decisive for its general shape. The beliefs about what man is —about what I am, you are, we are, they are, he is—are *in* the person, and are the most decisive for the makeup and outworking of the person. That theory, whatever it is, is both the final act, derived from all else, and the first act, the father of all others. In the beginning is the Word. *Im Anfang ist die That.*

I do not believe that a simple juxtaposition of what might be called Marxian views with Freudian views is good enough. Nor is any argument which purports to explain or explain away the other even remotely satisfactory. Nor is the effect of thirty years or more of interdisciplinary or cross-disciplinary research acceptable. The upshot is simply the "explanation" of bits and pieces of human behavior through an eclectic choosing now of this explanatory scheme, now of that one. In cases of doubt about convenience his favored explanatory scheme prevails whose personal force and social status is greater.

No light is visible, but I do not believe that no new light is to come. New light, if it is to be had, will come out of new relations and new enterprises, and the relation and the enterprise, as in psychoanalytic therapy itself, is the beginning both of the new theory and the new act. I therefore look to an encounter, more profound than any before it, between the best representatives of the two great perspectival systems, who are the possessors of great, rich chunks of profound acquaintance with how we do, personally and severally, behave: the psychologically sensitized social scientists and the socially and sociologically sensitized psychological theoretician-therapists.

If there is to be an encounter, respectively, between those oriented from men toward society and those oriented from society toward men, we must bring to the encounter a lively sense of who and what we are, our similarities and our differences, and what it behooves us to melt together, for a productive and happy relationship, and what to keep distinct. It would be sad if we aimed to incorporate each other, to lose all distinction of identity or, unduly bristling, refuse conjugation for fear of engulfment.

Let me go some distance toward laying the groundwork for a relationship. A psychoanalyst is a carer-helper-facilitator who attempts to encounter persons, commonly one at a time, so that, apart from counting the encounter valuable in itself, reorientation (of a certain kind) and reactivated self-activation (of a certain kind) occur in both, perhaps especially in the person ostensibly being helped. An applied sociologist, I submit, is a carer-helper-facilitator who attempts to encounter persons, face-to-face or otherwise, commonly in numbers as in groups or publics, so that, apart from the value of the encounter, reorientation (of a certain kind) and reactivated, personal or group self-activation (of a certain kind) occur in both, again especially in those being helped. The psychoanalyst may direct conscious attention to the personal myth-making that serves and protects one part of the personal economy or drama-playing at the expense of another; the socioanalyst is occupied in precisely the analogical enterprise, the uncovering of the unwitting myth-making that goes to protect one part or aspect of the society at the expense of another. Both aim, not so much to uncover any particular myth or body of myth, but to ensure for each of their "subjects" such general and particular understanding of the myth-making process itself so that obscure needs or unilluminated preference no longer have *that* part of their sway attributable to the fact that they are *blind*. In the one case, the relations between the institutions of the mind, viewed as functional bundles, may in some respects be altered from what they would have been had the otherwise blind operation of personal history held sway; in the other case, for the socioanalyst, by a strictly analogical process, the going order of institutions is in some sense or degree altered from what "historical necessity" would otherwise have ensured. As in the one case, so in the other, psychological insight or self-insight and relational or social insight, is always (perhaps within measure) to be desired, but rarely necessary and never sufficient. In both cases, intellectual knowledge-about is by itself ordinarily worth very little, though not altogether to be discounted. There is in both cases, despite much good practice, tremendous difficulty in stating aims acceptably, whether in terms of product or process.

In both cases, a very thorough understanding of the one theory, practice, and body of fact is necessary to any high-level, or perhaps even acceptable, performance of the other. By "understanding" I do not mean the sort of academic knowledge about the other's theory or even body of facts which is frequently allowed to pass for "grasp" or mastery. I mean by understanding what flows (with luck) out of a long, hard, painful process: a process of detaching oneself to a sensible and significant degree from the accidents, fortunate and unfortunate, of one's history and make-up and mode of seeing and feeling and operation; and especially and particularly from those far-reaching, because unconscious, "basic" schemes that are the very structure respectively of the unexamined life of person and society. The one no more comes by the light of nature than the other. Indeed, these complementary detachment-reorganization processes have analogical difficulties, dangers, risks, and rewards; both kinds of reorganization can take place only in a context of skilled and informed *caring* competence. It is a poor psychoanalyst who is not knowledgeable about and to a sizable degree reoriented to society in general and to his society and culture in particular. It is a poor sociologist or socioanalyst who is not knowledgeable about and rather radically reoriented to himself in particular and to his intimate and remoter spheres of social operation in general. However, neither professional is for the most part equally or even adequately competent in the realm of the other; each tends to mistake sympathetic knowing-about for knowledge *of* (in the required, nearly carnal sense) and each tends to underestimate the degree of crippling and distortion he suffers because of his professional deficiency. Each tends to treat the other's foreground as mere background, and each normally tends to explain the other's data or phenomena "ultimately" or "basically" in terms of his professionally preferential focus of explanatory attention.

A collaboration so constituted cannot long endure. If there is to be an advance of any magnitude, there has to be a common theory; and a common theory will come only out of a joint or common practice, not from another interdisciplinary research. Theories generally develop best out of problems; and the problems most likely to develop theory are problems *for* people, problems faced, problems that follow upon commitment and accompany responsibility.

The joint and common practice I have in mind would require, in the context of committed meliorist action, the simultaneous attention by appropriate personnel to what are traditionally regarded as three problems: the desirable alteration of persons and processes seen as primarily "psychological"; the desirable alteration of societies and processes that are seen as primarily "social"; and the desirable alteration of the social and psychological "ontogenetic" process in which, as co-emergents, the "new" persons and the "new" society are "reproduced."

My view is that it is no longer profitable to talk about such things and to work at such alterations as though we had hold of three "problems," three "fields," or three "levels" of logical analysis. The worst intellectual heresy of the day (a genuine "scandal" in the medieval sense) is to pretend that they are separate, and in a way yet to be discovered, causally related. All this makes us do is hunt for metaphysical nonexistents and "intervening variables" that only intervene because we have put those words there to intervene between the object and the vision of the object.

It is not that these things—personality, society, human development—are causally related; it is that they are *logically* related, for the simple reason that they are different ways of stating the same thing (in the same sense that the equivalences on either side of a mathematical equation are statements of the same thing). If we say, for instance, that alteration in family behavior affects the behavior of members of the family, we are talking sheer animism: altered family behavior *is* altered family *member* behavior. We are talking about identities, not causal sequences.

To this joint and common, theoretical and practical enterprise, psychoanalysis brings a great deal that is unique and indispensable for the welfare of both concerns. So, I believe, does the activity that has gone under such varied labels as applied psychology and applied sociology. Both disciplines, like any other unreconstructed patient, bring a crushing burden of useless and counteruseful views, habits, investments, cripplings, blindnesses, nonorders, and disorders, but it is precisely out of engagement with such sad mixes of assets and liabilities that we have learned most of what little we do know about man, ourselves, and each other. I suggest we stop playing autistically in our corners and encounter each other.